CROCHET
Edgings & Insertions
from Early 20th Century Sources

by Eliza A. Taylor & Belle Robinson

The work of this book is taken, unabridged, from two of the most complete manuals of crochet edgings:

PRISCILLA CROCHET BOOK, EDGINGS & INSERTIONS (Book 1), Edited by Eliza A. Taylor, published by the Priscilla Publishing Company in 1913

and

PRISCILLA CROCHET BOOK NO. 2, EDGINGS & INSERTIONS, Edited by Belle Robinson, published by the Priscila Publishing Company in 1916

SUPPLIES: Fine crochet hooks, to size 16, Novelty Braid and fine crochet threads available from:
LACIS. 2990 Adeline Street, Berkeley, CA 94703

Note: Page numbers are unchanged from original publications
Edgings on Cover: Left - page 46 Book 1; Right - page 32 Book 2

LACIS
PUBLICATIONS
3163 Adeline Street, Berkeley, CA 94703

© 1996, LACIS
ISBN 0-916896-80-3

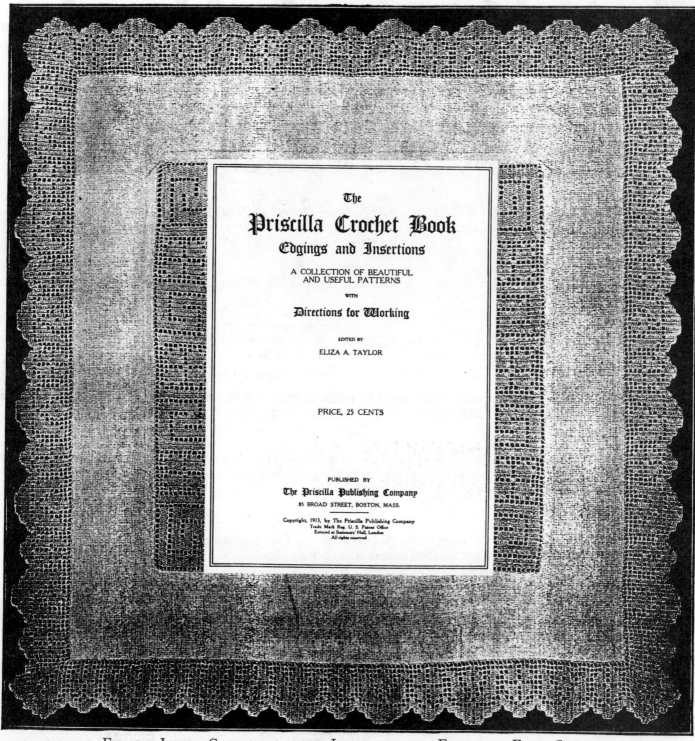

The

Priscilla Crochet Book
Edgings and Insertions

A COLLECTION OF BEAUTIFUL
AND USEFUL PATTERNS

WITH

Directions for Working

EDITED BY

ELIZA A. TAYLOR

PRICE, 25 CENTS

PUBLISHED BY

The Priscilla Publishing Company

85 BROAD STREET, BOSTON, MASS.

FIG. 1. LINEN CENTREPIECE WITH INSERTIONS AND EDGING IN FILET CROCHET

See directions on page 16

EDGINGS AND INSERTIONS

Explanation of Stitches

CHAIN (ch). Make a slip knot on needle, draw thread through this loop. Again draw thread through this second loop and continue till ch is of length required.

SLIP STITCH (sl st). Put hook through work at st indicated in directions; draw thread through work and loop on needle at same time.

DOUBLE (d). Put hook through work, thread over hook and draw through, making two loops on needle; thread over again and draw through both loops.

HALF TREBLE (h t). Thread over needle, hook through work, thread over and draw through, giving three sts on needle, thread over and draw through the three sts at once.

TREBLE (t). Thread over the needle, hook through work, thread over and draw through, giving three sts on needle; thread over, draw through two, over again and draw through remaining two.

DOUBLE TREBLE (d t). Thread over twice, hook through work, thread over and draw through, giving four sts on needle, * thread over and draw through two; repeat from * twice.

LONG TREBLE (l t). Thread over three times, hook through work, thread over and draw through, giving five sts on needle, thread over and work all off by twos.

PICOT (p). A p is formed on a ch by joining the last four sts (or any given number) in a ring by working a d in the fourth st, counting from hook. In making p on d around the edge of motifs, the d is worked in the top of the last d.

Directions

Materials.—All of the edgings shown in this book were made of No. 100 Cordonnet crochet cotton excepting those in which the number of cotton is specified in the directions.

For No. 100 cotton use a No. 13 hook, for No. 70 cotton a No. 12 hook; for coarser cottons use a hook that will carry the thread easily without splitting it.

Cover Design.— Directions for the Insertion on the cover of this book will be found on page 46.

FIG. 2. EDGING. See page 3

Figure 2.—Make a chain the length required. *1st row*—Make 1 d in 9th st from hook, * ch 3, skip 2, 1 t in next st, ch 1, 1 t in same st, ch 3, skip 2, 1 d in next st, repeat from * . *2d row*—Fasten thread with 1 d in 3d ch st to the right of 1st d, * ch 4, 1 d under 1 ch, ch 5, 1 d in same place, ch 7, 1 d in same place, ch 5, 1 d in same place, repeat from * to end.

Figure 3.—Chain 8. *1st row*—One t in 4th st, 1 t in 5th, 1 t in 6th, ch 2, 4 t in last st, with 2 ch between each, turn. *2d row*—* Chain 1, 1 d, 2 t, 1 d under 1st 2 ch, 1 d, 3 t, 2 ch, 3 t under next 2 ch, 1 d, 2 t, 1 d under last 2 ch, ch 2, 1 t on 1st of 4 t, 1 t on each of next 2 t, 1 t under 3 ch at end of row, turn. *3d row*—Chain 3, 1 t on 2d t, 1 t on each of next 2 t, ch 2, 4 t in shell with 2 ch between each, turn, and repeat from *.

FIG. 3. EDGING. See page 3

Figure 4.— Make a chain (ch) of 9 sts. *1st row*—Two treble crochet (t) in 4th st from hook, ch 2, skip 1 st on ch, 3 t in next st, skip 2 sts, 1 t in last st, turn. *2d row*—Chain 3, 3 t, 2 ch, 3 t under 2 ch (this makes a shell), turn. *3d row*—Chain 3, shell in shell, 1 t under 3 ch at end of row; turn. *4th row*—Chain 3, shell in shell, turn work over, ch 5, take hook out of work, insert under 3 ch, catch last loop of 5 ch and pull through; ch 5, catch in point of first shell and pull through in the same way, ch 1 to fasten, turn, make 8 d in loop just made, 3 d in next loop, ch 6, pull through 4th d of first loop, ch 1, 8 d in this ch, 5 d in second loop to finish. *5th row*—Shell in shell, 1 t under 3 ch at end of row. Repeat from 2d row for length desired.

Figure 5.— Make a chain of 19 sts. *1st row*—One d in 13th st from hook, ch 5, skip 3, 1 d in next st, ch 3, 1 d in next st, turn. *2d row*—Chain 1, make a shell of 4 t, 1 ch, 4 t, under 3 ch, 1 d in 5 ch, ch 7, 1 d in next ch, turn. *3d row*—Chain 8, 1 d under 7 ch, ch 5, 1 d, 3 ch, 1 d under the 1 ch in shell, turn. Begin again at 2d row.

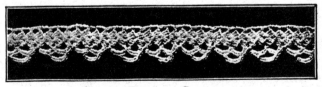

FIG. 4. EDGING. See page 3

Figure 6.— Chain 24 sts. *1st row*—Make 1 d in 10th st from hook, (ch 5, skip 4 sts, 1 d in next st) twice more, turn. *2d row*—Chain 6, 1 d in first space (sp), ch 5, 1 d in each sp to end of row, turn. *3d row*—Chain 6, 1 d in 1st sp, ch 5, 1 d in each of next 2 sps, ch 3, 10 t under 6 ch, 1 d in last sp in 1st row, turn. *4th row*—Chain 3, 1 d between 2d and 3d t, ch 3, 1 d between each t to end, making last d in top of last of 10 t; there should be nine small scallops; ch 2, make 3 t under each sp across, turn. *5th row*—Chain 6, 1 d between first and sec-

3

FIG. 5. EDGING. See page 3

ond cluster of t, ch 5, 1 d between each of next two clusters, ch 5, 1 d in 2 ch at end of last 3 t, turn. Begin again at 2d row, and repeat till you have length required.

Figure 7.—Make ch a little longer than the desired length. Turn, 1 t in 6th ch, 2 ch, 1 t in every 3d ch to end. This makes a row of squares. Turn, 5 ch, 1 t on t of first square, 2 ch, 1 t on t of next square; repeat to end. Turn, 2 d in first square. Turn, 10 ch, 1 sl st in last d. Turn, 4 d, 4 ch, 4 d, 4 ch, 4 d, 4 ch, 4 d, in ring just made, 2 d in first square, 4 d in each of next three squares, 2 d in next square, 10 ch, join as in first and repeat to end of squares. Turn, sl st up to 1st picot (p), 11 ch, fasten in 3d p, 4 ch, fasten with sl st in 1st p of next ring; repeat to end. Turn, 4 d, 5 ch, 4 d, 5 ch, 4 d, 5 ch, 4 d, over 11 ch, fasten with sl st in p, 3 d, 5 ch, 3 d over 4 ch; repeat to end.

Figure 8.—Chain 13. *1st row*—Make 1 t in 4th st from needle, 5 t in next 5 sts, ch 2, skip 2 sts, 1 t in next st, turn. *2d row*—Chain 6, 3 t under 2 ch, ch 2, skip 2 t, 4 t in next 4 t, back loops only except last t, which you make in the two loops of t below, turn. *3d row*—Chain 3, 1 t in each of 4 t, 3 t under 2 ch, ch 2, 15 t under 6 ch, 1 d in last st of foundation ch, turn. *4th row*—One d in each of 15 d (back loops), ch 1, 2 t under 2 ch, 1 t in each of next 6 t, turn. *5th row*—

FIG. 6. EDGING. See page 3

Chain 3, 1 t in each of next 6 t, ch 2, 1 t in 1-ch space before scallop, turn, and repeat from 2d row for length required, making the 1 d at end of 15 t, in the 1-ch space before scallops.

Figure 9.—Chain 15. *1st row*—One t in 4th st from hook, ch 5, skip 5 sts, 1 t in next, ch 3, 1 t in same st, ch 5, skip 5, 1 t in next st, turn. *2d row*—Three d t (thread over twice) under 3 ch, ch 5, 1 t under same ch, ch 5, 4 d t in same ch, ch 2, 2 t in 2 t, turn. *3d row*—Chain 3, t in t, ch 2, 4 t in 4 d t, ch 5, 1 t in t, ch 5, 4 t in 4 d t, turn. *4th row*—Slip stitch in each of 4 d t, ch 3, 3 t under 5 ch, ch 3, t in t, ch 3, 3 t under 5 ch, t in next t, ch 5, 2 t in 2 t, turn. *5th row*—Chain 3, t in t, ch 8, 1 t in last of 4 t's, 3 t under 3 ch, ch 3, 3 t under next 3 ch, 1 t in next t, turn. *6th row*—Slip stitch in each of 4 t, ch 3, 3 t under 3 ch, ch 4, thread over hook twice, insert hook in 4th t, * thread over hook, draw a loop through, thread over again, draw through two loops, thread over, draw

through two loops. * thread over hook twice, insert in 3d st of ch, repeat from * to *, thread over hook and draw through three remaining sts on hook. (This is a cross treble.) Chain 5, 2 t in 2 t, turn. *7th row*—Chain 3, t in t, ch 4, t in cross treble, ch 3, 1 t in same place, ch 5, 1 t in 1st t, turn. Repeat from 2d row.

Figure 10.—Chain 10, join with sl st. *1st row*—Chain 3, 11 t in ring, turn. *2d row*—Chain 3, 1 t in top of 2d t, 1 t in each of next 3 t, (ch 2, 1 t in next t) 6 times, ch 2, 1 t under 3 ch at end of row, turn. *3d row*—Chain 6, 1 d in top of 1st t (where ch of 6 began), * ch 5, 1 d in top of next t, 7 times, ch 6, 1 d under 3 ch at end of row, turn *. This finishes first scallop. Begin again at 1st row, making the 11 t under 6-ch loop, and repeat for length desired; be-

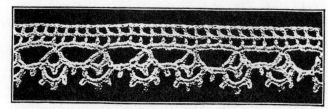

FIG. 7. EDGING. See page 4

ginning at end of 2d row in third scallop connect each scallop to previous one as follows: Chain 3, 1 d in 2d loop of 5 ch on scallop below, turn, ch 3, 1 d on 1st t (where ch of 3 began), then repeat from * to *.

Figure 11. *1st row*—Make a chain as long as you wish the edge to be. *2d row*—One t in 7th st from hook, ch 2, miss 2, 1 t in next to end of chain. *3d row*—Two d in each space to end. *4th row*—Turn, sl st to 2d st, ch 1, d in 13 d, * ch 6, thread over hook twice, skip 2, insert hook in next d and draw a loop through, thread over hook and draw through 2 loops, thread over, draw through 2 loops, leaving 2 loops on hook; thread over twice, skip 1 st, insert hook in next and draw a loop through, thread over, draw through 2 loops, thread over, draw through next 2 loops, leaving 3 loops on hook; thread over twice, skip 1 d, insert hook in next, draw loop through, thread over, draw through 2 loops, thread over, draw through 2 loops, thread over, draw through all loops on hook; ch 6, insert hook in top st and draw last loop of 6 ch through, ch 5, skip 3 d, 13 d in next 13 d on chain; repeat from * to end. *5th row*—Turn, skip 1 d, 10 d in next 10 d of last row, * ch 5, 16 t in ring of 5 ch, ch 5, 10 d in d of last row, skipping 1 d on each end; repeat from * to end. *6th row*—Turn, skip 1 d, 8 d in next d, * ch 7, d in 1st t, ** ch 7, 1 d in 3d st from hook, 1 d in next, 1 t in next, 1 t in next, 1 d t in next, 1 d in 3d t; repeat from ** 4 times. Chain 7, skip 1 d, 8 d in d of last row; repeat from

FIG. 8. EDGING. See page 4

* to end. *7th row*—Turn, * skip 1 d, 6 d in 6 d, ** ch 8, 1 d in ring at top of pyramid; repeat from ** to end of pyramids. Chain 8; repeat from * to end. *8th row*—Turn, * skip 1 d, 3 d in next 3 d, ch 5, 1 d in 3d st to pyramid, ** ch 5, 1 d in d on top of pyramid; repeat from ** to end of pyramids, ch 5; repeat from * to end. *9th row*—Turn, sl st to end of 1st 5 ch, (5 d, 3 ch, 5 d,) over each 5-ch loop to end of row.

Figure 12.—Chain 8, 1 t in 1st st made, ch 3, 1 t in same st, turn. *2d row*—Chain 3, 7 t in 1st space, ch 2, 1 t in 3d st of next space, ch 3, 1 t in same st, turn. *3d row*—Chain 3, 7 t under first space, ch 2, 1 t in 1st of 7 t below, ch 3, 1 t in same st, turn, and repeat last row for length desired, then make a heading by working 1 d in top of 3 ch before 7 t, ch 6, 1 d in next 3 ch, the length of edge.

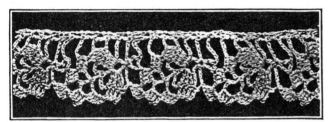

FIG. 9. EDGING. See page 4

Figure 13.—Make a chain a little longer than the desired length, to allow for taking up in making. *1st row*—Turn, miss 3 ch, 1 t in each ch to end. *2d row*—Turn, in 4th st 2 t, then 3 ch, 2 t, in same place; repeat in every 4th st. *3d row*—Turn, 4 d, 4 ch, 4 d, in first ring, sl st between rings. Work in each ring to end. *4th row*—Turn, sl st up to 1st p, 9 ch, fasten with sl st in 3d p; repeat to end of work. *5th row*—Turn, 4 d, 4 ch, 4 d, 4 ch, 4 d, over 9 ch, fasten with sl st between; repeat to end.

Figure 14.—Chain 16, form in a ring by making 1 d in the 1st ch st, make 17 d in this ring, turn. *1st row*—Make 1 d in each of 17 d, back loops only, turn. *2d row*—Eight d in next 8 d, ch 5, 1 d in next d, ch 5, 1 d in same d, ch 5, 1 d in each of next 5 d, turn. *3d row*—Chain 9, 1 d in middle picot, ch 9, 1 d in 4th d after picots, turn. *4th row*—Thirteen d in first arch, and 7 d under second arch, turn. *5th row*—Chain 10, 1 d in the 7th d of first arch, turn, and repeat from 1st row. Without breaking thread, when you have the length of edge you wish, ch 5, 1 d in point of scallop, * ch 5, 1 t under ch, ch 5, 1 d in next point, repeat to end of edge.

Figure 15.—Chain 10, join with sl st. *1st round*—Chain 4, 5 d t in ring, (ch 5, 6 d t in ring), 3 times, ch 5, 1 sl st in last st of 4 ch. *2d round*—One d in each of next 2 sts, taking up both loops of st, ch 9,

FIG. 10. INSERTION. See page 4

FIG. 11. EDGING. See page 4

1 d in same st with last d, 1 d in each of next 4 sts, 3 d in next st, (which is the 3d st of 5 ch), (1 d in each of next 10 sts, 3 d in next st) 3 times, 1 d in each of next 2 sts, 1 sl st in sl st, break thread and fasten.

NEXT STAR.—In the 2d round after making "1 sl st in last st of 4 ch, 1 d in each of next 2 sts," join to first star as follows: ch 5, take hook out of work, insert in d on 3d d t of the second cluster of 6 d t, catch the 5th ch and pull through, ch 9, 1 d in same st with last d on second star, 4 d in next 4 sts, 3 d in next st, (10 d in next 10 sts, 3 d in next st), twice, 10 d in next 10 sts, 2 d in next st, join in the corresponding st on first star with 1 sl st, ch 1, 1 d in same st with last d on second star, 1 d in each of next 2 sts, 1 sl st in last st of 4 ch. Make as many star motifs as you require for length of lace, joining each to preceding one in the manner described. In the last motif you make for end of lace, after making the 3d d in the second cluster of 6 t, ch 9, 1 d in same st with last d, 4 d in next 4 sts, 3 d in next st, and finish round like the preceding ones.

HEADING.—Holding wrong side of lace towards you, make 1 d in 9-ch loop, ch 7, 1 sl st in each of the 3 d made in centre st of 5 ch, ch 7, 1 d under 9 ch; repeat to end of row, turn. *2d row*—Chain 3, 1 t in 2d st of preceding row, * ch 1, miss 1, 1 t in next st; repeat from * to end of row.

EDGE.—Holding right side towards you, make * 1 t, 3 ch, 1 t in the d over the 3d d t in cluster, miss 2, 1 t, 3 ch, 1 t in next d, (miss 1, 1 t, 3 ch, 1 t in next d), 3 times, miss 2, 1 t, 3 ch, 1 t in next d, twice. Repeat from * to end.

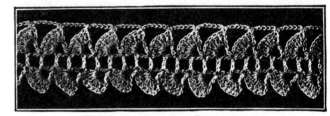

FIG. 12. EDGING. See page 5

Figure 16.—Make a chain as long as you wish your lace to be, allowing 2¼ inches more in length on foundation chain for every yard. *1st row*—Make 1 d t (thread over twice) in 5th st from hook, 1 d t in each of next 3 sts, keeping the last loop of each st on the hook till you have them all made, then put thread over the hook and draw through all the loops at once, then insert the hook under the 1st d t made, and make a d around all three d t at the top to secure them closely; ch 4, 1 d t in each of the next 3 sts, you will then have four loops on your needle, thread over hook and draw through all four at once. One d around all three at the top, inserting the hook under the 4 ch. Repeat the length of foundation chain.

5

FIG. 13. EDGING. See page 5

Without breaking thread, ch 5, 1 d in the end of foundation ch, ch 5, 1 d t between the 1st and 2d d t of last row, 1 d t between next 2 d t, 1 d t between the clusters, thread over needle and draw through all the loops, 1 d around them all at the top, * ch 4, 1 d t between next 2 d t, 1 d t between next 2, 1 d t between clusters, thread over, draw through all the loops, 1 d around the top of them. Repeat from * to end of row, turn, ch 5, 1 d under 1st ch of 4 (ch 3, 1 d under next ch of 4), repeat to end of row, turn, ch 5, 1 t under 1st ch (ch 1, 1 t in next d, ch 1, 1 t under next 3 ch), repeat to end.

Figure 17.— Foundation of Figs. 18, 19, 20. Chain 9, turn, make 1 t in first ch, * 3 ch, 1 t in same

FIG. 14. EDGING. See page 5

st *. Make from * to * three times altogether. * Five ch, turn, 1 t in second mesh below, 3 ch, 1 t in same mesh, 3 ch, 1 t in same mesh, 3 ch, 1 t in same mesh *. Repeat from * to * for the desired length.

Figure 18.— A lace that is like Fig. 20 as far as the 2d row. The 3d row is omitted from the upper edge, and the 3d row below is, 3 ch over each group of 4 t, 1 d over the next chain, a picot of 3 ch, 1 d over same chain.

Figure 19.— Make foundation of Fig. 17, as above, and when the required length is made, turn and double crochet all along one edge, making 4 d in the smaller meshes and 6 or 7 d in the larger meshes of 5 ch. The other edge is to be overcast to the material and will fit any edge, straight, circular, or around a corner. If preferred, a chain and double crochet or treble crochet can be made along this edge to sew to the material, but it is not quite so adjustable, unless the chains are adapted to the curves or corners.

Figure 20.— An appliqué with picots at both edges. After making the foundation (Fig. 17) the required length, make, *1st row*—A group of 4 t over each scallop of 5 ch with 2 ch between groups, along each edge. *2d row*—Like 1st. *3d row*—Make 1 d over the middle of group of 4 t, 1 t over next chain, 3 ch, 1 t over same chain, picot of 3 ch, 3 ch, 1 t over same chain.

Figure 21.— Chain 21. *1st row*—One d in 12th st from hook, ch 7, skip 3 sts on ch, 1 d in 4th st, ch 7, skip 3 sts, 1 d in last st of ch, turn. *2d row*—Chain 9, 1 d under first space (sp), (ch 7, 1 d in next sp) twice, turn. *3d row*—Chain 9, 1 d under first sp, (ch 7, 1 d under next sp) twice, turn. *4th row*—Chain 2, insert hook under first sp, thread over, draw a loop through, sl st in this loop, thread over hook and draw through both sts on hook. Through these 2 sts the 3 picots are made. Chain 6, 1 d through the 2 sts, twice, ch 5, 1 d in the same place, 8 t, 1 d under sp, 1 d, 7 t, 1 d under next sp, 1 d, 6 t, under next sp, turn. *5th row*—Chain 9, 1 d in 4th t of first group, ch 7, 1 d in 4th t of second group, ch 7, 1 d in 4th t of last group. Repeat from 2d row for length.

HEADING.—Without breaking thread ch 4, 1 t under first sp, ch 3, 1 t under next sp, ch 3, 1 t in last t of group, inserting hook under the two loops of st at the top. Repeat to end of row.

Figure 22.— Chain 13. * *1st row*—Skip 3 sts on ch, 10 t in next 10 sts, taking up only 1 l of sts, turn. *2d row*—(Chain 5, skip 2 t, 1 d in 3d t) 3 times, ch 5, 1 d in centre stitch of 3 ch at end, ch 5, 1 d in same st; ch 5, 1 d between 1st and 2d t, taking up two loops of st, * (ch 5, skip 2 t, 1 d in 3d t) 3 times, turn. *3d row*—Chain 5, 1 d in first loop (l), (ch 5, 1 d in next l), 3 times, ** ch 5, 1 t in centre l, ch 4, make a close picot (p) by inserting hook in t, using the two upper loops, putting hook down through top of 1st l, and out through side of 2d one, thread over hook, and make a sl st through the 2 l's and st

FIG. 15. EDGING. See page 5

on hook, (1 t, p of 4 ch in same l) 3 times, 1 t in same l, ch 5, 1 d in next l, 4 times, **. *2d scallop*—Chain 18, repeat from * to *, (ch 5, skip 2 t, 1 d in next), twice, ch 2, 1 d over centre of ch between scallops, (ch 2, 1 d in 1st l on 1st scallop, ch 2, 1 d in opposite l on 2d scallop) twice, so that the two first l's on both are connected; ch 5, 1 d in next l, repeat from ** to **. Begin again at second scallop, and repeat for length.

HEADING.—Without breaking thread, ch 5, 1 d under 1st l on top, * ch 5, 1 d under l past row of t sts, (ch 5, 1 d in next l) twice, repeat from * to end of row, break thread. *2d row*—Begin at right-hand corner with 1 d in 1st l, ch 3, 1 d in next l all across to

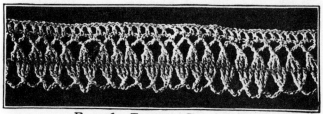

FIG. 16. EDGING. See page 5

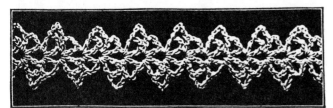

FIG. 17. INSERTION. See page 6

end, break thread. *3d row*—Make 1 d in 1st l at right hand, ch 4, 1 t in 1st l, ch 2, 1 t in next l, to end. Break thread, and fasten all loose ends securely.

Figure 23. — Chain 12, turn. *1st row*—One t in 5th st from hook, ch 6, 1 t in each of last 2 sts of 12 ch, turn. *2d row*—Chain 3, 1 t in 2d t, 6 t over 6 ch, 1 t in next t, 1 t in top of 3 ch at end of last row, turn. *3d row*—Chain 3, 1 t in 2d t, ch 6, 1 t in last t, 1 t in top of 3 ch at end, ch 5, fasten with sl st in 3 ch at end of 2d row (for scallop), ch 1, turn. *4th row*—Five d, 4 ch, 5 d over 5 ch, 1 sl st in top of next t, ch 3, 1 t in next t, 6 t over 6 ch, 1 t in next t, 1 t in 3 ch at end; ch 5, fasten in 3 ch with sl st, ch 1, turn. *5th row*—Five d, 4 ch, 5 d over 5 ch, 1 sl st in top of next t, ch 3, 1 t in next t, ch 6, 1 t in last t, 1 t in 3 ch at end, ch 5, sl st in 3 ch, ch 1, turn. Repeat from 4th row for length desired.

FIG. 18. EDGING. See page 6

Figure 24. — *1st row*—Chain 21, 2 t in 4th ch from hook, ch 2, 2 t in same st, making shell (sh), 1 t in 7th ch, ch 8, miss 7 sts, 1 t in next ch, miss 2 sts, make sh in next st, 1 t in last st of foundation ch, ch 4, turn. *2d row*—One sh in sh, 1 t in next t, 10 t over 8 ch, 1 t in next t, 1 sh in sh, 1 t in 4 ch at end of shell, ch 4, turn. Repeat rows 1 and 2 until at end of 5th row, ch 5, fasten in 1st loop of 4 ch with sl st (for scallop), ch 5, fasten in 2d loop of 5 ch with sl st, ch 1, turn, 10 d over 5 ch, 5 d over part of next 5 ch, ch 5, turn, fasten back between 10 d of scallop below with sl st, ch 1, turn, 5 d, 4 ch, 5 d over last 5 ch, 5 d over rest of 5 ch, fasten with sl st in top of last t, ch 4. Make 1 row of work. At end of this make another scallop. Repeat to desired length.

Figure 25. — Chain 39. *1st row*—* Draw a loop through 2d st from needle, draw a loop through next st; repeat till you have 7 loops on needle, counting the one you had at first; thread over hook and draw through 6 loops, thread over and draw through remaining 2 loops on needle, this ties the knot. Chain 9 and repeat from * to *, ch 3, miss 7 sts, 1 d in next st; repeat to end of foundation chain, when you should have 5 knots, turn. *2d row*—Chain 9; repeat from * to *, ch 3, catch with 1 d in first end of knot below; repeat to end of row, and from beginning of 1st row for length desired.

Figure 26. — Use novelty braid, No. 100 thread, and No. 12 hook.
1st row—Make * 1 t in first picot on medallion, ch 3, 1 t in next p, 4 times, ch 5, thread over hook 3 times, insert hook in end of medallion close to last p, thread over and pull a loop through (thread over, pull through 2 loops) 3 times, thread over 3 times, insert hook in end of next medallion close to first p, pull a loop through, (thread over, pull through 2 loops) 5 times, ch 5; repeat from * for length desired.
EDGE.— Make 1 d in 1st p of medallion on the other side of braid, (ch 2, 1 d in next p) 4 times, ch 9; repeat from * to end. The thread should be broken at end of each row, beginning each row at right-hand end.

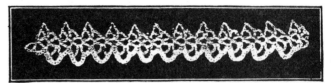

FIG. 19. EDGING. See page 6

2d row—One sl st in 1st d, * 2 d under 2 ch, (ch 2, 2 d under next 2 ch) 3 times, 14 d under 9 ch; repeat from * to end of row. *3d row*—One d in 1st d, * ch 2, 2 d under 2 ch, 3 times, ch 2, 1 d between 2d and 3d d, ch 12, 1 d between last d under ch, and next d under 2 ch; repeat from * to end of row. *4th row*—One d under 1st sp, * (ch 2, 2 d under next sp) twice, ch 2, 1 d under next sp, 20 d under ch, 1 d in next sp; repeat from * to end. *5th row*—* One d under 1st 2 ch, ch 2, 2 d under next 2 ch, ch 2, 1 d under next 2 ch, ch 19; repeat from * to end. *6th row*—* One d in 1st sp, ch 7, 1 d in 5th st from hook for a p, ch 2, 1 d in 2d sp, 6 d under ch, p of 5 sts, 3 d, p, 4 times, 6 d under ch; repeat from * to end.

Figure 27. — Chain 6, and join. Chain 6, 18 d t in ring, ch 6, turn, 3 d t in 1st 3 d t of previous row. Chain 6, 1 d t in each of next 3 d t, ch 6, 3 d t till there are 5 spaces and 6 clusters of 3 d t. Turn, fasten in 3d d t from needle, * 12 h t in space of 6 ch, fasten in 3d d t; repeat from * until all spaces are used. Chain 6 and join. Make second fan as the first to end of 2d row; fasten in centre of first fan. Last row like last row of first fan. After the second fan all others should be fastened between the first and second scallops of the last fan on the same side of the work.

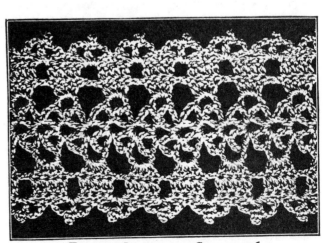

FIG. 20. INSERTION. See page 6

Figure 28A. — Chain 6, 2 d t in 1st st, * ch 6, 2 d t in same st, turn, fasten in 2d d t from middle; 12 h t in ch 6, fasten in last st of 1st ch. Turn, 1 sl st in each h t, fasten, ch 6, fasten in st in which the 4 d t were made. Chain 6, 2 d t at top of last d t, ch 6, fasten in same d t; repeat from *.

Figure 28B. — Make chain as long as desired. *1st row*—Chain 6, 2 d t in 7th st from needle, ch 6, skip 4, 3 d t in 5th st; repeat to end of ch, turn. *2d row*—Twelve h t in each ch 6, fastening in 3d d t each time. Slip stitch along foundation ch.

Figure 29. — Chain 14. *1st row*—Make a shell of 3 t, 3 ch, 3 t in 5th st from hook, ch 4, skip 4 sts, 1 d in 5th st, skip 2 sts, a shell in next st, turn. *2d row*—Chain 5, shell in shell, ch 4, tie down with 1 d in

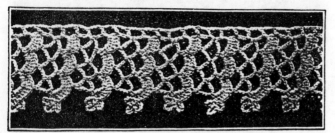

FIG. 21. EDGING. See page 6

top of 1st t of shell, shell in shell, turn. *3d row*—Chain 5, shell in shell, ch 4, tie, shell in shell, 2 t under 5 ch between rows, (ch 2, 2 t under same ch) 4 times, 1 d in last st of foundation chain, turn. *4th row*—* One d between first 2 t, 4 t under 2 ch between t, repeat 4 times, 1 d between last 2 t, ch 3, shell in shell, ch 4, tie down, shell in shell, turn *.

FIG. 22. EDGING. See page 6

5th row—Chain 5, and repeat from 1st row for length. After making last t under 5 ch in 3d row of 2 d and all succeeding scallops, make 1 d under same 3 ch where last shell of 5th row was made, then turn and repeat from * to *. When you have length desired, without breaking thread, ch 5, 2 d under 1st 5 ch between shells (ch 4, 2 d under next 5 ch), to end of row.

Figure 30. — Use No. 50 Cordonnet crochet cotton, a No. 12 hook. Make 1 d in first point of braid, * ch 8, give a downward twist of chain from left to right, insert hook in 4th st from beginning of ch, or 5th st from hook, thread over hook and pull a loop through st and the st on hook (this makes a downward turning picot), ch 2, 1 d in next point of braid. Repeat from * till you have length desired. Take another piece of braid, make 1 d in first point, ch 3, take hook out of work, pick up first piece of

FIG. 23. BEADING. See page 7

braid, insert hook in 1st st at left of 1st p, * catch 3d st of 3 ch just made and pull through, ch 4, twist ch around to the right, insert hook in same st. the 3d st was pulled through, thread over hook and pull through st and loop on hook together, ch 2, 1 d in next point of braid; ch 3, take hook out and insert downwards through 1st st to the left of next p on top piece of braid and repeat from * to end of first piece of braid.

HEADING.—Make 1 t in first point of braid, * ch 7, make a downward turning p by twisting ch to the right, inserting hook in 3d st from beginning of ch or 5th st from hook and pulling a loop through st, and loop on hook together, ch 2, 1 t in next point. Repeat from * to end of row. *2d row*—One t on 1st t, ch 2, 1 t in st close to p, ch 2, 1 t in next t, repeat to end, and on second edge. Fasten off ends securely.

Figure 31. — Use No. 40 Cordonnet crochet cotton, a hook that will carry the thread easily without splitting it. *1st row*—Make 1 d in first point of braid, * ch 8, make an inverted picot by twisting ch around underneath to the right, insert hook in 5th st from hook, thread over and pull through 5th st and loop on hook together, ch 3, 1 d in next point, ch 3, 1 d t in next point, (ch 3, 1 d t in same point) 3 times, ch 3, 1 d in next point; repeat from * till you have length desired. *2d row*—One d in centre of 1st p, taking up two threads of sts, * ch 4, 6 t under first 3 ch in second point, take hook out, insert it in top of first of 6 t, catch last st and pull through, (ch 5, 6 t under next 3 ch, take hook out of work, insert in first of 6 t, pull last st through) twice, ch 4, 1 d in centre of next p, repeat from * to end of row. *3d row*—* Five d under 4 ch, 7 d under 5 ch, 3 d under next 5 ch, ch 7, take hook out of work, insert in 4th d of first 7 ch, catch 7th st and pull through, ch 1, 9 d under ch, 3 d in unfinished sp, 5 d under 4 ch; repeat from * to end of row.

HEADING.—One d in first point of braid at right hand, * ch 7, downward turning p in 5th st from

FIG. 24. BEADING. See page 7

hook, ch 2, 1 d in next point; repeat from * to end of braid. *2d row*—Begin again at right-hand end, 1 t in d on first point, * ch 2, 1 t in centre of p, ch 2, 1 t in d on next point; repeat from * to end.

Figure 32. WHEEL.— Chain 20, join with sl st. *1st round*—Chain 1, 40 d in ring, join to 1st d with sl st. *2d round*—Chain 7, miss 4 d, 1 d in 5th d, (ch 6, miss 4 d, 1 d in 5th d) around, join last 6 ch to 1st st of 7 ch with sl st. *3d round*—Make 9 d under each chain-loop around, join to 1st d. Break thread and fasten. Join each wheel as you make it to preceding one, at the 5th d in a loop. Take hook out of work, insert in a 5th d in preceding wheel, catch 5th loop and pull through, then proceed with d, making four more in loop, join next 1 in same manner, always leaving two free loops at top and bottom of wheel.

Make a row of wheels as long as you wish your edge to be, leaving an end of thread at beginning of each wheel long enough to make the needlework stitches in the centre with.

HEADING. — Fasten thread with 1 d in 5th st of 2d l to the right on first wheel, ch 5, 1 d in 5th st on next l, * ch 8, 1 d in 5th st of first free loop on next wheel, ch 5, 1 d in 5th st on next l, repeat from * to end of row. Break thread and fasten at end of each row, for it has to be worked all one way, from right to left. *2d row*—Beginning at right-hand corner, make 1 d in each st to end of row, taking up two loops of each st. *3d row*—Make 1 t in 1st d at right-hand corner, ch 1, miss 1 d, 1 t in next d, repeat across. *4th row*—Make 1 d under first space, ch 1, 1 d under next sp, * ch 6, miss 1 sp, 1 d under next sp, ch 1, 1 d under next sp, repeat from * to end of row. *5th row*—One d between first 2 d, 9 d under 6 ch, repeat across. *6th row*—One d in 5th d of 1st l, ch 5, 1 d in 5th d on next l, repeat across. *7th row*—One t in 1st d, (ch 1, miss 1 st of ch, 1 t in next st) repeat across. *8th row*—One d in each st to end of row.

INSERTION TO MATCH EDGING.—Make a chain the length required, then repeat directions for heading from 2d row.

Figure 33. *Roll Stitch.* — Thread around the needle 12 times, insert needle in work, thread over, draw through the work; thread over, pull through the coil, thread over, draw through the loop on needle. The roll when complete is straight with a string the length of the roll on its left side. The length of the rolls are regulated by the number of times the thread is put around the needle.

Chain 10, join with 1 t in 4th st from hook, ch 6,

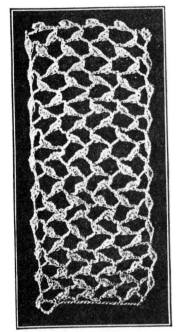

FIG. 25. INSERTION
See page 7

FIG. 26. EDGING. See page 7

turn. Make 4 roll sts of 12 overs each, with 3 ch sts between each roll, (not counting the one made first to fasten the st), in ring just made, turn. Chain 2, make a scallop of 1 d, 3 t, 1 d, between each roll, 1 d under 6 ch, turn. Chain 8, 4 roll sts with 3 ch between each in the middle scallop of last fan, ch 1, 6 roll sts with 3 ch between each in the 2 ch at bottom of last scallop of first fan made, join to 1st st of foundation ch with sl st, turn. Chain 2, make a scallop between each roll of 6, 1 d under 1 ch between fans, ch 2, 3 scallops in next fan, 1 d under 8 ch, turn. *Chain 8, make a fan of 4 roll sts in centre of last fan, turn, ch 3, 1 d, 3 t, 1 d between each roll, 1 d under 8 ch, turn. Chain 8, make another fan in centre of last fan, ch 1, fan of 6 roll sts in 3 ch at bottom of preceding fan, 1 d under 2 ch at end of pre-

FIG. 27. INSERTION. See page 7

vious 6-roll fan, turn, ch 2, make scallops in 6-roll fan, 1 d under 1 ch, ch 2, 3 scallops on next fan, turn. Repeat from * for length desired.

A pretty insertion can be made by omitting the 6-roll scallops and working an edge on both sides of the row of small fans.

Figure 34. — Make a chain of 14 sts. *1st row*—One t in 4th st, 2 more t in same st, ch 2, 3 t in next st, ch 8, skip 7 sts, 3 t in next st, ch 2, 3 t in next st, turn. *2d row*—Chain 5, shell in shell, ch 8, shell in shell, turn. *3d row*—Chain 5, shell in shell, ch 8, shell in shell, ch 1, 1 t under 5 ch, turn. *4th row*—Chain 5, shell in shell, ch 7, 1 d over all 3 chs, turn, ch 2, 7 t under 7 ch, turn, ch 2, 7 t between 7 t (last one being made under 2 ch at end), twice more, shel'

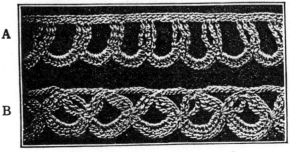

FIG. 28. EDGINGS. See page 8

FIG. 29. EDGING. See page 8

in shell, turn. *5th row*—Chain 5, shell in shell, ch 8, shell in shell, ch 1, 1 t under 5 ch, turn. *6th row*—Chain 5, shell in shell, ch 8, shell in shell, turn. *7th row*—Chain 5, shell in shell, ch 8, shell in shell, ch 1, 1 t under 5 ch, turn. *8th row*—Like 4th row, making 1 d over 3 chains into point of diamond, turn. *9th row*—Like 5th row, turn. *10th row*—Like 6th to last shell in shell, then ch 5, 1 shell under 5 ch between 8th and 9th rows, ch 2, 3 t under next 5 ch, ch 5, 3 t under next 5 ch, ch 2, shell in next 5 ch, ch 5, 1 sl st in 3 ch at end of 1st row, turn; 9 d under 5 ch, shell in shell, ch 2, 10 t under next 5 ch, ch 2, shell in shell, turn, ch 5, shell in shell, ch 1, 1 d between first 2 t on 5 ch (ch 4, 1 d between next 2 t), repeat to end of t's, ch 1, shell in shell, ch 5, 1 sl st between last t of shell and next d, ch 1, 9 d over 5 ch, shell in shell, ch 2, 1 d under first 4 ch (ch 4, 1 d under next 4 ch), repeat in each loop, ch 2, shell in shell, turn; ch 5, shell in shell, ch 2, 1 d under first loop (ch 4, 1 d in next), in each loop, ch 2, shell in shell, ch 5, 1 sl st at end of last t, ch 1, 9 d under 5 ch, shell in shell, ch 2, 1 d under first loop, ch 4, 1 d under remaining loops, ch 2, shell in shell, turn, ch 5, shell in shell. Continue working back and forth in this manner till you have but one loop at the top, then ch 5, shell in shell, ch 2, 1 t in centre loop, ch 2, shell in shell, ch 5, 1 sl st between 3d t and d, ch 1, 9 d in loop of 5 ch, 6 t in place of shell, 1 t on t, 6 t in next 3 ch, turn, ch 6, 1 d in t, ch 6, 1 sl st at end of 6 t, ch 1, 9 d under 6 ch, 5 d under next ch, without turning, ch 5, pull last st through 5 d of first loop, ch 1, 9 d over loop, 4 d over next loop, 9 d over each loop to bottom of scallop. *11th row*—Shell in shell, ch 8, shell in shell, ch 1, 1 t under 5 ch. Repeat from 4th row for length required.

Figure 35.—Chain 45. *1st row*—One t in 8th st from hook, (ch 2, miss 2, 1 t in next st), 11 times, turn. *2d row*—Chain 5, 1 t in next t, (ch 2, miss 2, 1 t in next t), twice. Thread over hook, take a st under next 2 ch, thread over, take a st in the same place 3 times more, drawing the sts all up the same length, thread over and draw through all the sts on the hook, ch 1 to fasten, 1 t in next t, this forms what is called a bean st, (ch 2 1 t in next t), 5 times, 1 bean in next sp, 1 t in next t, (ch 2, 1 t

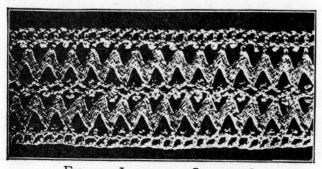

FIG. 30. INSERTION. See page 8

in next t), 3 times, turn. *3d row*—Chain 5, make 2 sps, 1 bean in next sp, 1 sp, 1 bean, 3 sps, 1 bean, 1 sp, 1 bean, 2 sps, turn. *4th row*—One sp, 1 bean in each alternate sp until 6 beans are made, 1 sp at end, turn. *5th row*—Two sps, 2 beans with 1 sp between, 3 sps, 2 beans with 1 sp between, 2 sps, turn. *6th row*—Three sps, 1 bean, 5 sps, 1 bean, 3 sps, turn. *7th row*—Thirteen sps like 1st row. Repeat from 2d row for length desired.

Figure 36.—Make a chain the length desired. *1st row*—One t in 8th st from hook, ch 2, miss 2, 1 t in next st to end of chain, turn. *2d row*—Chain 3, 1 t on next t, ch 5, 1 t in the two loops at top of the first 3 ch and the 1 t, inserting hook under the upper loops of sts, * ch 2 and make a double cross

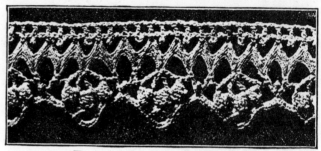

FIG. 31. EDGING. See page 8

treble as follows: Thread over hook three times, insert hook in top of next t, thread over and work off 2 sts twice, thread over once, insert hook in next t, thread over and work off sts by twos, 4 times, ch 2, 1 t in upper loops of two centre sts, as you did in first double cross treble (d c t). Repeat from * to end of row, turn. *3d row*—Chain 5, 1 t on 2d t of d c t, * ch 1, 1 t under 2 ch, ch 1, 1 t in 1st t of d c t, ch 2, 1 t in 2d t of d c t, repeat from * to end of row, turn. *4th row*—Chain 5, 3 1 t under first space (sp), 1 1 t on next t, * ch 2, miss the t made under 2 ch on preceding row, make a d c t in top of next two t, making 5 ch between the top t's instead of two as made in 2d row, ch 2, miss 1 t, 1 1 t on next t, 3 1 t under 2 ch, 1 1 t on next t, repeat from * to end, turn. *5th row*—Slip stitch to 3d 1 t, * ch 2, 1 t in first t of d c t, ch 3, 1 t in 3d st of 5 ch, ch 5, 1 t in same st, ch 3, 1 t on 2d t of d c t, ch 2, 1 d in top of 3d 1 t; repeat from * to end, and turn. *6th row*—Two d under 2 ch, 1 d under 3 ch, ch 4, make 1 d in top loops of last d to form a p, 1 d under same ch, 1 d, p, 1 d, p, 1 d, under 5 ch, 1 d, p, 1 d, under 3 ch, 2 d under 2 ch; repeat from * to end.

Figure 37.—Make 7 chain, join in a ring. *1st row*—Chain 5, 1 t in ring (ch 3, 1 t in ring) 4 times. ch 3, catch in the 2d of 1st 5 ch. *2d row*—One d, 5 t, 1 d under each 3-ch loop in turn. *3d row*—Chain 4, 1 d in top of t of 1st row at back of previous row,* ch 4, 1 d in top of next t; repeat this from * around. *4th row*—One d, 7 t, 1 d under each 4-ch loop at back of previous row in turn. *5th row*—Chain 5, 1 d in top of 1st d at back of previous row, * ch 5, 1 d in top of next d; repeat from * around. *6th row*—One d, 9 t, 1 d under each 5-ch loop in turn. *7th row*—Slip stitch up to 3d of 9 t, * ch 9, p in 4th st from hook, ch 3, miss 3, 1 d in next t, ch 9, p, ch 3, 1 d in 3d t of next petal; repeat from * around and fas-

FIG. 32. EDGING. See page 9

ten off. Make another rose like one finished and join to first one as follows: After making the last loop sl st up 3 sts on 1st loop, ch 7, p in 4th st, ch 7, p, ch 1, 1 d under next loop, ch 9, p, ch 1, 1 d t, under next loop, take up first rose made, and holding it next you, right side upwards, work 1 d t under one of the loops, ch 9, p, ch 1, 1 d in next loop on same rose, ch 9, p, ch 1, 1 d between picots on first joining loop, ch 9, p, ch 1, 1 d in next loop on opposite rose, finish off. Join each rose as you make it to the sixth free loop from joining loop on last rose joined, in order to have the first joining loop with the 2 p's always in the same position at the top; repeat for length desired.

HEADING.— Holding work right side towards you, using for the top the edge where the joining loops with 2 p's are, make 1 t in 4th loop from joining loop, * ch 3, 1 d in next loop, 3 times, ch 3. 1 t in next loop, (ch 3, 1 d t in next loop), twice, ch 3, 1 t in next t; repeat from * to end, break thread. 2d row—Begin again at right-hand end, 1 t on 1st t, ch 3, 1 t on next t, to end.

EDGE.— One d in first loop at bottom edge, holding right side towards you, making the d before the p in the loop, * ch 8, p in 4th st, ch 4, 1 d in next loop before the p; repeat from * 5 times in first and last scallops, but only 4 times in all others, ch 5, 1 d in next loop at side of p on next rose; repeat from * to end. 2d row—Make 1 d in loop at side of p, ch 9, 1 sl st in 5th st from hook, (ch 5, 1 sl st in same st twice, forming a triple p), ch 4, 1 d in next loop at side of p; repeat to end.

Figure 38. ROSE.—Chain 6, join with sl st. 1st row—Chain 6, 1 t in ring (ch 3, 1 t in ring), repeat three times, ch 2, 1 sl st in 3d st of 6 ch. 2d row—One d, 5 t, 1 d under each loop all around, join with sl st in 1st d. 3d row—Chain 5, catch in back of petal in last d of petal, repeat 5 times. 4th row—Make 1 d, 8 t, 1 d under each loop in this row, join with sl st in 1st d. 5th row—Loops of 6 ch, fasten back of petals. 6th row—One d, 11 t, 1 d under loops all around. 7th row—Loops of 7 ch.

FIG. 33. EDGING. See page 9

8th row—Chain 5, 1 t in 1st 7-ch loop, (ch 2, 1 t in same loop) once more; ch 2, 1 t in next loop, twice more, repeat around, joining last 2 ch to 3d st of 5 ch, with sl st. You should have nineteen loops or spaces in this row. 9th row—Chain 5, 1 d under first loop, ch 5, 1 d under next loop, repeat around. 10th row—Chain 5, 1 d under 5 ch, all around, break thread and fasten off.

WHEEL.—Chain 6, join with sl st. 1st row—Chain 3, for 1st t, make 17 more t in ring, join to 3 ch with sl st. 2d row—Chain 5, 1 t in next t, (ch 2, 1 t in next t) repeat 16 times, ch 2, fasten in 3d st of 5 ch. 3d row—Chain 5, for 1st d t (thread over twice), make a d t under first 2-ch loop, working off two loops twice, retaining last two on needle, make two more d t in same loop, working off two loops twice each time. You should have remaining on the needle four loops, work off by two's; ch 3, * make a cluster of 4 d t under next loop, you will have five loops left on needle, work off 2 sts twice, then thread over hook and work off three remain-

FIG. 34. EDGING. See page 9

ing stitches, ch 3 and repeat from * around, joining last 3 ch with sl st in 5 ch; you should have eighteen clusters of d t. 4th row—Chain 5, 1 d under 3 ch between clusters of d t, repeat around, ch 5, 1 d in same sp, ch 1, 1 d in first 5 ch made. This completes the wheel motif; now, without breaking thread, join the two finished motifs together as follows: Place the two right sides together, having the loop of rose where the last loop was fastened off, opposite the last loop on wheel, ch 3, 1 sl st in d fastening last loop of rose motif, ch 3, 1 d in loop on wheel, ch 3, 1 d in next loop on rose. Continue alternating 3 ch, 1 d on wheel and rose till four loops have been joined on each, the last joining d, being on the wheel. All the motifs are to be joined in the same manner. When you have a sufficient number joined, fasten thread with 1 d in sixth free loop from joining, beginning at right-hand upper corner of work. 1st row—Chain 5, 1 d in next loop, repeat four times more, * ch 5, make a cluster of 3 d t under loop where the motifs were joined, leaving two loops on needle, make another cluster of 3 d t in centre, under the d joining motifs, you now have three loops on needle; make a third cluster under next loop, leaving four loops on needle; thread over and draw through two loops, thread over and draw through remaining three loops; ch 5, 1 d in next loop, make four more 5-ch loops across the top of wheel; repeat from * to the end of row, turn. 2d row—Chain 6, 1 d under first loop (ch 5, 1 d under next loop), repeat to end of row, turn. 3d row—Slip stitch up 3 sts on 5-ch loop, ch 5, one cluster of 4 d t, counting 5 ch as 1st d t, under first loop (ch 3, another cluster of 4 d t under next loop), repeat to end of row, turn. *4th row*—Chain 6, 1 d under 3 ch between clusters, ch 5, 1 d under next 3 ch, to end of row, turn. *5th row*—Chain 7, 1 t in first loop, (ch 4, 1 t in next loop) to end of row; break thread, and fasten off. Go back to beginning of row, make 1 d in 7 ch, ** ch 5, 1 d under next 4-ch loop, ch 5, 1 d in next loop, ch 1, 1 t under next loop, (ch 1, 1 t in same loop) repeat six times more, 1 d under next 4-ch loop, turn. *2d row*—Chain 5, 1 t between 1st and 2d t, * ch 2, 1 t between next t, repeat from * six more times, 1 d under next loop at bottom, turn. *3d row*—Chain 5, make clusters of 4 d t with 3 ch

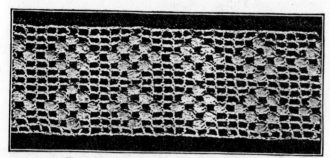

FIG. 35. INSERTION. See page 10

between each cluster, under each 2 ch around scallop, making eight clusters in all, ch 3, 1 d under 4 ch of preceding row at bottom, turn. *4th row*—Chain 6, 1 d under 3 ch preceding first cluster, ch 5, 1 d under next 3 ch, repeat 5-ch loops around scallop, making 5 ch, 1 d under 5 ch at beginning of d t, ch 3, 1 d under 4 ch at bottom, turn. *5th row*—Chain 6, 1 d under 3 ch, ch 5, 1 d under next loop, repeat 5-ch loops around scallop, ch 3, 1 d under 4 ch at bottom. This completes the first scallop, repeat from ** to end of row.

In all scallops after the first one, at the end of the 4th row, after making the last 5 ch, 1 d at end of d t cluster, make 1 ch, 1 d under 4-ch loop at bottom. Then to connect the scallops, ch 3, 1 d under the opposite 5-ch loop on first or preceding scallop, then turn, ch 3, 1 d under first 5-ch loop on second scallop, and complete the row like 5th row of first scallop. Finish the upper edge of lace the same as lower from the 1st row after the motifs are all joined, where you join in your thread under sixth free loop, to where you break thread and fasten off.

Figure 39.— Use No. 40 Cordonnet crochet cotton. In first loop on medallion of braid make 3 d t, retaining last loop of each st on the hook, (thread over hook, pull through 2 loops) 4 times, thread over and pull through last 3 loops; ch 3, and repeat in each of the next 5 loops. This makes 6 petals in all with 3 ch between each. Chain 3, make 1 sl st through the 1st 3 loops on next medallion, 1 sl st through next 3 loops, drawing the st up closely; this makes an inverted flower; ch 3, repeat from * till you have the length desired, ending with the inverted flower. Chain 3, 1 sl st in the end of this last medallion, ch 3; repeat from * to end of row on second side of braid. Chain 3, 1 sl st in end of medallion. *2d row*—Chain 3, sl st along the d t sts to 1st ch of 3, under this work ** 1 d, 2 t, ch 3, 1 sl st in last t, to form a picot (p), 2 t, 1 d; repeat in each 3-ch space to end of medallion, 1 d under next 3 ch, ch 7, 1 d under next 3 ch,

close to cluster of d t; repeat from ** to end of row. Chain 6, 1 d under 3 ch at end of ch 6, 1 d under 3 ch close to d t. Under each of next five 3-ch spaces, work 1 d, 3 t, 1 d, ch 2, 1 d t in centre of inverted flower, ch 2, 1 d under 3 ch close to cluster of d t; repeat to end of row, ending with 1 d t in centre of inverted flower. *3d row*—Chain 8, turn, * 1 d t in first scallop, ch 3, 1 t in next scallop, ch 3, 1 d in centre scallop, ch 3, 1 t in next, ch 3, 1 d t in last scallop; ch 1, 1 l t (thread over 3 times), in d t below, ch 1; repeat from * in 3d row to end of row, turn. *4th row*—Chain 6, * 1 t on next t, (ch 3, 1 t on next t), twice, ch 3, 1 d t on next d t, ch 3, miss centre 1 t below and make 1 d t on next d t, ch 3, 1 t on next t; repeat from * to end of row and break thread. *5th row*—Begin at right-hand end and make 4 t under each sp, with 1 ch between to end of row.

Figure 40. — Follow directions given for Fig. 39 to 2d row. In making the scallops on the 2d row of petals, make them like the 1st row, with a p in the centre; break thread at end of 2d row, as it finishes the appliqué.

FOR INSERTION.— Finish both sides alike, making the scallops without the picots, and adding the heading on both sides.

Figure 41. — Use No. 50 Cordonnet crochet cotton and medium size braid. Join a piece of braid of 20 points, sewing together firmly between two points, so that the joining will be invisible. Chain 6, join with sl st. * Chain 13, take hook out of work, insert in a point on the inside circle of braid, 4 sl sts in next 4 sts of ch, ch 5, fasten in the same way in next two points, putting hook down through second point, then through the next one, 4 sl sts in next 4 sts of ch, ch 5, fasten in next point, 4 sl sts in next 4 sts, reach over centre ch and make 1 sl st on 1st ch, putting hook down through centre of sl st, and through st of main ch the sl st was worked in; then 3 d over ch, ch 6, 1 sl st in last d to make a picot (p), 9 d over remainder of ch, 1 d in ring. Chain 10, fasten in next point, 3 d over ch, p of 6 sts, 9 d to ring, 1 d in ring; repeat from * 3 times and fasten off. Make as many diamonds as you desire for length of lace and sew points together on the wrong side. *2d row*—At beginning of first diamond, make a half block and one whole one as follows: Chain 10, miss 1st st, 9 d in next 9 sts of ch, * ch 1 to turn, 9 d in 9 d, using back loops of sts only; repeat from * once more, this brings you to the end of 3d row; make 1 d in fourth point of braid from top point, then another row of 9 d in 9 d. Make a long st by putting ** thread over hook 4 times, insert hook in next point, thread over

Fig. 36. EDGING. See page 10

12

hook and pull through, (thread over hook and pull through 2 loops) 5 times, ** ch 10, miss 1st st, 9 d in next 9 sts, ch 1 and work 6 more rows, which makes a full block of 7 rows, 1 d in next point, fasten off.

BETWEEN DIAMONDS.— Make 3 whole bls of 7 rows each. Begin the 1st bl with 1 d in second point of braid from top, ch 10, miss 1st st and work back and forth for 7 rows, 9 d in each row, make a long st in next point (directions from ** to **), ch 10, 1 d in

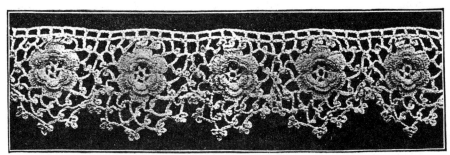

FIG. 37. EDGING. See page 10

next point, make another bl to end of 6th row, 1 d in opposite point on next diamond, then make the 7th row; repeat from ** to ** in next point. Chain 10, work another bl of 7 rows, 1 d in next point, fasten off; repeat to end, making 1 bl and ½ bl at end of lace.

HEADING. *1st row*—Repeat from ** to ** in the top of the long st between the half bl and the block, ch 5, 1 sl st in first end of bl, make 6 more sl sts along the top of bl; *** repeat from ** to ** in next point of braid, ch 12, 1 d in top point, ch 12; repeat from ** to ** next point, 7 sl sts across bl, ch 5, thread over hook, 4 times, insert hook in top of long st at right of lower bl, work off 2 loops 4 times, leaving 2 on hook, thread over 4 times, insert hook in top of next loop-stitch, work off sts by two's, 6 times, insert hook under 5 ch and make 1 tight d st around the top of the long st, ch 5, 7 sl sts across next bl; repeat from *** to end of row. *2d row*—Begin at right hand again, 1 t in top of first long st, ch 2, 1 t in centre st of 5 ch, ch 2, 1 t in 1st sl st on bl, (ch 2, 1 t between next 2 ribs of bl) twice, ch 2, 1 t in last sl st on bl, ch 2, miss 2, 1 t in next st to next bl, make the 2 ch, 1 t across the bl the same as on the first one, ch 2, 1 t in 3d st of 5 ch, ch 2, 1 t on the 1 st, ch 2, 1 t in 3d st of next 5 ch, ch 2, 1 t in 1st sl st on bl; repeat directions from 1st bl to end of row, do not break thread. *3d row*—Without turning, ch 11, and working from left to right, take hook out of work, miss 2 sps, insert hook in next t, and pull 11th st through, ch 1 to fasten, 3 d under ch, p of 6 sts, 3 d under ch, the last one made through the 5th st of ch; * ch 9, miss 1 t, fasten 9th st in next t, 3 d, p, 3 d under ch, the last one in the 5th st of 9 ch; repeat from * to end of row. *4th row*—Chain 5, 1 t in 2d st, ch 2, 1 t in side of next d, ch 2, 1 t in 2d st; repeat to end.

Figure 42.—Follow directions for insertion (Fig. 41) "between diamonds," making the 1st d in third point of braid. At the end of 6th row in 2d bl, miss 2 points on braid and make 1 d in next point, after the length desired is completed, these two points should be sewed together, making the

point of scallop. The directions of heading are also right for the edging.

BOTTOM EDGE. *1st row*—Chain 7, pull 7th st through first point at the left, and holding the top of the lace towards you make 3 d, p, 3 d, (last one being worked through last st of 7 ch), * ch 6, fasten in next point, 3 d, p, 3 d under ch, (you need fasten no other 3d d through ch), ch 12, fasten in next point to the right, 3 d, p, 3 d under ch; repeat in each point to centre, in that after making the 12 ch, 3 d, p, 3 d under it, make 15 ch, 1 d in same point, 3 d, p, 3 d under ch; repeat the 12 ch, 3 d, p, 3 d, 4 times, which brings you to the last point on first scallop, ch 6, fasten in next two points, putting hook through second point first, 3 d, p, 3 d under ch; repeat from * to end of scallop.

Figure 45.— Make a ch of 30 sts. *1st row*—One t in 4th st from hook, 1 t in next st, ch 5, miss 4, 1 d in each of next 3 sts, ch 5, miss 4, 1 d t in next st, ch 5, miss 4, 1 d in each of next 3 sts, ch 5, miss 4, 1 d in next 3 sts, turn. *2d row*—* Chain 5, 1 d in top of 1st t for a picot (p), ch 3, t in next 2 sts, ch 5, d in next 3 d, ch 5, d on each side and into d t, ch 5, d in next 3 d, ch 5, t in next 2 t, 1 t under 3 ch at end, turn. *3d row*—Chain 5, 1 d in 1st t, ch 3, t in next 2 sts, ch 5, d t in 2d d, ch 5, d in 3 d, ch 5, d t in 2d d, ch 5, t in 2 t, 1 t under 3 ch. turn. *4th row*—Picot, ch 3, t in 2 t, ch 5, d on each side and into d t, ch 5, d t in 2d d, ch 5, d in 3 d, ch 5, t in 2 t, 1 t under 3 ch, turn; repeat from *.

Figure 47.— Twist a 3d section of braid around underneath to form a ring, 1 d over crossed braid to fasten, make 2 more underneath twists of sections, fastened in the same manner with 1 d over crossed ends of braid in each. Bring the ends of braid together at the top of the 3 rings, bring working thread up back of them and make 1 sl st across, then 5 d over the 2 cords, break thread and fasten. Pass 2 sections; repeat from beginning for length required. *2d row*—Fasten thread with 1 t in centre of first section above the 3 rings at right hand, * ch 5, 1 d in centre of section in first ring, ** (ch 6, 1 d in 5th st for p) 3 times, ch 1, ** 1 d in first end of section in next ring; repeat from **, 1 d in the end of same section; repeat from ** to **, 1 d in centre of third section, ch 5, 1 cross treble in the two sections between as follows: Thread

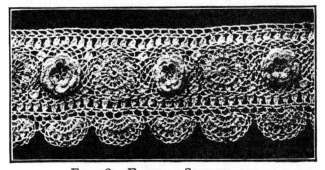

FIG. 38. EDGING. See page 11

over hook twice, insert hook in centre of first section, (thread over hook, draw through 2 loops) twice, thread over twice, insert hook in centre of next section, (thread over and draw through 2 loops) twice, thread over and draw through last 3 loops at once, ch 5; repeat from * to end. *3d row*—Begin at the right side at the top, holding the 3 rings next to you; make 5 d under the cord between first and second sections, * ch 9, make 1 l t in centre of second section, (thread over hook 3 times,

FIG. 39. EDGING. See page 12

thread over and work off loops by two's 3 times), leaving 2 loops on needle, make 2 more l t, fastening each one as you work it through the 2 threads of 1st l t at the bottom, and working off 2 loops 3 times; you will have 4 sts left on needle, thread over, work off 2 sts, thread over and work off last 3; repeat in next section, then make 1 tight d around the 2 clusters at the top; ch 9, 5 d between sections; repeat from * to end.

HEADING.—* One t in 1st d, ch 2, 1 t in 3d d, ch 2, 1 t in 5th d, (ch 2, 1 t in 3d st), 5 times, ch 2; repeat from * to end.

Figure 48.—Use medium coronation braid, and No. 20 Cordonnet crochet cotton. Holding the end of the braid in the right hand, with the left * make a downward pointing loop composed of two sections, hold the loop in place with the thumb and forefinger while you make another loop of four sections, crossing at the same point as the first loop, make 3 t at the point of crossing to fasten the loops together, ch 4, skip one section of braid and repeat from * until you have required length. Fasten the ends of lace together to form a circle. Break thread. *2d row*—Holding the lace so the loops point upwards, fasten the thread between the first and second section of the first large loop, * ch 4, 1 sl st at the top of the inside loop, (ch 4, 1 sl st in same place) twice, ch 4 and fasten together with sl st the first large loop and the adjoining one between the sections. Repeat from * to end of row, turn. *3d row*—* Chain 9, 4 t between sections on first large loop, ch 9, fasten with sl st at the point where the large loops join; ch 6, make a sl st in joining sl st to form a picot; repeat from * to end of row, break thread and turn. *4th row*—Insert hook in 5th st of the first chain of 9 in the 3d row, and fasten thread; * ch 4, 1 sl st in top of next t, ch 4, 1 sl st in top of 4th t, (ch 4, 1 sl st in 5th st of next 9 ch) twice; repeat from * to end, turn. *5th row*—Chain 4, 1 sl st in first loop of previous row, ch 4, 1 sl st in next loop, ch 6, 1 sl st in same place to form a p. Repeat to the

end, making 4 ch, 1 sl st in each loop, making a 6-ch p in each loop over the 4 t group below.

HEADING.—Holding lace with scallops pointing downwards, make 1 t in top of 1st t, * ch 1, 1 t in top of 3d t, ch 1, 1 t in centre of 4-ch loop, ch 1, 1 t in next t; repeat from * to end, turn. *2d row*—Make a row of solid t, that is, 1 t in each st of previous row. To make a neat finish where the linen centre and the lace join, make another row of t on the back of the lace, always inserting the hook in the base of the last row of t. This makes a double row of t to slip the edge of linen centre between.

Figure 49.—Medium size braid and No. 40 Cordonnet crochet cotton, No. 10 hook. Wind p c 20 times around tip of little finger, make 48 d in this ring, join to 1st d with sl st. *2d row*—* Two d in next 2 d in ring, ch 9, 1 d in 7th st from hook, ch 2, miss 2 d in ring, * repeat from * to * 4 times. Take up braid, ** ch 6, and working from left to right, insert hook in ninth point of braid (holding braid in left hand and working on the upper points), pull 6th st through, ch 3, 1 d in 3d st of ch, ch 2, miss 2 d on ring, 2 d in next 2 d; repeat from ** 6 times, pulling the 6th ch st through next point each time, joining last 2 ch to 1st d in ring with sl st. Make another ring, then repeat from * to * 5 times. Holding work in left hand, with the circle inside the scallop at the lower edge, ch 6, fasten 6th ch in eighth point of braid, counting from first point on lower edge of scallop, ch 3, 1 d in 3d st of 6 ch, ch 2, miss 2 d on ring, 2 d in next 2 d, repeat 6 times, join last 2 ch to 1st d made in 2d row. For the next scallop, reverse the braid, holding the circle of the second scallop at the bottom, count 11 points from the point in which the last

FIG. 40. INSERTION. See page 12

p of ring in first scallop was joined, pull the 6th st of ch on third circle through and finish like two preceding scallops. Repeat till you have scallops enough for length desired.

HEADING.—Beginning at first point at right hand, make 1 t in this point, * ch 11, thread over hook 6 times, insert hook in next point, ** (thread over hook, pull loop through, thread over, pull through two loops) 3 times, thread over hook 3 times, insert hook in 1st p on centre ring, thread over, pull a loop through, (thread over, pull through two loops) twice, thread over, pull through 3 loops, (thread over, pull through 2 loops) 4 times, which should be all the loops remaining on hook, ** ch 11, 1 t in next p on ring, ch 6, 1 h t in next p, ch 6, 1 t in next p, ch 11, thread over hook 6 times, insert in last p on ring, repeat from ** to **, inserting hook, after putting thread over hook 3 times, the second time, in the next free point on braid, ch 11, 1 t in next point, ch 9, 1 t in next point, repeat from * to end. *2d row*—Make * 12 d under first 11 ch at right-hand end, 1 d in top of long st, 11 d under next ch, 1 d on t, 6 d under next ch, 1 d on h t, 6 d under next ch, 1 d on t, 11 d under next ch, 1 d on long st, 12 sts under next ch, 1 d

FIG. 41. INSERTION. See page 12

on t, 10 d under next ch, 1 d on t; repeat from * to end. *3d row*—Begin again at right hand, 1 t in 1st d, (ch 2, miss 2, 1 t in next d) to end. *4th row*—At right again, make * 3 d under each of next 4 sps, without turning ch 7, take hook out of work, insert between d sts, over the 2 d t to the right, catch 7th st and pull through, ch 1, make 11 d under the 7 ch. Repeat from * to end.

Figure 50.— Chain 22. *1st row*—Make 1 d in 8th st from hook, make an arch with a loop as follows: * Chain 9, 1 d in 6th st from hook, ch 3, skip 5 sts in foundation ch, 1 d in next, * 1 d in each of next 2 sts, repeat from * to *, turn. *2d row*—Chain 8, 6 t in loop of arch, ch 7, make a reversed loop by taking hook out of work, insert in 2d st from 6 t (or 6th from hook), catch 7th loop with hook and make 1 d, ch 1, 6 t in loop of next arch, * ch 1, 13 t in the loop of 8 ch at the end of row, turn. *3d row*—Make 1 d in the top of each of the 13 t (using back loops only), turn, 1 d in each of 13 d (in every scallop after the first one, make 1 d in the 3 ch after the scallop before it to join them together), turn, 1 d in each of 1st 2 d, picot of 4 ch, 3 d in next 3 d, p, 3 d in next 3 d, p, 3 d in next 3 d, p, 2 d in last 2 d, ch 3, 1 d in the 1st of 6 t in loop, ** 1 arch with loop, putting the 1 d at end of arch in the st before reversed loop, 1 d in loop, 1 d in 1 ch after loop, make another arch with loop, making the 1 d at end of arch in the 1st st after the 6 t below, turn **. *4th row*—Like the 2d row, stopping at the *, turn. *5th row*—Chain 8, 1 d in 1st of the 6 t in loop, repeat from ** to ** in 3d row. Repeat from 2d row. When you have desired length make a heading by fastening thread in the end t at right-hand end of edge, ch 5, 1 t under 8 ch, ch 2, 1 t under same ch, ch 2, * 1 t under next ch, ch 2, 1 t under same ch, ch 2, repeat from * to end of edge.

Figure 51.— Use No. 150 Cordonnet crochet cotton and No. 13 steel hook. Double braid in centre and cross the first two medallions, and fasten securely with needle and thread, ch 9, join with sl st. *1st round*—Eighteen d in ring, join to 1st d with sl st. *2d round*—* Chain 13, take hook out of work, insert in first medallion on lower side next joining, a little more than one-eighth of an inch from the end, catch 13th st and pull through, 1 sl st in each of next 4 sts of ch, ch 5, pull 5th st through medallion on the other side of joining, the same distance from the end, 1 sl st in each of next 4 sts of ch, 1 sl st across into next st of main ch, 1 d, 1 h t, 2 t, 2 d t, 1 l t in next 7 sts of ch, miss 1 d on ring, 1 t in next d; repeat from * (crossing the fourth medallions, the upper over the lower one but not fastening together), to first point, join, break thread, and fasten. Repeat till you have length desired.

BOTTOM EDGE.—One d in end of medallion next to joining at right, * ch 5, 1 d t between medallions, ch 5, 1 d in first end of next medallion, ch 5, 1 d in centre of same medallion, ch 5, 1 d in end of same, ch 5, 1 d t between medallions, ch 5, 1 d t in same place, ch 5, 1 d in end of next medallion, ch 5, 1 d in centre, ch 5, 1 d in end of same medallion, ch 5, 1 d t between next medallion, ch 5, 1 d in end of next medallion, ch 3, 1 d in first medallion in next circle. Repeat from * to end. *2d row*—Three d under first 5 ch, ch 7, picot in 6th st from hook, ch 2, 3 d under next 5 ch, repeat to 3 ch between circles, then ch 2, 1 d under 3 ch, ch 2, repeat from * to end.

HEADING.—Chain 7, 1 d in top end of first medallion next joining, ch 7, 1 sl st in 1st st of 7 ch, ch 7, 1 d in first end of next medallion, ch 7, 1 sl st in same st with last sl st, ch 15, 1 d in the end of same medallion, * ch 7, 1 t between medallions, ch 7, 1 d in end of next medallion, ch 32, 1 d in second end of next medallion, repeat from * to end. *2d row*—One t in 4th st of 19 ch, ch 2, miss 2, 1 t in next st, repeat to end. *3d row*—Make stars between each circle as follows: One sl st in 1st st to the left of 5th t between circles, ch 11, 1 sl st in end of medallion to the right, ch 7, sl st in 8th st of ch, counting from sl st in medallion, ch 7, sl st in first end of next medallion, ch 7, sl st in same st of ch with last sl st, repeat in next two medallions, ch 4, pull 4th st through 2d st from

FIG. 42. EDGING. See page 13

centre t, between medallions, sl st along sts to 1st sl st, break thread, and fasten. Repeat between each circle.

Figure 52.— Chain 5, 2 t in 1st st of 5 ch, ch 4, 1 sl st in same st, ch 5, 1 sl st in each of the 2 t, taking up both loops of st. *2d cluster*—Chain 5, 2 t in 1st st of 5 ch, ch 4, * insert hook down through same

[CONTINUED ON PAGE 16]

Figure 1 (page 2). Centrepiece.

DIRECTIONS FOR USING THE TABLES.—Each horizontal row of figures represents one entire row of crochet. Every row is read from left to right. When you come to the end of a row of figures, turn your crochet. The letters at the top of each column tell what the figures in that column represent. Thus a "4" in the column under a "T" represents 4 treble crochet, while if it were under an "S" it would mean 4 spaces. Throughout these directions, "S" means "spaces," and "T" means "treble crochet." To start the crochet, a chain must be made. For the edging it should be 32 stitches, and for first space, make the first t in 8th st from hook. For the insertion work 45 ch, and for the centre, 105 ch. Use 2 ch for each space and 5 when turning.

No specific dimensions can be given for cutting out the linen. It should be cut to fit the crochet. The best way is to lay the crochet on the linen the way it is to go, and mark it, cut out the linen, allowing 1/4 inch for a hem. Hem it and sew the crochet in.

Use cream linen. For the crochet use unbleached linen machine thread No. 40 with a No. 11 steel crochet needle.

INSERTION FOR CENTREPIECE.—Each of these tables, Nos. 1 to 5 inclusive, represents a section of the crochet, and, when worked, one after another, in the following order, will make a strip of insertion: No. 4, No. 1, No. 2, No. 1, No. 3, No. 1, No. 5. Break the thread. Join on again, 13 spaces from the break, and crochet from table No. 4, fastening into the side of the strip and working toward the end. Repeat the patterns in the above order. When you have made 4 strips all joined together at right angles, sew the two ends together and you will have a square of insertion.

No. 1

S	T	S	T	S	T	S	T	S
2	4	1	4	3	4	1	4	2
3	10	1	10	3				
2	13	1	13	2				
3	10	1	10	3				
6	4	6						
3	10	1	10	3				
2	13	1	13	2				
3	10	1	10	3				
2	4	1	4	3	4	1	4	2

No. 2

S	T	S	T	S	T	S
11	4	1				
1	34	1				
1	34	1				
10	7	1				
1	7	1	25	1		
1	25	1	7	1		
1	7	1	7	4	7	1
1	7	1	16	1	7	1
1	7	1	16	1	7	1
1	7	1	7	4	7	1
1	25	1	7	1		
1	7	1	25	1		
10	7	1				
1	34	1				
1	34	1				
11	4	1				

No. 3

S	T	S	T	S	T	S
1	4	11				
1	34	1				
1	34	1				
1	7	10				
1	25	1	7	1		
1	7	1	25	1		
1	7	4	7	1	7	1
1	7	1	16	1	7	1
1	7	1	16	1	7	1
1	7	4	7	1	7	1
1	7	1	25	1		
1	25	1	7	1		
1	7	10				
1	34	1				
1	34	1				
1	4	11				

No. 4

S	T	S
1	34	1
1	34	1
1	4	11

No. 5

S	T	S	T	S	T	S
11	4	1				
1	34	1				
1	34	1				
10	7	1				
1	7	1	25	1		
1	25	1	7	1		
1	7	1	7	4	7	1
1	7	1	16	1	7	1
1	7	1	16	1	7	1
1	7	1	7	4	7	1
1	25	1	7	1		
1	7	1	25	1		
10	7	1				
1	37					
X	37	1				
13						

Figure 43. Edging for Centrepiece.

TO TURN A CORNER IN THE CROCHETED EDGING.—After completing the pattern for crocheted edging (Fig. 43) once, you turn a corner according to the following directions:

Seven S, 7 T, chain 5, turn, 1 T in 4th stitch from needle, make 1 T in next st, then make 4 T more, 5 S, 4 T, 2 S, turn.

Slip stitch back 1 space, make chain of 5, fasten a T in the first T, 15 T more, 2 S, 4 T, chain 5, turn.

One T in 4th stitch from needle, make 1 T in next stitch, then make 4 T more, 1 S, 16 T, 1 S, turn.

Slip stitch back 1 space, make a chain of 5, fasten a T in the 4th T, 1 S, 10 T, 1 S, 7 T, chain 5, turn.

Fasten in 4th stitch from needle with 1 T, make 1 T in next st, then make 7 T more, 1 S, 7 T, 1 S, 4 T, turn.

Slip stitch back over 4 T, make a chain of 3, 3 T, 1 S, 4 T, 1 S, 10 T, turn.

Slip stitch back over 4 T, make chain of 3, 12 T, 1 S, turn.

Slip stitch back 1 S, make a chain of 3, 3 T, 1 S, 7 T, turn.

Slip stitch back over 4 T, make a chain of 3, make 6 T more along row, turn.

Slip stitch back over 4 T, chain 3, 3 T, turn.

Slip stitch back over the 4 T, chain 3, 2 T in side of last T of last row, slip stitch in corner, chain 2, and make 1 T into next corner, turn.

Three T, slip stitch down edge of last T, chain 5, turn.

Two T in chain, slip stitch in corner, turn.

Slip stitch back over 3 T, chain 3, turn.

Twelve T, slip stitch to corner, chain 2, fasten 1 T into next corner, turn.

Three T, 1 S, 7 T, slip stitch down edge of last T, chain 5, turn.

Two T in chain, slip stitch in corner, turn.

Slip stitch back to outer end of row, chain 3, turn. Nine T, 1 S, 7 T.

Chain 2, slip stitch in corner, chain 2, fasten 1 T in 3d stitch of 5 ch in next corner, turn, 9 T, 1 S, 7 T, ch 3, turn.

Six T, 1 S, 15 T, slip stitch in corner, chain 3, 2 T in next space, slip stitch in corner, turn.

Slip stitch back over the 4 T, 12 T, 2 S, 4 T, turn.

Seven T, 5 S, 4 T, chain 2, slip stitch in corner, slip stitch forward, 1 S, turn.

Begin with row marked with *. There should be 13 scallops between each corner, 6 large and 7 small. (See Fig. 46, page 17, for detail of corner.)

S	T	S	T	S	T	S
7	7	C				
X	7	5	4	2		
2	16	2	4	C		
X	7	1	16	3		
5	10	1	7	C		
X	10	1	7	2	4	3
2	10	2	4	1	10	
X	13	1	10	1	7	1
2	10	2	4	1	10	
X	10	1	7	2	4	3
5	10	1	7			
X	7	1	16	3		
2	16	2	4			
X	7	5	4	2		
* 7	7	C				
X	7	2	4	1	4	3
2	7	1	7	2	4	C
X	7	1	10	1	10	1
4	4	3	10			
X	7	1	10	1	10	1
2	7	1	7	2	4	
X	7	2	4	1	4	3

FIG. 43. TABLE FOR WORKING EDGING ON FIG. 1, PAGE 2

C Wherever "C" occurs, you must chain 5, turn, and make 1 T in 4th st from hook, and 1 T in 5th st. This widens the pattern.

X This is only to call attention to the fact that this row begins with a T.

* After turning a corner, begin at star.

[CONTINUED FROM PAGE 15]

st with 2 t, and bring it out underneath on the opposite side, catch thread and pull through work and st on hook, making a sl st, * ch 5, 1 sl st in each of the 2 t on top. 3d cluster—Chain 5, 2 t in 1st st of 5 ch, ch 4, repeat from * to *, ch 5, 2 sl sts in the 2 t on top, ch 4, insert hook in the 4th st of first 4 ch of cluster, then through the same st with 2 t (which appears like a connecting st between the clusters), and make 1 sl st. 4th cluster—Like 2d cluster. 5th cluster—Chain 5, 2 t in 1st st of 5 ch, ch 4, repeat

FIG. 44. TABLE FOR WORKING CENTRE DESIGN OF CENTREPIECE, FIG. 1, PAGE 2. See page 16

33																				
1	4	1	4	12	4	12	4	1	4	1										
2	10	1	4	1	4	1	4	4	10	4	4	1	4	1	4	1	10	2		
1	7	1	25	2	16	2	25	1	7	1										
2	10	1	4	1	4	1	4	2	10	1	10	2	4	1	4	1	4	1	10	2
3	4	8	10	3	10	8	4	3												
2	10	1	25	2	4	2	25	1	10	2										
3	4	2	22	2	10	2	22	2	4	3										
2	10	1	7	6	16	6	7	1	10	2										
3	4	2	7	1	4	4	16	4	4	1	7	2	4	3						
2	10	1	7	2	10	1	16	1	10	2	7	1	10	2						
3	4	2	7	2	13	1	10	1	13	2	7	2	4	3						
5	10	2	13	1	10	1	13	2	10	5										
4	10	4	10	2	4	2	10	4	10	4										
3	10	2	10	3	4	1	4	1	4	3	10	2	10	3						
2	10	2	19	2	10	2	19	2	10	2										
1	10	2	31	1	31	2	10	1												
2	10	2	19	2	10	2	19	2	10	2										
3	10	2	10	3	4	1	4	1	4	3	10	2	10	3						
4	10	4	10	2	4	2	10	4	10	4										
5	10	2	13	1	10	1	13	2	10	5										
3	4	2	7	2	13	1	10	1	13	2	7	2	4	3						
2	10	1	7	2	10	1	16	1	10	2	7	1	10	2						
3	4	2	7	1	4	4	16	4	4	1	7	2	4	3						
2	10	1	7	6	16	6	7	1	10	2										
3	4	2	22	2	10	2	22	2	4	3										
2	10	1	25	2	4	2	25	1	10	2										
3	4	8	10	3	10	8	4	3												
2	10	1	4	1	4	1	4	2	10	1	10	2	4	1	4	1	4	1	10	2
1	7	1	25	2	16	2	25	1	7	1										
2	10	1	4	1	4	1	4	4	10	4	4	1	4	1	4	1	10	2		
1	4	1	4	12	4	12	4	1	4	1										
33																				

from * to *. Repeat 2d, 3d, 4th, and 5th clusters, over and over till you have the length desired, ending with what should be the 5th cluster, but making it just like the second to bring the hook and thread in proper position. *2d row*—To finish out the diamonds, repeat the 2d, 3d, and then the 2d clusters, joining the last second cluster to the first centre cluster with 2 sl sts in the 2 t in centre cluster. Repeat to end of row, joining the second cluster at the end to the first cluster made with 2 sl sts. *3d row*—*** Chain 4, 1 d in the 4th st of the 5 ch of first cluster made, ch 12, 3 t in 5th st from hook, ch 4, repeat from * to *, ch 5, 2 sl sts in 1st 2 t, ch 2, 1 d in top of centre cluster, ** ch 7, repeat cluster in 5th st of 7 ch (making it the same as last cluster), ch 5, make another cluster in 1st st of 5 ch, ch 2, 1 d in top of centre cluster. Repeat from ** to end of row, then ch 7, and make one more cluster in 5th st of 7 ch, ch 7, 1 d in 1st st at beginning of centre cluster at end of lace. Repeat from *** around the other side. *4th row*—Make 10 d under 7 ch, 2 d in 2 sts at end of cluster, * ch 4, 1 p in last d made, putting hook down through top, and out at side of st, catch thread and draw loop through and make a d st, (ch 4, p in d just made) 4 times, making 5 picots in all, 1 d in last st of 5 ch on cluster, ch 3, 1 d in 2d st of 5 ch on next cluster, * repeat from * to * to end of row, 1 d in last st of 5 ch, 1 d in next st, 10 d under 7 ch, 1 d in 1st st of 4 ch, ch 4, 1 d in last st of 4 ch. Repeat from first of 4th row for the second side.

CHAINS FOR RIBBON.—Holding wrong side of lace towards you, insert hook (having a loop on hook), in centre of top cluster of diamond (the width of the last ch row from edge), and make a sl st, ch 17, take hook out of work, insert in opposite centre cluster, the same distance from top edge, pull a loop through, make 1 sl st in each of next 3 sts of 17 ch, ch 11, 3 sl sts in last 3 sts of 17 ch, break thread, and fasten. Repeat in each diamond. You may omit the chains if you do not wish to run a ribbon through.

Figure 53.—Chain 35. *1st row*—Two t in 4th st of ch, ch 1, 2 t in same st, forming a shell, ch 4, skip 4 sts, 1 t in each of next 9 sts, ch 2, skip 2, 1 t in 3d st, ch 2, skip 2, 1 t in each of next 9 sts, ch 4, shell in last st, ch 3, to form loop for scallop, turn. *2d row*—shell in shell, ch 4, * skip 1st t to narrow leaf, 1 t in each of next 7, * ch 2, 3 t in 1 t, ch 2, repeat from * to *, ch 4, shell in shell, 1 d in top of last t of shell to form straight edge, ch 3, turn. *3d row*—Shell in shell, ch 4, * skip 1 t, 1 t in each of next 5 t, * ch 2, 2 t in 1st t, 1 t in 2d t, ch 2, 1 more t in 2d t, 2 t in 3d t, ch 2, repeat from * to *, ch 4, shell in shell, ch 2, 3 d in 3-ch loop at end, ch 2, 3 more t in same loop, ch 3, turn. *4th row*—Skip first 3 t, 3 t on ch 2, ch 2, skip 3 t, 3 t on next ch 2, ch 2, shell in shell, ch 4, skip 1st t, 1 t in each of next 3 t, ch 2, * 2 t in 1st t to widen new leaf, 1 t in 2d t, 2 t in 3d t, * ch 3, repeat from * to *, ch 2, skip 1st t, 1 t in each of next 3 t, ch 4, shell in shell, 1 t in top of last t of shell, ch 3, turn. *5th row*—Shell in shell, ch 4, 1 t in centre of 3 t, ch 2, * 2 t in 1st t, 1 t in each of next 3 t, 2 t in last, * ch 2, 1 t on 3 ch, ch 2, repeat from * to *, ch 2,

FIG. 45. INSERTION
See page 13

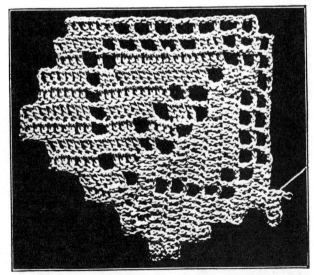

FIG. 46. MITRED CORNER OF EDGING FOR CENTREPIECE
See Frontispiece, page 16 and Fig. 43

1 t in centre of 3 t, ch 4, shell in shell, ch 2, 3 t on ch 2, ch 2, skip 3 t, 3 t on ch 2, ch 2, 3 more t on same ch, ch 3, turn. *6th row*—Skip 3 t, 3 t on ch 2, (ch 2, skip 3 t, 3 t on ch 2) twice, ch 2, shell in shell, ch 4, skip the lone t, * 2 t in 1st t of widening leaf, 1 t in each of next 5 t, 2 t in last t, * ch 2, 3 t in 1 t, ch 2, repeat from * to *, ch 4, shell in shell, 1 t in top of shell, ch 3; turn. *7th row*—Shell in shell, ch 4, skip 1 t, 1 t in each of next 7 t, ch 2, 2 t in 1st t, 1 t in 2d t, ch 2, 1 more t in 2d t, 2 t in 3d t, ch 2, skip 1 t, 1 t in each of next 7 t, ch 4, shell in shell, (ch 2, 3 t on next ch 2) twice, ch 2, skip 3 t, 3 t on ch 2, ch 2, 3 more t on same ch, ch 3, turn. *8th row*—Skip 3 t, 3 t on ch 2 (ch 2, skip 3 t, 3 t on ch 2) 3 times, ch 2, shell in shell, ch 4, skip 1 t, 1 t in each of next 5 t, ch 2, * 2 t in 1st t, 1 t in 2d t, 2 t in 3d t, * ch 3, repeat from * to *, ch 2, skip 1 t, 1 t in each of next 5 t, ch 4, shell in shell, 1 t in top of shell, ch 3, turn. *9th row*—Shell in shell, ch 4, skip 1 t, 1 t in each of next 3 t, ch 2, * 2 t in 1st t, 1 t in each of next 3 t, 2 t in last t, * ch 2, 1 t on ch 3, ch 2, repeat from * to *, ch 2, skip 1st t, 1 t in each of next 3 t, ch 4, shell in shell, (ch 2, 3 t on next ch 2) 3 times, ch 2, skip 3 t, 3 t on ch 2, ch 2, 3 more t on same ch, ch 3, turn. *10th row*—* Six t on ch 2 to form a shell, skip 3 t, fasten shell with a d on ch 2, ch 2, * which is counted as 1st t of shell, repeat from * to * 3 times, always starting new shell on same chain where last shell was fastened, ch 3, for loop for new scallop, shell in shell, ch 4, 1 t in centre of 3 t, ch 2, ** 2 t in 1st t, 1 t each in next 5 t, 2 t in last t, ** ch 2, 3 t in 1 t, ch 2, repeat from ** to **, ch 2, 1 t in centre of 3 t, ch 4, shell in shell, 1 t in top of shell. Repeat from 2d row.

Figure 54A.—Chain 10. *1st row*—One t in 9th st from hook, 6 t in same st, turn. *2d row*—Chain 5, 1 t in 3d t of last row, (ch 2, miss 1 t, 1 t in next st) twice, ch 4, 7 t under loop of ch, turn. *3d and 4th rows*—Like 2d row. *5th row*—Like 2d row to end, then ch 8, fasten with 1 d under 5 ch of 4th row, ch 1, turn. *6th row*—Make 13 d under 8 ch, ch 2, 1 t on 3d t, (ch 2, miss 1, 1 t on next t) twice, ch 4, 7 t under 4 ch, turn. *7th row*—Like 2d row to end, then ch 1, 1 d t in each of the 13 d of preceding row, with 1 ch between each, making 13 d t in all; fasten last d t to the 5 ch with 1 d, turn. *8th row*—Chain 3, 1 d under first 1 ch between d t, (ch 4, 1 d under next 1 ch) 11 times, ch 1, 1 d under 1 ch, finish row like 2d row. Begin again at 3d row and repeat for length desired.

FIG. 47. EDGING. See page 13

HEADING.—Having finished last row of edge with 7 t, without breaking thread ch 7, 1 d under 5 ch at end of preceding row, * ch 7, 1 d under next 5 ch, repeat from * to end of row, break thread. *2d row*—One t in 5th st of 7 ch at right-hand edge, * ch 1, miss 1, 1 t in d made in 5 ch, (ch 1, miss 1, 1 t in next st) twice, repeat from * to end of row.

Figure 54B.—Leave off the scallops, and make one row of 7 ch, 1 d in 5 ch, on each side of lace.

FIG. 48. EDGING. See page 14

Figure 55.—Wind the cotton 20 times around tip of little finger and make 54 d in ring thus made, join last d to first one with sl st, ch 1, 10 d in next 10 d, taking up both threads of st, * ch 8, take hook out of work, insert in 7th d back, catch 8th st and pull through, ch 1, 3 d, p of 4 sts, 4 d, p, 4 d, p, 3 d under 8 ch, 1 d in ring, turn, (ch 8, 1 d in centre between p's) twice, ch 8, pull through d in ring, ch 1, 1 d 12 t, 1 d under each 8 ch-loop, 1 sl st in side of last d made under 1st 8 ch; 13 d in next 13 d in ring *. Repeat from * to * twice, then d in d around, 1 sl st in 1st d to join. Break thread, leaving thread long enough to finish centre with needlework stitches.

Make as many of these motifs as you require for the length of your lace, joining the motifs together as follows: After making the 6th t in the 2d ch of 8 on 2d motif, ch 3, take hook out of work, insert between 6th and 7th t of corresponding scallop on preceding motif, pull st through, ch 9, take hook out and insert in 3d st of 9 ch, pull st through (ch 5, 1 d in ring thus formed) 5 times, 1 sl st in same st where ch was pulled through, to make the ring, ch 3, pull 3d st through last t made in 2d ring and finish out scallop with 6 t, 1 d like the others.

UPPER PART OF EDGE.—Make 1 d between 6th and 7th t in 1st scallop at right-hand side, * (ch 10, miss 6 d on ring, 1 d in next d) twice, ch 10, 1 d between 6th and 7th t on next scallop, ch 10, 1 d in 3d loop in little ring between motifs, ch 10, 1 d between 6th and 7th t on next scallop. Repeat from * to end of row and break thread. The thread is broken at the end of each row and joined again at the right-hand upper edge. *2d row*—Join thread in same st with 1st d, ch 16, 1 d under 1st ch-loop, (ch 5, 1 d in same sp) twice * ch 10, 1 d under next loop, (ch 5, 1 d in same loop) twice. Repeat from * to end of row, making 16 ch after last 5 ch-loop, 1 sl st in d in scallop. *3d row*—Begin with 1 d under 16 ch-loop at right-hand end, then * ch 10, 1 d under next loop, (ch 5, 1 d in same loop) twice. Repeat

18

FIG. 49. INSERTION. See page 14

from * to end of row, ending with 1 d in 16 ch space. *4th row*—One sl st in the d under 16 ch-loop, ch 16, 1 d under 1st loop, (ch 5, 1 d under same loop) twice, * ch 10, 1 d under next loop (ch 5, 1 d under same loop) twice. Repeat from * to end of row, ending with 16 ch, 1 sl st in the d at end of last row. *5th row*— Like 3d row. *6th row*—Like 4th row. *7th row*—Join thread with 1 d under 1st loop, ch 9, 1 d under 2d loop, ch 9, 1 d under next loop to end of row. *8th row*—One t in 1st d, * ch 2, miss 2 sts, 1 t in next st to end of row and fasten off.

Figure 56. — Chain as long as desired, turn. *1st row*—One t in 5th and 6th st. Chain 2, miss 2, 1 t in each of next 2; repeat to end, break thread and start at other end. *2d row*—Chain 8, 1 t in first space, (ch 1, 1 t in next space, ch 8, 1 t in next sp), to end, break thread. *3d row*—Start at right end by fastening thread in loop of 8 ch, 5 d in middle of 8-ch loop, ch 4, and repeat same in next ch, etc., to end. *4th row*—Chain 12, turn, and fasten in centre of 5 d on ch, turn, make 5 d in this ch. Chain 11, turn, and fasten in next centre d; repeat to end, break thread. *5th row*—Fasten thread at opposite end, 1 d 7 times across ch, make 1 st at the bar of d, then continue 7 d over ch as before. Follow these same instructions on the other side of t row, thus making the t row the centre one.

Figure 57. — No. 50 Cordonnet crochet cotton, No. 12 hook, and a large size braid.

Baste the braid on strong paper or cambric, holding braid in right hand, with the left twist the third section over and upwards to form a ring, basting securely at the intersection of the cord so that it will not turn or twist. Skip the next section, and twist the next one under, fastening at intersection of cord; repeat the length of your paper or cambric, bringing the cord going upwards *over,* the cord

coming down *under.* *1st row*—Make 1 d in cord before first section, * (ch 5, p in 4th st) 3 times, ch 1, 1 d in centre of section, (ch 5, p in 4th st) 3 times, 1 d under cord at end of section, ch 5, ** thread over hook twice, insert hook in centre of next section (the one going down), thread over, pull a loop through, (thread over, pull through 2 loops) twice, thread over twice, insert hook in centre of opposite section, thread over, pull a loop through, (thread over, pull through 2 loops) 4 times, ** ch 5, 1 d under cord at beginning of next section. Repeat from * to end. *2d row*—Beginning at right hand again, make 1 d t under ch between first and second p, * ch 7, 1 t in the d made in centre of section, ch 7, and make another cross-treble (directions from ** to **) inserting hook first between 2d and 3d p's on p 1 on first section, then after working off 2 loops twice, and putting thread over hook again twice, insert in loop on next section between the first 2 p's. Repeat from * to end. *3d row*—Make 8 d under each 7-ch loop to end. On the other side, work three rows the same.

Figure 58. *To make Knot Stitch.*—Having a loop on hook, draw it out one-quarter of an inch in length, thread over hook and draw a loop through, reach back of long loop and insert hook under thread you have just drawn through, thread over and draw a loop through, you now have 2 sts on your hook, thread over and draw through both sts. To make a loop of 2 knots sts, pull out the loop just drawn through, one-quarter of an inch, and make another loop just like the first one, and fasten at point indicated, with 1 d or t as directed.

Chain 40. *1st row*—One t in 4th st from hook, 1 t in each of next 2 sts, 1 loop of 2 knot sts, skip 4 sts on foundation ch, 1 d in 5th st, 1 d in next st, 6 t in next 6 sts, 2 d in next 2 sts, 6 t in next 6 sts, 2 d in next 2, 1 loop of 2 knot sts, skip 4 sts, 2 t in next 2, ch 2, skip 2 sts, 3 t in next, ch 2, 3 t in next st, turn. *2d row*—Chain 3, shell in shell, ch 2, 1 t in last t of shell, ch 2, 2 t on 2 t, 1 knot st, catch with 1 d before the knot in loop below, 1 d after the loop (you use the two upper threads of the loop in making the d under them), loop of 2 knot sts, catch with 1 d in 3d t of cluster of 6 t, 1 d in next t, 3 t in each of next 2 d, 1 d in each of two centre t of group (the 3d and 4th), 2 knot sts, catch with 1 d before the knot in next loop, 1 d after knot, 1 knot st, 3 t in 3 t at end of row, turn. *3d row*—Chain 3, 3 t on 3 t, loop of 2 knot sts, 1 d before and after knot in next loop, 3 t in each of 2 d in centre of next 6 t, 2 d in centre sts of next 6 t, 3 t in each of next 2 d

FIG. 50. EDGING. See page 15

FIG. 51. EDGING. See page 15

at end of cluster of 6 t, 1 d each side of knot in next loop, loop of 2 knot sts, 2 t on 2 t, ch 2, 1 t on next t, ch 2, 1 t on 1st t of shell, ch 2, shell in shell, turn. *4th row*—Chain 2, shell in shell, ch 2, 1 t on last t of shell, (ch 2, 1 t on next t) twice, ch 2, 2 t on 2 t, 1 d each side of knot in next loop, 6 t in next 2 d, 2 d in 2 centre sts of 6 t, loop of 2 knot sts, 1 d in each of 2 centre sts of 6 t, 6 t in next 2 d at end of group, 1 d each side of knot in next loop, 3 t in 3 t, turn. *5th row*—Chain 1, 3 d on 3 t, 6 t in next 2 d, 2 d in centre sts of 6 t, loop of 2 knot sts, 1 d before and after knot in next loop, 2 knot st loop, 2 d in centre sts of 6 t, 6 t in next 2 d, 2 d in 2 t, (ch 2, 1 t on next t) 3 times, 2 t under 2 ch, 1 t on next t, turn. *6th row*—Chain 3, 1 t on 4th t, 2 t under 2 ch, 1 t on next t, ch 2, 1 t on next t, ch 2, 2 t on 2 d, 2 d in 2 centre sts of 6 t, 6 t in next 2 d in knot at end of group, 1 d each side of knot in next loop, 2 knot sts, 1 d each side of knot in next loop, 6 t in next 2 d, 2 d in centre sts of 6 t, 3 t in 3 t, turn. This completes one scallop. *7th row*—Chain 3, 3 t in 3 t, 2 knot sts, 2 d in centre sts of 6 t, 6 t in next 2 d, 1 d each side of knot in next loop, 6 t in next 2 d, 2 d in centre of next 6 t, 2 knot sts, 2 t on 2 t, ch 2, 1 t on next t, 2 t under 2 ch, ch 2, 3 t under same ch. Repeat from 2d row for length required.

Figure 59. *Centre part.*—Chain 6, join with sl st. *1st row*—Chain 5, 1 t in ring, (ch 2, 1 t in ring) twice, ch 5, turn. *2d row*—Chain 5, 1 t in centre sp, (ch 2, 1 t in same sp) 3 times, turn; repeat from beginning of row for length desired. Do not break thread. *3d row*—Chain 5, 4 t under 1st 5-ch loop on side, ch 2, 4 t under next loop. to end of row. Break thread, and begin again at right-hand end. *4th row*—Make 4 t under 5-ch loop at end, (ch 2, 4 t in 2-ch sp), to end; repeat on the other side of centre, ch 2, 1 t in last of 4 t in previous row, turn. Chain 6, 1 t under next 2 ch; repeat to end of row, turn, ch 1, * 10 d under 1st 6 ch, 5 d under next 6 ch, ch 6 without turning, take hook out of work, insert in 5th st on 1st 6-ch loop, thread over hook, pull through, ch 1, 10 d under 6 ch, 5 d under unfinished loop; repeat from * to end of row.

Figure 60. *Materials.*—Either Macramé thread or a coarse mercerized crochet thread in écru or cream, and as fine a hook as can be used without splitting the thread.

PICOT WHEEL.—Chain 7, join. Over ring work 2 d, p, and repeat 5 times more, join. *2d row*—Chain 3 for a t, then ch 5 more, * 1 t between next 2 p be-

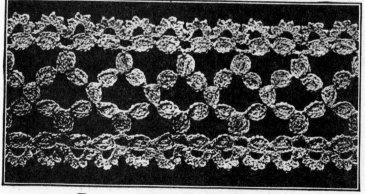

FIG. 52. INSERTION. See page 15

low, ch 5, repeat from * around, join to 3d st of 1st ch. *3d row*—Over the ch space work 4 d, p, 4 d, then a p over the t below; repeat around, and join.

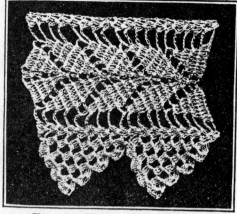

SMALL MEDALLION.

FIG. 53. EDGING. See page 17

—Chain 6, join, 10 d over ring, join. *2d row*—Work 1 d into the next d of preceding row, ch 5, 1 d into the same st, 1 d into next d below, ch 1, turn; *2 d into d below, ch 1, turn; * 2 d into 1st d below, 1 d into each remaining d, ch 1, turn; repeat from * until you have 7 d in the row, then work one more d into last d below, ch 1, and sl st down the side of triangle back to ring. Repeat from beginning of 2d row. There should be five triangles with points turning centreward, and five picots.

RING FOR THIS MEDALLION.—Work d over a cord of 6 strands until the piece (which reaches two-thirds of the distance around medallion), measures about one inch larger in diameter than the medallion; leave cord and turn. *2d row*—Chain 4, miss 2, 1 d into next d, * ch 3, miss 2, 1 d into next to end of row; turn. *3d row*—Chain 5, 1 d into next loop, * ch 4, 1 d into next loop to end of row; turn. Pick up cord and over it work 1 d, 1 t, 1 ch, and 1 d into each loop of preceding row. Adjust to a perfect two-thirds of a circle by means of the cord and fasten off carefully. Baste the medallion and circle on the pattern and join with twisted bars and knots.

STAR MEDALLION WITH PICOT WHEEL CENTRE.—Make a Picot Wheel as above. Work a circle of six triangles, each one having a base of 12 d. Chain 12 for base, ch 1 more to turn, miss 1 ch, into the next 12 ch work 12 d, * ch 1, turn; miss the 1st d, and work 1 d into each succeeding d of the row; repeat from * until you have but 1 d at the point; make 5 more triangles and join. The wheel and circle are basted in place on the pattern and joined with twisted bars and knots.

BORDER.—First work a row of triangles, the base of each being 8 d. *2d row*—Baste in place along the side of band, work 1 d into the point of first triangle, ch 10, 1 d into point of next triangle, repeat to end. Increase or diminish the number of chain sts between the triangles, if necessary, to make a straight edge. *3d row*—Work 1 d into each st of preceding row. *4th row*—Work 1 d into each of four succeeding sts below, then a p; repeat to end. After all motifs are basted in place on the cambric pattern, join with twisted bars and picots. For picot, work a loose buttonhole st (over bar), into which work 6 buttonhole sts. Repeat on the other side from beginning of border.

Figure 61.—Make a chain of 92 sts, turn

1st row—Make 1 t in 8th st, * ch 2, skip 2, 1 t in next st, repeat from * 27 times, thus forming 28 spaces (sps), turn. *2d row*—Chain 5, t on next t, make ten more sps, ch 2, 3 t under next sp, 14 sps, ch 2, 3 t, 2 ch, 3 t (a shell), in last sp, turn. *3d row*—Chain 3, shell in shell, ch 2, 3 t in next sp, 12 sps, ch 2, 3 t in next sp, ch 2, 3 t in next sp, 10 sps, ch 2, 1 t

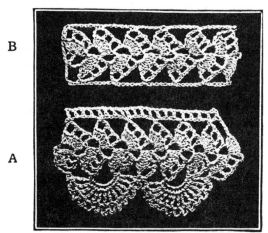

FIG. 54. INSERTION AND EDGING
See page 18

in 3d st in last sp, turn. *4th row*—Chain 5, t on next t, 8 spaces, ch 2, 3 t in next sp, ch 4, 1 d t in next sp, ch 4, 3 t under next sp, 10 sps, ch 2, 3 t under next sp, ch 4, 1 d t in next sp, ch 4, shell in shell, turn. *5th row*—Chain 3, shell in shell, * ch 5, 1 d under 4th st of ch, 1 d on d t, 1 d under 1st st of next 4 ch, ch 5, 3 t in next sp, * 8 sps, ch 2, 3 t in next space, repeat from * to *, then sps to end of row. *6th row*—Chain 5, t on t, 6 sps, ** ch 2, 3 t in next sp, ch 6, 5 d in centre (1 d under ch, 3 d on 3 d, 1 d under ch), ch 6, ** 3 t in next sp, 6 sps; repeat from ** to **, shell in shell, turn. *7th row*—Chain 3, shell in shell, * ch 2, 3 t under 6 ch, ch 5, 3 d in 3 centre sts of 5 d, ch 5, 3 t under 6 ch, ch 2, 3 t under next sp; * 4 sps, ch 2, 3 t under next sp, repeat from * to *, 7 sps to end of row. *8th row*—Chain 5, 5 sps, * ch 2, 3 t in next sp, ch 4, 1 d t in next sp, ch 4, 3 t under 5 ch, ch 4, 1 d t in centre d of 3 d, ch 4, 3 t under 5 ch, ch 4, 1 d t in next sp, ch 4, * 3 t under next sp, 2 sps, repeat from * to *, shell in shell, turn. *9th row*—Chain 3, shell in shell, ch 5, 3 d in centre, ch 5, 3 t under 4 ch, ch 2, 3 t under next 4 ch, ch 5, 3 d in centre, ch 5, 3 t in next 2-ch sp, 1 sp, 3 t in next sp, repeat from * to *, 5 sps to end of row, turn. *10th row*—Chain 5, 3 sps, ch 2, * 3 t in next sp, ch 6, 5 d in centre, ch 6, repeat from * 3 times, shell in shell, turn. *11th row*—Chain 3, 6 t under 2 ch, ch 2, * 3 t under 6 ch, ch 5, 3 d in centre, ch 5, 3 t under 6 ch, ch 2, repeat from * 3 times, 5 sps, turn. *12th row*—Chain 5, 5 sps, ch 2, 3 t under 5 ch, * ch 4, 1 d t in centre, ch 4, 3 t under 5 ch, ch 4, 1 d t under 2 ch, ch 4, 3 t under 5 ch, ch 4, 1 d t in centre, ch 4, 3 t under 5 ch,* 2 sps, ch 2, 3 t under 5 ch, repeat from * to * once, ch 2, 3 t under 2 ch, turn. *13th row*—Chain 3, 3 t under 2 ch,

ch 2, * 3 t under 4 ch, ch 2, 3 t under next 4 ch, ch 5, 3 d in centre, ch 5, 3 t under 4 ch, ch 2, 3 t under 4 ch, * 4 sps, ch 2, repeat from * to * once, 7 sps to end of row, turn. *14th row*—Chain 5, 7 sps, ch 2, * 3 t under 2 ch, ch 6, 5 d in centre, ch 6, 3 t under 2 ch, * 6 sps, ch 2, repeat from * to * once, ch 2, 3 t under 2 ch, turn. *15th row*—Chain 3, 3 t under 2 ch, ch 2, * 3 t under 6 ch, ch 5, 3 d in centre, ch 5, 3 d under 6 ch, * 8 sps, ch 2, repeat from * to * once, 9 sps to end, turn. *16th row*—Chain 5, 9 sps, * ch 2, 3 t under 5 ch, ch 4, 1 d t in centre, ch 4, 3 t under 5 ch, * 10 sps, repeat from * to *, ch 2, 3 t under 2 ch, turn. *17th row*—Chain 3, 3 t under 2 ch, ch 2, 3 t under 4 ch, ch 2, 3 t under 4 ch, 12 sps, ch 2, 3 t under 4 ch, ch 2, 3 t under 4 ch, 11 sps, turn. *18th row*—Chain 5, 11 sps, ch 2, 3 t under 2 ch, 14 sps, ch 2, 3 t under 2 ch, ch 2, 3 t under 2 ch, turn. *19th row*—Begin again at 3d row, and repeat for length required.

EDGE.—Beginning at the lower right-hand corner, fasten thread in top of 1st t, make 7 t under each 3 ch, all across the edge, with 1 d in the top of each t preceding the 3 ch.

Figure 62.—Chain 30. *1st row*—One t in 4th st from hook, 2 t in next 2 ch, skip 2 ch, 1 t in each of next 4 sts, ch 6, t in 6th ch, ch 2, t in same st, ch 2, t in same st, ch 2, t in same st, ch 6, t in 6th ch, 3 t in next 3 ch, ch 2, 3 t, turn. *2d row*—Chain 3, 2 t, ch 2, 4 t, ch 6, (1 d, 4 t, 1 d) in each space of 2 ch, ch 6, 4 t, ch 2, 3 t, turn. *3d row*—Chain 3, 2 t, ch 2, 4 t, ch 6, t in centre st of middle petal, ch 2, t in same st, ch 2, t in same st, ch 2, t in same st, ch 6, 4 t, ch 2, 3 t, turn. Repeat 2d and 3d rows for length desired.

Figure 63.—Chain 16. *1st row*—One t in 4th st from hook, 2 t in next 2 ch, skip 2 ch, t in next 3 sts, ch 6, t in last st in foundation ch, (ch 2, t in same st) 3 times, turn. *2d row*—(One d, 4 t, 1 d) in 1st space; repeat in next two spaces. Chain 6, 2 t over 6 ch of previous row, 3 t over 3 t, ch 2, 3 t, turn. *3d row*—Chain 3, 2 t, ch 2, 5 t over 5 t, 2 t over ch, ch 6, t in centre stitch of middle petal of leaf, 2 ch, t in same st, ch 2, t in same st, ch 2, t in same st, turn. *4th row*—(One d, 4 t, 1 d), in each space, ch 6, 2 t over ch, 7 t over 7 t, ch 2, 3 t, turn. *5th row*—Chain 3, 2 t, ch 2, 9 t over 9 t, 2 t over ch, ch 6, t in centre stitch of petal, * ch 2, d in same st; repeat from * twice. *6th row*—(One d, 4 t, 1 d), in each space, ch 6, 2 t over ch, 11 t over 11 t, ch 2, 3 t, turn. *7th*

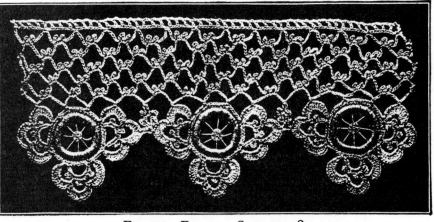

FIG. 55. EDGING. See page 18

21

row—Chain 3, 2 t, ch 2, 3 t, ch 6, t in 13 t of preceding row, * ch 2, t in same stitch; repeat from * twice, turn. Repeat from beginning of 2d row.

Figure 64. — Use No. 100 Cordonnet crochet cotton. Chain 9, join with sl st to form a ring, ch 4, 1 d t (thread over twice), in ring, (ch 1, 1 d t in ring) 6 times; you should have 8 d t in all, the first 4 ch counting as 1 d t. * Chain 17, insert hook in 9th st from hook, with the end of hook pointing to the

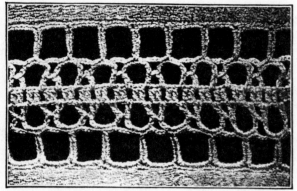

FIG. 56. INSERTION. See page 19

left, swing work so that the thread comes underneath the chain, then make a sl st through both sts on hook; without turning, ch 4, 1 d t in ring, (ch 1, 1 d t in ring) 6 times. Repeat from * for length required, then ch 1 and fill out last ring with 8 d t with 1 ch between each. After last d t, insert hook in 3d st of 4 ch, then through 3d st on 17 ch, and make 1 d through both sts together, ** ch 2, skip 2 sts (there should be 5 sts of the 17 ch left), 1 d in 3d st on 17 ch, ch 2, 1 d through two upper threads of last t on next ring, 1 d t in ring, ch 1, and make 7 d t in ring, with 1 ch between each. Repeat from ** to end of row, joining with 1 sl st in 3d st of 4 ch. *Next row*—* Chain 5, 1 d under 1 ch between t, ch 5, 1 d under next 1 ch, to end of half circle. There will be seven loops (1) on the first half circle, but only 6 on each subsequent one till the last one on the row, which will have 7, ch 3, 1 d under first 1 ch in next circle. Repeat from * to end of row. Fill out last circle with 5-ch loops under each 1 ch, then ch 3, 1 d under first 1 ch in next circle, and repeat from * to end of row as on first side, and break thread.

HEADING.—Join thread in the 6th l to the right of the 3 ch between circles, ch 8, miss 1 l, 1 d in next l, ch 3, 1 d in next l, * ch 5, miss 1 l, thread over hook twice, insert in next l, thread over hook, pull through l, (thread over hook, pull through 2 l's) twice, thread over hook twice, insert in opposite l, thread over, pull through l, (thread over hook, pull through 2 l's) twice, thread over, pull through remaining 3 loops. This forms a cross treble st. Chain 5, miss 1 l, 1 d in next, ch 3, 1 d in next l, repeat from * to end of row; at end, ch 5, miss 1 l, 1 d t in next; break thread. *2d row*—Begin at right-hand side again, fasten thread in 3d st of 8 ch, ch 5, miss 2 sts on chain, 1 t in next st, * ch 2, 1 t in d on l, ch 2, 1 t on next d, ch 2, miss 2, 1 t in 3d st of 5 ch, ch 2, 1 t on cross treble, ch 2, 1 t in 3d st of 5 ch, repeat from * to end. Break thread at end of each row. Repeat the two rows of heading on the other side of circles,

then begin ruffle. *3d row*—Fasten thread in 3d st of 5 ch at right-hand side, with 1 d, 1 d in each of next 10 sts, taking up two threads of sts, * ch 5, miss 5 sts, 1 d in next st, 20 d in next 20 sts, repeat from * to end of row. *4th row*—At right-hand side fasten thread with 1 d in 1st d, 9 d in next 9 d, using back loops only, * ch 3, 1 t in 3d st of 5 ch, ch 3, 1 t in same st, ch 3, miss 1 d, 19 d in next 19 d; repeat from * to end of row. *5th row*—Nine d in 9 d, * ch 3, 1 t under 3 ch, ch 3, 1 t under centre 3 ch, ch 3, 1 t in same place, ch 3, 1 t under next space (sp), ch 3, miss 1 d, 17 d in 17 d, repeat from * across. As all the rows are worked in the same way, decreasing 1 d in the group at the right-hand end, and 2 d in the others, and increasing in the sps in each scallop, it is unnecessary to give directions for each row in detail. Continue working till you have but 3 d between each scallop, and 9 3-ch sps each side of the centre sp (which is the 10th sp). *Last row*—Make 1 d in d at right-hand end, 1 d in 1st sp, * ch 8, 1 d in 6th st from hook for a picot (p), ch 2, 1 d in next sp, repeat to end of scallop. There should be 18 of these little points on each scallop. Make 1 d in the centre d between scallops, 1 d in 1st sp on next scallop. Repeat from * to end of row, break thread, and fasten off all the loose threads at the end and beginning of the rows.

Figure 65. — This insertion matches Fig. 64. It is the top of the edging finished with 1 d in each st on top and bottom.

Figure 66. — Chain 48, turn. *1st row*—One t in 14th st from hook, 12 t in next 12 sts, ch 7, miss 7, 13 t in next 13 sts, turn. *2d row*—Chain 12, 1 t in 3d ch st from last t in preceding row, ch 4, insert hook in top of t just made, thread over hook, pull through, thread over hook, and pull through both loops on hook, 1 t in same st with last t, ch 7, miss 3 t, 7 t in next 7 t, ch 7, 1 t in 4th st of 7 ch, p, 1 t in same st, ch 7, miss 3 t, 7 t in next 7 t, ch 7, 1 t in 3d st of ch, p, 1 t in same st, turn. *3d row*—Chain 12, 1 t in 3d st from 1st t, p, 1 t in same st, ch 7, 1 t in 4th st of next 7 ch, p, 1 t in same st, ch 7, 1 l t, (thread over hook 3 times), in 4th t, ch 7, 1 t in 4th st of next 7 ch, p, 1 t in same st, ch 7, 1 t in 4th st of next 7 ch, p, 1 t in same st, ch 7, 1 l t in 4th t, ch 7, 1 t, p, 1 t in 3d st of next 7 ch, turn. *4th row*—Chain 12, 1 t, p, 1 t in 3d st from t in previous row, ch 7, 3 t in the 3 sts before 1 t, 1 t in 1 t, 3 t in next 3 sts,

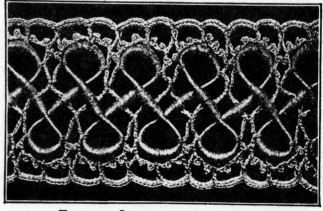

FIG. 57. INSERTION. See page 19

22

ch 7, 1 t, p, 1 t in 4th st of next 7 ch, ch 7, 1 t, p, 1 t in 4th st of next 7 ch, ch 7, 3 t in 3 sts before 1 t, 1 t in 1 t, 3 t in next 3 sts, ch 7, 1 t, p, 1 t in 4th st of next 7 ch, turn. *5th row*—Chain 12, * 3 t in 3 ch sts before 7 t, 7 t on 7 t, 3 t in next 3 sts,* making 13 t in all, ch 7. Repeat from * to *, turn, and repeat from 2d row for length desired. Complete your lace at the end of the 5th row, the one with two groups of 13 t, do not break thread.

HEADING.—Chain 12, 1 d in 1st ch-loop on top, ch 6, 1 d in next l. Repeat to end, ch 12, fasten with

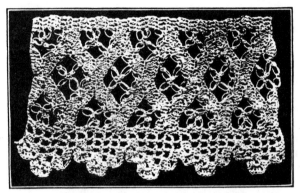

FIG. 58. EDGING. See page 19

sl st in bottom of last t of 1st row. Break thread. *2d row*—Fasten at right hand at top in 10th st of 12 ch, ch 5, miss 2 sts, 1 t in next st, ch 2, miss 2, 1 t in next st to end of row.

EDGE.—Fasten thread with 1 d under 1st loop at right, 2 more d in same loop, * ch 2, 1 t in next loop, (1 p on t, 1 t in same loop), 7 times, ch 2, 3 d under next loop). Repeat from * to end.

Figure 67.—Use No. 50 Cordonnet crochet cotton and No. 10 steel hook. Make 1 t between **first** two points of braid, (ch 11, 1 t between next) 11 times, ch 6, (1 t on next point) 6 times, ch 6, 1 t between next point, (ch 6, take hook out of work, insert in 6th st of opposite 11 ch, pull 6th st through, ch 5, 1 t between next points) 4 times, repeat from * for length desired, finishing after the third connection of 11 chs. Make 1 t between first two points on the other side of braid at end where you finished first row, the t alternating with the t's on the other side, and repeat from * to end.

BOTTOM EDGE.—One d in 6th st of 2d ch loop at end where you first began, * ch 6, (3 d t in 6th st of next 11 ch, ch 7 1 t in 6th st from hook, ch 2, 3 d t in same st) 5 times, making 3 ch between each. After making fifth cluster, ch 2, miss one loop on next scallop, 1 d in 6th st of next loop. Repeat from * to end.

HEADING. *1st row*—Having a loop on hook, insert in 6th st of first free loop at right hand, draw a loop through 6th st, and loop on hook, ch 7, * thread over hook 4 times, insert hook in 5th st of 7 ch, draw a loop through, (thread over hook and draw through two loops) 4 times, repeat from *, thread over and draw through two loops; ch 15, 1 d t in 6th st of next loop, **** ch 9, 1 t in 6th st of next loop, ch 13, thread over hook 5 times, insert hook in 6th st of next loop, pull loop through, (thread over and pull through two loops) 5 times, ** thread over 4 times, insert hook in first two loops

of last st, draw a loop through, (thread over and draw through 2 loops) 4 times, ** repeat from **, thread over and draw through 3 loops on hook; thread over 6 times, insert hook in 6th st of next loop, draw a loop through, thread over and draw through 2 loops, thread over twice, insert hook in 6th st of opposite loop, leaving one free loop below it, draw loop through, (thread over, draw through 2 loops) 7 times, *** thread over 4 times, insert in 2 loops at top of cross t at bottom of last st, draw a loop through, (thread over and draw through 2 loops) 4 times; repeat from ***, thread over and draw through 3 loops, thread over hook 5 times, insert hook in 6th st of next loop, make another cluster of 3 sts, repeating from ** to **, thread over, draw through 3 loops, thread over and draw through last 2 on hook. Chain 13, 1 d t in 6th st of next loop. Repeat from **** to end.

Figure 68.—Popcorn stitch (p c) is made by putting 1 t in t of previous row, 6 t under next 2 ch, take needle out, put it through 1st of 6 t and draw the loop of 6th t through, ch 1, 1 t in next t of previous row.

Begin insertion with 96 ch, turn. *1st row*—One t in 7th st from needle, ch 2, miss 2, 4 t in next 4 sts, * ch 2, 1 t in 3d st from last t; repeat from * until there are 25 spaces (sp), 1 block (bl), 2 sps, ch 5, turn. *2d row*—One t in 2d t of 1st row, 1 bl, made by putting 1 t in t of previous row, 2 t under 2 ch and 1 t in next t, 13 sp, 1 p c, 13 sp, 1 bl, ch 2, 1 t in 3d st of 5 ch, ch 5, turn. *3d row*—Same as 1st row; ch 5, turn. *4th row*—One sp, 1 bl, 7 sp, 1 p c, 4 sp, 1 p c, 1 sp, 1 p c, 4 sp, 1 p c, 7 sp, 1 bl, 1 sp, 1 t in 3d st of 5 ch, ch 5, turn. *4th, 6th, 8th, 10th, 12th, 14th rows*—The same on the edges, but increase the number of p c sts until there are 6 in each diamond and 1 sp between. *The odd rows—5th, 7th, 9th, 11th, 13th, etc.*, are alike throughout the work. *16th row*—Like 12th row, having 5 p c. *18th row*—Like 10th row, having 4 p c in diamond. *20th row*—Like 8th row, having 3 p c in diamond. *22d row*—Like 6th row, having 2 p c in diamond and 1 p c in centre. *23d row*—Like 4th row, having 1 p c in diamond and 2 p c in centre. *24th row*—Like 2d row. *25th row*—Plain, except the edges. *26th row*—Like the 24th row. Continue as in first pattern.

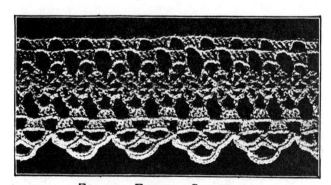

FIG. 59. EDGING. See page 20

Figure 69.—Chain 49. *1st row*—One t in 4th st, 1 t in each of next 5 sts, 9 sps, 1 bl, 2 sps, 3 t in last 3 sts, ch 3, turn. *2d row*—Three t on 3 t, 1 sp, 1 bl, 7 sps, 1 p c, 2 sps, 6 t on 6 t, ch 8, turn. *3d row*—One t in 4th st, 1 t in each of next 4 sts, 1 t in next t, 11 sps, 1 bl, 2 sps, 1 bl, ch 3, turn. *4th row*—Three t on 3 t, 1 sp, 1 bl, 6 sps, 1 p c, 1 sp, 1 p c, 3 sps, 6 t on 6 t, ch 8, turn. *5th row*—Like 3d row, except there are 13 sps. *6th row*—Three t on 3 t, 1 sp, 1 bl, 5 sps, 1 p c, 1 sp, 1 p c, 1 sp, 1 p c, 4 sps, 6 t on 6 t, ch 8, turn. *7th row*—Like 3d row, except there are 15 sps. *8th row*—Three t on 3 t, 1 sp, 1 bl, 4 sps, 4 p c with 1 sp between each, 5 sps, 6 t on 6 t, ch 8, turn. *9th row*—Like 3d row, with 17 sps. *10th row*—Three t on 3 t, 1 sp, 1 bl, 3 sps, 5 p c, with 1 sp between each, 6 sps, 6 t on 6 t, ch 8, turn. *11th row*—Like 9th row, except increase in sps. *12th row*—One bl, 1 sp, 1 bl, 2 sps, 6 p c, with 1 sp between each, 7 sps, 6 t on 6 t, ch 3, turn. *13th row*—Six t on 6 t, the rest of row like 11th row. Beginning with the 14th row, the remaining rows to the 23d, are like the rows from 10th to 1st rows. Repeat from 2d row.

Figure 70.—Make balls first (see below). Chain 16. *1st row*—A t in the 4th st from the needle, 12 t in the next 12 sts, turn. *2d row*—Chain 3, 3 t in the 1st t for a scallop; 1 t in each of next 12 t. This makes the solid panel, turn. *3d row*—Chain 5, a t in the 3d t, (2 ch, a t in 3d t) 3 times. This makes four spaces, turn. *4th row*—Chain 3, 3 t in 1st t for a scallop, 2 ch, a t in next t, now a dot-stitch as follows: Chain 3 (thread over the needle, pull up a loop as long as the 3 chs through the first of the 3 ch), repeat this 6 times in all, thread over the needle and draw through all the loops, 1 ch to close the dot. This is the eye of the dot; thread over and make a dot in the next t, ch 3, and make a dot in the eye of the last dot; a t on the next t, 2 ch, a t in the 3d st of the 5 ch on the end. *5th row*—Chain 5, a t on the 2d t, 2 ch, a dot in the centre of where the three dots come together, 2 ch, a t in next t, 2 ch, a t in next t. *6th row*—Chain 3, 3 t in 1st t, 2 ch and t 4 times. Now make the point on the edge of four rows. First, 1 ch, then 3 d in each space for four rows. (Turn, ch 1 and a d in each d except last.) Repeat this until only 1 d is left. Fasten the vandyke by pulling a loop through the last chain on the vandyke, then, (ch 2 and sl st in the missed d up the side) 6 times, then 1 sl st into the first space. *7th row*—Chain 3, in each sp 2 t, and 1 t in each t, making 13 with the 3 ch. Repeat from the 2d row. *To make a ball:* Chain 3, 6 d in the second chain, work 2 d in each of 6 d, then 1 d in 1 d 45 times; now make a little cotton ball and place in this cup, and make a d in every other d until closed. Chain 5, leave about one-half inch of thread and work this in with the crochet-needle when making the stitches down the side of the point.

FIG. 61. EDGING. See page 20

Figure 71.—In this edge a stitch is employed which is rather unusual and is called a high treble (not a half treble). It is made as follows: Thread over hook and hook through work as in ordinary treble, catch thread, pull loop through, thread over hook and pull through *one* loop only, (thread over hook and pull through two loops) twice. All the t sts used in this edge, with the exception of the 2d st at beginning of star point, and the st next the last d at bottom of star point (which are ordinary t sts), are high t. STAR.—Chain 6, join with sl st to form a ring, * 1 d in ring, ch 9, 1 d in 3d st from hook (use only upper loops of ch sts), 1 t in next st, 3 high t in next 3 sts, 1 t in next st, 1 d in next st, repeat from * 7 times, 1 sl st in 1st d made in ring, break thread, and fasten off. The stars are all made separately, so it is well to make a quantity of them before beginning the edge. Chain 40, 1 d in 15th st from hook, ch 5, miss 4, 1 high t in next st, ch 5, miss 4, 1 d in next st, ch 5, miss 4, 1 high t in next st, ch 5, miss 4, 1 d in next st, ch 5, miss 4, 1 high t in last st, turn. * Chain 7, 1 high t in 1st st of 5 ch of preceding row, 1 high t in last st of next 5 ch, ch 4, 1 high t in next high t, ch 4, 1 high t in 1st st of next 5 ch, insert hook in a point of a star and pull st through, 1 high t in last st of next 5 ch, ch 4, 1 high t in next high t, ch 4, 1 high t in 1st st of next 5 ch, insert hook in next point of star, pull loop through, miss 4 sts on end loop, 1 high t in next st, ch 4, 1 high t in same st, turn. Chain 18, 1 d in 14th st from hook, ch 5, 1 high t in next high t, 1 sl st in next point of star, turn, ch 7, 1 high t in 1st st of 5 ch, miss 4 sts on end loop, 1 high t in next st, ch 4, 1 high t in same st, turn. Chain 9, 1 d between next 2 high t, ch 5, 1 high t in 4th st of 7 ch, 1 sl st in next point of star, turn, ch 9, 1 high t in 1st st of last 5 ch, miss 4 sts, 1 high t in next st of end loop, ch 4, 1 high t in same st, break thread. Having wrong side of work next to you, fasten thread in first free point of edge (at top of lace) with 1 sl st, 1 high t in next high t on edge, ch 5, 1 d between next 2 high t, ch 5, 1 high t in centre st of end loop, turn. Chain 7, 1 high t in 1st st of 5 ch, 1 high t in last st of next 5 ch, ch 4, 1 high t in next high t,

FIG. 60. INSERTION. See page 20

24

ch 4, sl st in next point of star, turn. Chain 5, I d between next 2 high t, ch 5, I high t in centre st of end loop, turn, ch 7, I high t in 1st st of 5 ch, I high t in last st of next 5 ch, ch 4, I high t in ch joining point of star, ch 4, I d in next point of star, ch 7, I d in last point of star, ch 4, join with I d in centre of next chain-loop, turn. Chain 9, I d in the d

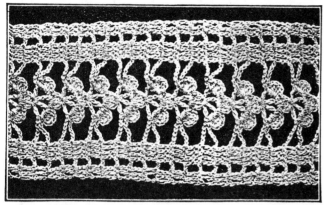

FIG. 62. INSERTION. See page 21

made in point of star, ch 5, I high t in centre of 7 ch, ch 5, I d in next d at point of star, ch 5, I high t in next high t, ch 5, I d between next 2 high t, ch 5, I high t in centre of end loop, turn. Chain 7, I high t in 1st st of 5 ch, I high t in last st of next 5 ch, ch 4, I high t in next high t, ch 4, I high t in 1st st of next 5 ch, I high t in last st of next 5 ch, ch 4, I high t in next high t, ch 4, I high t in 1st st of next 5 ch, I high t in centre st of end loop, ch 4, I high t in same st, turn, I sl st in each of next 4 sts, I sl st between 2 high t, I sl st in each of next 4 sts, I d in next high t, ch 9, I d between next 2 high t, ch 5, I high t in next high t, ch 5, I d between next 2 high t, ch 5, I high t in centre of end loop, turn. Chain 7, I high t in 1st st of 5 ch, I high t in last st of next 5 ch, ch 4, I high t on high t, ch 4, I high t in 1st st of next 5 ch, I high t in centre of next chain-loop, ch 4, I high t in same st. This completes first scallop. Turn. Chain 18, I d in 14th st from hook, ch 5, I high t in next high t, ch 5, I d between next 2 high t, ch 5, I high t in next high t, ch 5, I d between next 2 high t, ch 5, I high t in centre st of end loop. This completes the 1st row of second scallop. Repeat from *.

EDGE FOR BOTTOM.—*Three d under first space, I picot of 4 sts, I d on next st, (3 d under next sp) twice, I p, I d on next st, 4 d, p, 4 d in corner space, I p, I d on next st, (3 d under next sp) twice, I p, I d in same sp with last 3 d, I d in next st, 4 d, p, 4 d under corner sp, I p, I d in next st, 3 d in next sp, I p, I d on next st, 3 d in next sp, I p, I d on next st, 4 d, p, 4 d in corner sp, I p, I d on next st, 3 d under next sp. Repeat from * to end.

Figure 72.—Chain 45. *1st row*—Make I d in 4th st from hook to form a picot, ch 4, I t in 11th st from p, in foundation ch; * without turning, ch 8, take hook out of work, insert under loop just made, beyond the p towards the end of loop, catch the last st of 8 ch, pull through under loop, ch I to fasten, then under this 8 ch make I d, 11 t, I d, I d under the t at end of first loop; * ch 9, p in 4th st, ch 4, miss 6 sts, I d in 7th st of ch, ch 9, p in 4th st, ch

4, miss 6 sts, I t in 7th st, repeat from * to *, ch 9, p in 4th st, ch 4, miss 6 sts, I d in 7th st, ch 9, p in 4th st, I t in last st of ch, repeat from * to *, omitting the I d under the t at end of loop at the top, turn. *2d row*—Slip stitch 3 sts on shell, making 1st sl st in the 2d st, make a picot loop (p l) of 10 sts, p in 4th, ch 4 (always make I extra st before p in turning at top and bottom of edge, the other p l's are all made with 9 ch at the beginning), miss 3 sts on shell, I d in 4th st, I p l, I t beyond p in next l, I p l, I d in 8th st of shell, counting the I d under the t at end of l as I st, I p l, I t in next l beyond p, I p l, miss 3 sts on shell, I d in next st, I p l, miss 3 sts on shell, I d in 4th st, turn. *3d row*—One p l (remember to ch 10 in turning), I t past p in 1st l, repeat from * to * in 1st row, I p l, I d in next l, I p l, I t in next l, repeat from * to *, I p l, I d in next l, I p l, I t in next l, repeat from * to *, I p l, I t in last l, turn. *4th row*—One p l, I t in 1st l, I p l, I d in 8th st of shell, I p l, I t in next l, I p l, I d in 8th st of shell, I p l, I t in next l, I p l, miss 3 sts on shell, I d in next st, I p l, miss 3 sts on shell, I d in 4th st, turn. *5th row*—One p l, I t in 1st l, repeat from * to *, I p l, I d in next l, I p l, I t in next l, repeat from * to *, I p l, I d in next l, I p l, I t in next l, repeat from * to *, I p l, I d in next l, I p l, I t in next l, repeat from * to *, turn. *6th row*—Slip stitch 3 sts on shell, I p l, miss 3 sts, I d in 4th st on shell, I p l, I t in next l, I p l, I d in 8th st of shell, I p l, I t in next l, I p l, I d in 8th st of shell, I p l, I t in next l, I p l, I d in 6th st of shell, turn. *7th row*—One p l, I d in 1st l, I p l, I t in next l, repeat from * to *, I p l, I d in next l, I p l, I t in next l, repeat from * to *, I p l, I d in next l, I p l, I t in next l, repeat from * to *, I p l, I t in last l, turn. *8th row*—One p l, I t in 1st l, I p l, I d in 8th st of shell, I p l, I t in next l, I p l, I d in 6th st of shell, turn. *9th row*—One p l, I d in 1st l, I p l, I t in next l, repeat from * to *, I p l, I d in next l, I p l, I t in next l, repeat from * to *, I p l, I d in next l, I p l, I t in last l, repeat from * to *, and do not forget to omit the I d under the t at the end, turn. Repeat from 2d row for length required, and after making shell at top of last 9th row, turn, and sl st 3 sts on shell.

HEADING.—Without breaking thread, ch 5, * I t in 3d sl st, ch 2, I t under next t, ch 2, I t under

FIG. 63. EDGING. See page 21

next loop, ch 2, I t in same l, ch 2, I t under next t, ch 2, I t under next l, ch 2, I t in 1st sl st on shell, ch 2, repeat from * to end, break thread. *2d row*—Begin at right hand and make 3 d

25

under each space to end. Edge.—Make * 1 d in 2d st of 1st shell at right hand at bottom of edge, ch 2, 1 t under next 1, ch 2, 1 t in same 1, ch 2, 1 t in 2d st on shell, ch 2, skip 2, 1 t in 3d st, ch 2, 1 t in st next the d joining next 1 to shell, ch 2, 1 t under next 1, ch 2, 1 t under same 1, ch 2, 1 t in 2d st of next shell, ch 2, skip 1, 1 t in next st, ch 2, skip 2, 1 t in next st, ch 2, skip 2, 1 t in next t on shell, ch 2, 1 t under next 1, ch 2, 1 t in same 1, ch 2, 1 t in 2d st on next shell, ch 2, skip 2, 1 t in next st, ch 2, 1 t in next st, ch 2, 1 t under next 1, ch 2, 1 t under same 1, ch 3, repeat from * to end of row, break thread. *2d row*—Begin at right hand again, * make 3 d under 1st 2 ch, ** 3 d under each of next 3 spaces, without turning, (ch 5, take hook out of work, and pull 5th st through 4th d) twice, ch 1 to fasten, 3 d under 1st 5 ch, ch 4, 1 d in top of last d to make a p, 1 d under same ch, (ch 5, p in 1st st) 3 times, 1 d under next 5 ch, p of 4 sts, 3 d under same ch, repeat from ** 4 times, making five little scallops in all, 3 d under each of next 2 sps, 4 d under next sp *. Repeat from * to * in each scallop to end of row and fasten off.

Figure 73.—Chain 6, holding braid in left hand make a downward twist with second section, bringing the long end of braid up underneath; holding crossed ends with thumb and finger, make 1 d over

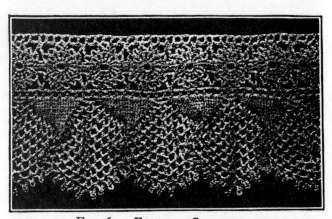

Fig. 64. Edging. See page 22

them to fasten. * Chain 9, 1 d in centre of next section, ch 9, twist next section underneath, 1 d over crossed ends; repeat from * for length desired, ch 6, and break thread. *2d row*—Begin at right hand, make 3 sl sts in the 1st 3 sts of 6 ch, ch 4, take up a piece of braid, twist second section upwards and bring end over, 1 d over crossed braid, * ch 4, 1 sl st in 4th st of 9 ch, using 2 threads of ch st, 1 sl st in each of next 4 sts, which brings you to the d in centre of section on 1st row of braid rings, 1 d into centre of opposite section, 5 sl sts in 5 sts of next 9 ch, ch 4, twist another section, 1 d over crossed cord; repeat from * to end of row, make 3 sl sts in last 3 sts of 6 ch. *3d row*— Fasten thread in first ring at the right with 1 d at bottom of first section, * ch 9, 1 d in centre of section, ch 9, 1 d at lower end of section in ring, ch 3, 1 d in next ring at lower end; repeat from * to end of row, and break thread. *4th row*—Make 3 d in 1st 9 ch at right, 3 d under next 9 ch, * ch 5, 3 d under next 9 ch, 3 d under next 9 ch; repeat from

* to end. *5th row*—One t in 1st d at right-hand end, * (ch 2, 1 t in 3d d,) 3 times, ch 2, 1 t in centre st of 5 ch, ch 2, 1 t in next d; repeat from * to end. Sew ends of braid at beginning and end of the 2 rows, over and over the cord of ring.

Figure 74.—This edging is worked lengthways, and the thread broken at the end of each row, beginning again at right-hand end. Make a chain as long as you wish your edge to be, allowing an inch or two over in length. *1st row*—Make 1 t in 1st st of ch, ch 5, make a picot by inserting hook under two upper threads, draw a loop through, thread over hook and draw through both loops on hook. This method of making a p is used when it is desirable to have the p lie perfectly flat. Make another t in same st as last t, * ch 5, miss 4 sts on ch, 1 t in 5th st, p in last t, 1 t in same st with last t, repeat from * to end of row. *2d row*—One t on 1st t before p, * ch 5, 1 t in

Fig. 65. Insertion. See page 22

3d st of 5 ch, p on t, 1 t in same st with last t, repeat from * to end of row. Make five more rows the same. *8th row*—One d in 3d st of 5 ch (ch 9, 1 d in 3d st of next 5 ch), repeat to end of row. *9th row*—One d under 9 ch, * ch 5, ** thread over hook twice, insert under next 9 ch, thread over, draw loop through, (thread over, draw through two loops) twice, thread over hook twice, insert under same 9 ch, draw loop through, thread over and draw through two loops till all the loops are worked off by twos, ch 3, ** repeat from ** to ** 3 times. You should have four clusters of 2 d t, with 3 ch between each cluster. Chain 5, 1 d under next 9 ch, ch 9, 1 d under next 9 ch, * repeat from * to * to end of row. *10th row* —Make * a cluster of d t under 5 ch, like those in last row, but making three of them in the cluster instead of two, and working the sts all off by twos after making the 3d d t, ch 3, 2 clusters of 3 d t under next ch, with 3 ch between. Repeat in each 3 ch between clusters of 2, ch 3, 1 cluster under 5 ch, ch 7, 1 d under 9 ch, ch 7, repeat from * to end of row. *11th row*—One d between first 2 clusters of d t (ch 5, 1 d under next 3 ch), to end of scallop, * ch 5, 2 d under first 7 ch, 2 d under next 7 ch, ch 5, 1 d under first 3 ch between clusters, (ch 5, 1 d under next 3 ch) 5 times, repeat from * to end of row. *2d ruffle*—Fasten thread in 3d row with 1 d in the same st that the first 2 t in 4th row were made in, ch 9, 1 d in same st with next 2 t of 4th row, ch 9, 1 d in st with next 2 t, repeat across, then repeat from 9th row of edge for remainder of ruffle.

Heading.—Make 1 t in 1st st to the right of first 2 t, * ch 2, 1 t in st after 2 t, ch 2, 1 t in st before next 2 t, repeat from * to end of row. Fasten off all ends with needle.

Figure 75.—Chain 53. *1st row*—Make 1 t in 8th st, ch 2, skip 2, 1 t in next st, make 22 more spaces (sps) like this, turn. *2d row*—Chain 5, 1 t on next t for 1st sp, 5 more sps, make a puff by putting thread over hook, put hook under sp, thread over hook and draw up a long thread, repeat three times more, then thread over hook and draw through all the loops on the hook, then make 1 ch to fasten, 1 t on next t, 9 sps, 1 puff, 6 sps, turn. *3d row*—Make 5 sps, always making 5 ch for first one, 1 puff, 1 sp, 1 puff, 7 sps, 1 puff, 1 sp, 1 puff, 5 sps, turn. *4th row* —Four sps, 3

FIG. 66. EDGING. See page 22

puffs with 1 sp between each, 5 sps, 3 puffs with 1 sp between, 4 sps, turn. *5th row*—Three sps, 4 puffs with 1 sp between each, 3 sps, 4 puffs, 1 sp between each, 3 sps, turn. *6th row*—Two sps, 10 puffs, 1 sp between each, 2 sps, turn. *7th row*—Like 5th row. *8th row*—Like 4th row. *9th row*—Like 3d row. *10th row*—Like 2d row.

After completing the 10th row, you begin the scallop for the edge; ch 6, 1 d under the edge of 9th row (you turn your work over), ch 6, 1 d under 7th row, 2 more chs of 6, fastening them with 1 d under the 5th and 3d row. Turn work, and make 11 d under next three loops, 6 d under 4th loop; without turning work ch 6, take hook out of work, insert in 6th d of 3d loop, repeat twice for next two loops; 11 d in each of two loops, 6 d in 3 d, repeat in next row, making but two loops of 6 ch each, 11 d in the first loop, 6 d in next one, in the next row make only one loop, make 12 d in it, then fill each unfinished loop with 5 d, turn, ch 4, skip 2 d, on first loop, 1 t in next d, make five more t with 1 ch between each, up the side to the top loop, having a sp of 2 or 3 d between them; in the top loop make 5 t, with 1 ch between, continue down the other side of scallop the same, making 6 or 7 t as the space requires, ch 1, 1 sl st in top of 1st t of 1st row, turn, ch 4, 1 t between 1st and 2d t, ch 2, 1 t between next t, repeat around scallops with 2 ch between each t, making 17 t in all, ch 2, 1 sl st in 2d st of 3 ch at end. *11th row*—Chain 1, 1 t on next t for 1st sp, 10 more sps, 1 puff, 11 sps, turn. *12th row*—Ten sps, 1 puff, 1 sp, 1 puff, 9 sps, ch 2, 2 t under 3 ch on scallop (ch 2, 2 t under 2 ch), repeat around scallop, making 2 t under last 3 ch at end, 1 d in sp in 1st row, turn (ch 4, 1 d in 2 ch between t's), repeat to end of scallop, catch last 4 ch with sl st in top of last t. *13th row*—Chain 5, 1 on t, 8 more sps, 3 puffs with 1 sp between each, 9 sps, turn. *14th row* —Eight sps, 4 puffs, 1 sp between each, 8 sps, make last sp by catching last 2 ch with t in 3d st of 5 ch below, turn. *15th row*—Make 7 sps, 5 puffs, 1 sp between each, 7 sps, turn. *16th row*—Eight sps, 4 puffs, 1 sp between each, 3 sps, 4 puffs, 1 sp between

each, 8 sps, turn. *17th row*—Nine sps, 3 puffs, 1 sp between each, 9 sps, turn. *18th row*—Ten sps, 2 puffs, 1 sp between, 10 sps, turn. *19th row*—Eleven sps, 1 puff, 11 sps, turn. *20th row*—Like 2d, repeat for length desired. Scallops begin every 14th row.

Figure 76.—Join a piece of braid so that you have a circle of 12 points. Wind p c 7 times around 3 matches, make 18 d in ring. *2d row*—* Chain 6, take hook out of work, insert in a point of braid, then through the point of braid to the left, catch 6th st with hook and pull it through the two points together, ch 1, 1 d in next st of ch, 1 h t in next, 1 t in each of next 2 sts, 1 d t in next, miss 2 d on ring, 1 sl st in next d; repeat from * 5 times, when you will have a star with 6 points enclosed in a circle of braid. Make as many of these circles as you require for length desired, joining them together with needle and thread at the point of braid that was sewn together to make the circle.

HEADING. *1st row*—Join thread in 5th point from joining, at right hand, with 1 t, ch 7, make a downward turning picot by swinging chain around to the right underneath and making 1 sl st through the 5th st from hook, ch 11, p in 5th st from hook, (not a downward one), ch 3, 1 sl st in next point, * ch 7, downward p in 5th st, ch 11, a downward p in 5th st, ch 3, 1 sl st in next point; repeat from * once more, ch 7, p in 5th (not downward), ch 11, downward p in 5th st, ch 3, make a cross treble as follows: thread over hook, insert hook in last free point on 1st circle, thread over hook, pull through point, thread over, pull through two loops, thread over, insert hook in opposite point on next circle, thread over, pull through point, (thread over, pull through 2 loops) 3 times, ch 7, downward p in 5th st, ch 11, p in 5th st, ch 3, sl st in next point; repeat from * to end. *2d row*—Begin again at right hand, make 1 l t, (thread over 3 times), in centre st between p's in first p l at end, * ch 11, 1 d in centre st of next p l, ch 7, 1 t in sl st on next point, ch 7, 1 d in centre st of next p l, ch 11, thread over hook 3 times, insert hook in centre st of next p l, thread over and pull a loop through, thread over, pull through 2 loops, thread over, insert hook in centre st of first p l on next circle, thread over, pull a loop through, (thread over, pull through 2 loops) 5 times; repeat from * to end. *3d row*—At right hand, make 1 t on 1 t, (ch 2, miss 2, miss 2 sts, 1 t in next st) to end.

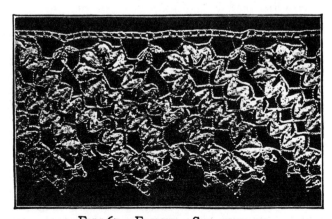

FIG. 67. EDGING. See page 23

Figure 77.— Chain 16. *1st row*—One t in 4th st from hook, ch 7, make 1 d in 5th st from hook to form a picot, ch 2, miss 4 sts, 1 t in 5th, 1 t in next st, ch 12, 1 d in last st, turn. *2d row*—Chain 2, 20 t under 12 ch, 2 t on next 2 t, ch 7, p in 5th st, ch 2, 2 t at end of row, turn. *3d row*—* Chain 3, 1 t on next t, ch 7, p in 5th st, ch 2, 2 t on next 2 t, * (ch 5, miss 3 t, 1 d in next t) 5 times, turn. *4th row*—Chain 5, 1 d in centre of first 5 ch, ch 9, p in 5th st, ch 6, p in 5th, ch 7, p in 5th, ch 6, p in 5th, ch 2, 1 d in 3d st from beginning of the 4 ch before 1st p, ch 3, 1 d in centre of next 5 ch, * ch 11, and make a p as before in the 5th st from hook, ch 6, p, ch 7, p, ch 6, p, ch 2, 1 d in 4th st from beginning of 11 ch, ch 4, 1 d in centre of 5 ch, * repeat from * to * 3 times, ch 3, 2 t on 2 t, ch 7, p,

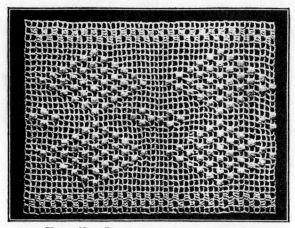

FIG. 68. INSERTION. See page 23

ch 2, 2 t at end, turn. *5th row*—Repeat from * to * in 3d row, ch 5, 1 d between p's at centre of first picot loop, ch 7, 1 d between p's in next loop, ch 9, 1 d between p's in next loop, ch 11, 1 d in next loop, ch 9, 1 d in last 5-ch loop, turn. *6th row*—Under the 9 ch, make * 1 d, 3 t, p of 4 sts, fastened in top of t with 1 d (2 t, p) 3 times, 3 t, 1 d *. In next loop, which is the 11-ch loop, make 1 d, 3 t, p (2 t, p), 4 times, 3 t, 1 d in next loop, repeat from * to * next loop, 1 d, 3 t, p, (2 t, p) twice, 1 d, last loop, 1 d, 3 t, p, 2 t, p, 3 t, 2 t in next 2 t, ch 7, p, ch 2, 2 t at end, turn. *7th row*—This corresponds to 1st row, and you start a new scallop. Repeat from * to * in 3d row, ch 12, 1 d in 1st p of second small scallop, turn, and repeat from 2d **row** for length. Do not break thread but begin heading.

HEADING. *1st row*—Chain 5, 1 t in side of 1st t, ch 2, 1 t in side of next t, repeat to end, turn. *2d row*—Chain 5, * thread over hook 3 times, insert hook in top of next t, pull a loop through, (thread over and pull through 2 loops) twice, thread over hook, insert in next t, (thread over, pull through 2 loops) 4 times, ch 2, thread over, insert hook in centre of st, pull a loop through (thread over, pull through 2 loops) twice, ch 2, repeat from * to end of row, turn. *3d row*—Chain 5, 1 t on next t, ch 2, 1 t on next t, to end of row.

Figure 78.— Chain 44. *1st row*—Make 1 t in 6th st from hook, 1 t in next st, ch 4, miss 4, 1 d in next st, 1 d in each of next 26 sts, ch 4, miss 4, 2 d in last 2 sts, turn. *2d row*—Chain 5, 2 d in 2 d, ch 7,

beginning in 4th d, make 21 d in 21 d, using only lower or back loops to give a ribbed effect; ch 7, 2 d on 2 t, turn. *3d row*—Chain 5, 2 t on 2 d, ch 4, 1 d in centre of 7 ch, ch 7, 15 d in 21 d, making the 1st one in the 4th d, ch 7, 1 d in centre of 7 ch, ch 4, 2 d on 2 t, turn. *4th row*—Chain 5, 2 t on 2 d, ch 7, 1 d in 7 ch, ch 7, 9 d in 15 d, beginning at 4th d, ch 7, 1 d in 7 ch, ch 7, 2 d on 2 t, turn. *5th row*—Chain 5, 2 t on 2 d, ch 4, 1 d in next 7-ch sp, ch 7, 1 d in next 7 ch, ch 7, 3 d in 3 centre d of 9 d, (ch 7, 1 d in 7 ch), twice, ch 4, 2 d on 2 t, turn. *6th row*—Chain 5, 2 t on 2 d, (ch 7, 1 d in 7 ch), 4 times, ch 7, 2 d on 2 t, turn. *7th row*—In this row the next diamond is begun. Chain 5, 2 t on 2 d, ch 4, 1 d in 7 ch, ch 7, 1 d in 7 ch, ch 7, 3 d in 3 centre sts of next 7-ch sp, (ch 7, 1 d in 7 ch) twice, ch 4, 2 d on 2 t, turn. *8th row*—Chain 5, 2 t on 2 d, ch 7, 1 d in 7-ch sp, ch 7, 9 d across the 3 d, 3 extending over the sides worked into the chains, ch 7, 1 d on 7-ch sp, ch 7, 2 d on 2 t, turn. *9th row*—Chain 5, 2 t on 2 d, ch 4, 1 d in 7 ch, ch 7, 15 d across the 9, 3 extending over the sides; ch 7, 1 d in 7 ch, ch 4, 2 d on 2 t, turn. *10th row*—Chain 5, 2 t on 2 d, ch 7, 21 d across 15 d, ch 7, 2 d on 2 t, turn. *11th row*—Chain 5, 2 t on 2 d, ch 4, 27 d across 21 d, ch 4, 2 d on 2 t, turn. *12th row*—Chain 5, 2 t on 2 d, ch 4, 27 d on 27 d, ch 4, 2 d on 2 t, turn. Repeat from 2d row.

Figure 79A.— Chain 84, turn. *1st row*—Make 1 t in 5th st from needle, 3 festoons (see directions for Fig. 79B), ch 2, skip 2 sts, 1 t in next, ch 2, skip 2, 4 t in next 4 sts, ch 5, skip 4 sts, 28 d in next 28 sts, ch 5, skip 4 sts,

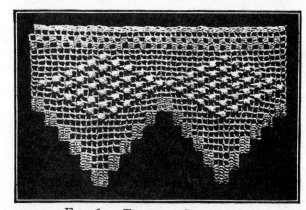

FIG. 69. EDGING. See page 23

4 t in next 4 sts, ch 2, skip 2, 1 t in next st, 1 f, 1 t in next st, turn. *2d row*—Chain 3, 1 t on next t, 2 sq m, 4 t (the first t of this group is the t of the sq m), ch 5, 22 d, ch 5, 4 t, ch 14, 4 t, ch 2, 1 t, 3 sq m, 1 t on 3 ch at end of row, turn. *3d row*—Chain 3, 1 t on t, 3 festoons, 4 t (the last t of festoon is the first of this group), ch 6, 4 d, ch 6, 4 t, ch 6, 16 d, ch 6, 4 t, ch 2, 1 t, 2 festoons, 1 t in 3 ch, turn. *4th row*—Chain 3, 1 t on t, 3 sq m, 4 t, ch 6, 10 d, ch 6, 4 t, ch 6, 10 d, ch 6, 4 t, ch 2, 1 t, 2 sq m, 1 t on t, turn. *5th row*—Chain 3, 1 t on t, 2 festoons, 3 t in next 3 sts, ch 5, 16 d, ch 5, 4 t, ch 8, 4 d, ch 8, 4 t, ch 2, 1 t, 3 f, 1 t on 3 ch, turn. *6th row*—Chain 3, t on t, 4 sq m, 3 t in next 3 sts, ch 2, 4 t on last 3 sts of next ch, and 1st t of group below, ch 5, 22 d, ch 5, 4 t, ch 2, 1 t, 1 sq m, 1 t in 3 ch, turn. *7th row*—Chain 3, 1 t on t, 1 f, 3 t, ch 5, 28 d, ch 5, 4 t, ch 2, 1 t, 4 f, 1 t, turn. *8th*

row—Chain 3, 1 t on t, 4 sq m, 3 t, ch 14, 4 t, ch 5, 22 d, ch 5, 4 t, ch 2, 1 t, 1 sq m, 1 t on 3 ch, turn. *9th row*—Chain 3, 1 t on t, 2 f, 4 t, ch 6, 16 d, ch 5, 4 t, ch 6, 4 d, ch 6, 4 t, ch 2, 1 t, 3 f, 1 t, turn. *10th row* —Chain 3, 1 t on t, 3 sq m, 4 t, ch 6, 10 d, ch 6, 4 t, ch 6, 10 d, ch 6, 4 t, ch 2, 1 t, 2 sq m, 1 t, turn. *11th row*—Chain 3, 1 t on t, 3 f, 4 t, ch 8, 4 d, ch 8, 4 t, ch 5, 16 d, ch 5, 4 t, ch 2, 1 t, 2 f, 1 t in 3 ch, turn. *12th row*—Chain 3, 1 t on t, 2 sq m, 3 t, ch 5, 22 d, ch 5, 4 t, ch 2, 4 t, ch 2, 1 t, 3 sq m, 1 t, turn. *13th row*—Chain 3, 1 t on t, 3 f, ch 2, 1 t, ch 2, 4 t, ch 5, 28 d, ch 5, 4 t, ch 2, 1 t, 1 f, 1 t, turn. Repeat from 2d row.

FIG. 70. FRINGE. See page 24

Figure 79B.—Chain 59 sts. *1st row*—Make 1 t in 5th st from needle, * ch 3, skip 2 sts, 1 sl st in 3d st, ch 3, skip 2, 1 t in next st * (from * to * is called a festoon [f]), ch 2, skip 2 sts, 4 t in next 4 sts, ch 5, skip 5, 28 d in next 28 sts, ch 5, skip 5, 4 d in last 4 sts, turn. *2d row*—Chain 11, 1 t in 9th st from needle, 1 t in each of next 2 sts, 1 t on 1st t of group below, ch 14, 4 t, the first of this group in the last t of group below, ch 5, 22 d beginning with the 4th d of preceding row, and using back loops only. (Both d and t sts should be taken in the back loops of sts, except the treble st of the f or the square mesh; these should be taken under both threads of the st or chain below; when 4 t are directed they should be always joined in the four consecutive sts of the preceding row, and when a group of 4 t comes after a f or square mesh, the last t of either of them is counted as the 1st t of the group), ch 5, 4 t on the last 3 ch and 1st t, * ch 5, skip 3 t and 2 ch sts, 1 t on t, * from * to * is called a square mesh (sq m), ch 5, skip 1 f, 1 t on last t, 1 t in 3 ch at end of row, turn. *3d row*—Chain 3, 1 t on 2d t, 2 f's, ch 2, 4 t, ch 6, 16 d, beginning on 4th d below, ch 6, 4 t, (3 on last 3 ch, and the 4th on 1st t), ch 6, 4 d, beginning on 6th st of 14 ch, ch 6, 4 t (on last t, and 3 following ch below), turn. *4th row* —Chain 11, 3 t in

last 3 sts of 11 ch, 1 t on next t, ch 6, 10 d, 3 on the ch, 4 on the d's, and 3 on the ch beyond, ch 6, 4 t, ch 6, 10 d (begin on 4th d below), ch 6, 4 t, 3 sq m, 1 t on the 3 ch at end of row, turn. *5th row*—Chain 3, 1 t on t, 3 f, ch 2, 4 t, ch 8, 4 d in centre of 10 d, ch 8, 4 t, ch 5, 16 d (1st 3 on ch), ch 5, 4 t, turn. *6th row*—Chain 11, 4 t, ch 5, 22 d, ch 5, 4 t, ch 2, 4 t, 4 sq m, 1 t on 3 ch at end of row, turn. *7th row*—Chain 3, 1 t, 4 f, ch 2, 4 t, ch 5, 28 d, ch 5, 4 t, turn. *8th row*—Chain 5, 4 t, ch 5, 22 d, ch 5, 4 t, ch 14, 4 t, 4 sq m, 1 t in 3 ch at end, turn. *9th row* —Chain 3, 1 t on t, 3 f, ch 2, 4 t, ch 6, 4 d (beginning on 6th st of 14 ch), ch 6, 4 t, ch 6, 16 d, ch 6, 4 t, turn. *10th row*—Chain 5, 4 t, ch 6, 10 d, ch 6, 4 t, ch 6, 10 d, ch 6, 4 t, 3 sq m, 1 t on 3 ch, turn. *11th row*—Chain 3, 1 t, 2 f, ch 2, 4 t, ch 5, 16 d, ch 5, 4 t, ch 8, 4 d, ch 8, 4 t, turn. *12th row*—Chain 5, 4 t, ch 2, 4 t, ch 5, 22 d, ch 5, 4 t, 2 sq m, 1 t on 3 ch, turn. *13th row*—Chain 3, 1 t on t, 1 f, ch 2, 4 t, ch 5, 28 d, ch 5, 4 t, turn. *14th row*—Like 2d row. *15th row*—Like 3d row, etc.

EDGE FOR SCALLOP.—Join thread in the 1st t at the right-hand edge of first scallop, * make 9 t over the first loop between blocks, make a sl st at the intersection of the next two blocks, * repeat the length of edging, making 1 sl st in the centre of block at the bottom of scallops and between scallops at the top.

Figure 80.— For this insertion, make a row of circles the length desired (see directions for Fig. 81), joining two loops of one circle to two loops of next circle, with d. For the edge on each side make 1 d in a loop, * 1 ch, p, 3 ch, p, 1 ch, 1 d in next loop, 1 ch, p, 3 ch, p, 2 ch, 1 d in first loop on next circle, repeat from * to end. *2d row*—Two d under 3 ch between picots, * 8 ch, 2 d under next 3 ch, repeat from * to end. *3d row*—Two d under 8 ch, * 3 ch, 2 d under same 8 ch, 3 ch, 2 d under next 8 ch, repeat from * to end. *4th row*—Two d under 3 ch, * 2 ch, 2 d under next 3 ch, repeat from * to end.

Figure 81.— For the circles make 9 ch and join. *1st row*—Twenty-four d in the ring, sl st in 1st d. *2d row*—One d in 2 sts, * 3 ch, skip 1, 1 d in next 2, repeat from * to end. *3d row*—Slip stitch to first 3 ch, 2 d under 3 ch, * 5 ch, 2 d under next 3 ch. Repeat from * all around. Join 2 loops of 5 ch to 2 loops of 5 ch on next circle with 1 d, make each row three circles in length. To join the rows make 1 d in first loop of 5 ch on side, * (1 ch, p)

FIG. 71. EDGING. See page 24

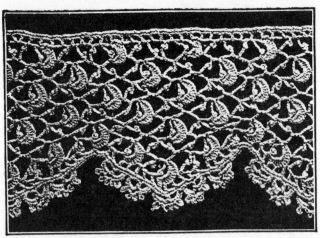

FIG. 72. EDGING. See page 25

3 times, 1 ch, 1 d in next loop, (1 ch, p) 3 times, 2 ch, 1 d in first loop on next circle, repeat from * once. (A picot is made by working 4 ch, then 1 d in the first chain), 3 d in first loop on lower circle, 6 ch, 1 d in third and second, 1 t in first, 1 t in top of 3d d, * 5 d under next loop, 7 ch, 1 d in fourth and third, 1 t in second and first, 1 t in top of 5th d, repeat from * twice, 5 d under fifth loop, 6 ch, 1 d in third and second, 1 t in first, 1 t in top of 5th d, 3 d under sixth loop, work up second side same as first. After making 2 d in last loop on top circle, make 2 ch, p, 5 ch, p, 2 ch, 1 d in first side loop on next row of circles, when working down the first side of 2d row, join 3d st of centre p's to centre p's of opposite loops of 1st row with d and centre st of first point on lower circle, to centre st on fifth point on opposite circle with d. Work around each row and join in same manner. For the top edge, 2 d in first loop, * 4 ch, 2 d in next loop, 8 ch, 2 d under 5 ch, 8 ch, 2 d under first loop on next row of circles, repeat from * to end. *2d row*—* Two d under 4 ch, 3 ch, 2 d under 8 ch, 3 ch, 2 d under 8 ch, 3 ch, 2 d under next 8 ch, 3 ch, 2 d under same 8 ch, 3 ch, repeat from * to end. *3d row*—Two d under 3 ch, * 3 ch, 2 d under next 3 ch, repeat from * to end.

Figure 82.—Chain 31, turn. *1st row*—Make a shell of 3 t, 2 ch, 3 t in 4th st of ch, miss 3, 1 d in 4th st of ch, draw out st on hook one-quarter of an inch, take up thread and draw through this loop, put hook under thread just drawn through, between it and the long st, thread over hook, draw through, thread over and draw through both sts on hook. This makes 1 knot st, make another in same way, miss 4

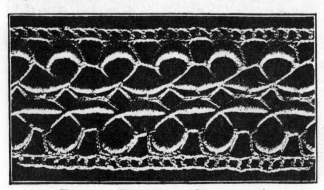

FIG. 73. INSERTION. See page 26

sts on ch, 1 d in 5th st, ch 3, 1 d in same st, working off two loops only, 1 d t in same st, working off two loops, thread over hook, work off 4 sts, thread over and work off last 2 sts, miss 4 sts, 2 d t in next st, working off loops in same way, then thread over, draw through 4 sts, thread over, draw through last 2 sts, ch 3, 1 d in same st, 2 knot sts, miss 4 sts, 1 d in next st, miss 3 sts, shell in next st, 1 d in last st of chain, turn. *2d row*—Chain 6, shell in shell, 1 knot st, 1 d in centre of 2 knot sts of last row, 1 knot st, 2 d t as before in centre st of the clusters of d t of last row, ch 3, 1 d in same st, ch 3, 2 d t in same st, 1 knot st, 1 d in centre knot of last row, 1 knot st, shell in shell, ch 7, 1 sl st in top of first shell made, ch 1, turn; * under 7 ch make 3 d (a picot consisting of 3 ch, put hook down through the top, and out front of last d made, under two threads of the st, catch thread and draw through the two threads and st on hook), 4 d, ch 6, turn, 1 sl st in last d made, ch 1, turn, under 6 ch make 3 d, 1 p, 5 d, 1 p, 3 d, under last half of 7 ch make 3 d, 1 p, 3 d *. *3d row*—Shell in shell, 1 d in last st of shell in preceding row, 2 knot sts, 1 d in st at end of first cluster of d t in last row, ch 3, 2 d t in same st (always working as described in previous rows), 2 d t in st at end of second cluster, ch 3, 1 d in same st, 2 knot sts, 1 d in 1st st of next shell, shell in shell, 1 d in last st of

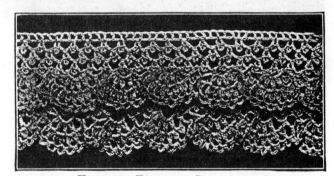

FIG. 74. EDGING. See page 26

shell, turn. *4th row*—Like 2d row, making the sl st after the 7 ch at bottom, between the two shells on the edge. *5th row*—Like 3d row. Repeat the 4th and 5th rows till you have 12 rows and 6 little scallops across the bottom edge, leaving the 6th scallop partly unfinished, making under it 3 d, p, 4 d, ch 6, turn, 1 sl st in last d made, ch 1, turn, under 6 ch make 3 d, p, 2 ch. You now begin the 2d row of points by making * (7 ch, take hook out of work, insert in 3d st of 5 d in the 6 ch ring of fifth scallop, catch 7th ch st with hook and pull through, ch 1 to fasten) * 5 times, finish each 7 ch by repeating from * to * in 2d row, leaving last 7 ch at right-hand side of point unfinished in each row, repeating from * to * (in the parenthesis), in turning. Repeat till you have but one loop at the bottom, make 3 d, p, 3 d, p, 3 d, p, 3 d in last 6-ch loop at bottom of point, then finish the loops up the side, and repeat from 2d row for length required.

Figure 83.—Make a chain of 15 sts. *1st row*—Make 3 t in 5th st of ch, ch 2, skip 1 st on ch, 3 t in next st (this makes a shell), ch 6, skip 4 sts on ch, 3 t in next st, ch 2, 3 t in last st of ch, turn. *2d row*—Chain 5, shell in shell, ch 5, shell in shell, turn. *3d row*—Chain 3, shell in shell, ch 3, 1 d over two chains below, ch 3, shell in shell; * ch 13, 1 d in 7th st from hook, turn, ch 6, 1 d in loop, twice, ch 6, 1 d in st where first loop was joined, taking up two threads, turn, 1 d, 5 t in first loop, take hook out of work, insert it in 5 ch between two previous rows, pull loop you took hook out of through, and make 1 ch to fasten, 5 t, 1 d in loop to finish, 1 d, 10 t, 1 d in next loop, 1 d, 5 t in next, repeat from * for another leaf, joining it to first leaf at 5th st of centre petal, then finish petal with 5 t, 1 d; in next two loops make 1 d, 10 t, 1 d, making the last d in third loop in same d that joined first loop to the 7th st of ch, 8 d under 6 ch; then finish first leaf with 5 t, 1 d in the d joining first loop to ch. 8 d over stem. *4th row*—Shell in shell, ch 5, shell in shell, turn. *5th row*—Chain 3, shell in shell, ch 6, shell in shell, turn. Begin again at 2d row and repeat for length required. Join the third leaf to the first one as you make it, pulling the loop of the 5th t in the second loop through the st where the stem of the second leaf begins. Begin the fourth leaf at the 5th t in the last loop of third leaf, joining the 5th t of first loop

FIG. 76. EDGING. See page 27

3 t, 3 ch, 3 t in next sp, repeat in every other sp around, ch 1, 1 d in last t of shell in previous row, turn. *11th row*—Chain 1, 9 t under each 3 ch between shells all around scallop excepting bottom shell, make 10 t in that; after making last 9 t, ch 1, 1 d in 1 ch between next shell, ch 2, shell in shell, ch 3, tie, shell in shell, turn. *12th row*—Like 2d. *13th row*—Like 3d. Repeat from 4th row for length required, then, without breaking thread, work along the top as follows: Chain 6, 2 d under 1st 4 ch, * ch 4, 2 d under next 4 ch, repeat from * to end. To make the purl edge on the bottom of scallops, fasten thread in 3 ch at beginning of 1st row, ch 4, 1 d under 1 ch before 9 t, ch 2, 1 sl st in 1st t, ch 2, 1 sl st in next t, repeat to 9th t, ch 2, skip 9th t, 1 sl st between scallops, ch 2, skip 1st t, 1 sl st in next, ch 2, 1 sl st in next. Repeat to end, skipping last t of each scallop and first of next one, making 1 sl st between scallops; when you reach the end of large scallop, ch 3, 1 d in centre of next two rows, ch 3, 1 d under 1 ch before 9 t on next scallop.

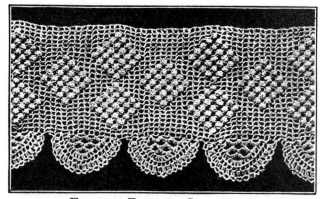

FIG. 75. EDGING. See page 27

in same st where stem of second leaf began, and the 5th t in centre loop, to 5th t of last loop of second leaf.

Figure 84.—Chain 14. *1st row*—Make 3 t in 5th st from hook, ch 2, 3 t in same st; this makes a shell and will be described as such hereafter. Chain 3, skip 3 sts, 1 d in next st, turn. *2d row*—Chain 4, shell in shell, ch 3, tie down with 1 d in 1st t of next shell, shell in shell, turn. *3d row*—Chain 3, shell in shell, ch 3, tie with 1 d in next shell, shell in shell, turn. *4th row*—Chain 4, shell in shell, ch 3, tie, shell in shell, ch 2, 1 t in top of t (take up both threads of st), at end of shell in previous row, turn. *5th row*—Chain 5, 1 t in 1st t of shell, ch 2, shell in shell, ch 3, tie, shell in shell, turn. *6th row*—Like 4th row from * to *, ch 2, 1 t in next t, ch 2, 1 t in 3d st of 5 ch, turn. *7th row*—Chain 5, 1 t on 1st t, ch 2, 1 t on next t, ch 2, 1 t on 1st t of shell, ch 2, shell in shell, ch 3, tie, shell in shell, turn. *8th row*—Like 6th from * to *, (ch 2, 1 t on next t) 3 times, ch 2, 1 t in 3d st of 5 ch, turn. *9th row*—Chain 5, 1 t on next t, (ch 2, 1 t on next t) 4 times, ch 2, shell in shell, ch 3, tie, shell in shell, turn. *10th row*—Chain 4, shell in shell, ch 3, tie, shell in shell, ch 1, skip 1 space on scallop, and make a shell of

Figure 85.—Chain 60. *1st row*—* Make 1 d in 2d st, 1 h t, 5 t, 1 h t, 1 d, in next 8 sts, * of foundation ch, putting each st *into* not *under* ch; this completes one leaf. One d in next st, 1 d, 1 h t, 5 t, 1 h t, 1 d, in next 9 sts, 1 d in next st, ch 3, miss 3 sts, 1 d in next, ch 5, 1 d in same st, miss 3 sts, 7 t in next st, miss 3 sts, 1 d in next st, ch 5, 1 d in same st, ch 7, miss 4 sts, 1 d in next, ch 5, 1 d in same st, miss 3, 7 t in next st, miss 3, 1 d in next st, ch 5, 1 d in same st, ch 7, miss 4, 1 d in next st, ch 5, 1 d in same st, ch 7, miss 4, 1 t in each of last 2 sts, turn. *2d row*—** Chain 3, 1 t on 2d t, ch 3, 1 d in 1st space (sp), ch 5, 1 d in same sp, ch 7, 1 d in next sp, ch 5, 1 d in same sp, **, ch 7, 1 d in 4th t of

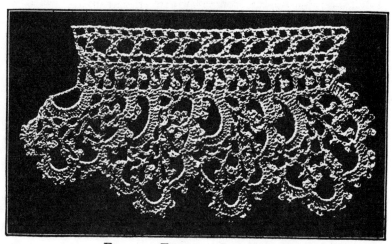

FIG. 77. EDGING. See page 28

shell, ch 5, 1 d in same st, ch 7, 1 d in next sp, ch 7, 1 d in 4th st of shell, ch 5, 1 d in same st, ch 3, 1 d between the 2 d at point of leaf. below, turn, *** ch 12, take hook out of work and insert in centre d between the two leaves. below, catch 12th ch and pull through, ch 1, 4 d under 12 ch for stem, ch 10, repeat from * to *, 1 d in side of 4th d on stem, push

FIG. 78. INSERTION
See page 28

4 d on stem as closely together as you can, and make 1 d in next st of ch, then 1 h t, 5 t, 1 h t, 1 d, in next 8 sts, 1 d in t at end of leaf. *3d row*—Chain 15, pull last st through centre d on stem, ch 1, 4 d under ch, ch 10, repeat from * to *, 1 d in side of 4th d on stem, repeat from ** to **, making 1st d in 3d st of 15 ch, by pushing the 4 d on stem closely together and making the d in next visible st of ch, 1 d in next st, leaving 2 sts free to represent a t, ch 3, 1 d under next 7 ch, ch 5, 1 d in same sp, 7 t in next d, 1 d in next sp, ch 5, 1 d in same sp, *** (ch 7, 1 d in next sp, ch 5, 1 d in same sp)

twice, ch 7, 2 t on 2 t, the last 3 ch at end of row representing the 1st t, turn. *4th row*—Repeat from ** to **, ch 7, 1 d in next sp, ch 7, 1 d in 4th t of shell, ch 5, 1 d in same st, ch 3, 1 t between 1st and 2d d at end of leaf. The 5th row began in 3d row at ch 15, in repeating from *** to *** and has been completed, therefore the next row is the 6th. *6th row*—Repeat from *** to ***, ch 7, 1 d in 4th t of shell, ch 5, 1 d in same st, ch 3, 1 t between 2 d at end of leaf, turn. *7th row*—Chain 12, pull last st through centre d between leaves, ch 1, 4 d under 12 ch, 1 d in 4th st of 12 ch (push 4 d on ch close together so that 3 of them will be covered by them), 1 h t, 5 t, 1 h t, 1 d, in next 8 sts, 1 d on t at end of leaf, (ch 7, 1 d in next sp, ch 5, 1 d in same sp) twice, ch 7, 2 t on 2 t, turn. *8th row*—Repeat from ** to **, ch 7, 1 d in next sp, ch 5, 1 d in same sp, turn. *9th row*—Chain 12, pull last st through centre d on stem, ch 1, 4 d under 12 ch, 1 d in 4th st of 12 ch, (the three first sts being covered with the last 4 d), 1 h t, 5 t in next 5 sts, (ch 7, 1 d in the next sp, ch 5, 1 d in same sp) twice, ch 7, 2 t on 2 t, turn. *10th row*—Repeat from ** to **, ch 7, 1 d in next sp, ch 5, 1 d in same sp, turn. *11th row*—Chain 15, pull last st through 4th d on stem, ch 1, 4 d under 15 ch, push last 4 d closely together and make 1 d in next st of ch, 1 h t, 5 t, 1 h t, 1 d, in next 8 sts, 1 d in next st leaving 2 ch for t, (ch 7, 1 d in next sp, ch 5, 1 d in same sp) twice, ch 7, 2 t on 2 t, turn. *12th row*—Repeat from ** to **, ch 7, 1 d in next sp, ch 7, 1 t between 2 d at end of leaf, turn, ch 12, pull last st through centre d on stem, ch 1, 4 d under 12 ch, ch 9, turn work wrong side toward you, thread over hook 4 times, miss 4 d,

insert hook between next 2 d (in the centre of leaf stem), thread over hook, pull through 2 loops, thread over again, pull through 2 more loops, thread over twice, miss 8 d, insert hook between next sts (in centre of leaf stem), thread over, pull through 2 loops, and repeat till all the loops on hook are worked off by twos, 1 sl st in top of 5th leaf, turn. *13th row*—Make 1 d on the long st just made, 1 d, 1 h t, 5 t, 1 h t, 1 d, in next 9 sts, 1 d on centre d between leaves, 1 d in 4th st of ch, 1 h t, 5 t, 1 h t, 1 d, in next 8 sts of ch, 1 d on next t at end of leaf, ch 15, pull last st through centre d between leaves, 4 d under 15 ch, ch 10, repeat from * to *, 1 d in centre d, 1 d in next st of ch after pushing 4 d together, 1 h t, 5 t, 1 h t, 1 d, in next 8 sts, 1 d in next st, leaving 2 sts for t, ch 7, 1 d in 1st sp, ch 5, 1 d in same sp, 7 t in next d, 1 d in next sp, ch 5, 1 d in same sp, ch 7, 1 d in next sp, ch 5, 1 d in same sp, ch 7, 2 t on 2 t, turn. *14th row*—Repeat from ** to **, ch 7, 1 d in 4th t of shell, ch 5, 1 d in same st, ch 7, 1 d in next sp, ch 7, 1 t between 2 d at end of leaf, turn, ch 12, pull last st through centre d, ch 1, 4 d under 12 ch, ch 10, repeat from * to *, 1 d in side of 4th d on stem, 1 d in 4th st of 12 ch, 1 h t, 5 t, 1 h t, 1 d, in next 8 sts, 1 d in next t. *15th row*—Chain 15, pull last st through centre d, 4 d under 15 ch, ch 10, repeat from * to *, 1 d in side of 4th d on stem, 1 d in 1 d in next st of ch, 1 h t, 5 t, 1 h t, 1 d, in next 8 sts, 1 d in next st, leaving 2 ch for t, ch 7, 1 d in next sp, ch 5, 1 d in same sp, 7 t in next d, 1 d in next sp, ch 5, 1 d in same sp, (ch 7, 1 d in next sp, ch 5, 1 d in same sp) twice, ch 7, 2 t on 2 t. *16th row*—Repeat from ** to **, ch 7, 1 d under next sp, ch 7, 1 d in 4th t of shell, ch 5, 1 d in same st, ch 7, 1 d in next sp, ch 7, 1 t between 2 d at end of leaf, turn, ch 12, pull last st through centre d on stem, 4 d under 12 ch, ch 10, repeat from * to *, 1 d in side of 4th d on stem, 1 d in 4th st of 12 ch, 1 h t, 5 t, 1 h t, 1 d, in next 8 sts, 1 d in t. This row completes first scallop, the next row is the beginning of second one. *17th row*—Chain 30, repeat from * to *, 1 d in next st, 1 d, 1 h t, 5 t, 1 h t, 1 d, in next 9 sts, 1 d in next st, ch 3, 1 d in next sp on last row, ch 5, 1 d in same sp, 7 t in next d, 1 d in next sp, ch 5, 1 d in same sp, ch 7, 1 d in next sp, ch 5, 1 d in same sp, 7 t in next d, 1 d in next sp, ch 5, 1 d in same sp, ch 7, 1 d in next sp, ch 5, 1 d in same sp, ch 7, 2 t on 2 t. Repeat from 2d row. To finish lower edge of lace: Holding the lace, with right side towards you, fasten thread with 1 d in right-hand lower

A   B

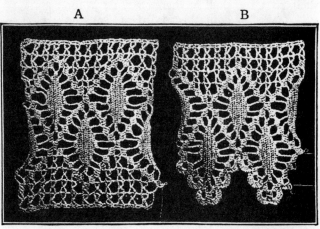

FIG. 79. INSERTION AND EDGING. See page 28

corner, between 2 d at beginning of first leaf, ch 6, 1 d t in centre st between leaves, * (ch 5, 1 p in 1st st, 1 d t in same st) 4 times *, ** ch 6, 1 d in point of leaf, (ch 4, 1 d in point of next leaf) 8 times, ch 6, 1 d t in centre st between leaves, repeat from * to *, ch 3, 1 d in 9 ch between scallops, ch 3, 1 d t in centre st between leaves, repeat from * to *, then repeat from ** to end of row. SQUARE.—Chain 8, 1 t in 1st st made (ch 5, 1 t in same st) twice, ch 5, 1 sl st

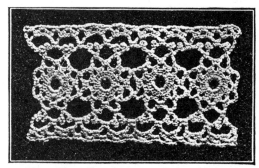

FIG. 80. INSERTION. See page 29

in 3d st of 8 ch. *2d row*—Chain 1, * 1 d in each of first 2 sts, 3 d in 3d st, 1 d in each of next 2 sts, 1 d on t, repeat from * 3 times, making 1 sl st in the joining sl st of last row, after making the last d. *3d row*—Chain 4, 1 d t in sl st, ch 5, ** thread over hook twice, insert hook in the centre st of the 3 d at corner, thread over hook, draw a loop through, thread over again, draw through two loops, thread over, draw through two loops, retaining two loops on hook, put thread over hook twice, insert in same st, thread over, draw a loop through, (thread over, draw through two loops) 4 times, when the loops should be all worked off, ch 6, repeat from ** in same corner st, ch 5, repeat the 2d t in centre d on t, repeat around, making 4 d t sts in each corner st with 6 ch between them, between the 2 d t sts in the sides make but 5 ch between; after making the last 5 ch, make 1 sl st in top of 1st d t, ch 1. *4th row*—Four d under 1st sp, 5 ch, 4 d in same sp, in next sp which is the corner sp, make 4 d, 5 ch, 4 d, ch 2, now join square to lace, as follows: Take hook out of work, insert in last leaf on lace, putting hook down through the d at the point, from the right side, catch the 2d st with hook and draw through the d, ch 3, 4 d in same sp on square (4 d, ch 2 in next sp and connect the same as in previous sp, 4 d in same sp), repeat in next 2 sps, making 4 d after joining 1st p of corner sp to 4th leaf, then join 2d p of same sp to point of first leaf on opposite side, join next 3 picots in same manner to next three leaves, then make 4 d, 5 ch, 4 d to finish corner sp, and finish remainder of square around bottom, with 4 d, 5 ch, 4 d in each side sp, and 4 d, 5 ch, 4 d, 5 ch, 4 d in corner square, join with sl st, and fasten off. Join squares in same manner across the length of the lace.

Figure 86.—Chain 150 for foundation. *1st row* —One t in 5th st, 1 t in each of next 3 sts, ch 2, 1 t in 3d st, which forms a space (sp) make 46 more sps, 4 t on last 4 sts, ch 3, turn. *2d row*— Three t on first 3 t below, 27 sps, 10 t, 18 sps, 4 t in 5 ch of last row, ch 8. *3d row*—Four t made on last 3 ch and 1st t, 10 sps, 10 t, 5 sps, 16 t, 15 sps, 7 t, 2 sps, 4 t, 1 sp, 13 t, 1 sp, 4 t, ch 3. *4th row*—Three

t, 1 sp, 22 t, 1 sp, 10 t, 14 sps, 16 t, 4 sps, 16 t, 10 sps, 4 t, ch 8. *5th row*—Eleven sps, 16 t, 4 sps, 16 t, 9 sps, 4 t, 4 sps, 10 t, 1 sp, 22 t, 1 sp, 4 t, ch 3. *6th row*—Three t, 2 sps, 10 t, 1 sp, 22 t, 2 sps, 10 t, 1 sp, 7 t, 6 sps, 10 t, 1 sp, 10 t, 1 sp, 16 t, 6 sps, 7 t, 4 sps, 4 t, ch 8. *7th row*—Four t, 4 sps, 13 t, 3 sps, 7 t, 1 sp, 10 t, 1 sp, 16 t, 3 sps, 7 t, 4 sps, 19 t, 2 sps, 13 t, 1 sp, 4 t, 1 sp, 13 t, 2 sps, 4 t, ch 3. *8th row*—Three t, 4 sps, 10 t, 2 sps, 4 t, 1 sp, 7 t, 1 sp, 22 t, 3 sps, 13 t, 2 sps, 16 t, 4 sps, 13 t, 2 sps, 13 t, 1 sp, 7 t, 2 sps, 4 t, ch 8. *9th row*—Four t, 2 sps, 13 t, 1 sp, 7 t, 3 sps, 13 t, 1 sp, 7 t, 1 sp, 16 t, 2 sps, 13 t, 3 sps, 10 t, 1 sp, 10 t, 1 sp, 7 t, 1 sp, 4 t, 1 sp, 19 t, 2 sps, 4 t, ch 3. *10th row*—Three t, 2 sps, 13 t, 5 sps, 13 t, 2 sps, 10 t, 2 sps, 7 t, 1 sp, 7 t, 1 sp, 7 t, 1 sp, 10 t, 1 sp, 13 t, 1 sp, 7 t, 2 sps, 7 t, 3 sps, 13 t, 3 sps, 4 t, ch 8. *11th row*—Four t, 5 sps, 7 t, 3 sps, 13 t, 4 sps, 13 t, 4 sps, 13 t, 4 sps, 4 t, 3 sps, 10 t, 2 sps, 10 t, 3 sps, 16 t, 3 sps, 4 t, ch 3. *12th row*— Three t, 5 sps, 16 t, 2 sps, 4 t, 2 sps, 16 t, 1 sp, 7 t, 4 sps, 13 t, 1 sp, 10 t, 1 sp, 7 t, 1 sp, 10 t, 1 sp, 13 t, 1 sp, 7 t, 8 sps, 4 t, ch 3. *13th row*—Four t made in first space, 6 sps, 13 t, 1 sp, 7 t, 1 sp, 16 t, 2 sps, 16 t, 1 sp, 7 t, 1 sp, 10 t, 2 sps, 4 t, 1 sp, 19 t, 1 sp, 4 t, 3 sps, 4 t, 8 sps, 4 t, ch 3. *14th row*—Three t, 5 sps, 22 t, 4 sps, 10 t, 2 sps, 4 t, 1 sp, 4 t, 7 sps, 16 t, 2 sps, 16 t, 4 sps, 13 t, 5 sps, 4 t, ch 3. *15th row*—Four t, 5 sps, 7 t, 2 sps, 7 t, 1 sp, 16 t, 2 sps, 16 t, 2 sps, 10 t, 1 sp, 13 t, 3 sps, 16 t, 3 sps, 19 t, 4 sps, 4 t, ch 3. *16th row*—Three t, 4 sps, 13 t, 5 sps, 4 t, 7 sps, 7 t, 2 sps, 16 t, 2 sps, 10 t, 1 sp, 7 t, 1 sp, 10 t, 1 sp, 13 t, 7 sps, 4 t, ch 3. *17th row*—Four t, 6 sps, 13 t, 4 sps, 13 t, 5 sps, 16 t, 2 sps, 4 t, 7 sps, 4 t, 1 sp, 22 t, 6 sps, 4 t, ch 3. *18th row*—Three t, 5 sps, 25 t, 2 sps, 4 t, 3 sps, 4 t, 2 sps, 7 t, 1 sp, 16 t, 1 sp, 7 t, 2 sps, 13 t, 5 sps, 7 t, 6 sps, 4 t, ch 3. *19th row*— Four t, 13 sps, 7 t, 2 sps, 13 t, 1 sp, 10 t, 2 sps, 4 t, 4 sps, 4 t, 1 sp, 4 t, 3 sps, 13 t, 1 sp, 13 t, 4 sps, 4 t, ch. *20th row*—Three t, 4 sps, 10 t, 2 sps, 10 t, 5 sps, 7 t, 4 sps, 7 t, 5 sps, 13 t, 16 sps, 4 t, ch 3.

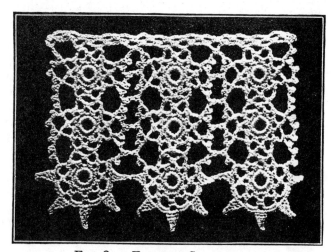

FIG. 81. EDGING. See page 29

21st row—Four t, 16 sps, 7 t, 5 sps, 7 t, 3 sps, 7 t, 8 sps, 4 t, 10 sps, 4 t, ch 3. *22d row*—Three t, 21 sps, 10 t, 1 sp, 13 t, 19 sps, 4 t, ch 3. *23d row*— Four t, 18 sps, 13 t, 1 sp, 10 t, 21 sps, 4 t, ch 3. *24th row*—Three t, 10 sps, 4 t, 8 sps, 7 t, 3 sps, 7 t, 5 sps, 7 t, 15 sps, 4 t in loop at end, ch 8. *25th row* —Four t on ch, 15 sps, 13 t, 5 sps, 7 t, 4 sps, 7 t,

5 sps, 10 t, 2 sps, 10 t, 4 sps, 4 t, ch 3. *26th row* —Three t, 4 sps, 13 t, 1 sp, 13 t, 3 sps, 4 t, 1 sp, 4 t, 4 sps, 4 t, 2 sps, 10 t, 1 sp, 13 t, 2 sps, 7 t, 12 sps, 4 t, ch 8. *27th row*—Four t, 5 sps, 7 t, 5 sps, 13 t, 2 sps, 7 t, 1 sp, 16 t, 1 sp, 7 t, 2 sps, 4 t, 3 sps, 4 t, 2 sps, 25 t, 5 sps, 4 t, ch 3. *28th row*—Three t, 6 sps, 22 t, 1 sp, 4 t, 7 sps, 4 t, 2 sps, 16 t, 5 sps, 13 t, 4 sps, 13 t, 5 sps, 4 t, ch 8. *29th row*—Four t, 6 sps, 13 t, 1 sp, 10 t, 1 sp, 7 t, 1 sp, 10 t, 2 sps, 16 t, 2 sps, 7 t, 7 sps, 10 t, 3 sps, 13 t, 4 sps, 4 t, ch 3. *30th row*—Three t, 4 sps, 19 t, 3 sps, 16 t, 3 sps, 13 t, 1 sp, 10 t, 2 sps, 16 t, 2 sps, 16 t, 1 sp, 7 t, 2 sps, 7 t, 4 sps, 4 t, ch 8. *31st row*—Four t, 4 sps, 13 t, 4 sps, 16 t, 2 sps, 16 t, 7 sps, 4 t, 1 sp, 4 t, 2 sps, 10 t, 4 sps, 22 t, 5 sps, 4 t, ch 3. *32d row*— Three t, 8 sps, 4 t, 3 sps, 4 t, 1 sp, 19 t, 1 sp, 4 t, 2 sps, 10 t, 1 sp, 7 t, 1 sp, 16 t, 2 sps, 16 t, 1 sp, 7 t, 1 sp, 13 t, 5 sps, 4 t, ch 8. *33d row*—Four t, 7 sps, 7 t, 1 sp, 13 t, 1 sp, 10 t, 1 sp, 7 t, 1 sp, 10 t, 1 sp, 13 t, 4 sps, 7 t, 1 sp, 16 t, 2 sps, 4 t, 2 sps, 16 t, 5 sps, 4 t, ch 3. *34th row*—Three t, 3 sps, 19 t, 2 sps, 10 t, 2 sps, 10 t, 3 sps, 4 t, 4 sps, 13 t, 4 sps, 13 t, 4 sps, 13 t, 3 sps, 7 t, 6 sps, 4 t, ch 3. *35th row*—Four t in 1st sp, 4 sps, 13 t, 3 sps, 7 t, 2 sps, 7 t, 1 sp, 13 t, 1 sp, 10 t, 1 sp, 7 t, 1 sp, 7 t, 1 sp, 7 t, 2 sps, 10 t, 2 sps, 13 t, 5 sps, 13 t, 2 sps, 4 t, ch 3. *36th row*— Three t, 2 sps, 19 t, 1 sp, 4 t, 1 sp, 7 t, 1 sp, 10 t, 1 sp, 10 t, 3 sps, 13 t, 2 sps, 16 t, 1 sp, 7 t, 1 sp, 13 t, 3 sps, 7 t, 1 sp, 13 t, 3 sps, 4 t, ch 3. *37th row*— Four t, 3 sps, 7 t, 1 sp, 13 t, 2 sps, 13 t, 4 sps, 16 t, 2 sps, 13 t, 3 sps, 22 t, 1 sp, 7 t, 1 sp, 4 t, 2 sps, 10 t, 4 sps, 4 t, ch 3. *38th row*—Three t, 2 sps, 13 t, 1 sp, 4 t, 1 sp, 13 t, 2 sps, 19 t, 4 sps, 7 t, 3 sps, 16 t, 1 sp, 10 t, 1 sp, 7 t, 3 sps, 13 t, 5 sps, 4 t, ch 3. *39th row*—Four t, 5 sps, 7 t, 6 sps, 16 t, 1 sp, 10 t, 1 sp, 10 t, 6 sps, 7 t, 1 sp, 10 t, 2 sps, 22 t, 1 sp, 10 t, 2 sps, 4 t, ch 3. *40th row*—Three t, 1 sp, 22 t, 1 sp, 10 t, 4 sps, 4 t, 9 sps, 16 t, 4 sps, 16 t, 12 sps, 4 t, ch 3. *41st row*—Four t, 11 sps, 16 t, 4 sps, 16 t, 14 sps, 10 t, 1 sp, 22 t, 1 sp, 4 t, ch 3. *42d row*—Three t, 1 sp, 13 t, 1 sp, 4 t, 2 sps, 7 t, 15 sps, 16 t, 5 sps, 10 t, 11 sps, 4 t, ch 3. *43d row*— Four t, 19 sps, 10 t, 27 sps, 4 t, ch 3. *44th row*— Three t, 48 sps, 4 t, ch 3. Repeat from 1st row;

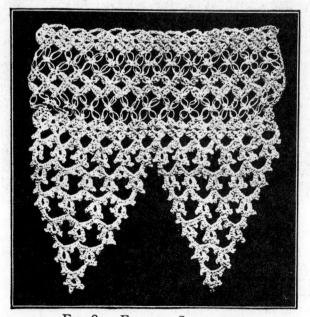

FIG. 82. EDGING. See page 30

finish edge by making shells of 9 t each in chains.

Figure 87.—Chain 6, join with sl st. *1st row*— Chain 6, 1 d in ring 7 times, ch 6, 1 sl st in 1st st of 1st 6 ch, 1 sl st in each of next 2 sts, 1 d under ch. *2d row*—Chain 6, 1 d in next ch, 7 times, ch 6, 1 sl st in 1st st of next ch, 1 sl st in each of next 2 sts,

FIG. 83. EDGING. See page 30

1 d under ch. *3d row*—Chain 7, 1 d in each chain-loop around. *4th row*—Chain 1, 4 d under 1st ch, ch 8, 1 sl st in fifth st from hook, 1 sl st in each of next 3 sts taking up only one loop of st; reach across ch and make 1 sl st to bring thread on right side of ch, ch 3, 1 t in 1st st of ch, 1 t in each of next 3 sts (taking up one loop only), 5 t in 4 ch at end, 1 t in each of next 4 sl sts down side of ch, ch 3, 1 sl st in the sl st taken across end of ch, taking up both loops of st, 4 d under ch. Repeat in each sp around, join to 1st d with sl st. Break thread and fasten end. *5th row*—Join thread with 1 d in the 3d of the 5 t made at end of leaf, * ch 9, thread over hook twice, insert hook in 3d t from the d in end of leaf, ** thread over hook, pull a loop through, thread over, pull through two loops, thread over, pull through two loops, ** leaving two on hook, thread over hook twice, insert hook in 4th t on next leaf, repeat from ** to **, thread over hook and pull through remaining 3 sts on hook, ch 9, 1 d in the 3d of the 5 t on top of leaf *. Repeat from * to * around, joining last 9 ch to 1st d with sl st. Break thread, and fasten. The circles are joined together as they are made, in the 5th row, as follows: Work the 5th row in a 2d circle to the 4th leaf, after making 9 ch, 1 d in top of it, ch 4, take hook out of work, insert in corresponding loop on another circle (having them both right side up), pull 4th ch st through loop, ch 1 over the loop, ch 4, thread over hook twice, insert hook in 3d t from d on top of leaf, repeat from ** to **, thread over hook twice, insert in 4th t on next leaf, repeat from ** to **, thread over hook and pull through remaining 3 sts on hook; ch 4, take hook out of work, insert in next loop on opposite circle, ch 1 over loop, ch 4, 1 d in 3d t on top of leaf. Fill remainder of circle by repeating from * to * in 5th row. Join each subsequent circle in same manner, at the 7th free loop from joining to previous circle.

HEADING.—When you have length required, join thread with 1 d in 5th free loop back from joining at right-hand side of edge, * (ch 7, 1 d in next loop) 3 times, ch 15, 1 d in next l, ch 5, 1 d in next l, ch 5, take hook out of work, insert in 15 ch, catch 5th st on hook and pull through, 1 st over ch, ch 8, 1 d in next loop *. Repeat from * to * to end; break thread. *2d row*—Fasten thread with 1 t in 1st d at right-hand side, ch 2, skip 2 sts on ch, 1 t in next st, ch 2, skip 2, 1 t in next st to end of row. Break thread and fasten. Edge.—Fasten thread with 1 d in 6th free loop from joining, * ch 10, 1 d in next 1 6 times, ch 5, 1 d in first loop on next scallop, repeat from * to end, and break thread. 2d row—Begin again at right hand, * 4 d under first loop, ch 5, make a picot (p) with 1 sl st taken through the two loops of last d, ch 5, 1 sl st in same place, 4 d, 2 p's, 4 d under same chain-loop, repeat from * 5 times on scallop, 5 d under 5 ch between scallops **. Repeat from * to ** to end.

FIG. 84. EDGING. See page 31

Figure 88. — Make 53 chain. *1st row*—Miss 2, 1 t in the 3d, 5 ch, miss 5, d in the next, * 3 ch, miss 1 st, 1 d in the next, and repeat (rep) from * once, ** 10 ch, sl st into the 6th of the foundation ch, reckoning from where you are working; now turn the work over, work 5 d up the lower half of the 10 ch, turn the work, make 5 ch, miss 5 of foundation ch, then d into the 6th, * 3 ch, miss 1, d in the next and rep from * once. Repeat from ** once, then 5 ch, miss 5, 1 snug t in each of the next 2. Turn. *2d row*—Three fairly tight ch, 1 snug t between the 2 at beginning of previous row, * 6 d under the next 5 ch, 1 d into the first small hole; 3 ch, 1 d in next small hole, 6 d under the next ch, 3 ch and rep from * once, 6 d under the next ch, 1 d in the next hole, 3 ch, 1 d in the next hole, 6 d under the next ch, 2 snug t at end of row. *3d row* —Three snug ch, 1 rather snug t between the 1st and 2d st of previous row, * 10 ch, catch into middle of next centre hole in the row below; turn the work as before, and make 5 d on the lower part of the ch; turn the work to its proper position, make 5 ch, 1 d in the last or 6th st of the next set below, 3 ch, 1 d in centre hole, 3 ch, 1 d in 1st d of next set of 6; rep from * once, 10 ch, catch in hole of 3 ch; turn and work the 5 d; then turn again, make 5 ch, 2 snug t at end of row. *4th row*—Three snug ch, 1 t in 2d st or between 1st and 2d, as you prefer, * 6 d under ch, 3 ch, 6 d under next ch, 1 d in the first of two holes, 3 ch, 1 d in next hole, rep from * once, 6 d under next ch; 3 ch, 6 d under the next ch; finish with 2 snug t to match what you began the row with. *5th row*—Three ch, 1 t in 2d st, 5 ch, 1 d in 6th st, * 3 ch, 1 d in small hole, 3 ch, 1 d in first of next set of six, 10 ch, catch in the 3-ch hole; turn the work and put 5 d over upright part of the 10 ch, turn the work to usual position and make 5 ch; 1 d in 6th d of next set, rep from * once, 3 ch, 1 d in small hole, 3 ch, 1 d in 1st st of next set of 6 sts, 5 ch, 1 t in each of last 2 sts. Begin again

at 2d row and continue till the proper length is reached. NOTE.—It is much better to make the pieces the length needed for their expected position, but if this is done, measure amply. If a length is made and it has to be cut, it is better to cut along one row and gather up the ends neatly and strongly, particularly strongly sewing all ends with fine cotton.

Figure 89.—This insertion is composed mostly of blocks and open spaces, and will be alluded to as bls and sps, to simplify directions. *1st row*—Chain 93, 1 t in 8th st from hook, 3 t in next 3 sts, (this makes 1 bl), ch 2, miss 2 sts, 4 t in next 4 sts, (ch 2, miss 2, 1 t in next st) 3 times, ch 2, miss 2, 10 t in next 10 sts, (ch 2, miss 2, 1 t in next st) 6 times, ch 2, miss 2, 10 t in next 10 sts, (ch 2, miss 2, 1 t in next st) 3 times, ch 2, miss 2, 4 t in next 4 sts, ch 2, miss 2, 4 t in next 4 sts, ch 2, miss 2, 1 t in last st of foundation ch, turn. *2d row*—Chain 5, 1 t on 1st t, ch 2, 1 t on last of 4 t, 2 t under 2 ch, 1 t on next t, 4 sps, ch 2, 4 t on next 4 t, 7 t in next t to form a cup, take hook out of work, insert in 1st of 7 t, draw st through, ch 1, 5 t in next 5 t, 2 sps, 1 bl, 1 sp, 1 bl, 2 sps, 5 t in next 5 t, a cup in 6th t, 4 t in next 4 t, 5 sps, 1 bl, 2 sps, turn. *3d row*—One sp, 1 bl, 1 sp, 1 bl, 4 sps, 10 t on t, making the 5th t in st connecting the 1st and 7th sts of cup, 1 sp, 2 bls, (7 t's make 2 bls), 1 sp, 2 bls, 1 sp, 10 t, making one of them in the connecting st of cup, 4 sps, 1 bl, 1 sp, 1 bl, 1 sp, turn, always chaining 5 sts in turning. *4th row*— One sp, 1 bl, 1 sp, 1 bl, 4 sps, 10 t on t, making cup in 5th t, 3 sps, 1 bl, 3 sps, 10 t, cup in 6th t, 4 sps, 1 bl, 1 sp, 1 bl, 1 sp, turn. *5th row*—Like 2d row, omitting cup and making 1 t in the connecting st of cups. *6th row*—Like 3d row, making cups in the 5th, and 6th sts of the 10 t, turn. *7th row*—Like 1st row. *8th row*—Like 2d row to centre, when it should be 3 sps, 1 bl, 3 sps. *9th row*—Like 3d row to centre, when it should be 2 sps, 3 bls, 2 sps. *10th row*— Like 4th row to centre, then make 1 sp, 2 bls, 1 sp, 2 bls, 1 sp. *11th row*—Two sps, 1 bl, 5 sps, 16 t, ch 6, 1 d under 2 ch in centre, ch 6, miss 3 t, 16 t, 5 sps, 1 bl, 2 sps. *12th row*—One sp, 1 bl, 1 sp, 1 bl, 4 sps,

FIG. 85. EDGING. See page 31

13 t, (ch 6, 1 d under next ch-loop) twice, ch 6, miss 3 t, 13 t, in next 13 t, 4 sps, 1 bl, 1 sp, 1 bl, 1 sp. *13th row*—Like 3d row to centre then (ch 6, 1 d in next loop) 3 times, ch 6, miss 3 t, then repeat remainder of 3d row. *14th row*—Two sps, 1 bl, 5 sps, 7 t in next 7 t, (ch 6, 1 d under next loop) 4 times, ch 6, miss 3 t, 7 t on next 7 t, 5 sps, 1 bl, 2 sps.

15th row—One sp, 1 bl, 1 sp, 1 bl, 3 sps, 2 bls, (ch 6, 1 d under next loop) twice, ch 6, 4 t under next loop, (ch 6, 1 d under next loop) twice, ch 6, miss 3 t, 2 bls, 3 sps, 1 bl, 1 sp, 1 bl, 1 sp. *16th row*—One sp, 1 bl, 1 sp, 1 bl, 2 sps, 2 bls, (ch 6, 1 d under next loop) twice, ch 6, 3 bls, (ch 6, 1 d under next loop) twice, ch 6, miss 3 t, 2 bls, 2 sps, 1 bl, 1 sp, 1 bl, 1 sp. *17th row.*—Two sps, 1 bl, 2 sps, 2 bls, (ch 6, 1 d under next

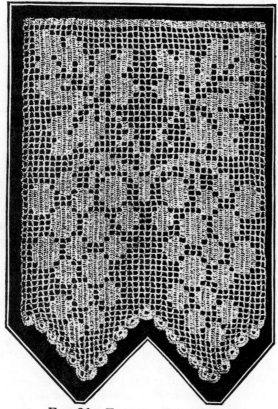

FIG. 86. EDGING. See page 33

loop) twice, 2 bls, 1 sp, 2 bls, (ch 6, 1 d under next loop) twice, ch 6, miss 3 t, 2 bls, 2 sps, 1 bl, 2 sps. *18th row*—One sp, 1 bl, 1 sp, 1 bl, 2 sps, 2 bls, ch 6, 1 d under next loop twice, ch 6, miss 3 t, 3 bls, (ch 6, 1 d under next loop) twice, ch 6, 2 bls, 2 sps, 1 bl, 1 sp, 1 bl, 1 sp. *19th row*—One sp, 1 bl, 1 sp, 1 bl, 3 sps, 2 bls, (ch 6, 1 d under next loop) twice, ch 6, miss 3 t, 4 t in next 4 t, (ch 6, 1 d under next loop) twice, ch 6, 2 bls, 3 sps, 1 bl, 1 sp, 1 bl, 1 sp, *20th row*—Two sps, 1 bl, 5 sps, 2 bls, (ch 6, 1 d under next loop) 4 times, ch 6, 2 bls, 5 sps, 1 bl, 2 sps. *21st row*—Like 13th row. *22d row*—Like 12th row. *23d row*—Like 11th row. *24th row*—Like 10th row. *25th row*—Like 9th row. *26th row*—Like 8th row. *27th row*—Like 7th row. *28th row*—Like 6th row. *29th row*—Like 5th row. *30th row*—Like 4th row. *31st row*—Like 3d row. *32d row*—Like 2d row. *33d row*—Like 1st row.

In the 34th row begins the second diamond, for that you can follow the directions for centre, the portion between the two rows of 10 t, from the 8th row, but the border of the 8th row does not correspond to that of the 34th row, but you can easily continue the pattern of that, as it does not vary.

Figure 90. *Wheel.*—Chain 9, join with sl st. *1st round*—Make a cluster of 3 d t, working 4 ch to represent first d t, in the second d t, work off 2 loops

twice, leaving third loop on hook, make another d t, working off 2 loops twice, then the last 3 loops altogether; * ch 8, make another cluster of d t, working off 2 loops of each twice in the first two d t sts, in the 3d one work off two loops 3 times, then the last three loops altogether; repeat from * 4 times, ch 8, join with sl st in top of first cluster of d t. *2d round*—Chain 1, make 13 d under each ch-loop around, join with sl st to first d, break thread and fasten off. Make another wheel and join to first one in working last row of d as follows: After making the 7th d under a 13-ch loop, take hook out of work and insert in a 7th d on first wheel, draw the loop of d you took hook out of, through, and finish remainder of loop with 6 d under it. Join each wheel in a similar manner, leaving one free scallop between joining, alternating the point of joining at top and bottom of wheels to form a scallop. Repeat for length required.

1st row at bottom—Chain 38, turn, 1 t in 5th st from hook, (ch 1, miss 1, t in next st) 6 times, (ch 5, miss 3, 1 d in next st) 3 times, ch 2, miss 1, 1 t in next st, (ch 1, miss 1, 1 t in next st) 3 times, turn. *2d row*—Chain 2, 4 t on 4 t with 1 ch between each t, (ch 5, 1 d under 5-ch loop) 3 times, ch 5, miss 1 space, 1 t in next sp, (ch 1, 1 t under next sp) 4 times, (ch 1, 1 t in last sp) twice, ch 3, pick up the row of wheel scallops and holding wheel at point downward, make 1 sl st in 7th d of scallop next joining to lower wheel, beginning at first wheel at the left, turn. *3d row*—Chain 3, 1 t under 3 ch, ch 1, 1 t under same ch, (ch 1, 1 t, 1 t under 1 ch sp) 5 times, (ch 5, 1 d under 5-ch loop) 4 times, ch 2, 4 t on 4 t, with 1 ch between each, turn. *4th row*—Chain 2, 4 t on 4 t with 1 ch between each t, (ch 5, 1 d under 5-ch loop) 3 times, ch 5, 1 t under next loop, ch 1, 1 t in same loop, (ch 1, 1 t under 1 ch) 5 times, ch 2, sl st in 4th d on next free scallop of next wheel, turn. *5th row*—Chain 1, miss 1 sp, 1 t in next, (ch 1, 1 t in next sp) 4 times, ch 1, 2 t under 5-ch loop with 1 ch between t's, (ch 5, 1 d under next loop) 3 times, ch 2, 4 t on 4 t, with 1 ch between each t, turn. *6th row*—Chain 2, 4 t on 4 t, with 1 ch between, (ch 5, 1 d under next loop) twice, ch 5, 2 t under next loop, with 1 ch between, (ch 1, 1 t under next sp) 5 times, ch 2, miss 4 d from last d on scallop, sl st in next, turn. *7th row*—Chain 1, miss 1 sp, 1 t in next, (ch 1, 1 t under next sp) 4 times, ch 1, 2 t under next loop with 1 ch between, (ch 5, 1 d under next loop) twice, ch 2, 4 t on 4 t, with 1 ch between each, turn. *8th row*—Chain 2, 4 t on 4 t, 1 ch between each, ch 5, 1 d under next loop, ch 5, 2 t under next loop with 1 ch between, (ch 1, 1 t under 1 ch) 5 times, ch 2, sl st in 4th d on next scallop, turn. *9th row*—Chain 1, miss 1st sp, 1 t under next sp, (ch 1, 1 t under next sp) 4 times, ch 1, 2 t under next loop with 1 ch between, ch 5, 1 d under next loop, ch 2, 4 t on 4 t with 1 ch between each, turn. *10th row*—Chain 2, 4 t on 4 t, 1 ch between each, ch 5, 2 t under next loop, with 1 ch between, (ch 1, 1 t under next 1 ch) 5 times, ch 4, miss 4 d on scallop, sl st in next, turn. *11th row*—Chain 3, 1 t under 4 ch, ch 1, 1 t under same ch, (ch 1, 1 t under 1 ch) 5 times, ch 5, 1 d under next loop, ch 2, 4 t on 4 t with 1 ch between, turn. *12th row*—Chain 2, 4 t on 4 t, with 1 ch between, ch 5, 1 d under next loop, ch 5, miss 1 sp, 1 t under next sp, (ch 1, 1 t under next 1 ch) 4 times, (ch 1, 1 t under last sp) twice, ch 3, sl st in 4th d on next scallop, turn. *13th* row—Chain 3, (1 t under 3 ch) twice, with 1 ch between, (ch 1, 1 t under 1 ch) 5 times, (ch 5, 1 d under next loop) twice, ch 2, 4 t on 4 t, with 1 ch between, turn. *14th row*—Chain 2, 4 t on 4 t, with 1 ch between, (ch 5, 1 d under next loop) twice, ch 5, miss 1 sp, 1 t in next, (ch 1, 1 t under next 1 ch) 4 times, (ch 1, 1 t under last sp) twice, ch 3, sl st in 4th d from last d made on scallop, turn. *15th row*—Chain 3, 1 t under 3 ch, ch 1, 1 t in same ch, (ch 1, 1 t under 1 ch) 5 times, (ch 5, 1 d under next loop) 3 times, ch 2, 4 t on 4 t, with 1 ch between.

UPPER EDGE.—Chain 30; holding work right side up, pull the last st of ch through the 4 d on top scallop at the left, ch 3, miss 1 st on ch, 1 t in next st, ch 1, 1 t in next st, (ch 1, miss 1, 1 t in next st) 5 times, ch 5, miss 3, 1 d in next st, ch 2, miss 1, 1 t in next st, (ch 1, miss 1, 1 t in next st) 3 times, turn. *2d row*—Chain 2, 4 t on 4 t with 1 ch between each t, ch 5, 2 t under 5 ch, with 1 ch between, (ch 1, 1 t in next sp) 5 times, ch 4, miss 4 d on scallop, 1 sl st in next d, turn. *3d row*—Chain 3, 2 t under 3 ch with 1 ch between, (ch 1, 1 t under next sp) 5 times, ch 5, 1 d under next loop, ch 2, 4 t on 4 t, with 1 ch between, turn. *4th row*—Chain 2, 4 t on 4 t, with 1 ch between, ch 5, 1 d under next loop, ch 5, miss 1 sp, 1 t under next sp, (ch 1, 1 t under next sp) 4 times, (ch 1, 1 t under next sp) twice, ch 4, sl st in 5th d on next scallop. *5th row*—Chain 3, 2 t under 4 ch, with 1 ch between each t, (ch 1, 1 t in next sp) 5 times, (ch 5, 1 d under next loop) twice, ch 2, 4 t on 4 t, with 1 ch between, turn. *6th row*—Chain 2, 4 t on 4 t, with 1 ch between, (ch 5, 1 d under next loop) twice, ch 5, miss 1 sp, 1 t in next sp, (ch 1, 1 t in next sp) 4 times, (ch 1, 1 t under last sp) twice, ch 4, miss 3 d on scallop, sl st in next d, turn. *7th row*—Chain 3, 2 t under 3 ch, with 1 ch between, (ch 1, 1 t under next sp) 5 times, (ch 5, 1 d under next loop) 3 times, ch 2, 4 t on 4 t, with 1 ch between, turn. *8th row*—Chain 2, 4 t on 4 t, with 1 ch between, (ch 5, 1 d under next loop) 3 times, ch 5, miss 1 sp, 1 t in next, (ch 1, 1 t under next sp) 4 times, (ch 1, 1 t under last sp) twice, ch 3, sl st in 7th of free scallop on next wheel, turn. *9th row*—Chain 3, 2 t under 3 ch, with 1 ch between, (ch 1, 1 t in next sp) 5 times, (ch 5, 1 d under next loop) 4 times, ch 2, 4 t on 4 t, with 1 ch between, turn. *10th row*—Chain 2, 4 t on 4 t, with 1 ch between, (ch 5, 1 d under next loop) 3 times, ch 5, 2 t under next loop, with 1 ch between, (ch 1, 1 t in next sp) 5 times, ch 3, sl st in 4th d on next free scallop on next wheel, turn. *11th row*—Chain 1, miss 1 sp, 1 t in next, (ch 1, 1 t in next sp) 4 times, ch 1, 2 t under 5-ch loop, with 1 ch between, (ch 5, 1 d under next loop) 3 times, ch 2, 4 t on 4 t, with 1 ch between, turn. *12th row*—Chain 2, 4 t on 4 t with 1 ch between, (ch 5, 1 d under next loop) twice, ch 5, 2 t under next loop, with 1 ch between, (ch 1, 1 t in next sp) 5 times, ch 2, sl st in 5th d on scallop, turn.

13th row—Chain 2, miss 1 sp, 1 t in next sp, (ch 1, 1 t in next sp) 4 times, (ch 1, 1 t in next loop) twice, (ch 5, 1 d in next loop) twice, ch 2, 4 t on 4 t, with 1 ch between, turn. *14th row*—Chain 2, 4 t on 4 t, ch 5, 1 d under next loop, ch 5, 2 t under next, with 1 ch between, (ch 1, 1 t in next sp) 5 times, ch 2, sl st in 4th d on next scallop, turn. *15th row*—Chain 1, miss 1 sp, 1 t in next sp, (ch 1, 1 t in next sp) 4 times, (ch 1, 1 t in 5-ch loop) twice, ch 5, 1 d under next loop, ch 2, 4 t on 4 t. Repeat from 2d row.

Figure 91.—Chain 25. *1st row*—In the 5th st from hook make a shell of (3 t, 2 ch, 3 t), ch 4, skip 4, 1 t in next st, ch 2, 1 t in same st, ch 4, skip 4, shell in next st, ch 2, skip 2, 1 t in next st, ch 5, skip 4, 1 d in next st, turn. *2d row*—Chain 3, 12 t under 5 ch, ch 2, shell in shell, ch 3, 7 t under 2 ch, ch 3, shell in shell, turn. *3d row*—* Chain 3, shell in shell, ch 2, 6 t with 1 ch between each, between next 7 t, ch 2, shell in shell, ch 2, * 13 t with 1 ch between each, between 13 t, making 13th t under 3 ch at end of 12 t's, turn. *4th row*—Chain 3, 12 t between last 12 t, with 1 ch between each, ch 2, shell in shell, ch 1, 3 t under each 1 ch between t's on fan, ch 1, shell in shell, turn. *5th row*—* Chain 3, shell in shell, ch 4, 1 t in 8th t on fan, ch 2, 1 t in same st, ch 4, shell in shell, ch 2, * 1 t under each 1 ch, with 2 ch between them, turn. *6th row*—* Chain 3, 2 t under first 2 ch, ch 2, 2 t under same ch, skip 1 sp, shell of 2 t, 2 ch, 2 t in next sp, repeat to end of fan, ch 2, * shell in shell, ch 3, 7 t under 2 ch, ch 3, shell in shell, turn. *7th row*—* Chain 3, shell in shell, ch 2, 1 t between each of next 7 t with 1 ch between, ch 2, shell in shell, ch 2, * shell in shell of 3 t, 2 ch, 3 t across fan, turn. *8th row*—Chain 3, shell in shell of 4 t, 2 ch, 4 t across fan, ch 2, shell in shell, ch 1, 3 t under each 1 ch across fan, ch 1, shell in shell, turn. *9th row*—Like 5th row from * to * shell in shell across fan (4 t, 3 ch, 4 t in each shell), turn. *10th row*—Chain 3, 10 t under each

FIG. 87. EDGING. See page 34

next sp) 4 times, (ch 1, 1 t under last sp) twice, ch 3, sl st in 7th of free scallop on next wheel, turn. *11th row*—Chain 1, miss 1 sp, 1 t in next, (ch 1, 1 t in next sp) 4 times, ch 1, 2 t under 5-ch loop, with 1 ch between, (ch 5, 1 d under next loop) 3 times, ch 2, 4 t on 4 t, with 1 ch between, turn. *12th row*—Chain 2, 4 t on 4 t with 1 ch between, (ch 5, 1 d under next loop) twice, ch 5, 2 t under next loop, with 1 ch between, (ch 1, 1 t in next sp) 5 times, ch 2, sl st in 5th d on scallop, turn.

3 ch in shells on fan, ch 2, shell in shell, ch 3, 7 t under 2 ch, ch 3, shell in shell, turn. *11th row*—Like 3d row, from * to *, 1 t on 1st of 10 t, ch 5, 1 d in 5th t, ch 3, sl st in 3d t on next scallop, turn. *12th row*—Twelve t under 5 ch, ch 2, shell in shell, ch 1, 3 t under each 1 ch on fan, ch 1, shell in shell, turn. *13th row*—Like 5th from * to *, 13 t with 1 ch between each, between 13 t; after making 13th t, make sl st in 3 t from last sl st, ch 3, 1 sl st in 2d t

on next scallop, turn. *14th row*—Chain 2, 1 t between next 2 t, ch 2, 1 t between next 2 t, repeat across fan, ch 2, shell in shell, ch 3, 7 t under 2 ch, ch 3, shell in shell, turn. *15th row*—Like 7th from * to *, 1 t under each 1 ch, with 2 ch between; after last t make 1 sl st in 3d t from last sl st, turn. *16th row*—Like 6th from * to *, shell in shell, ch 1, 3 t under each 1 ch across fan, ch 1, shell in shell, turn. *17th row*—Like 5th row from * to *, shell in shell (3 t, 2 ch, 3 t) across fan, turn. *18th row*—Chain 3, shell in shell, of 4 t, 2 ch, 4 t across fan, ch 2, shell in shell, ch 3, 7 t under 2 ch, ch 3, shell in shell, turn. *19th row*—Like 3d, from * to *, shell in shell across fan (4 t, 3 ch, 4 t), turn. *20th row*—Chain 3, 10 t under each 3 ch across fan, ch 2, shell in shell, ch 1, 3 t under each 1 ch across fan, ch 1, shell in shell. Repeat for length.

Figure 92.—The directions are the same as for insertion, Fig. 56, for 3 rows. *4th row*— Begin at opposite end, ch 12, make a p in 6th st; ch 3, 3 t in space between the 5 d's of 3d row; ch 9, p in 6th st; ch 3, 3 t in next space to end, always making the ch 9, the ch of 12 only made at beginning of row, turn. *5th row*— Chain 8, 1 d in 1st p; ch 7, from p to p across length, turn. *6th row*— Make 11 d

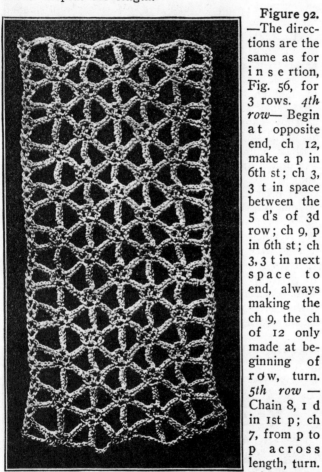

FIG. 88. INSERTION. **See page 35**

in 1st ch of 7, and 5 d, or half across next ch; ch 11, turn, fasten in 5th st of first scallop, turn, and make 15 d over this chain, on the unfinished chain of 6 d and 5 d to middle of next; ch 11, turn and catch in middle of second scallop, turn, 7 d on half of this ch, then ch 11, turn, catch in top of first scallop on 2d row, turn, 15 d in this, 8 d in the next, 6 d in next, this completes first scallop. Repeat from 1st of the row to end of edge.

Figure 93.— Use No. 80 Cordonnet crochet cotton. Chain 7, join to form a ring. Chain 1, * 3 d in ring, ch 5, d in the 5th st from hook to form a picot (p), ch 9, d in the 5th st from hook, ch 1, sl st in the top of the last d in centre ring; repeat from *

until you have 4 loops of ch with 3 d between each loop, join first and last d, sl st up to the centre of loop, (ch 12, d in next loop) 4 times, ch 1, 17 d, in each 12-ch space, join first and last d.

· FIRST PYRAMID.— Holding wrong side of work next you, work 1 d in each of 8 sts, turn; work in the back loops of the sts throughout, ch 1, ** 1 d in each of 8 d, turn; ch 5, 1 d in each of 8 d, turn; ch 1, 1 d in each of 7 d, turn; ch 5, 1 d in each of 7 d, turn; miss 1, 1 d in each of 4 d, turn; ch 5, 1 d in each of 4 d, turn, miss 1, 1 d in each of 2 d, turn; ch 5, 1 d in each of 2 d, sl st down side of point to centre.

SECOND PYRAMID.— One d in each of 9 d on centre, ch 1, turn; * 1 d in each of 8 d, turn; ch 1, 1 d in each of 8 d, turn; ch 5, 1 d in each of 8 d, turn; ch 1, 1 d in each of 7 d, turn; ch 5, 1 d in each of 7 d, turn; miss 1, 1 d in each of 4 d, turn; ch 5, 1 d in each of 4 d, turn; miss 1, 1 d in each of 2 d, ch 5, turn; 1 d in each of 2 d.

THIRD PYRAMID.—Chain 9, 1 d beside end p on first pyramid, turn; 1 d in each of 9 sts of ch, turn; miss 1, 1 d in each of 8 d, turn; ch 5, 1 d in each of 8 d, turn; ch 5, 1 d in each of 7 d, turn; ch 5, 1 d in each of 6 d, turn; ch 5, 1 d in each of 5 d, turn; ch 5, 1 d in each of 4 d, turn; ch 5, 1 d in each of 3 d, turn; ch 5, 1 d in each of 2 sts, fasten off at back of work.

For the second group of pyramids, having wrong side of work next you, work 1 d in each of the 1st 8 sts of next group of 17 d; repeat from ** until you have four groups of pyramids.

The second and following motifs must be joined to the previous ones in working the third and fourth groups of pyramids as follows: Instead of working the 4th p on the third point, ch 2, and work 1 t in the corresponding p on previous motif, ch 2, 1 d in each of 5 d on point, finish as usual, join the *3d* p of the next group (always counting p on both sides of point) to the corresponding p on opposite point.

The picot chains in the diamond-shaped space are worked as follows: Join the thread to the 2d p as shown by the illustration. Chain 9, d in the 5th st from hook, ch 4, d on ch before p, p of 5 ch, d on ch after p, ch 3, d in p on pyramid, fasten off.

HEADING.— *1st row*—Join the thread to the end p on first point, * ch 22, d in the 5th st from hook for p, ch 6, 1 d in the 2d p on a point (counting from centre), ch 6, 1 d on ch before p, ch 5, d in 1st of 5 ch, for another p, 1 d on ch after 1st p, ch 13, d in the 5th st from hook, ch 6, d in 2d p on next point, ch 6, 1 d on ch before p, 1 p of 5-ch, d on ch at other side of 1st p, ch 17, 1 d in end p of pyramid, ch 1, d in next pyramid; repeat from * to end. *2d row*— One d in each st of ch across top of lace. *3d row*— Treble in 1st st, (ch 1, miss 1, t in next st); repeat across, fasten off.

EDGE.— *1st row*—Like 1st row of heading. *2d row* —Chain 1, turn, miss 1, *** 1 d in each of 9 sts, turn, miss 1, like "first pyramid" (pyr) from **, after finishing pyr, work 1 d in each of 10 sts of ch, turn; miss 1, like "second pyr" from * to end of third pyr, then miss 3 sts of ch and repeat from *** to end of lace.

Figure 94.—Chain 78. *1st row*—One d in 9th st from hook, ch 3, miss 2 sts, 7 t in next 7 sts (ch 3, miss 2, 1 d in next st, ch 3, miss 2, 1 t in next st), this is called a festoon, and will be represented hereafter by f. Repeat 4 times more, 6 t in next 6 sts, 3 f, 6 t in last 6 sts, turn. *2d row*—* Chain 9, miss 4 sts of ch, 5 t in next 5 sts, 1 t on next t, ch 5, miss 5 t, 1 t on next t, (ch 5, t on next t), 3 times, * 6 t on 6 t, make 5 sps of 5 ch, 1 t on next t, 6 t on 6 t, ch 5, 1 t in 4th st of last loop of f, turn. *3d row*—Chain 7, 1 d in 3d st of 5 ch, ch 3, 1 t on next t, ch 3, miss 2 t, 1 d in next, ch 3, 1 t on last t of group, 4 more f, 5 t in sp, 7 t on 7 t, 5 t in next sp, t on t, 3 f, 6 t on 6 t, turn. *4th row*—Repeat from * to *, 18 t on 18 t, 6 sps to end of row, turn. *5th row*—Chain 7, 5 f, 5 t in sp, 7 t on 7 t, ch 5, miss 5 t, 7 t on next 7 t, 5 t in sp, 1 t on next t, 3 f, 6 t on 6 t, turn. *6th row*—Repeat from * to *, 6 t on 6 t, 1 sp, 1 f, 1 sp, 6 t on 6 t, 5 sps, turn. *7th row*—Chain 7, 2 f, 5 t in sp, 1 t on next t, 2 f, 6 t on 6 t, 1 f, 1 sp, 1 f, 6 t on 6 t, 4 f, 6 t on 6 t, turn. *8th row*—** Chain 3, 6 t on 6 t, 4 sps, ** 6 t on 6 t, 1 sp, 1 f, 1 sp, 6 t on 6 t, 2 sps, 6 t on 6 t, 2 sps, turn. *9th row*—Chain 7, 5 f, 6 t on 6 t, 5 t in sp, 1 t on t, ch 5, 1 t on next t, 5 t in next sp, 7 t on 7 t, 3 f, 5 t in sp, 1 t on next t, turn. *10th row*—Repeat from ** to **, 6 t on 6 t, 5 t in sp, 7 t on 7 t, 6 sps, turn. *11th row*—Six f, 18 t on 18 t, 3 f, 5 t in sp, t on t, turn. *12th row*—Repeat from ** to **, 6 t on 6 t, 7 sps, turn. *13th row*—Seven f, 6 t on 6 t, 3 f, 5 t in sp, t on t, turn. *14th row*—Chain 3, 6 t on 6 t, 11 sps. This completes one scallop. In the next row the corner begins. For length of edge repeat from 1st row. *1st row*—One f, 5 t in sp, t on next t, 5 f, 5 t in sp, t on t, 3 f, 6 t on 6 t, turn. Repeat from the 2d row to end of 7th row. *8th row*—In this you begin the corner by omitting last sp at end of row, turn. *9th row*—Make 4 f and finish row from directions of 9th row, the 1st f being omitted, turn. *10th row*—Repeat from directions, making but 4 sps at end, turn. *11th row*—Make 4 f and finish row, turn. *12th row*—Repeat row from directions, making but 4 sps at end, turn. *13th row*—Four f, finish row. *14th row*—Chain 3, 6 t on 6 t, 7 sps, turn. *15th row*—Three f, 5 t in sp, t on t, 3 f, 6 t on 6 t, turn. *16th row*—Repeat from * to *, 6 t on 6 t, 2 sps, turn. *17th row*—One f, 5 t in sp, 7 t on 7 t, 5 t in sp, t on t, 3 f, 6 t on 6 t, turn. *18th row*—Repeat from * to *, 18 t on 18 t, turn. *19th row*—Chain 3, 6 t on 6 t, ch 5, miss 5 t, 7 t on next 7 t, 5 t in sp, t on next t, 3 f, 6 t on 6 t, turn. *20th row*—Repeat from * to *, 6 t on 6 t, 1 sp, 1 f, turn. *21st row*—Chain 8, 1 t on last t of f, 1 f, 6 t on 6 t, 4 f, 6 t on 6 t, turn. *22d row*—Chain 3, 6 t on 6 t, 4 sps. 6 t on 6 t, 1 sp, turn. *23d row*—Chain 3, 5 t in sp, 7 t on 7 t, 3 f, 5 t in sp, 1 t on t, turn. *24th row*—Chain 3, 6 t on 6 t, 4 sps, turn. *25th row*—Three f, 5 t in 5 ch, t on t, turn. *26th row*—Chain 3, 6 t on 6 t, 2 sps, turn. *27th row*—One f, 5 t in sp, 1 t on t, turn. *28th row*—Chain 3, 6 t on 6 t, turn. This concludes first half of corner. *1st row of second half*—Chain 9, miss 4 sts of ch, 5 t in next 5 sts, 1 t on next t, sl st in 4th st of second loop of next f, turn. *2d row*—Slip stitch in 1st t, ch 3, 6 t on 6 t, turn. *3d row*—Chain 9, miss 4 sts, 5 t in next 5 sts, 1 t on t, ch 5, miss 5 t, 1 t on next, ch 5, 1 t in the t at end of sp preceding next f, 1 sl st in 4th st of second loop of next f, turn. *4th row*—Two f, 6 t on 6 t, turn. *5th row*—Chain 9, miss 4 sts, 5 t in next 5 sts, 1 t on t, 2 sps, ch 5, 1 t in 4th st of second loop of next f, ch 5, 1 t

in t of sp preceding next f, ch 3, miss 3 t of next group, sl st in each of last 3 t, turn. *6th row*—Three t in 3 ch, 1 t on t, 5 t in sp, t on next t, 3 f, 6 t on 6 t, turn. *7th row*—Repeat from * to *, 6 t on 6 t, ch 5, 1 t in bottom of t at corner of the two rows of 13 t, sl st in 3d st of next ch, ch 3, 1 t in next 3d st of same ch, turn. *8th row*—Chain 7, 1 f, 6 t on 6 t, 4 f, 6 t on next 6 t, turn. *9th row*—Chain 3, 6 t on 6 t, 4 sps, 6 t on 6 t, ch 5, 1 t at end of f, ch 3, 1 d in end of t of next f, ch 3, 1 t in end of next f (where 8 ch began), ch 3, miss 2 t, sl st in each of next 3 t to end, turn. *10th row*—Three t in 3 ch, t on t, 1 sp, 5 t in next sp, 7 t on 7 t, 3 f, 5 t in next sp, t on t, turn. *11th row*—Chain 3, 6 t on 6 t, 3 sps, ch 5, miss 5 t, 7 t on next 7 t, 5 t in sp, 4 t in next 4 t, 3 t in side of next t, ch 5, 1 d in 4th st of last loop of next f, turn. *12th row*—Make 1 f, 18 t on 18 t, 3 f, 5 t in sp, t on t, turn. *13th row*—Chain 3, 6 t on 6 t, 3 sps, ch 5, miss 5 t, 7 t in next 7 t, ch 5, miss 5 t, 1 t on next t, ch 5, 1 t in 4th st of second loop of f, ch 5, 1 t in end of next f, sl st in 4th st of second loop of next f, turn. *14th row*—Three f, 6 t on 6 t, 3 f, 5 t in sp, t on t, turn. *15th row*—Chain 3, 6 t on 6 t, 7 sps, ch 5, 1 t in 4th st of second loop of f, 1 t in 4th st of

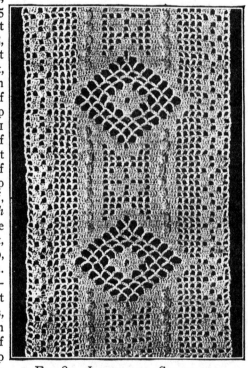

FIG. 89. INSERTION. See page 35

second loop of next f, turn. *16th row*—Four f, 5 t in sp, t on t, 3 f, 6 t on 6 t, turn. *17th row*—Repeat from * to *, 6 t on 6 t, 4 sps, ch 5, 1 t in next f (in same st with t of last row), 1 t in 4th st of second loop of next festoon. *18th row*—Four f, 5 t in sp, 7 t on 7 t, 5 t in sp, t on t, 3 f, 6 t on 6 t, turn. *19th row*—Repeat from * to *, 18 t on 18 t, 4 sps, ch 5, 1 t in same st with t in next f, 1 t in 4th st of second loop of next f, turn. *20th row*—Four f, 5 t in sp, 7 t in 7 t, ch 5, miss 5, 7 t in next 7 t, 5 t in sp, t on t, 3 f, 6 t on 6 t, turn. *21st row*—Repeat from * to *, 4 sps, 6 t on 6 t, 1 sp, 1 f, 1 sp, 6 t on 6 t, 4 sps, ch 5, 1 t in f below, 1 t in 4th st of second loop of next f, turn. This row completes the corner. Repeat from 7th row to finish scallop.

Figure 95.—For this insertion, begin with 55 ch sts. *1st row*—One t in 8th st from hook, (ch 2, miss 2, 1 t in next st) twice, ch 2, miss 2, 7 t in next 7 sts, (ch 2, miss 2, 7 t in next 7 sts) twice, 4 sps, turn. The remainder of the pattern may be worked from the cut, as the method of working is given in directions for Fig. 96.

Figure 96. — Chain 40. *1st row* — One t in 8th st from hook, 6 t in next 6 sts, (ch 2, miss 2 sts on foundation ch, 7 t in next 7 sts) twice, (ch 2, miss 2, 1 t in next st) 3 times, turn. *2d row* — Chain 5, 1 t on next t, ch 2, 1 t on next t, ch 2, 1 t on next t, ch 2, miss 2 t, 4 t on 4 t, 2 t in sp, 1 t on t, 2 t

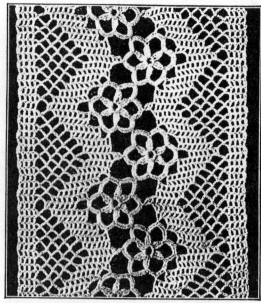

FIG. 90. INSERTION. See page 36

in sp, 4 t on 4 t, ch 2, 1 t on last t, ch 2, 1 t on next t, ch 2, 1 t on last t of row, turn. *3d row* — Chain 8, 1 t in 6th st from hook, 1 t in each of next 2 sts, 1 t on t, ch 2, 1 t on 4th t, ch 2, 1 t on next t, ch 2, miss 2 t, and make 13 t, 5 sps, turn. *4th row* — Three sps (making 5 ch in turning), 10 t, 1 festoon (f) as follows: ch 3, miss 2 t, 1 d in 3d t, ch 3, miss 2, 1 t on next t, 9 more t, 2 sps. 3 t under ch at end of row, turn. *5th row* — Chain 8, 3 t, 3 t in last 3 sts of ch, 1 t on t, 2 sps, 7 t (counting t of last sp as 1 t), 1 f, ch 5, 1 t on next t, 1 f, 7 t, 2 sps, turn. *6th row* — * Chain 5, 1 t on next t, 4 t, 1 f, 5-ch sp, 1 f, 5-ch sp, 1 f, 4 t, * 2 sps, 3 t under ch at end, turn. *7th row* — Chain 8, 3 t in last 3 sts of ch, 1 t on t, 3 sps, ** 4 t, 5-ch sp, 1 f, 5-ch sp, f, 5-ch sp, 4 t, 1 sp, ** turn. *8th row* — Repeat from * to *, 4 sps, 4 t, turn. *9th row* — Chain 8, 3 t in last 3 sts of ch, 1 t on t, 2 sps, 4 t, 2 sps; repeat from ** to **, turn. *10th row* — Repeat from * to *, 1 sp, 4 t, 1 sp, 4 t, 2 sps, 3 t under ch, turn. *11th row* — Chain 5, 1 t on 4th t, 2 t in sp, 1 t on next t, 2 sps, 4 t, 2 sps; repeat from

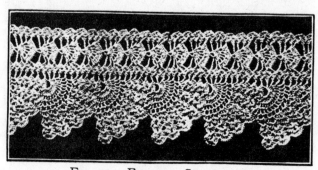

FIG. 91. EDGING. See page 37

** to **, turn. *12th row* — Repeat from * to *, 4 sps, 4 t, turn. *13th row* — Chain 5, 1 t on 4th t, 2 t in sp, 1 t on t, 3 sps; repeat from ** to **, turn. *14th row* — Repeat from * to *, 2 sps, 4 t, turn. *15th row* — Chain 5, 4 t, 2 sps, 7 t, (making the 2d and 3d under the 1 sp of f, 1 on d, 2 under next sp, and the last one on next t), 1 f, 1 sp of 5 ch, 1 f, 2 sps, turn. *16th row* — Three sps, 10 t, f, 10 t, 2 sps, 4 t, turn. *17th row* — Chain 5, 4 t, 3 sps, 13 t, 5 sps, turn. *18th row* — Four sps, 7 t, 2 sps, 7 t, 1 sp, 4 t, turn. *19th row* — Chain 5, miss 3 t, t on next t, 2 t in sp, 4 t on next 4 t, 1 sp, 7 t, 1 sp, 7 t, 3 sps, turn. *20th row* — Three sps, 7 t, 1 sp, 7 t, 1 sp, 7 t, turn. *21st row* — Chain 5, 1 t on 1st t, 6 more t, 1 sp, 7 t, 1 sp, 7 t, turn. In the next scallop you begin the corner. Repeat from 2d row to end of 10th row, then work the 11th row to end of last 5-ch sp, turn.

CORNER. *1st row* — Chain 6, 1 d under 5-ch sp, ch 3, t on t, finish row like 12th from 1st 5-ch sp, turn. *2d row* — Work 13th row to end of 2d f, turn. *3d row* — Chain 8, t on last t of f below, finish row like 14th row, beginning with 2d f, turn. *4th row* — Repeat 15th row to end of 1st 5-ch sp, turn. *5th row* — Chain 6, 1 d under 5-ch sp, ch 3, t on t, 9 more t, 2 sps, 4 t, turn. *6th row* — Chain 5, miss 3 t, t on next t, 2 t in sp, t on next t, 3 sps, 4 t, turn. *7th row* Chain 3, for 1st t, 6 more t, 1 sp, 4 t, turn. *8th row* — Chain 5, miss 3 t, t on next t, 2 t in sp, t on t.

SECOND HALF OF CORNER. *1st row* — Chain 8, 3 t in last 3 sts of ch, t on t, ch 2, miss 2 t on 7 t of 7th row of corner, 1 t in next t, sl st over 3 t, turn. *2d row* — Two t under last t made, t on next t, ch 2, miss 2 t, t on next t, 3 t under ch at end, turn. *3d row* — Chain 8, 3 t in last 3 sts of ch, t on t, 3 sps, 4 t in side of next t, counting last t of sp as 1; 1 t in 3d st of 2d section of f, turn. *4th row* — Slip stitch on 1st t, ch 3, 9 more t, 2 sps, 3 t under ch at end, turn. *5th row* — Chain 8, 3 t in last 3 sts of ch, t on t, 2 sps, 7 t, f, 5-ch sp, making the t in the end of f after the 10 in first half of corner, 1 d in 3d st of next 5-ch sp, turn. *6th row* — Chain 6, 1 d in 5-ch sp, ch 3, t on t, 5-ch sp, f, 4 t, 2 sps, 3 t under ch, turn. *7th row* — Chain 8, 3 t in last 3 sts of ch, t on t, 3 sps, 4 t, 5-ch sp, f, 5 ch, 1 t in 4th st of 2d section of f, ch 3, 1 d in same st with d in 5-ch sp, ch 3, t in end of t of next f in first half of corner, turn. *8th row* — Chain 5, t on next t, f, 5-ch sp, f, 4 t, 4 sps, 3 t under ch, turn. *9th row* — Chain 8, 3 t in last 3 sts, t on t, 2 sps, 4 t, 2 sps, 4 t, 5-ch sp, f, 5 ch, f, 5 ch, 3 t in next sp, sl st in end of 4th t, sl st in 2 sts of ch at end, turn. *10th row* — Three t in 3 t; repeat 10th row, beginning with 1st f, turn. Repeat from 11th row to end of 21st row; which will finish scallop, and make one row on the next. Repeat from 2d row for length desired, making each corner in the same manner.

EDGE. — Fasten thread with 1 d in end of first t at right-hand lower edge, 7 t under 5 ch, ch 2, 1 d between next two rows, * ch 2, 7 t under 5 ch, ch 2, 1 d between rows, * 3 times, ch 2, 7 t under 5 ch, ch 2, 1 d in side of t at end of scallop; repeat from * to * 4 times; ch 2, 7 t, 1 d under 5 ch, ch 1, 1 d, 7 t under next 5 ch; repeat from 1st * to end of edge.

Figure 97. — This pattern was worked in cream white twofold zephyr and may be used on a flannel skirt or as a finish to a crocheted one. Chain

86; allow a few extras. Treble in 8th ch from the hook, t in next 3 ch sts, ch 2, t in 3d ch, ch 2, t in 3d, repeat until you have 5 sps (counting the ch sts from last st placed in a ch st, and not from one at beginning), work 3 t in next 3 ch, ch 2, t in 3d,

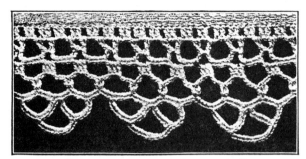

FIG. 92. EDGING. See page 38

ch 2, work a shell in the 3d ch (2 t, ch 2, 2 t), ch 5, (1 t, ch 3, 1 t) called a half shell (h s), in 5th ch, ch 5, shell in 5th ch, ch 2, t in 3d, ch 2, 4 t followed by 5 sps, 4 t, 3 sps, ch 5, turn. *2d row*—Three sps, 1 t in each of the 4 t, 2 in the sp. 1 in t, fill in the sps, all but 1, ch 2, 1 t in each of 4 t, sp over sp, ch 2, shell in shell, ch 3, 6 t in h s, ch 3, shell in shell, ch 2, t in t, ch 2, t in each of 4 t, 2 t in each of next 4 sps with 1 t in each t, sp over 5th sp, 4 t, 1 sp, ch 5, turn. *3d row*—Four t, sp, 4 t, 3 sps, 4 t, 2 sps, shell in shell, t in each of the 6 t, with 1 ch between, shell in shell, 2 sps, 4 t, 1 sp, 4 t, 3 sps, 4 t, 2 sps, 9 t in last sp, which with the 1 t just made to form last sp, makes 10 t. Skip 2 t of ch, catch by sl st into 3d, ch 5, turn. *4th row*—Skip 1 t, t in next, ch 2, t in 2d, ch 2, t in next, ch 2, t in next, ch 2, t in 2d, ch 2, t in 2d, which will give you 6 sps (2 skipping 1 t, 2 without skipping, 2 skipping 1 t), 2 sps over next 2, 4 t, 1 sp, 4 t, 1 sp, 4 t, 1 sp, 4 t, 2 sps, shell in shell, d between 1st and 2d d, ch 3, d back in same sp, repeat in each sp, making 5 picots, shell in shell, 2 sps, 4 t, 1 sp, 4 t, 1 sp, 4 t, 1 sp, 4 t, 1 sp. ch 5, turn. *5th row*—One sp, 4 t, 3 sps, 4 t, 1 sp, 4 t, 2 sps, shell in shell, ch 5, h s in centre picot, ch 5, shell in shell, 2 sps, 4 t, 3 sps, 4 t, 1 sp, 4 t, 2 sps 2 t in each of the 6 sps with 1 ch between each group of 2, sl st into 4th ch of foundation. *6th row*—Chain 5, catch back into 1st ch made by a d, making a p, t between first and second groups, make another picot, t in same sp, another picot, t in next sp, another p, t in same sp. Proceed thus until you reach last sp, t twice in this, with no p between, ch 2, 2 t in 2d t of group beneath, 2 sps, 4 t, 1 sp, 16 t, 2 sps, shell in shell, ch 3, 6 t in half shell, ch 3, shell in shell, 2 sps, 4 t, 1 sp, 16 t, 1 sp, ch 5, turn. With the next row you start a new scallop and a new design in the Grecian border. The fan insertion is far enough along to show you how to go on with it.

Figure 98.—Chain 22. *1st row*—Make 1 sl st in 10th st

from hook, ch 5, 1 sl st in same st, ch 7, skip 5 sts on foundation chain, 1 sl st in next st, ch 5, 1 sl st in same st, ch 7, 1 sl st in last st of ch, turn. *2d row*—* Chain 7, 1 sl st under 1st 7-ch space (sp), ch 5, 1 sl st in same sp, ch 7, 1 sl st under next sp, ch 5, 1 sl st in same sp, ch 7, 1 sl st in last sp, * turn; repeat from * to * till you have 8 rows. You now begin the scallop. ** Chain 3, 1 l t (thread over 3 times and work off by twos) under the loop formed at the end of the 4th row in turning, (ch 2, 1 l t under same loop) 7 times; skip 1 loop at end, and make 1 sl st in end loop, turn; ch 7, 1 sl st between 1st and 2d l t, (ch 7, 1 sl st between next 2 l t) 6 times, ch 7, 1 sl st under 3 ch at beginning of t **. You should have 8 loops in all. Repeat from * to * 8 times, then from ** to ** for scallop. At the end of 2d scallop, and each subsequent one, after having made the last 7 ch, and 1 sl st under 3 ch, ch 2, 1 sl st under opposite 7 ch on preceding scallop, turn, ch 4, 1 sl st between 1st and 2d l t; this counts as one loop, make 7 more, and repeat from * for length desired.

Figure 99.—Chain 13, 1 d in 3d st from hook, ch 5, miss 4 sts, 1 d t in next st, ch 5, miss 4, 1 d in last st of ch, turn. Chain 10, 1 d in st next d t, 1 d in d t, 1 d in next st, ch 4, 1 d t in last d, turn. Chain 10, 1 d t in d t just made, ch 5, 1 d in each of 3 d, ch 4, miss 4, 1 d t in 5th st of 10 ch, turn. Chain 1, 1 d on d t just made, ch 4, 1 d t in centre d, ch 4, 1 d in ch st next d t, 1 d on d t, 1 d in next ch st, ch 4, 1 d t in centre of 10 ch, turn, * ch 10, 1 d t on d t, ch 5, 1 d in each of 3 d, ch 4, 1 d t on next d t, turn, ch 1, 1 d on d t, ch 4, 1 d t in centre d, ch 4, 1 d in st next d t, 1 d on d t, 1 d in next ch st, ch 4, 1 d t in 5th st of 10 ch. Repeat from * for length desired, in last square to finish, making 10 ch, 3 d on 3 d, ch 4, 1 d t on next d t, turn, ch 1, 1 d t on d t, ch 4, 1 d t in centre d, ch 4, 1 d in 5th st of 10 ch, break thread.

FOR BOTTOM EDGE. *1st row*—Holding lace right side towards you, begin at right-hand upper corner of square, in the space next to centre d t, make * 4 d, 3 d at end of d t, 4 d under next chain-space, repeat from * to end of lace. *2d row*—* One

FIG. 93. EDGING. See page 38

d in centre of 3 d at beginning of preceding row, * ch 9, make a cluster of t as follows: (Thread over hook once, insert hook in next centre d, pull a loop through, thread over, pull through 2 loops) 4 times in same d, thread over and pull through 4 loops, thread over and pull through remaining sts, ch 5, put hook through two upper loops of cluster and make 1 d, ch 9, 1 d in next centre d, repeat from * to end, and break thread. 3d row—Begin again at right hand, fasten thread in 1st d, ch 9, * (thread over hook twice, insert hook in 7th st from hook, pull loop through, thread over, pull through two loops, thread over, miss 2 sts on next ch, insert hook in next st, pull loop through, thread over, pull through two loops, thread over, pull through two more loops, thread over, pull through two loops, thread over and pull through last two loops. Chain 5, thread over, insert hook in two centre loops of cross treble, make 1 t), this makes a cross t, ch 3, miss 2 sts on ch, 1 sl st in each of next 4 sts, make 1 d in little ring of 5 ch, ch 4, make a cluster of 3 t in the

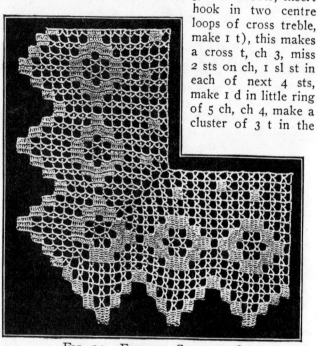

FIG. 94. EDGING. See page 38

same manner as in preceding row, ch 17, insert hook in 13th st from hook, in the outside part of st on the right-hand side and sl st through it, 1 d, 1 h t, 8 t in ring, ch 3, 8 t, 1 h t, 1 d in same ring, 1 sl st in st where ring was joined, to secure it closely, ch 4, make a second cluster of t's, ch 4, 1 d in little ring, 1 sl st in each of next 4 sts of ch, ch 3, and repeat from * to end of lace, break thread. 4th row—* One d under 5 ch at top of cross t, ch 5, 1 d t in centre of first cluster, 1 t in 1st t in ring (missing the 1st d and h t), ** ch 3, miss 1 t, 1 t in next st, repeat from ** twice more, (ch 3, 1 t under centre ch) 3 times, (ch 3, miss 1 t, 1 t in next st) 4 times, 1 d t in centre of second cluster, * repeat from * to * to end of row, break thread. 5th row—Fasten thread in the d in cross t, at right-hand end, ch 3, 2 t under next ch, * (ch 3, 3 t under next 3 ch) 10 times, ch 3, 3 t under next ch, repeat from * to end, break thread. 6th row—One d top of 3 ch in last row, * ch 3, 1 d in next sp, ch 3, 1 t in centre t of 3 t, (ch 5, 1 d on top of t just made) 3 times, repeat from * 10 times, ch 3, 1 d under next sp, ch 3, 1 d in centre between t's, repeat from * to end of row and fasten off. HEADING.—Leave two free spaces at right-hand end of lace, repeat directions in 1st row of bottom edge. 2d row—Fasten thread in centre d at top of square, ch 10, 1 t in next centre d, * ch 7, 1 t in next centre d, repeat from * to end of row, break thread. 3d row—Fasten thread in 3d st of 10 ch of preceding row, ch 4, miss 1 st, 1 t in next st, * ch 1, miss 1, 1 t in next st, repeat from * to end.

A pretty insertion may be made by finishing both edges of the row of squares with the heading, leaving off the scallops at the bottom edge.

Figure 100.—Chain 92. 1st row—One t in 4th ch from hook, 2 t in next 2 ch; ch 2, skip 2 on foundation chain, t in 3d st; ch 2, 4 t, ch 2, until you have 21 open meshes or spaces, 4 t, ch 2, t, ch 2, 3 t. 2d row—Chain 3, 2 t, ch 2, t, ch 2, 4 t, 21 sps, 4 t, ch 2, t, ch 2, 3 t. 3d row—Chain 3, 2 t, ch 2, t, ch 2, t, ch 2, 4 t, 9 sps, 4 t, 9 sps, 4 t, 3 sps, 3 t. 4th row—Chain 3, 2 t, 3 sps, 4 t, 8 sps, 10 t, 8 sps, 4 t, 3 sps, 3 t. 5th row—Chain 3, 2 t, 5 sps, 4 t, 4 sps, 4 t, 1 sp, 10 t, 1 sp, 10 t, 1 sp, 4 t, 4 sps, 4 t, 5 sps, 3 t. 6th row—Chain 3, 2 t, 4 sps, 7 t, 1 sp, 4 t, 2 sps, 10 t, now make 5 t all in the next t, take hook out of work, insert in first of 5 t, catch 5th st and pull through (this will hereafter be called a tuft), ch 1, 11 t, 2 sps, 4 t, 1 sp, 7 t, 4 sps, 3 t. 7th row—Chain 3, 2 t, 7 sps, 7 t, 1 sp, 7 t, tuft in 8th t, 6 t, tuft, 7 t, 1 sp, 7 t, 7 sps, 3 t. 8th row—Chain 3, 2 t, 5 sps, 13 t, 1 sp, 10 t, 1 sp, 10 t, 1 sp, 13 t, 5 sps, 3 t. 9th row—Chain 3, 2 t, 6 sps, 10 t, 2 sps, 4 t, 1 sp, ch 3, d in middle of sp in 8th row, ch 3, 1 sp, 4 t, 2 sps, 10 t, 6 sps, 3 t. 10th row—Chain 3, 2 t, 9 sps, 7 t, ch 3, d in 4th t below, ch 3, t in t, ch 5, t on t, ch 3, d in t below, ch 3, 7 t, 9 sps, 3 t. 11th row—Chain 3, 2 t, 4 sps, 13 t, 1 sp, 4 t, 1 sp, ch 5, t, ch 3, d, ch 3, t, ch 5, t, 1 sp, 4 t, 1 sp, 13 t, 4 sps, 3 t. 12th row—Chain 3, 2 t, 5 sps, 13 t, ch 5, t, ch 3, d, ch 3, t, ch 5, t, ch 3, d, ch 3, t, ch 5, 13 t, 5 sps, 3 t. 13th row—Chain 3, 2 t, 3 sps, 11 t, tuft, 4 t, 1 sp, ch 3, d, ch 3, t, ch 5, t, ch 3, d, ch 3, t, ch 5, t, ch 3, d, ch 3, 1 sp, 4 t, tuft, 11 t, 3 sps, 3 t. 14th row—Chain 3, 2 t, 2 sps, 11 t, tuft, 4 t, 2 sps, ch 5, t, ch 3, d, ch 3, t, ch 5, t, ch 3, d, ch 3, t, ch 5, 2 sps, 4 t, tuft, 11 t, 2 sps, 3 t. 15th row—Like 13th. 16th row—Like 12th. 17th row—Like 11th. 18th row—Like 10th. 19th row—Like 9th. 20th row—Like 8th. 21st row—Like 7th. 22d row—Like 6th. 23d row—Like 5th. 24th row—Like 4th. 25th row—Like 3d. 26th row—Like 2d. 27th row—Like 1st. Repeat from beginning of 2d row. If you desire border, fasten thread in end of 1st t, holding work wrong side towards you, ch 7, miss 1 row, 1 d in end of next row; repeat to end, turn. 2d row—Three d, picot of 4 ch, 3 d, p, 3 d; repeat to end, and on second side.

Figure 101.—Chain length desired, turn. 1st row—One t in 7th st from hook, 1 t in every other st, with 2 ch between each, to end of ch, turn. 2d row—Chain 4, 1 t under 1st 2 ch, 1 t under each 2 ch, with 2 ch between each t, to end of row, turn. 3d row—Chain 4, 1 t on next t, * ch 12, miss 2 t, 1 t on next t, ch 1, 1 t on next t; repeat from * to end, turn. 4th row—Chain 12, 6 d under 12 ch, 6 d under next 12 ch; repeat to end, turn. 5th row—Chain 12, 4 t under 1st 12 ch, * ch 10, 4 d in centre 4 d of the 12 d in preceding row, ch 10, 4 t under next 12 ch; repeat to end of row, turn. 6th row—Chain 4, 1 t on 2 d t, 1 t on each of next 2 t with

2 ch between each, ch 2, miss 2, 1 t in next t; repeat to the 4 t at top of scallop, in these you do not miss, but make 1 t in each of the 4 t with 2 ch between each; between scallops, make 4 t in the 4 d, without any sts between; repeat to end, turn. *7th row*—Chain 12, 1 t in 7th st from hook, ch 5, miss 1 t, 1 d in next t, * ch 5, turn, 1 t in the t made in 7th st of 12 ch, turn, ch 7, 1 t in t just made, ch 5, miss 1 t, 1 d in

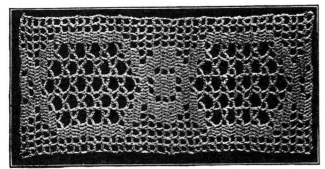

FIG. 95. INSERTION. See page 39

next t; repeat from * to end of scallop. Between scallops, draw a st through each of the 4 t, retaining them on the hook, thread over and draw through all at once; repeat from beginning of row.

Figure 102. — Chain 92. *1st row*—One t in 4th ch from hook, 2 t in next 2 ch, ch 2, skip 2 on foundation chain, t in 3d ch, ch 2, skip 2, 4 t, (ch 2, skip 2, 1 t on t) until you have 21 spaces, 4 t, ch 2, 1 t, ch 2, 4 t. *2d row*—Chain 3, 3 t, ch 2, 1 t, ch 2, 4 t, 21 sps, 4 t, ch 2, 1 t on t, ch 2, 4 t on 4 t. *3d row*—Chain 3, 3 t, 3 sps, 4 t, 9 sps, 4 t, 9 sps, 4 t, 2 sps, 7 t. *4th row* —Slip stitch back on 3 t, ch 3, 3 t, 2 sps, 4 t, 8 sps, 10 t, 8 sps, 4 t, 3 sps, 4 t. *5th row*—Chain 3, 3 t, 5 sps, 4 t, 4 sps, 4 t, 1 sp, 10 t, 1 sp, 4 t, 4 sps, 4 t, 3 sps, 7 t. *6th row*—Slip stitch back on 3 t, ch 3, 3 t, 2 sps, 7 t, 1 sp, 4 t, 2 sps, 10 t, tuft (see 6th row of directions for Fig. 100), 11 t, 2 sps, 4 t, 1 sp, 7 t, 4 sps, 4 t. *7th row* —Chain 3, 3 t, 7 sps, 7 t, 1 sp, 7 t, tuft, 6 t, tuft, 7 t, 1 sp, 7 t, 5 sps, 4 t. *8th row*—Chain 3, 3 t, 3 sps, 13 t, 1 sp, 10 t, 1 sp, 10 t, 1 sp, 13 t, 5 sps, 4 t. *9th row*—Chain 3, 3 t, 6 sps, 10 t, 2 sps, 4 t, 1 sp, ch 3, 1 d in middle of sp below, ch 3, 1 t on next t, 1 sp, 4 t, 2 sps, 10 t, 4 sps, 4 t. *10th row*—Chain 5, 1 t in 4th ch from hook, 1 t in next ch, 4 more t, 7 sps, 7 t, ch 3, 1 d on 4th t, ch 3, 1 d on next t, ch 5, 1 d on next t, ch 3, d on next t, ch 3, 7 t, 9 sps, 4 t. *11th row*—Chain 3, 3 t, 4 sps, 13 t, 1 sp, 4 t, 1 sp, ch 5, 1 t on next t, ch 3, 1 d under 5 ch, ch 3, 1 t on t, ch 5, 1 t on t, 1 sp, 4 t, 1 sp, 13 t, 3 sps, 4 t. *12th row*—Chain 5, t in 4th and 5th ch, 4 more t, 4 sps, 13 t, ch 5, skip 3 t and 1 sp, 1 t on next t, ch 3, d in 5 ch, ch 3, t on t, ch 5, t on t, ch 3, d in 5 ch, ch 3, t on t, ch 5, skip 1 sp and 3 t, 13 t, 5 sps, 4 t. *13th row*—Chain 3, 3 t, 3 sps, 11 t, tuft, 4 t, 1 sp, ch 3, 1 d under 5 ch, ch 3, 1 t on next t, ch 5, 1 t on t, ch 3, d in 5 ch, ch 3, t on t, ch 5, t on t, ch 3, d under 5 ch, ch 3, t on next t, 1 sp, 4 t, tuft, 11 t, 3 sps, 4 t. *14th row*—Chain 3, 3 t, 2 sps, 11 t, tuft, 4 t, 2 sps, ch 5, t on next t, ch 3, d under 5 ch, ch 3, t on next t, ch 5, t on t, ch 3, d under 5 ch, ch 3, t on t, ch 5, t on t, 2 sps, 4 t, tuft, 11 t, 2 sps, 4 t. *15th row*— Like 13th. *16th row*—Chain 3, 6 t, 4 sps, 13 t, ch 5, t on t, ch 3, d under 5 ch, ch 3, t on t, ch 5, t on next t, ch 3,

d under 5 ch, ch 3, t on t, ch 5, 13 t, 5 sps, 4 t. *17th row*—Chain 3, 3 t, 4 sps, 13 t, 1 sp, 4 t, 1 sp, ch 5, t on t, ch 3, d under 5 ch, ch 3, t on t, ch 5, t on t, ch 2, 3 t under 5 ch, 1 t on next t, 1 sp, 13 t, 3 sps, 4 t. *18th row*—Chain 3, 6 t, 7 sps, 7 t, ch 3, d under ch, ch 3, t on t, ch 5, t on t, ch 3, d under 5 ch, ch 3, t on next t, 6 more t, 9 sps, 4 t. *19th row*—Chain 3, 3 t, 6 sps, 10 t, 2 sps, 4 t, 3 of them made under 3 ch, 1 sp, ch 3, d in 5 ch, ch 3, t on next t, 1 sp, 4 t, 2 sps, 10 t, 4 sps, 4 t. *20th row*—Chain 3, 3 t, 3 sps, 13 t, 1 sp, 10 t, 1 sp, 10 t, 1 sp, 13 t, 5 sps, 4 t. *21st row*—Chain 3, 3 t, 7 sps, 7 t, 1 sp, 7 t, tuft, 6 t, tuft, 7 t, 1 sp, 7 t, 5 sps, 4 t. *22d row*—Chain 7, turn, sl st over 1st 4 ch (remaining 3 ch stand for 1 t), miss 1 t of last row and work 1 t over each of next 3 t, 2 sps, 7 t, 1 sp, 4 t, 2 sps, 10 t, tuft, 11 t, 2 sps, 4 t, 1 sp, 7 t, 4 sps, 4 t. *23d row*—Chain 3, 3 t, 5 sps, 4 t, 4 sps, 4 t, 1 sp, 10 t, 1 sp, 4 t, 4 sps, 4 t, 3 sps, 7 t. *24th row*—Chain 7, turn, sl st over 1st 4 ch, miss 1 t of last row and work 1 t over each of next 3 t, 2 sps, 4 t, 8 sps, 10 t, 8 sps, 4 t, 3 sps, 4 t. *25th row*—Chain 3, 3 t, 3 sps, 4 t, 9 sps, 4 t, 9 sps, 4 t, 2 sps, 7 t.

FIRST SIDE OF CORNER. *1st row*—Chain 3, 3 t, 2 sps, 4 t, 21 sps, 4 t, 1 sp. *2d row*—Turn, ch 5 (to stand for 1 sp), 4 t, 21 sps, 4 t, 2 sps, 4 t. *3d row* —Chain 3, 3 t, 2 sps, 4 t, 21 sps. *4th row*—Chain 3, 3 t, 9 sps, 4 t, 9 sps, 4 t, 2 sps, 7 t. *5th row*—Slip stitch over 4 t of last row, ch 3, 3 t, 2 sps, 4 t, 8 sps, 10 t, 7 sps. *6th row*—Chain 3, 3 t, 4 sps, 4 t, 1 sp, 10 t, 1 sp, 4 t, 4 sps, 4 t, 3 sps, 7 t. *7th row*—Slip stitch over 4 t of last row, ch 3, 3 t, 2 sps, 7 t, 1 sp, 4 t, 2 sps, 10 t, tuft, 11 t, 2 sps, 4 t. *8th row*—Chain 3, 6 t, 1 sp, 7 t, tuft, 6 t, tuft, 7 t, 1 sp, 7 t, 5 sps, 4 t. *9th row*—Chain 3, 3 t, 3 sps, 13 t, 1 sp, 10 t, 1 sp, 10 t, 1 sp. *10th row*—Chain 5 (to stand for 1 sp), 1 more sp, 4 t, 3 sps, 4 t, 2 sps, 10 t, 4 sps, 4 t. *11th row*—Chain 5, t in 4th ch from hook, t in next, 4 more t, 7 sps, 7 t, 5 sps. *12th row*—Chain 5, 5 more sps, 4 t, 1 sp, 13 t, 3 sps, 4 t. *13th row*—Chain 5, t in 4th st from hook, t in next, 4 more t, 4 sps, 13 t, 5 sps. *14th row*—Chain 5, 5 more sps, 4 t, tuft, 11 t, 3 sps, 4 t. *15th row* —Chain 3, 3 t, 2 sps, 11 t, tuft, 4 t, 5 sps. *16th row* —Chain 5, 3 more sps, 4 t, tuft, 11 t, 3 sps, 4 t. *17th row*—Chain 3, 6 t, 4 sps, 13 t, 1 sp. *18th row*— Chain 3, 3 t, 1 sp, 13 t, 3 sps, 4 t. *19th row*— Chain 3, 6 t, 6 sps. *20th row*—Chain 3, 6 t, 4 sps,

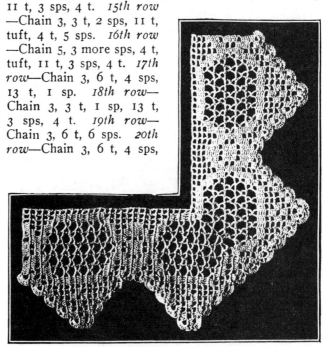

FIG. 96. EDGING. See page 40

4 t. *21st row*—Chain 3, 6 t, 2 sps, 4 t. *22d row*—Chain 5, 2 more sps, 4 t. *23d row*—Chain 3, 6 t, 1 sp, *24th row*—Chain 5, 4 t. This completes one-half of corner.

SECOND SIDE OF CORNER. *1st row*—Four t, ch 7, turn, sl st over 1st 4 ch. *2d row*—Two t into side of t just made, sl st in 3d st of 5 ch. *3d row*—Slip stitch to next t, ch 2, t into 5 ch. *4th row*—Turn, ch 2, 7 t. *5th row*—Slip stitch to end of t, ch 7, sl st over 1st 4 ch, skip 1st t, 3 t, 4 sps, 2 t into side of t. *6th row*—Turn, 9 t, 2 sps, 7 t. *7th row*—Chain 7, sl st over 1st 4 ch, 3 t, 4 sps, 10 t, 4 t into 4 t of first side of corner. *8th row*—Turn, 7 sps, 7 t. *9th row*—Chain 7, sl st over 1st 4 ch, 3 t, 3 sps, 13 t, 1 sp, 4 t, 1 sp, t into t of first side of corner, ch 2, t into 5 ch. *10th row*—Turn, 2 sps, 13 t, 4 sps, 7 t. *11th row*—Chain 3, 3 t, 3 sps, 11 t, tuft, 4 t, 5 sps, t into t of first side of corner, ch 2, t into 5 ch. *12th row*—Turn, 6 sps, 4 t, tuft, 11 t, 2 sps, 4 t. *13th row*—Chain 3, 3 t, 3 sps, 11 t, tuft, 4 t, 7 sps, t into t of first side of corner, ch 2, t into 5 ch. *14th row*—Turn, 6 sps, 13 t, 4 sps, 7 t. *15th row*—Slip stitch over 3 t, ch 3, 3 t, 3 sps, 13 t, 1 sp, 4 t, 7 sps, 3 t, sl st into t of first side of corner, sl st on 2 ch. *16th row*—Turn, 6 t, 5 sps, 7 t, 7 sps, 7 t. *17th row*—Slip stitch over 3 t, ch 3, 3 t, 4 sps, 10 t, 2 sps, 4 t, 3 sps, 4 t, 2 sps, 6 t, sl st into t on first side of corner, sl st to end of t. *18th row*—Turn, 6 t, 1 sp, 10 t, 1 sp, 10 t, 1 sp, 13 t, 3 sps, 4 t. *19th row*—Chain 3, 3 t, 5 sps, 7 t, 1 sp, 7 t, tuft, 6 t, 1 sp, 7 t, 1 sp, 4 t into 4 t of first side of corner. *20th row*—Turn, 1 sp, 4 t, 2 sps, 11 t, tuft, 10 t, 2 sps, 4 t, 1 sp, 7 t, 2 sps, 4 t. *21st row*—Chain 5, t into 4th ch from hook, t in next ch, 4 more t, 3 sps, 4 t, 4 sps, 4 t, 1 sp, 10 t, 1 sp, 4 t, 4 sps, 4 t, 1 sp, 4 t into 4 t on first

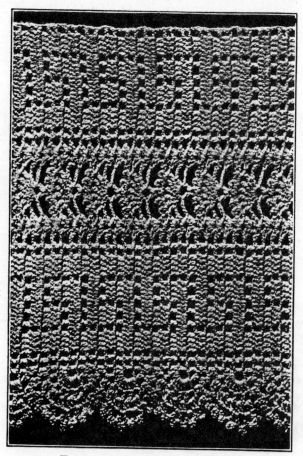

FIG. 97. EDGING. See page 40

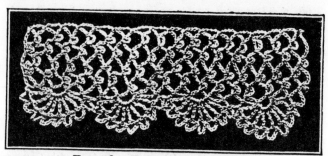

FIG. 98. EDGING. See page 41

side of corner. *22d row*—Turn, 8 sps, 10 t, 8 sps, 4 t, 2 sps, 4 t. *23d row*—Chain 5, t in 4th ch from needle, t in next, 4 more t, 2 sps, 4 t, 9 sps, 4 t, 9 sps, 4 t, 1 sp, 3 t, sl st into t on first side of corner, sl st into 2 ch. *24th row*—Turn, ch 2, 4 t, 21 sps, 4 t, 2 sps, 4 t. *25th row*—Chain 3, 3 t, 2 sps, 4 t, 21 sps, 4 t, 2 sps, 4 t into 4 t on first side of corner. *26th row*—Turn, 2 sps, 4 t, 21 sps, 4 t, 2 sps, 4 t. This completes corner. Continue with edging for length desired, repeating from 1st row, and make second corner the same as the first, and so on.

Figure 103.—Use No. 70 Cordonnet crochet cotton and a No. 11 steel hook. Chain 8, join with sl st. *1st round*—Chain 8, 1 d t in ring, (ch 4, 1 d t in ring) 6 times, ch 4, sl st in 4th st of 8 ch. *2d round*—Chain 5, 5 d t in 1st space (sp), 1 d t on d t, * 6 d t in next sp, 1 d t on d t, repeat from * around, making 56 d t in all, join to top st of 5 ch with sl st. *3d round*—Chain 5, 6 d t on next 6 d t, ch 5, * 7 d t on next 7 d t, ch 5, repeat from * around, joining last 5 ch with sl st in top st of 5 ch. *4th round*—One sl st in next d t, ch 3, * (thread over hook, insert hook in next d t, pull a loop through, thread over, pull through two loops on hook) 5 times; when you will have six loops on hook, thread over and pull through five loops, thread over, pull through last two loops, ch 7, repeat from * around, joining last 7 ch with sl st in top of first cluster. *5th round*—Slip stitch up 3 sts on 7 ch, 1 d in 4th st, ch 9, 1 d in 4th st of next 7 ch, repeat around, sl st in 3d d. *6th round*—Slip stitch 5 sts on 9 ch, ch 7, 1 t in 6th st from hook, * (ch 7, thread over hook twice, insert hook in 4th st of 9 ch and make a d t, ch 2, thread over once and make a t in the 1st st of d t (which is the loop that was pulled through the 9th st of 9 ch), inserting hook under the two upper threads of st. Repeat from * around, joining last 7 ch to 5th st of first 7 ch. Break thread and fasten securely.

Make another wheel like this, but in last row make but 13 of the cross treble stitches, then join to the first wheel as follows: Chain 29, take hook out of work, insert it in centre st of 7 ch between 5th and 6th cross t from beginning of row on first wheel. catch 29th st and pull through, ch 1, being careful that both wheels are right side up, sl st in each of first 3 sts of ch, ch 3, miss 1, 1 h t in next st, (ch 1, miss 1, 1 h t in next st) 8 times, ch 3, miss 1, sl st in three last sts of ch, ch 3, and finish out row of cross t sts (3 more in all), fastening last 7 ch to 5th st of 1st t in cross t.

Make as many wheels as required for length of lace you wish, making 13 cross t sts with 7 ch between, in last row, and join as before, finishing row of cross t sts, and breaking thread.

On the last wheel you make when you have length you wish, after completing the row of cross t's, do not break thread, but begin the next round. *7th round*—Chain 3, * 1 t in each of the 2 sts in cross t, using only one loop of sts, 1 t on t of cross t, 1 t in each of the 7 sts of ch; counting the first 3 ch made as 1 t, this makes 11 sts, and there must be just 11 sts between the beginning of each cross t and the beginning of next, around to the last cross t on wheel before the joining ch, in that one make 1 t on 1st t of cross t, 1 t in each of next 2 sts, 1 t on 2d t of cross t, 3 t in next 3 sts of ch, then join to 3d sl st on connecting ch with 1 sl st, 1 d under 1st sp, 1 d on h t, 1 d under next sp till you have 19 d (this takes you into the last sp), 1 sl st in last sl st on ch, 3 t in next 3 sts on wheel, 1 t on 1st t of the cross t, * and repeat from * to * all along the row of wheels around to the first joining on second side; when you reach that, after making the ** 3 t in 3 sts of last sp, join to 1st st of 3 ch on joining chain with sl st, 1 sl st in next st of 3 ch, 1 d under same 3 ch, 1 d on h t, 1 d under next sp, till you have 19 d (the last one should be under the 3 ch at end), 1 sl st in next st of 3 ch, 1 sl st in next sl st, 1 sl st in the top of last t made before joining. Three t in next 3 t, ** then repeat row of t all around, at each joining, repeating from ** to **, join with sl st to top st of 3 ch. *8th round*—Chain 3, 1 t in next t, * 4 t in next t, take hook out of work, insert in first of 4 t, pull last st through, 1 t in each of next 10 t, repeat from * 13 times, 3 t in next 3 t, which leaves two free t before connecting ch, ** ch 5, miss 2 d on connecting ch, 16 d in next 16 d, taking both loops of sts, ch 5, miss 2 t on wheel, 3 t in next 3 t, repeat from * 8 times, 3 t in next 3 t, repeat from ** to next wheel, then alternately from * to * and from ** to ** all around to beginning of round, join with sl st to 1st st of 3 ch. *9th round*—Chain 3, 7 t in next 7 t, (ch 2, miss 1, 10 t in next 10 t) 11 times, making 5 of the t on each side of st composed of 4 t, ch 2, 9 t in next 9 t, * ch 5, miss 2 d, 12 d in next 12 d, ch 5, 9 t in next 9 t, (ch 2, miss 1, 10 t in next 10 t) 6 times, ch 2, miss 1, 9 t in next 9 t, repeat from *, repeat from * all around to beginning of round, working all around end wheel to joining, making 2 ch, 2 t after last cluster to make 10 t in cluster at beginning, join to first 3 ch with sl st. *10th round*—Chain 3, 7 t on 7 t, (ch 3, 10 t on 10 t) 11 times, ch 3, 9 t on 9 t, * ch 5, miss 2 d, 8 d in next 8 d, ch 5, 9 t in next 9 t, (ch 3, 10 t in next 10 t) 6 times, ch 3, 9 t in next 9 t, repeat from * all around to beginning of round, making 3 ch, 2 t in next 2 t after last 10 t, join to 3 ch with sl st. *11th round*—Slip stitch in each of next 2 t, ch 8, 1 d t in 7th st from hook, * ch 5, 1 d under 3 ch, ch 5, 1 d t in centre of next 10 t, ch 3, 1 t in 1st st of d t at the bottom of st, repeat from * to connection, ch 8, miss 2 d, 4 d in next 4 d, ch 3, take

hook out of work, insert in 3d st of 8 ch (counting up from 1st d), pull 3d st through, ch 5, 1 d t between 4th and 5th t of next cluster, ch 3, 1 t in 1st st of d t, ** repeat from * to ** all around, ch 5, 1 sl st in 5th st of cross t. Break thread and fasten.

FIGURE BETWEEN WHEELS.—Chain 8, join with sl st. *1st row*—Chain 5, (1 d t in circle) 14 times, turn. *2d row*—One sl st in 1st d t, ch 5, 4 d t in next 4 d t, ch 3, 5 d t in next 5 d t, ch 3, 4 d t in next 4 d t, 1 d t in 1st st of 5 ch at end, turn. *3d row*—Chain 1, 5 d in next 5 d t, ch 5, 5 t in next 5 d t, ch 5, 5 d in next 5 d t, turn. *4th row*—Chain 3, * (thread over hook once, insert in 1st d, pull a loop through, thread over, pull through two loops) 5 times, thread over, pull through five loops on hook, thread over and pull through last two loops, * ch 3, take up row of wheels, holding wrong side up, insert hook under the 3 ch of 2d cross t from joining on first wheel at the right, make 1 d, ch 3, 1 d under first 5 ch on figure, ch 4, repeat from * to * on 5 t, 1 1 t under 3 ch of cross t next to joining, 1 1 t in 3 ch of opposite cross t, ch 4, 1 d under next 5 ch on figure, ch 3, 1 d under 3 ch of next

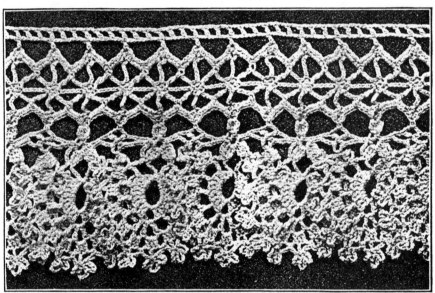

FIG. 99. EDGING. See page 41

cross t, ch 3, repeat from * to * in last 5 d on figure, break thread and fasten. Make one of these figures between each wheel on both sides, joining in the same manner.

HEADING. *1st row*—In the first stitch of fourth cross treble from joining in end wheel at right, having a slip knot on hook, fasten thread and ch 2, 1 t in 2d t of cross t, ch 16, 1 d under 3 ch of next cross t, ch 12, 1 d under 3 ch of next cross t, ch 12, * thread over four times, insert hook in 1st t of next cross t, draw a loop through, (thread over hook and draw through two loops) twice, thread over hook, insert hook in 2d t of cross t, pull loop through, (thread over, and pull through two loops) 5 times; * ch 9, make a 1 t in the end d of the row of 5 d in first petal of figure, ch 9, 3 d in ring at top of figure, ch 9, 1 1 t in end d of row in last petal, ch 9, repeat from * to *, (ch 12, 1 d under 3 ch of next cross t) twice, ch 12, ** repeat from * to ** ending on 4th cross t of last wheel, turn. *2d row*—Chain 4, miss 1, 1 t in next st, ch 1, miss

45

1, 1 t in next st to end of row, turn. *3d row*—Chain 3, 1 t in each st to end of row, turn. *4th row*—Like 2d row. Repeat heading on the other side.

Cover Design.—Chain 10, join in a ring with sl st. *1st round*—Chain 1, 2 d in ring, ch 5, 1 d in 1st st of 5 ch for a picot, (3 d in ring, p) 5 times, 1 d in ring, join to 1st d with sl st. *2d round*—Chain 8, 1 t in centre d between next 2 p's. (ch 5, 1 t in centre d between next 2 p's) 5 times, joining last 5 ch with sl st to 3d st of 8 ch. *3d round*—Nine d

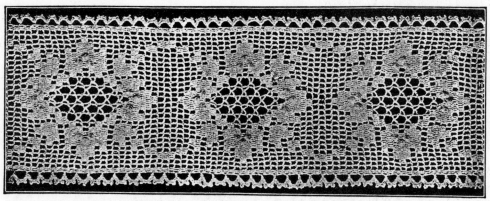

FIG. 100. INSERTION. See page 42

under each sp around, join with sl st to 1st d.

FIRST PETAL. *1st row*—Chain 1, 1 d in st where joined, (ch 3, miss 2, 1 d in next d) 3 times, turn. *2d, 3d, and 4th rows* the same, making 4 ch each time in turning. *5th row*—Chain 2, 1 d in next sp, (ch 3, 1 d in next sp) twice, turn. *6th row*—Chain 2, 1 d in 1st sp, ch 4, 1 d in next sp, turn, ch 2, 1 d in next sp, pull loop out and put ball through, letting thread lie loosely alongside of petal, insert hook in last d of petal and pull a loop through. Make 5 more petals in the same way, then make a row of d sts around each petal, making 1 d in bottom sp, 4 sps with 3 d, 7 d in top sp, the same on the other side. Slip stitch up over 2 sp, 1 d in next sp, and make a round of p loops as follows: ch 7, 1 d in 5th st from hook, ch 7, p in 5th st from hook, ch 2, miss 5 d, 1 d in next d, this brings you to the 1st d in top sp, make another p loop, miss 5 d, 1 d in next d, another p loop, miss 5 d, 1 d in next d, ½ p loop, (ch 7, p in 5th st, ch 2), miss 6 d on next petal, 1 d in next d; repeat around, join with sl st in 1st d on first petal.

Make another star like first one, joining between p's on p loop at top of a petal as follows: ch 7, p in 5th st, ch 1, take hook out of work, insert in top p loop between petals, pull st through, ch 6, p in 5th st, ch 2, 1 d in 6th d, then finish out p loops on second star.

Make as many stars as you require, joining each to preceding one, as you make it. Between the stars on each side make a little p ring as follows:

RING.—Chain 8, join with sl st, 2 d in ring, p, (3 d in ring, p,) 4 times, 1 d in ring, join to 1st d with sl st. Chain 8, p in 5th st, ch 7, p in 5th st, ch 2, 1 t in centre st between p's, ch 4, pick up row of stars, insert hook in p loop next top loop of a petal, next before joining petal, ch 4, 1 t in centre st between next 2 p's on ring; ch 4, insert hook in next p loop on joining petal, ch 4, 1 t in centre st between next 2 p's, ch 4, insert hook in corresponding p loop on next

star, ch 4, 1 t in centre st between next 2 p's on ring; ch 4, insert hook in corresponding p loop on next petal, ch 4, join with sl st in 3d ch of 1st p loop. Break thread and fasten off.

Figure 104.— Chain 115. *1st row*—Treble in 4th ch from hook, 3 treble in next 3 ch, ch 3, skip 2 on foundation, double in third ch, ch 3, treble in third ch. This is one festoon. Make three more festoons, ch 2, treble, until there are 19 spaces, 4 festoons, 4 treble.

2d row—Chain 3, 3 treble, ch 5, treble over treble (1 bar), 3 more bars, ch 2, 10 treble, 11 spaces, 10 treble, ch 2, 4 bars, 4 treble.

3d row—Chain 3, 3 treble, 3 festoons, 1 bar, 16 treble, 4 spaces, 4 treble, 4 spaces, 16 treble, 1 bar, 3 festoons, 4 treble.

4th row—Chain 3, 3 treble, 3 bars, ch 2, 7 treble, 3 spaces, 4 treble, 3 spaces, 4 treble, ch 2, 4 treble, 3 spaces, 4 treble, 3 spaces, 7 treble, (the last 3 being made under the 5 ch), ch 2, 3 bars, 4 treble.

5th row—Chain 3, 3 treble, 3 festoons, ch 2, 7 treble, 6 spaces, 4 treble, ch 5, treble over 2 ch of 4th row, ch 5, 4 treble, 6 spaces, 7 treble, ch 2, 3 festoons, 4 treble.

6th row—Chain 3, 3 treble, 3 bars, ch 2, 7 treble, 5 spaces, 4 treble, ch 5, 4 treble (2 on each side of treble in 5th row), ch 5, 4 treble, 5 spaces, 7 treble, ch 2, 3 bars, 4 treble.

7th row—Chain 3, 3 treble, 4 festoons, 7 treble, 3 spaces, 4 treble, ch 5, 10 treble, ch 5, 4 treble, 3 spaces, 7 treble, 4 festoons, 4 treble.

8th row—Chain 3, 3 treble, 4 bars, 4 spaces, 4 treble, ch 5, 16 treble, ch 5, 4 treble, 4 spaces, 4 bars, 4 treble.

9th row—Chain 3, 3 treble, 2 festoons, ch 2, 10 treble, 3 spaces, 4 treble, ch 5, treble over 5 ch, ch 2, 16 treble, ch 2, treble over 5 ch, ch 5, 4 treble, 3 spaces, 10 treble, ch 2, 2 festoons, 4 treble.

10th row—Chain 3, 3 treble, 2 bars, 16 treble, ch 2, 4 treble, ch 5, treble over 5 ch, ch 5, 16 treble, ch 5, treble, ch 5, 4 treble, ch 2, 16 treble, 2 bars, 4 treble.

11th row—Chain 3, 3 treble, 1 festoon, ch 2, 10 treble, ch 2, 7 treble, ch 2, 4 treble, ch 5, 7 treble, ch 2, 10 treble, ch 2, 7 treble, ch 5, 4 treble, ch 2,

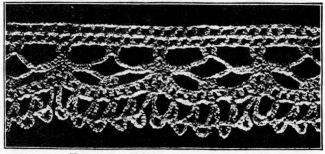

FIG. 101. EDGING. See page 42

46

7 treble, ch 2, 10 treble, ch 2, 1 festoon, 4 treble.

12th row — Chain 3, 3 treble, 1 bar, 10 treble, 5 spaces, 4 treble, ch 2, 13 treble, ch 2, 4 treble, ch 2, 13 treble, ch 2, 4 treble, 5 spaces, 10 treble, 1 bar, 4 treble.

13th row — Chain 3, 3 treble, 1 festoon, 10 treble, 5 spaces, 4 treble, ch 2, 34 treble, ch 2, 4 treble, 5 spaces, 10 treble, 1 festoon, 4 treble.

14th row — Like 12th row.

15th row — Like 11th row.

16th row — Like 10th row.

17th row—Like 9th row.

18th row—Like 8th row.

19th row—Chain 3, 3 treble, 3 festoons, 1 bar, 7 treble, 3 spaces, 4 treble, ch 5, 10 treble, ch 5, 4 treble, 3 spaces, 7 treble, 1 bar, 3 festoons, 4 treble.

20th row—Like 6th row.

21st row—Like 5th row.

22d row—Like 4th row.

23d row—Chain 3, 3 treble, 4 festoons, 16 treble, 4 spaces, 4 treble, 4 spaces, 16 treble, 4 festoons, 4 treble.

24th row—Chain 3, 3 treble, 4 bars, ch 2, 10 treble, 11 spaces, 10 treble, ch 2, 4 bars, 4 treble.

25th row—Chain 3, 3 treble, 4 festoons, 19 spaces, 4 festoons, 4 treble; this row is like first row.
Repeat from 2d row for length required.

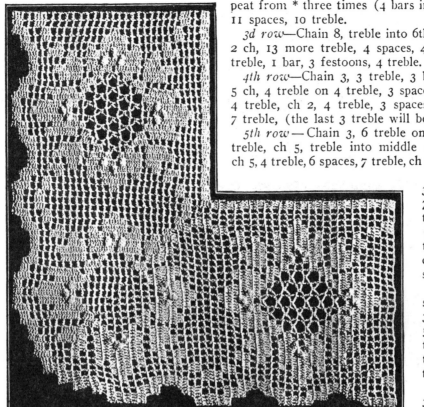

FIG. 102. EDGING. See page 43

peat from * three times (4 bars in all) ch 2, 10 treble, 11 spaces, 10 treble.

3d row—Chain 8, treble into 6th ch, treble into next 2 ch, 13 more treble, 4 spaces, 4 treble, 4 spaces, 16 treble, 1 bar, 3 festoons, 4 treble.

4th row—Chain 3, 3 treble, 3 bars, ch 2, 3 t under 5 ch, 4 treble on 4 treble, 3 spaces, 4 treble, 3 spaces, 4 treble, ch 2, 4 treble, 3 spaces, 4 treble, 3 spaces, 7 treble, (the last 3 treble will be in loop).

5th row — Chain 3, 6 treble on 6 treble, 6 spaces, 4 treble, ch 5, treble into middle of 2 ch of 4th row, ch 5, 4 treble, 6 spaces, 7 treble, ch 2, 3 festoons, 4 treble.

6th row—Chain 3, 3 treble, 3 bars, ch 2, 7 treble, 5 spaces, 4 treble, ch 5, 4 treble (2 on each side of treble of 5th row), ch 5, 4 treble, 5 spaces, 7 treble.

7th row—Chain 3, skip 3 treble, 7 treble, 3 spaces, 4 treble, ch 5, 10 treble, ch 5, 4 treble, 3 spaces, 7 treble, 4 festoons, 4 treble.

8th row—Chain 3, 3 treble, 4 bars, 4 spaces, 4 treble, 5 ch, 16 treble, 5 ch, 4 treble, 4 spaces.

9th row—Chain 15, treble into 7th ch, 8 more treble in next 8 stitches of ch, treble into treble, 3 spaces, 4 treble, ch 5, treble into 5 ch, ch 2, 16 treble, ch 2, treble into 5 ch, ch 5, 4 treble, 3 spaces, 10 treble, 6 of them under first 5 ch, 4 treble under next 5 ch, ch 2, 2 festoons, 4 treble.

10th row—Chain 3, 3 treble, 2 bars, 16 treble, ch 2, 4 treble, ch 5, treble into 5 ch, ch 5, 16 treble, ch 5, treble into 5 ch, ch 5, 4 treble, ch 2, 16 treble (last 3 treble into loop).

11th row—Chain 9, treble into 7th, 8th, and 9th ch, 7 more treble on treble, ch 2, miss 2, 7 treble on 7 treble, ch 2, 4 treble, ch 5, treble into treble, 5 treble into 5 ch, treble into treble, ch 2, miss 2, 10 treble in 10 treble, ch 2, 7 treble, ch 5, 4 treble, ch 2, 7 treble, ch 2, 10 treble, ch 2, 1 festoon, 4 treble.

Figure 105.— Chain 87. *1st row* —Treble into 9th ch, ch 2, skip 2 on foundation ch, treble into next, ch 2, skip 2, treble until there are 18 spaces, * ch 3, skip 2, double into third ch, ch 3, treble into third ch; * repeat from * three times (4 festoons in all), 3 more treble.

2d row—Chain 3, 3 treble, * ch 5, treble into treble of 1st row; * re-

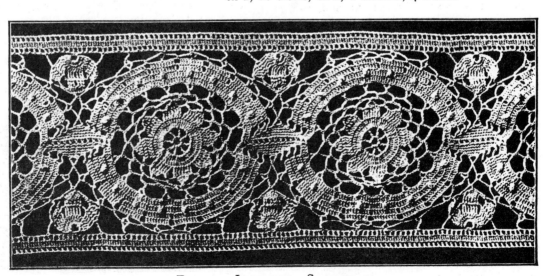

FIG. 103. INSERTION. See page 44

FIG. 104. INSERTION. See page 46

12th row—Chain 3, 3 treble, 1 bar, 10 treble, 5 spaces, 4 treble, ch 2, 13 treble, ch 2, 4 treble, 5 spaces, 10 treble.

13th row—Chain 3, 9 treble on 9 treble, 5 spaces, 4 treble, ch 2, 34 treble, ch 2, 4 treble, 5 spaces, 10 treble, 1 festoon, 4 treble.

14th row—Chain 3, 3 treble, 1 bar, 10 treble, 5 spaces, 4 treble, ch 2, 13 treble, ch 2, miss 2, 4 treble, ch 2, miss 2, 13 treble, ch 2, 4 treble, 5 spaces, 10 treble.

15th row—Chain 3, skip 3 treble, 10 treble, ch 2, 7 treble, ch 2, 4 treble, ch 5, 7 treble, ch 2, 10 treble, ch 2, 7 treble, ch 5, 4 treble, ch 2, 7 treble, ch 2, 10 treble, ch 2, 1 festoon, 4 treble.

16th row—Chain 3, 3 treble, 2 bars, 16 treble, ch 2, 4 treble, ch 5, treble, ch 5, 16 treble, ch 5, treble, ch 5, 4 treble, ch 2, 16 treble.

17th row—Chain 3, skip 3 treble, 10 treble, 3 spaces, 4 treble, ch 5, treble into second 5 ch, ch 2, 16 treble, ch 2, treble in 5 ch, ch 5, 4 treble, 3 spaces, 10 treble, ch 2, 2 festoons, 4 treble.

18th row—Chain 3, 3 treble, 4 bars, 4 spaces, 4 treble, ch 5, 16 treble, ch 5, 4 treble, 4 spaces.

19th row—Chain 5, 7 treble (into last 2 spaces of 18th row), 3 spaces, 4 treble, ch 5, 10 treble, ch 5, 4 treble, 3 spaces, 7 treble, 1 bar, 3 festoons, 4 treble.

20th row—Chain 3, 3 treble, 3 bars, ch 2, 7 treble, 5 spaces, 4 treble, ch 5, 4 treble, ch 5, 4 treble, 5 spaces, 7 treble (last 3 in loop).

21st row—Chain 3, 6 treble, 6 spaces, 4 treble, ch 5, treble into middle of 4 treble, ch 5, 4 treble, 6 spaces, 7 treble, ch 2, 3 festoons, 4 treble.

22d row—Chain 3, 3 treble, 3 bars, ch 2, 7 treble, 3 spaces, 4 treble, 3 spaces, 4 treble, ch 2, 4 treble, 3 spaces, 4 treble, 3 spaces, 7 treble.

23d row—Chain 3, skip 3 treble, 16 treble, 4 spaces, 4 treble, 4 spaces, 16 treble, 4 festoons, 4 treble.

24th row—Chain 3, 4 bars, ch 2, 10 treble, 11 spaces, 10 treble.

Repeat from 1st row.

Edging (not illustrated).—Chain 30. *1st row*—One t in 8th st, t in each of next 3 t, ch 2, t in 3d st, ch 2, miss 2, (1 t, 3 ch, 1 t) a half shell (h s), in 3d st, ch 2, t in 3d st, ch 2, miss 2, 4 t in next 4 sts, ch 2, t in last st, ch 5, turn.

2d row—One t on last t made, ch 2, * 4 t on 4 t, ch 2, t on t, ch 2, 1 d in next space (sp), ch 1, shell of (3 t, ch 1, 3 t) in h s, ch 1, 1 d in next sp, ch 2, t on t, ch 2, 4 t on 4 t, ch 2, t in 3d st of 5 ch, ch 5, turn. *

3d row—* Four t on 4 t, ch 2, t on t, ch 3, h s in 1 ch of shell, ch 3, t on t, ch 2, 4 t, ch 2, t on t, * 5 t in 5 ch, ch 3, turn.

4th row—One t on each t, making 2 in last 1 (7 in all, 1st 3 ch, representing 1), ch 2; repeat 2d row from * to *.

5th row—Repeat 3d row from * to *, t in each t, 2 in last t, ch 3, turn.

6th row—One t in each t, 2 in last t, ch 2; repeat 2d row from * to *.

7th row—Repeat 3d row from * to *, t in t, 2 in last t, ch 3, turn. *8th row*—Make t in t, 2 in last 1, (14 in all), ch 2; repeat 2d row from * to *. *9th row*—Repeat 3d row from * to *, ch 3, t in same st with last t, (ch 2, miss 3 t, h s in next t,) twice on side, once in point, 3 times on next side, making 1st h s on 2d side in bottom of t at end of 1st row; the others, miss one row of t and catch in end of next row, t in t at end of 1st row, turn. *10th row*—Six t in each h s, 1 d in each 2 ch between; after last 6 t, make 1 d in next t, ch 5; repeat 2d row from * to *. *11th row*—Repeat 3d row from * to *, making last t in 3d st of 5 ch.

Repeat from 2d row for length required.

FIG. 105. EDGING. See page 47

ERRATA

Figure 8, page 4.—The third row should read as follows: Chain 3, 1 treble in each of 3 treble, and so on.

Figure 76, page 27. (See illustration on page 31.) The lower edge was omitted and should follow the directions as given. LOWER EDGE.—Fasten thread with 1 double in first free point of braid at right-hand edge, * chain 5, 1 long treble between points, chain 8, 1 treble in top of next point, chain 8, 1 double long treble (thread over 4 times), between points, chain 8, 1 treble in top of next point, chain 8, 1 double long treble between points, chain 8, 1 treble on next point, chain 8, 1 double treble, between points, chain 5, 1 double in last point, chain 3, 1 double in first point on next scallop *. Repeat from * to end of row and cut thread.

2d row—Begin again at right, * 5 double in first space (5 double, picot of 5 chain, 5 double, in next space) 6 times, 5 double in last space, 2 double under 3 chain between scallops. Repeat from * to end.

Figure 77, page 28. The sixteenth line should read — from * to * twice, instead of "3 times." The sixth row should read—Under the 9 chain, make * 1 double, 3 treble, picot of 4 stitches, fastened in top of treble with 1 double, (2 treble, picot) 3 times, 3 treble, 1 double *. In next loop make 1 double, 3 treble, picot, (2 treble, picot) 4 times, 3 treble, 1 double; in next loop repeat from * to *; next loop, and so on.

Figure 85, page 31. At top of page 32, first column, the second line should read—1 d in 4th st of shell, ch 5, 1 d in same st, ch 3, 1 t, and so on. In the third row the seventh line should read—repeat from * to *, and so on. The fifth row should read—Repeat from *** to ***, ch 7, 1 d under next sp, ch 5, 1 d in same sp, ch 7, 2 t on 2 t, turn. The sixth row should read—Repeat from ** to **, and so on. The ninth row should read—Chain 12, pull last st through fourth d on stem, and so on. In the twelfth row, third line from bottom, "through centre d," should read—through fourth d, and so on.

Figure 102, page 43. The tenth row should read — Chain 5, 1 treble in 4th chain from hook, 1 treble in next chain, 4 more treble, 7 spaces, 7 treble, chain 3, 1 double on 4th treble, chain 3, 1 treble on next treble, chain 5, 1 treble on next treble, and so on. On page 44, first column, fourth line from top.—SECOND SIDE OF CORNER. The first row should read — Chain 3, 3 treble on 3 treble, chain 7, slip stitch over first 4 chain. The third row should read—Chain 7, slip stitch in first 4 chain, skip first treble, 3 treble, 4 spaces, 2 treble in side of treble, slip stitch from third treble at corner to end.

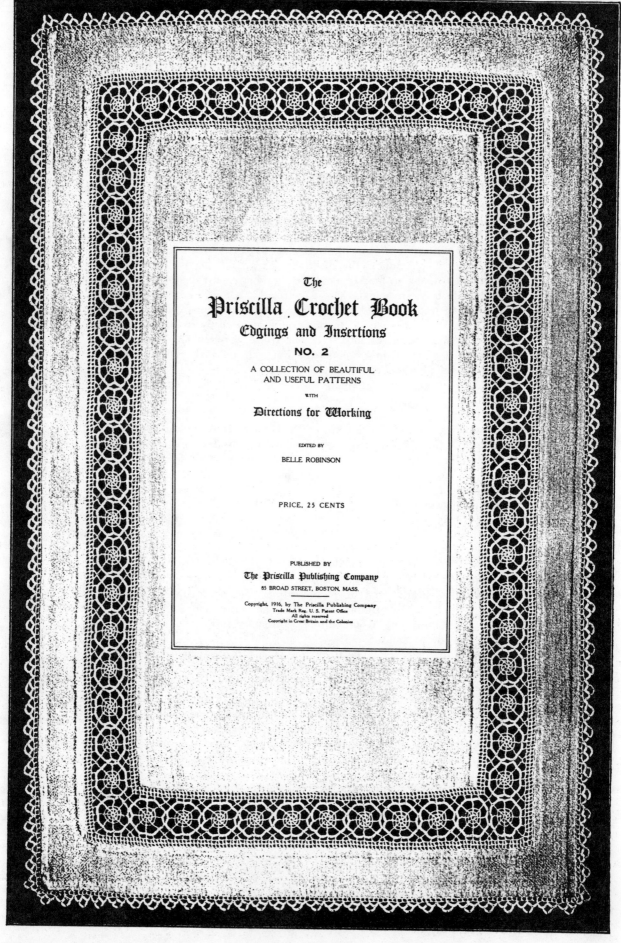

The

Priscilla Crochet Book
Edgings and Insertions
NO. 2

A COLLECTION OF BEAUTIFUL
AND USEFUL PATTERNS

WITH

Directions for Working

EDITED BY

BELLE ROBINSON

PRICE, 25 CENTS

PUBLISHED BY

The Priscilla Publishing Company

85 BROAD STREET, BOSTON, MASS.

FIG. 1. LINEN SCARF WITH INSERTION AND EDGING. See directions on page 25

EDGINGS AND INSERTIONS No. 2

Explanation of Stitches

CHAIN (ch). With a slip knot on the hook, draw thread through this loop; again draw thread through this second loop and continue until the chain is of the required length.

SLIP STITCH (sl). Having a st on the hook, put hook through work; draw thread through work and loop on the hook at the same time.

DOUBLE (d). Having a st on the hook, put hook through work, draw thread through work (making two loops on the hook); thread over again and through both loops. (This stitch has been, especially in wool crochet, called "single crochet." But it simplifies crocheting to call it "double crochet," after the custom of workers in Irish crochet; and that eliminates entirely the name "single crochet.")

HALF TREBLE (ht). Having a st on the hook, thread over hook, hook through work, thread over and through work (having three sts on the hook), thread over and through all three sts at once.

TREBLE (t). Having a st on the hook, thread over hook, hook through work, thread over and through work (having three sts on the hook), thread over and through two loops, thread over and again through two loops.

DOUBLE TREBLE (dt). Having a st on the hook, thread over twice, hook through work, thread over and through work (having four sts on the hook), thread over and through two, over and through two, over and through two.

LONG TREBLE (lt) OR TRIPLE TREBLE (tt). Like double treble, but thread over three times, and after thread through work, crocheting off by twos.

QUADRUPLE TREBLE (qt). Thread over four times, and crochet off by twos. Sometimes "long treble" is used for anything longer than dt, and the number of loops given.

PICOT (p). A p is formed on a ch by joining the last four sts (or any given number) in a ring by working a sl, or a d, in the fourth st from the hook. In the following directions a sl is understood unless otherwise designated. In a few cases the p is joined by a treble, but it is so stated in the directions.

CLUNY STITCHES, OR GROUPS OF CLUNY. Two, three, or four (any given number) trebles, dt, or long t are crocheted off, except the last loop of each, which is kept on the hook and one loop drawn through all together.

ROLL STITCH is made as follows: Thread over hook a given number of times, thread through work, thread over and through all the loops (but not through the st on the hook), thread over and through both on the hook. The hook for roll st should be of uniform thickness a considerable distance from the point.

BLOCK of 4, or BLOCK of 3, etc. A given number of t, dt, or long t worked without ch between.

SHELL. A group of t, ch 1 (or more), the same number of t, all joined in the same st or over same ch, as (4 t, ch 3, 4 t). The number of t, as well as the number of ch, may vary. "Shell over shell," the t are all made over ch of shell below.

KNOT STITCH (k st). To make a k st draw out the st on the hook until it is about ¼ of an inch long, catch working thread and draw through st, insert hook in front of the long st, and under the thread which was drawn through, and make one d. Two ks are usually made for a mesh, then joined to the work with a d. Second row of k st, * make 2 ks, join with d under the two threads of next open st and close to knot, one d in next open st (after k); repeat from *.

SPACE (sp). In filet crochet, "ch 2, miss 2 sts, t in next"; where the number of t is given, as 4 t, 7 t, etc., this t is included.

Directions

Materials. — Where the words "crochet cotton" are used in the text of this book, the cotton referred to is the hard-twisted cotton known by such names as Cordonnet, Cordonnet Special, Cordichet, Kord-net, etc., which can be purchased wherever needlework supplies are sold.

Figure 2. Border for Tea Cloth. — Crochet cotton No. 100, hook No. 14.

BORDER BEFORE CORNER. — Make a foundation chain of 148 stitches; always ch 3 for first treble. *1st row*—4 t, 1 sp, 4 t, 5 sp, 4 t, 1 sp, 7 t, 1 sp, 7 t, 7 sp, 10 t, 1 sp, 13 t, 2 sp, 10 t, 11 sp, 10 t. *2d row*—Ch 5, 13 t, 10 sp, 10 t, 3 sp, 10 t, 2 sp, 7 t, 9 sp, 4 t, 2 sp, 4 t, 5 sp, 4 t, 1 sp, 7 t. *3d row*—10 t, 1 sp, 4 t, 5 sp, 7 t, 10 sp, 4 t, 4 sp, 7 t, 3 sp, 10 t, 2 sp, 10 t, 4 sp, 13 t, omit 3 t. *4th row*—Ch 4, miss 3 t, 1 t in next, 12 more t, 2 sp, 4 t, 3 sp, 4 t, 1 sp, 10 t, 2 sp, 7 t, 4 sp, 4 t, 10 sp, 4 t, 2 sp, 4 t, 5 sp, 4 t, 1 sp, 7 t. *5th row*—4 t, 1 sp, 4 t, 29 sp, 10 t, 1 sp, 4 t, 1 sp, 7 t, 3 sp, 10 t, miss 3 t. *6th row*—Ch 4, miss 3 t, 1 t in next, 9 more t, 5 sp, 4 t, 1 sp, 10 t, 15 sp, 16 t, 8 sp, 4 t, 1 sp, 7 t. *7th row*—10 t, 1 sp, 4 t, 5 sp, 25 t, 5 sp, 10 t, 5 sp, 13 t, 2 sp, 22 t, miss 3 t. *8th row*—Ch 4, miss 3 t, 1 t in next, 15 more t, 4 sp, 10 t, 4 sp, 4 t, 3 sp, 4 t, 3 sp, 4 t, 5 sp, 13 t, 5 sp, 4 t, 1 sp, 7 t. *9th row*—4 t, 1 sp, 4 t, 4 sp, 13 t, 4 sp, 7 t, 1 sp, 4 t, 3 sp, 4 t, 1 sp, 7 t, 4 sp, 13 t, 5 sp, 10 t, miss 3 t. *10th row*—Increase—Ch 10, 1 t in 8th st from hook, 15 more t, 6 sp, 13 t, 5 sp, 4 t, 3 sp, 4 t, 3 sp, 4 t, 4 sp, 10 t, 3 sp, 4 t, 1 sp, 7 t. *11th row*—10 t, 1 sp, 4 t, 1 sp, 13 t, 5 sp, 10 t, 5 sp, 25 t, 6 sp, 22 t. *12th row*—Increase — Ch 10, 1 t in 8th st from hook, 9 more t, 5 sp, 4 t, 7 sp, 16 t, 15 sp, 10 t, 2 sp, 4 t, 1 sp, 7 t. *13th row*—4 t, 1 sp, 4 t, 3 sp, 10 t, 27 sp, 4 t, 1 sp, 7 t, 3 sp, 10 t. *14th row*—Increase—Ch 10, 1 t in 8th st from hook, 12 more t, 2 sp, 4 t, 3 sp, 4 t, 4 sp, 4 t, 2 sp, 4 t, 10 sp, 4 t, 4 sp, 7 t, 2 sp, 10 t, 2 sp, 4 t, 1 sp, 7 t. *15th row*—10 t, 1 sp, 4 t, 1 sp, 10 t, 3 sp, 7 t, 4 sp, 4 t, 10 sp, 7 t, 6 sp, 10 t, 4 sp, 13 t. *16th row*—Increase—Ch 8, 1 t in 6th st from hook, 12 more t, 13 sp, 4 t, 2 sp, 4 t, 9 sp, 7 t, 2 sp, 10 t, 3 sp, 10 t, 2 sp, 4 t, 1 sp, 7 t. *17th row*—4 t, 1 sp, 4 t, 3 sp, 10 t, 2 sp, 13 t, 1 sp, 10 t, 7 sp, 7 t, 1 sp, 7 t, 1 sp, 4 t, 13 sp, 10 t. (*16th to 26th rows, inclusive, are the same length.*) *18th row* — Ch 5, 10 t, 13 sp, 22 t, 7 sp, 25 t, 2 sp, 10 t, 2 sp, 4 t, 1 sp, 7 t. *19th row*—10 t, 1 sp, 4 t, 1 sp, 10 t, 3 sp, 4 t, 1 sp, 8 sp, 22 t, 13 sp, 10 t. *20th row*—Ch 5, 10 t, 12 sp, 10 t, 2 sp, 4 t, 1 sp, 7 t, 2 sp, 7 t, 7 sp, 4 t, 1 sp, 4 t, 2 sp, 10 t, 2 sp, 4 t, 1 sp, 7 t. *21st row*—4 t, 1 sp, 4 t, 3 sp, 10 t, 2 sp, 16 t, 4 sp, 4 t, 2 sp, 4 t, 1 sp, 4 t, 1 sp, 13 t, 1 sp, 7 t, 12 sp, 10 t. *22d row*—Ch 5, 10 t, 12 sp, 7 t, 1 sp, 4 t, 2 sp, 4 t, 1 sp, 4 t, 1 sp, 4 t, 3 sp, 4 t, 2 sp, 13 t, 2 sp, 4 t, 1 sp, 7 t, 3 sp, 4 t, 1 sp, 7 t. *23d row*—10 t, 1 sp, 4 t, 2 sp, 10 t, 3 sp, 13 t, 2 sp, 4 t, 2 sp, 4 t, 2 sp, 4 t, 1 sp, 4 t, 2 sp, 4 t, 1 sp, 7 t, 12 sp, 10 t. *24th row*—Ch 5, 10 t, 13 sp, 25 t,

5 sp, 4 t, 2 sp, 10 t, 3 sp, 13 t, 3 sp, 4 t, 1 sp, 7 t. *25th row*—4 t, 1 sp, 4 t, 5 sp, 16 t, 3 sp, 4 t, 2 sp, 4 t, 6 sp, 19 t, 14 sp, 10 t. *26th row*—Ch 5, 13 t, 15 sp, 10 t, 3 sp, 4 t, 2 sp, 4 t, 4 sp, 4 t, 1 sp, 19 t, 4 sp, 4 t, 1 sp, 7 t. *27th row*—10 t, 1 sp, 4 t, 4 sp, 7 t, 2 sp, 4 t, 5 sp, 10 t, 2 sp, 4 t, 1 sp, 7 t, 9 sp, 10 t, 4 sp, 13 t, miss 3 t. *28th row*—Ch 4, miss 3 t, 1 t in next, 12 more t, 2 sp, 4 t, 3 sp, 4 t, 10 sp, 7 t, 2 sp, 4 t, 1 sp, 4 t, 1 sp, 10 t, 2 sp, 10 t, 6 sp, 4 t, 1 sp, 7 t. *29th row*—4 t, 1 sp, 4 t, 8 sp, 10 t, 1 sp, 4 t, 1 sp, 4 t, 1 sp, 10 t, 2 sp, 10 t, 9 sp, 4 t, 1 sp, 7 t, 3 sp, 10 t, miss 3 t. *30th row*—Ch 4, miss 3 t, 1 t in next, 9 more t, 5 sp, 4 t, 8 sp, 4 t, 3 sp, 4 t, 2 sp, 4 t, 2 sp, 10 t, 1 sp, 7 t, 2 sp, 7 t, 4 sp, 4 t, 1 sp, 7 t. *31st row*—10 t, 1 sp, 4 t, 2 sp, 4 t, 2 sp, 4 t, 2 sp, 4 sp, 4 t, 3 sp, 4 t, 14 sp, 22 t, miss 3 t. *32d row* — Ch 4, miss 3 t, 1 t in next, 15 more t, 6 sp, 13 t, 1 sp, 10 t, 2 sp, 10 t, 2 sp, 10 t, 6 sp, 4 t, 3 sp, 4 t, 1 sp, 7 t. *33d row*—4 t, 1 sp, 4 t, 5 sp, 4 t, 4 sp, 7 t, 1 sp, 7 t, 1 sp, 10 t, 1 sp, 7 t, 1 sp, 7 t, 4 sp, 4 t, 6 sp, 10 t, miss 3 t. *34th row*—Increase—Ch 10, 1 t in 8th st from hook, 15 more t, 4 sp, 4 t, 6 sp, 10 t, 2 sp, 10 t, 1 sp, 13 t, 5 sp, 4 t, 1 sp, 7 t. *35th row*—10 t, 1 sp, 4 t, 13 sp, 4 t, 3 sp, 4 t, 4 sp, 4 t, 2 sp, 4 t, 3 sp, 22 t. *36th row* — Increase — Ch 10, 1 t in 8th st from hook, 9 more t, 5 sp, 4 t, 3 sp, 7 t, 2 sp, 7 t, 1 sp, 10 t, 2 sp, 4 t, 2 sp, 4 t, 3 sp, 4 t, 9 sp, 4 t, 1 sp, 7 t. *37th row*—4 t, 1 sp, 4 t, 11 sp, 10 t, 2 sp, 10 t, 1 sp, 4 t, 1 sp, 4 t, 1 sp, 10 t, 6 sp, 4 t, 1 sp, 7 t, 3 sp, 10 t. *38th row*—Increase—Ch 10, 1 t in 8th st from hook, 12

more t, 2 sp, 4 t, 3 sp, 4 t, 5 sp, 10 t, 2 sp, 10 t, 1 sp, 4 t, 1 sp, 4 t, 2 sp, 7 t, 11 sp, 4 t, 1 sp, 7 t. *39th row* —10 t, 1 sp, 4 t, 8 sp, 7 t, 1 sp, 4 t, 2 sp, 10 t, 5 sp, 4 t, 2 sp, 7 t, 5 sp, 10 t, 4 sp, 13 t. *40th row*—Increase—Ch 8, 1 t in 6th st from hook, 12 more t, 12 sp, 19 t, 1 sp, 4 t, 4 sp, 4 t, 2 sp, 4 t, 3 sp, 10 t, 7 sp, 4 t, 1 sp, 7 t *(40th to 50th rows, inclusive, are the same length).* *41st row*—4 t, 1 sp, 4 t, 6 sp, 19 t, 6 sp, 4 t, 2 sp, 4 t, 3 sp, 16 t, 13 sp, 10 t. *42d row*—Ch 5, 10 t, 12 sp, 13 t, 3 sp, 10 t, 2 sp, 4 t, 5 sp, 25 t, 4 sp, 4 t, 1 sp, 7 t. *43d row*—10 t, 1 sp, 4 t, 2 sp, 7 t, 1 sp, 4 t, 2 sp, 4 t, 1 sp, 4 t, 2 sp, 4 t, 2 sp, 4 t, 2 sp, 13 t, 3 sp, 10 t, 12 sp, 10 t. *44th row*—Ch 5, 10 t, 12 sp, 7 t, 1 sp, 4 t, 2 sp, 13 t, 2 sp, 4 t, 3 sp, 4 t, 1 sp, 4 t, 1 sp, 4 t, 2 sp, 4 t, 1 sp, 7 t, 3 sp, 4 t, 1 sp, 7 t. *45th row*—4 t, 1 sp, 4 t, 4 sp, 7 t, 1 sp, 13 t, 1 sp, 4 t, 1 sp, 4 t, 2 sp, 4 t, 4 sp, 16 t, 2 sp, 10 t, 11 sp, 10 t. *46th row*—Ch 5, 10 t, 11 sp, 10 t, 2 sp, 4 t, 1 sp, 4 t, 7 sp, 7 t, 2 sp, 7 t, 1 sp, 4 t, 2 sp, 10 t, 3 sp, 4 t, 1 sp, 7 t. *47th row*—10 t, 1 sp, 4 t, 2 sp, 22 t, 8 sp, 13 t, 1 sp, 4 t, 3 sp, 10 t, 11 sp, 10 t. *48th row*—Ch 5, 10 t, 11 sp, 10 t, 2 sp, 25 t, 7 sp, 22 t, 4 sp, 4 t, 1 sp, 7 t.

FOR THE CORNER. — The corner is arranged to follow next after 45 rows of the pattern which has been described.

For the first part, make 45 rows of "Border before the Corner." *46th row*—Ch 5, 10 t, 11 sp, 10 t, 2 sp. 4 t, 1 sp, 4 t, 7 sp, 7 t, 2 sp, 7 t, 1 sp, 4 t, 2 sp, 10 t, 3 sp, 4 t, 1 sp, miss 1 sp and 4 t. *47th row*—4 t, 1 sp, 4 t, 3 sp, 22 t, 8 sp, 13 t, 1 sp, 4 t, 3 sp, 10 t, 11 sp, 10 t. *48th row*—Ch 5, 10 t, 11 sp, 10 t, 2 sp, 25 t, 7 sp, 22 t, 4 sp, miss 1 sp, and 4 t. *49th row*—4 sp (ch 5 for first sp), 4 t, 1 sp, 7 t, 1 sp, 7 t, 7 sp, 10 t, 1 sp, 13 t, 2 sp, 10 t, 11 sp, 10 t. *50th row*—Ch 5, 13 t, 10 sp, 10 t, 3 sp, 10 t, 2 sp, 7 t, 9 sp, 4 t, 2 sp, 4 t, 3 sp, miss 2 sp. *51st row*—4 sp (ch 5 for first sp), 7 t, 10 sp, 4 t, 4 sp, 7 t, 3 sp, 10 t, 2 sp, 10 t, 4 sp, 13 t, miss 3 t. *52d row*—Ch 4, miss 3 t, 1 t in next, 12 more t, 2 sp, 4 t, 3 sp, 4 t, 1 sp, 10 t, 2 sp, 7 t, 4 sp, 4 t, 3 sp, 7 t, 5 sp, 4 t, 2 sp, 4 t, 1 sp, miss 2 sp. *53d row*—9 sp (ch 5 for first sp), 4 t, 2 sp, 4 t, 11 sp, 10 t, 1 sp, 4 t, 1 sp, 7 t, 3 sp, 10 t, miss 3 t. *54th row*—Ch 4, miss 3 t, 1 t in next, 9 more t, 5 sp, 4 t, 1 sp, 10 t, 11 sp, 4 t, 3 sp, 4 t, 4 sp, 4 t, 1 sp, miss 2 sp. *55th row*—1 sp (ch 5 for

Note.—To secure the unusual effect in this Border, the stitch is taken in the back loop, only, of stitch below.

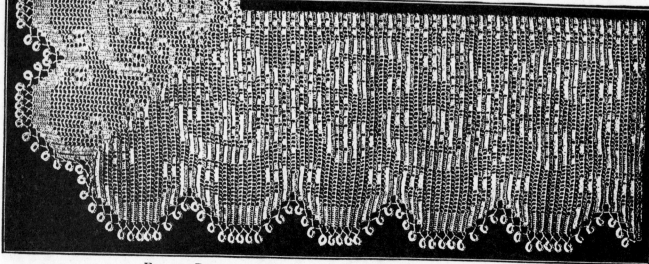

FIG. 2. BORDER FOR TEA CLOTH, SCROLL DESIGN. See page 3

sp), 4 t, 4 sp, 4 t, 2 sp, 4 t, 2 sp, 10 t, 5 sp, 13 t, 2 sp, 22 t, miss 3 t. *56th row*—Ch 4, miss 3 t, 1 t in next, 15 t, 4 sp, 10 t, 4 sp, 4 t, 3 sp, 4 t, 5 sp, 4 t, 4 sp, miss 4 t and 1 sp. *57th row*—4 t, 3 sp, 4 t, 5 sp, 4 t, 1 sp, 7 t, 4 sp, 13 t, 5 sp, 10 t. *58th row*—Increase—Ch 10, 1 t in 8th st from hook, 15 more t, 6 sp, 13 t, 5 sp, 4 t, 6 sp, 4 t, 1 sp, miss 1 sp and 4 t. *59th row*—10 t, 6 sp, 25 t, 6 sp, 22 t. *60th row*—Increase—Ch 10, 1 t in 8th st from hook, 9 more t, 5 sp, 4 t, 7 sp, 16 t, 2 sp, 4 t, 4 sp, 4 t, miss 7 t. *61st row*—4 t, 5 sp, 4 t, 13 sp, 4 t, 1 sp, 7 t, 3 sp, 10 t. *62d row*—Increase—Ch 10, 1 t, in 8th st from hook, 12 more t, 2 sp, 4 t, 3 sp, 4 t, 12 sp, 4 t, 1 sp, 4 t, 3 sp, miss 1 sp and 4 t. *63d row*—10 t, 16 sp, 10 t, 4 sp, 13 t. *64th row*—Ch 8, 1 t in 6th st from hook, 12 more t, 24 sp, 4 t, miss 7 t. *65th row*—4 t, 25 sp, 10 t. *66th row*—Ch 5, 10 t, 20 sp, 4 t, 3 sp, miss 1 sp and 4 t. *67th row*—10 t, 1 sp, 4 t, 19 sp, 10 t. *68th row*—Ch 5, 10 t, 21 sp, 4 t, miss 7 t. *69th row*—4 t, 21 sp, 10 t. *70th row*—Ch 5, 10 t, 18 sp, 4 t, 1 sp, miss 1 sp and 4 t. *71st row*—7 t, 5 sp, 10 t, 10 sp, 10 t. *72d row*—Ch 5, 10 t, 9 sp, 4 t, 3 sp, 4 t, 4 sp, miss 7 t. *73d row*—4 sp (ch 5 for first sp), 4 t, 1 sp, 4 t, 1 sp, 4 t, 9 sp, 10 t. *74th row*—Ch 5, 13 t, 8 sp, 4 t, 1 sp, 4 t, 1 sp, 7 t, 1 sp, miss 2 sp. *75th row*—1 sp (ch 5 for sp), 7 t, 2 sp, 4 t, 8 sp, 13 t, miss 3 t. *76th row*—Ch 4, miss 3 t, 1 t in next, 12 more t, 10 sp, 4 t, miss 4 t and 1 sp. *77th row*—7 t, 8 sp, 13 t, miss 3 t. *78th row*—Ch 4, miss 3 t, 1 t in next, 33 more t, miss 7 t. *79th row*—31 t, miss 3 t. *80th row*—Ch 4, miss 3 t, 1 t in next, 6 more t, turn, make 1 dt in top of 4th t just made, 7 t, turn, make 1 dt in top of 3d t just made, 7 t, turn, make 1 dt in top of 3d t just made. This completes the first part of corner.

FOR THE 2D PART OF CORNER. — *1st row*—Increase—Ch 3, turn, make 1 dt in 1st st from work, ch 6, turn and make 1 dt in 3d st, ch 6, turn, 1 dt in 3d st, making a foundation chain of 21 sts with 3 loops of dt on lower side of ch. *2d row*—Increase—Ch 10, 1 t in 8th st from hook, 20 more t on foundation ch, 3 t over end of upright row, join with sl to 4 t of next upright row. *3d row*—Sl to corner of upright row, 27 t. *4th row*—Increase—Ch 10, 1 t in 8th st from hook, 36 t, join with sl to 4th t in upright row. *5th row*—Sl to corner of upright row, 3 t, 8 sp, 13 t. *6th row*—Increase—Ch 10, 1 t in 8th st from hook, 12 more t, 10 sp, 7 t, join with sl to 4th t in upright row. *7th row*—Sl to corner of upright row, 6 t, 2 sp, 4 t, 8 sp, 13 t. *8th row*—Increase—Ch 8, 1 t in 6th st from hook, 12 more t, 8 sp, 4 t, 1 sp, 4 t, 1 sp, 7 t, 1 sp, join with 1 t to corner of sp in upright row. *9th row*—Ch 2, join with 1 t to corner of upright row, 2 sp, 4 t, 1 sp, 4 t, 1 sp, 4 t, 9 sp, 10 t. *10th row*—Ch 5, 10 t, 9 sp, 4 t, 3 sp, 4 t, 4 sp, 3 t, join with sl to 4th t in upright row. *11th row*—Sl to corner of 7th t in upright row, 3 t, 5 sp, 10 t, 10 sp, 10 t. *12th row*—Ch 5, 10 t, 18 sp, 4 t, 1 sp, 3 t, join with sl to corner of sp in upright row. *13th row*—Sl to corner of upright row, 21 sp, 10 t. *14th row*—Ch 5, 10 t, 21 sp, 4 t, 1 sp, join with sl to 4th t in upright row. *15th row*—Sl to corner of upright row, 6 t, 1 sp, 4 t, 19 sp, 10 t. *16th row*—

Ch 5, 10 t, 20 sp, 4 t, 3 sp, 3 t, join with sl to corner of sp in upright row. *17th row*—Sl to corner of upright row, 25 sp, 10 t. *18th row*—Ch 5, 13 t, 24 sp, 6 t, join with sl to 4th t in upright row. *19th row*—Sl to corner of upright row, 6 t, 16 sp, 10 t, 4 sp, 13 t, miss 3 t. *20th row*—Ch 4, miss 3 t, 1 t in next, 12 more t, 2 sp, 4 t, 3 sp, 4 t, 12 sp, 4 t, 1 sp, 4 t, 3 sp, 3 t, join with sl to corner of sp in upright row. *21st row*—Sl to corner of upright row, 5 sp, 4 t, 13 sp, 4 t, 1 sp, 7 t, 3 sp, 10 t, miss 3 t. *22d row*—Ch 4, miss 3 t, 1 t in next, 9 more t, 5 sp, 4 t, 7 sp, 16 t, 2 sp, 4 t, 4 sp, 4 t, 1 sp, join with sl to 4th t of upright row. *23d row*—Sl to corner of upright row, 6 t, 6 sp, 25 t, 6 sp, 22 t, miss 3 t. *24th row*—Ch 4, miss 3 t, 1 t in next, 15 more t, 6 sp, 13 t, 5 sp, 4 t, 6 sp, 4 t, 1 sp, 3 t, join with sl to corner of sp in upright row. *25th row*—Sl to corner of upright row, 3 sp, 4 t, 5 sp, 4 t, 1 sp, 7 t, 4 sp, 13 t, 5 sp, 10 t. *26th row*—Increase—Ch 10, 1 t in 8th st from hook, 15 more t, 4 sp, 10 t, 4 sp, 4 t, 3 sp, 4 t, 5 sp, 4 t, 4 sp, 3 t, join with sl to 4th t of upright row. *27th row*—Sl to corner of upright row, 3 t, 4 sp, 4 t, 2 sp, 4 t, 3

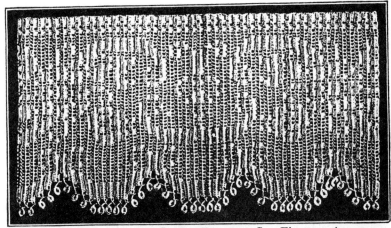

FIG. 3. TO REVERSE THE SCROLL DESIGN. See Fig. 2 and page 7

sp, 10 t, 5 sp, 13 t, 2 sp, 22 t. *28th row*—Increase—Ch 10, 1 t in 8th st from hook, 9 more t, 5 sp, 4 t, 1 sp, 10 t, 11 sp, 4 t, 3 sp, 4 t, 4 sp, 4 t, 1 sp, join with 1 t to corner of sp in upright row. *29th row*—Ch 2, join with 1 t to corner of upright row, 7 sp, 4 t, 2 sp, 4 t, 11 sp, 10 t, 1 sp, 4 t, 1 sp, 7 t, 3 sp, 10 t. *30th row*—Increase—Ch 10, 1 t in 8th st from hook, 12 more t, 2 sp, 4 t, 3 sp, 4 t, 1 sp, 10 t, 2 sp, 7 t, 4 sp, 4 t, 3 sp, 7 t, 5 sp, 4 t, 2 sp, 4 t, 1 sp, join with 1 t to corner of sp in upright row. *31st row*—Ch 2, join with 1 t to corner of upright row, 2 sp, 7 t, 10 sp, 4 t, 4 sp, 7 t, 3 sp, 10 t, 2 sp, 10 t, 4 sp, 13 t. *32d row*—Increase—Ch 8, 1 t in 6th st from hook, 12 more t, 10 sp, 10 t, 3 sp, 10 t, 2 sp, 7 t, 9 sp, 4 t, 2 sp, 4 t, 3 sp, join with 1 t to corner of sp in upright row. *33d row*—Ch 2, join with 1 t to corner of upright row, 2 sp, 4 t, 1 sp, 7 t, 1 sp, 7 t, 7 sp, 10 t, 1 sp, 13 t, 2 sp, 10 t, 11 sp, 10 t. *34th row*—Ch 5, 10 t, 11 sp, 10 t, 2 sp, 25 t, 7 sp, 22 t, 4 sp, 3 t, join with sl to corner of sp in upright row. *35th row*—Sl to corner of upright row, 1 sp, 4 t, 3 sp, 22 t, 8 sp, 13 t, 1 sp, 4 t, 3 sp, 10 t, 11 sp, 10 t. *36th row*—Ch 5, 10 t, 11 sp, 10 t, 2 sp, 4 t, 1 sp, 4 t, 7 sp, 7 t, 2 sp, 7 t, 1 sp, 4 t, 2 sp, 10 t, 3 sp, 4 t, 1 sp, 3 t, join with sl to corner of sp in upright row. *37th*

5

row—Sl to corner of upright row which is the 45th row of the pattern of the "Border before the Corner," 1 sp, 4 t, 4 sp, 7 t, 1 sp, 13 t, 1 sp, 4 t, 1 sp, 4 t, 2 sp, 4 t, 4 sp, 16 t, 2 sp, 10 t, 11 sp, 10 t. This completes the directions for the Corner.

FOR BORDER AFTER THE CORNER. — *1st row*—Ch 5, 10 t, 12 sp, 7 t, 1 sp, 4 t, 2 sp, 13 t, 2 sp, 4 t, 3 sp, 4 t, 1 sp, 4 t, 1 sp, 4 t, 2 sp, 4 t, 1 sp, 7 t, 3 sp, 4 t, 1 sp, 7 t. *2d row*—10 t, 1 sp, 4 t, 2 sp, 7 t, 1 sp, 4 t, 2 sp, 4 t, 2 sp, 4 t, 2 sp, 4 t, 2 sp, 13 t, 3 sp, 10 t, 12 sp, 10 t. *3d row*—Ch 5, 10 t, 12 sp, 13 t, 3 sp, 10 t, 2 sp, 4 t, 5 sp, 25 t, 4 sp, 4 t, 1 sp, 7 t. *4th row*—4 t, 1 sp, 4 t, 6 sp, 19 t, 6 sp, 4 t, 2 sp, 4 t, 3 sp, 16 t, 13 sp, 10 t. *5th row*—Ch 5, 13 t, 12 sp, 19 t, 1 sp, 4 t, 4 sp, 4 t, 2 sp, 4 t, 3 sp, 10 t, 7 sp, 4 t, 1 sp, 7 t. *6th row* —10 t, 1 sp, 4 t, 8 sp, 7 t, 1 sp, 4 t, 2 sp, 10 t, 5 sp, 4 t, 2 sp, 7 t, 5 sp, 10 t, 4 sp, 13 t, miss 3 t. *7th row*—Ch 4, miss 3 t, 1 t in next, 12 more t, 2 sp, 4 t, 3 sp, 4 t, 5 sp, 10 t, 2 sp, 10 t, 1 sp, 4 t, 1 sp, 4 t, 2 sp, 7 t, 11 sp, 4 t, 1 sp, 7 t. *8th row*—4 t, 1 sp, 4 t, 11 sp, 10 t, 2 sp, 10 t, 1 sp, 4 t, 1 sp, 4 t, 1 sp, 10 t, 6 sp, 4 t, 1 sp, 7 t, 3 sp, 10 t, miss 3 t. *9th row*—Ch 4, miss 3 t, 1 t in next, 9 more t, 5 sp, 4 t, 3 sp, 7 t, 2 sp, 7 t, 1 sp, 10 t, 2 sp, 4 t, 2 sp, 4 t, 3 sp, 4 t, 9 sp, 4 t, 1 sp, 7 t. *10th row*— 10 t, 1 sp, 4 t, 13 sp, 4 t, 3 sp, 4 t, 4 sp, 4 t, 2 sp, 4 t, 2 sp, 4 t, 3 sp, 22 t, miss 3 t. *11th row*— Ch 4, miss 3 t, 1 t in next, 15 more t, 4 sp, 4 t, 6 sp, 10 t, 2 sp, 10 t, 2 sp, 10 t, 1 sp, 13 t, 5 sp, 4 t, 1 sp, 7 t. *12th row*—4 t, 1 sp, 4 t, 5 sp, 4 t, 4 sp, 7 t, 1 sp, 7 t, 1 sp, 10 t, 1 sp, 7 t, 1 sp, 7 t, 4 sp, 4 t, 6 sp, 10 t, miss 3 t. *13th row*—Increase—Ch 10, 1 t in 8th st from hook, 15 more t, 6 sp, 13 t, 1 sp, 10 t, 2 sp, 10 t, 2 sp, 10 t, 6 sp, 4 t, 3 sp, 4 t, 1 sp, 7 t. *14th row* — 10 t, 1 sp, 4 t, 2 sp, 4 t, 2 sp, 4 t, 2 sp, 4 t, 4 sp, 4 t, 3 sp, 4 t, 14 sp, 22 t. *15th row* — Increase —Ch 10, 1 t in 8th st from hook, 9 more t, 5 sp, 4 t, 8 sp, 4 t, 3 sp, 4 t, 2 sp, 4 t, 2 sp,

10 t, 1 sp, 7 t, 2 sp, 7 t, 4 sp, 4 t, 1 sp, 7 t. *16th row* —4 t, 1 sp, 4 t, 8 sp, 10 t, 1 sp, 4 t, 1 sp, 4 t, 1 sp, 10 t, 2 sp, 10 t, 9 sp, 4 t, 1 sp, 7 t, 3 sp, 10 t. *17th row* —Increase—Ch 10, 1 t in 8th st from hook, 12 more t, 2 sp, 4 t, 3 sp, 4 t, 10 sp, 7 t, 2 sp, 4 t, 1 sp, 4 t, 1 sp, 10 t, 2 sp, 10 t, 6 sp, 4 t, 1 sp, 7 t. *18th row* — 10 t, 1 sp, 4 t, 4 sp, 7 t, 2 sp, 4 t, 5 sp, 10 t, 2 sp, 4 t, 1 sp, 7 t, 9 sp, 10 t, 4 sp, 13 t. *19th row*—In-crease—Ch 8, 1 t in 6th st from needle, 12 more t, 15 sp, 10 t, 3 sp, 4 t, 2 sp, 4 t, 4 sp, 4 t, 1 sp, 19 t, 4 sp, 4 t, 1 sp, 7 t. *20th row*—4 t, 1 sp, 4 t, 5 sp, 16 t, 3 sp, 4 t, 2 sp, 4 t, 6 sp, 19 t, 14 sp, 10 t. *21st row* —Ch 5, 10 t, 13 sp, 25 t, 5 sp, 4 t, 2 sp, 10 t, 3 sp, 13 t, 3 sp, 4 t, 1 sp, 7 t. *22d row*—10 t, 1 sp, 4 t, 2 sp, 10 t, 3 sp, 13 t, 2 sp, 4 t, 2 sp, 4 t, 2 sp, 4 t, 1 sp, 4 t, 2 sp, 4 t, 1 sp, 7 t, 12 sp, 10 t. *23d row*—Ch 5, 10 t, 12 sp, 7 t, 1 sp, 4 t, 2 sp, 4 t, 1 sp, 4 t, 1 sp, 4 t, 3 sp, 4 t, 2 sp, 13 t, 2 sp, 4 t, 1 sp, 7 t, 3 sp, 4 t, 1 sp, 7 t. *24th row*—4 t, 1 sp, 4 t, 3 sp, 10 t, 2 sp, 16 t, 4 sp, 4 t, 2 sp, 4 t, 1 sp, 4 t, 1 sp, 13 t, 1 sp, 7 t, 12 sp, 10 t. *25th row*—Ch 5, 10 t, 12 sp, 10 t, 2 sp, 4 t, 1 sp, 7 t, 2 sp, 7 t, 7 sp, 4 t, 1 sp, 4 t, 2 sp, 10 t, 2 sp, 4 t, 1 sp, 7 t. *26th row*—10 t, 1 sp, 4 t, 1 sp, 10 t, 3 sp, 4 t, 1 sp, 13 t, 8 sp, 22 t, 13 sp, 10 t. *27th row*—Ch 5, 10 t, 13 sp, 22 t, 7 sp, 25 t, 2 sp, 10 t, 2 sp, 4 t, 1 sp, 7 t. *28th row*—4 t, 1 sp, 4 t, 3 sp, 10 t, 2 sp, 13 t, 1 sp, 10 t, 7 sp, 7 t, 1 sp, 7 t, 1 sp, 4 t, 13 sp, 10 t. *29th row*—Ch 5, 13 t, 13 sp, 4 t, 2 sp, 4 t, 9 sp, 7 t, 2 sp, 10 t, 3 sp, 10 t, 2 sp, 4 t, 1 sp, 7 t. *30th row*— 10 t, 1 sp, 4 t, 1 sp, 10 t, 3 sp, 7 t, 4 sp, 4 t, 10 sp, 7 t, 6 sp, 10 t, 4 sp, 13 t, miss 3 t. *31st row*—Ch 4, miss 3 t, 1 t in next, 12 more t, 2 sp, 4 t, 3 sp, 4 t, 4 sp, 4 t, 2 sp, 4 t, 10 sp, 4 t, 4 sp, 7 t, 2 sp, 10 t, 2 sp, 4 t, 1 sp, 7 t. *32d row*—4 t, 1 sp, 4 t, 3 sp, 10 t, 27 sp, 4 t, 1 sp, 7 t, 3 sp, 10 t, miss 3. *33d row*— Ch 4, miss 3 t, 1 t in next, 9 more t, 5 sp, 4 t, 7 sp, 16 t, 15 sp, 10 t, 2 sp, 4 t, 1 sp, 7 t. *34th row*— 10 t, 1 sp, 4 t, 1 sp, 13 t, 5 sp, 10 t, 5 sp, 25 t, 6 sp, 22 t, miss 3 t. *35th row*—Ch 4, miss 3 t, 1 t in next, 15 more t, 6 sp, 13 t, 5 sp, 4 t, 3 sp, 4 t, 3 sp, 4 t, 4 sp, 10 t, 3 sp, 4 t, 1 sp, 7 t. *36th row*—4 t, 1 sp, 4 t, 4 sp, 13 t, 4 sp, 7 t, 1 sp, 4 t, 3 sp, 4 t, 1 sp, 7 t, 4 sp, 13 t, 5 sp, 10 t, miss 3 t. *37th row*—Increase—Ch 10, 1 t in 8th st from hook, 15 more t, 4 sp, 10 t, 4 sp, 4 t, 3 sp, 4 t, 3 sp, 4 t, 5 sp, 13 t, 5 sp, 4 t, 1 sp, 7 t. *38th row*—10 t, 1 sp, 4 t, 5 sp, 25 t, 5 sp, 10 t, 5 sp, 13 t, 2 sp, 22 t. *39th row*—Increase—Ch 10, 1 t in 8th st from hook, 9 more t, 5 sp, 4 t, 1 sp, 10 t, 15 sp, 16 t, 8 sp, 4 t, 1 sp, 7 t. *40th row* — 4 t

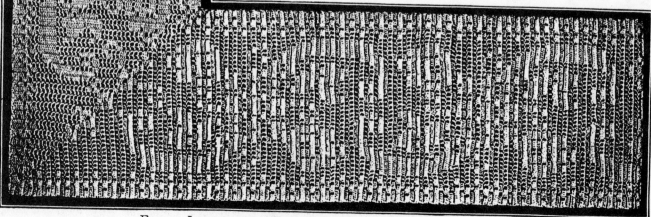

FIG. 4. INSERTION FOR TEA CLOTH, SCROLL DESIGN. See page 7

I sp, 4 t, 29 sp, 10 t, I sp, 4 t, I sp, 7 t, 3 sp, 10 t. *41st row*—Increase—Ch 10, I t in 8th st from hook, 12 more t, 2 sp, 4 t, 3 sp, 4 t, I sp, 10 t, 2 sp, 7 t, 4 sp, 4 t, 10 sp, 4 t, 2 sp, 4 t, 5 sp, 4 t, I sp, 7 t. *42d row*—10 t, I sp, 4 t, 5 sp, 7 t, 10 sp, 4 t, 4 sp, 7 t, 3 sp, 10 t, 2 sp, 10 t, 4 sp, 13 t. *43d row*—Increase—Ch 8, I t in 6th st from hook, 12 more t, 10 sp, 10 t, 3 sp, 10 t, 2 sp, 7 t, 9 sp, 4 t, 2 sp, 4 t, 5 sp, 4 t, I sp, 7 t. *44th row*—4 t, I sp, 4 t, 5 sp, 4 t, I sp, 7 t, I sp, 7 t, 7 sp, 10 t, I sp, 13 t, 2 sp, 10 t, 11 sp, 10 t. *45th row*—Ch 5, 10 t, 11 sp, 10 t, 2 sp, 25 t, 7 sp, 22 t, 4 sp, 4 t, I sp, 7 t. *46th row*—10 t, I sp, 4 t, 3 sp, 22 t, 8 sp, 13 t, I sp, 4 t, 3 sp, 10 t, 11 sp, 10 t. *47th row*—Ch 5, 10 t, 11 sp, 10 t, 2 sp, 4 t, I sp, 4 t, 7 sp, 7 t, 2 sp, 7 t, I sp, 4 t, 2 sp, 10 t, 3 sp, 4 t, I sp, 7 t. *48th row*—4 t, I sp, 4 t, 4 sp, 7 t, I sp, 13 t, I sp, 4 t, I sp, 4 t, 2 sp, 4 t, 4 sp, 16 t, 2 sp, 10 t, 11 sp, 10 t. This completes the pattern; for repetition commence again at first row of "Border after the Corner."

EDGE AROUND THE SCALLOPS.—Join thread to first loop on edge of scallop, ch 13, sl back in 5th st from work, forming a ring, over ring make 16 d, join with sl to first d on ring, ch 4, join to next loop on edge, repeat twice, making 3 rings on side of scallop, ch 3, join to first loop on opposite side of scallop. Repeat rings around Border, making 3 rings on each side and 5 rings on lower edge of scallops.

Figure 3. TO REVERSE THE PATTERN OF THE SCROLL BORDER. — The "Reverse" should come half way between corners. Make 40 rows of the "Border after the Corner" when the pattern of the "Reverse" will commence. *1st row*—Increase—Ch 10, I t in 8th st from hook, 12 more t, 2 sp, 4 t, 3 sp, 4 t, I sp, 10 t, 21 sp, 10 t, 4 sp, 4 t, I sp, 7 t. *2d row*—10 t, I sp, 4 t, 2 sp, 4 t, 3 sp, 4 t, 7 sp, 7 t, 11 sp, 10 t, 2 sp, 10 t, 4 sp, 13 t. *3d row*—Increase—Ch 8, I t in 6th st from hook, 12 more t, 10 sp, 10 t, 10 sp, 4 t, 2 sp, 4 t, 7 sp, 7 t, I sp, 4 t, 3 sp, 4 t, I sp, 7 t. *4th row*—4 t, I sp, 4 t, 4 sp, 4 t, 9 sp, 4 t, 2 sp, 4 t, 11 sp, 10 t, 11 sp, 10 t. *5th row*—Ch 5, 10 t, 11 sp, 10 t, 8 sp, 4 t, 5 sp, 4 t, 8 sp, 4 t, 4 sp, 4 t, I sp, 7 t. *6th row*—10 t, I sp, 4 t, 4 sp, 16 t, 3 sp, 4 t, 4 sp, 4 t, 3 sp, 4 t, 5 sp, 10 t, 11 sp, 10 t. *7th row*—Ch 5, 10 t, 12 sp, 10 t, 3 sp, 4 t, 3 sp, 10 t, 2 sp, 4 t, 2 sp, 19 t, 6 sp, 4 t, I sp, 7 t. *8th row*—4 t, I sp, 4 t, 8 sp, 34 t, I sp, 19 t, I sp, 10 t, 13 sp, 10 t. *9th row*—Ch 5, 10 t, 12 sp, 10 t, 3 sp, 4 t, 3 sp, 10 t, 2 sp, 4 t, 2 sp, 19 t, 6 sp, 4 t, I sp, 7 t. *10th row*—10 t, I sp, 4 t, 4 sp, 16 t, 3 sp, 4 t, 4 sp, 4 t, 3 sp, 4 t, 5 sp, 10 t, 11 sp, 10 t. *11th row*—Ch 5, 10 t, 11 sp, 10 t, 8 sp, 4 t, 5 sp, 4 t, 8 sp, 4 t, 4 sp, 4 t, I sp, 7 t. *12th row*—4 t, I sp, 4 t, 4 sp, 4 t, 9 sp, 4 t, 2 sp, 4 t, 11 sp, 10 t, 11 sp, 10 t. *13th row*—Ch 5, 13 t, 10 sp, 10 t, 10 sp, 4 t, 2 sp, 4 t, 7 sp, 7 t, I sp, 4 t, 3 sp, 4 t, I sp, 7 t. *14th row*—10 t, I sp, 4 t, 2 sp, 4 t, 3 sp, 4 t, 7 sp, 7 t, 11 sp, 10 t, 2 sp, 10 t, 4 sp, 13 t, miss 3 t. *15th row*—Ch 4, miss 3 t, I t in next, 12 more t, 2 sp, 4 t, 3 sp, 4 t, I sp, 10 t, 21 sp, 10 t, 4 sp, 4 t, I sp, 7 t. For continuation, commence at 5th row of "Border before the Corner," which is as follows: 4 t, I sp, 4 t, 29 sp, 10 t, etc.

Figure 4. Insertion to Match Border. — This is made like the Border, Fig. 2, except at the outer edge. And the directions for the Border may be followed, from the inner edge out, until the scroll of the design has been worked; then make 3 sp, 4 t, I sp, 4 t. Always reverse the pattern of the inner edge at the outer edge.

The insertion requires a ch of 121 beside the 3 to turn as I t. *1st row*—4 t, I sp, 4 t, 5 sp, 4 t, I sp, 7 t, I sp, 7 t, 7 sp, 10 t, I sp, 13 t, 2 sp, 10 t, 3 sp, 4 t, I sp, 4 t. *2d row*—7 t, I sp, 4 t, 2 sp, 10 t, 3 sp, 10 t, 2 sp, 7 t, 9 sp, 4 t, 2 sp, 4 t, 5 sp, 4 t, I sp, 7 t.

The foregoing illustrations, Figs. 2 and 4, of Border and Insertion for Tea Cloth are of remarkable pieces of work in the line of filet crochet. They differ from that work as it is usually made, in one minor point; the stitch is taken under the back loop, only, of stitch below, whereas the custom of taking the stitch under two threads is more generally followed. In the present instance it gives a very handsome ribbed effect, and as the work is exquisitely done, it adds much to the beauty of the piece. That plan, however, is to be adopted with caution and only by skilful workers; in the hands of the amateur it tends to draw the work out (in the length of the trebles) and it complicates very much the problem of making the

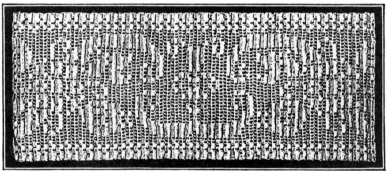

FIG. 5. TO REVERSE SCROLL DESIGN OF INSERTION. See Fig. 4

filet crochet square, which is absolutely essential.

While a great number of workers have no difficulty in copying from a block pattern, yet there are other numbers who plead for detailed directions; and it is with the purpose of pleasing the latter that the directions for this lace are written out in full. Since this piece is included in a collection of crochet embracing many varieties, special emphasis has not been put upon principles underlying filet crochet; the directions have been given in the simplest method possible in terms common to all the popular forms of crochet.

The work of filet crochet is among the most popular forms of crocheting, yet it is capable of more abuses than most other varieties. Most writers give an approximate scale of meshes to an inch with the different numbers of cotton. Without any doubt the same number of rows to an inch are required if the work approaches being square. In a circular piece and in making a mitre at corners one comes to grief if anything other than square work is produced. Filet crochet is at its best when the work is firmly drawn, even and very fine. The pieces here described are about 10 meshes and 10 rows to an inch.

Figure 6. Butterfly Edging with Corner.
MATERIALS. — No. 50 crochet cotton and No. 12 hook. The detail of work, Fig. 7, shows the corner as it should look when one-half is finished, ready for the rows of the next half to be joined.

While this is a good example of Filet Crochet, yet the long space (long sp) is introduced in the wings of the butterfly. A space (sp) is (ch 2, miss 2, 1 t), a long sp is (ch 5, miss 5, 1 t).

The models, Fig. 6 and Fig. 8 of Insertion are made as models containing the design, but when making a repeated border, the first row of work (at A) should be exactly like the second row, and the last row of Fig. 6 should be like the preceding row; the detailed directions are given with this point in view.

Commencing at A, chain 89, turn. *1st row*—T in 5th st from hook, 5 t in next 5 sts, 3 sp, 7 t, 21 sp, 1 t, ch 3, turn. *2d row*—T over t, 21 sp, 7 t, 3 sp, 7 t, ch 9, turn. *3d row*—T in 5th st from hook, 5 t, 4 sp, 4 t, 2 sp, 4 t, 5 sp, 10 t, 5 sp, 7 t, 5 sp, 1 t, ch 3, turn. *4th row*—One t, 6 sp, 19 t, 1 long sp, 1 sp, 4 t, 3 sp, 4 t, 8 sp, 7 t, ch 9, turn. *5th row*—T in 5th st from hook, 5 t, 11 sp, 4 t, 1 sp, 4 t, 1 sp, 7 t, 3 long sp, 4 t, 6 sp, 1 t, ch 3, turn. *6th row*—One t, 2 sp, 4 t, 4 sp, 4 t, 2 long sp, 1 sp, 7 t, 1 sp,

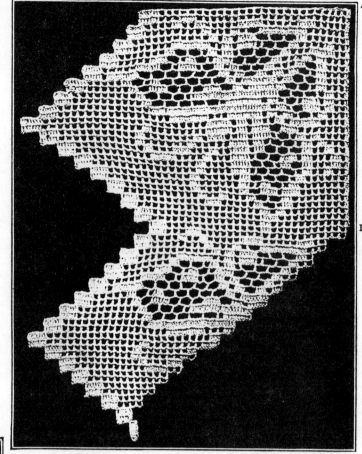

A FIG. 7. CORNER OF BUTTERFLY EDGING. See Fig. 6 and page 8

4 t, 2 sp, 16 t, 6 sp, 7 t, ch 9, turn. *7th row*—T in 5th st from hook, 5 t, 7 sp, 4 t, 2 long sp, 1 sp, 4 t, 1 sp, 4 t, 1 sp, 3 long sp, 4 t, 3 sp, 10 t, 2 sp, 1 t, ch 3, turn. *8th row*—One t, 3 sp, 4 t, 1 sp, 4 t, 3 sp, 4 t, 3 long sp, 7 t, 1 sp, 1 long sp, 4 t, 1 sp, 1 long sp, 7 t, 5 sp, 7 t, ch 9. *9th row*—T in 5th st from hook, 5 t, 5 sp, 10 t, 1 long sp, 1 sp, 7 t, 1 sp, 1 long sp,

FIG. 6. BUTTERFLY EDGING. See Fig. 7 and page 8

4 t, 1 sp, 4 t, 2 long sp, 4 t, 3 sp, 4 t, 1 long sp, 4 t, 3 sp, 1 t, ch 3. *10th row*—One t, 3 sp, 4 t, 1 sp, 1 long sp, 4 t, 1 sp, 4 t, 1 sp, 4 t, 1 long sp, 4 t, 1 sp, 4 t, 6 long sp, 13 t, 1 sp, 7 t, ch 9. *11th row* —T in 5th st from hook, 5 t, 5 sp, 4 t, 1 long sp, 1 sp, 4 t, 5 long sp, 4 t, 1 sp, 13 t, 1 sp, 4 t, 2 long sp, 4 t, 3 sp, 1 t, ch 3. *12th row*—One t, 3 sp, 4 t, 1 sp, 2 long sp, 13 t, 1 sp, 4 t, 1 long sp, 7 t, 3 long sp, 7 t, 1 long sp, 4 t, 6 sp, 7 t, ch 9. *13th row* —T in 5th st from needle, 5 t, 9 sp, 4 t, 3 long sp, 1 sp, 34 t, 3 long sp, 1 sp, 4 t, 2 sp, 1 t, ch 3. *14th row*—One t, 2 sp, 4 t, 1 sp, 7 t, 1 sp, 1 long sp, 1 sp, 4 t, 1 sp, 13 t, 1 sp, 5 long sp, 4 t, 10 sp, 7 t, ch 9. *15th row*—T in 5th st from hook, 5 t, 13 sp, 49 t, 1 sp, 4 t, 1 sp, 1 long sp, 7 t, 1 sp, 4 t, 2 sp, 1 t, ch 3. *16th row*—One t, 3 sp, 4 t, 1 sp, 1 long sp, 1 sp, 4 t, 1 sp, 4 t, 1 sp, 13 t, 3 sp, 16 t, 16 sp, 7 t, ch 9. *17th row*—T in 5th st from hook, 5 t, 24 sp, 7 t, 1 sp, 4 t, 1 sp, 4 t, 2 sp, 4 t, 1 sp, 13 t, 4 sp, 1 t, ch 3. *18th row*—One t, 7 sp, 7 t, 1 long sp, 7 t, 1 sp, 4 t, 1 sp, 10 t, 8 sp, 4 t, 14 sp, 7 t, ch 1. *19th row* — Sl over 7 t, ch 3, 6 t, 11 sp, 4 t, 7 sp, 4 t, 1 sp, 7 t, 2 sp, 4 t, 1 sp, 7 t, 1 sp, 1 long sp, 1 sp, 4 t, 1 sp, 4 t, 4 sp, 1 t, ch 3. *20th row*—One t, 3 sp, 4 t, 1 sp, 4 t, 1 sp, 2 long sp, 1 sp, 4 t, 1 sp, 7 t, 5 sp, 4 t, 6 sp, 4 t, 11 sp, 7 t, ch 1. *21st row*—Sl over 7 t, ch 3, 6 t, 10 sp, 4 t, 3 sp, 7 t, 3 sp, 4 t, 2 sp, 7 t, 1 sp, 4 t, 3 long sp, 4 t, 2 sp, 4 t, 2 sp, 1 t, ch 3. *22d row*— One t, 1 sp, 4 t, 3 sp, 4 t, 1 sp, 7 t, 2 long sp, 1 sp, 7 t, 3 sp, 4 t, 4 sp, 10 t, 11 sp, 7 t, ch 1. *23d row*— Sl over 7 t, ch 3, 6 t, 15 sp, 4 t, 4 sp, 7 t, 2 long sp, 1 sp, 4 t, 1 long sp, 4 t, 3 sp, 4 t, 1 sp, 1 t, ch 3. *24th row*—One t, 2 sp, 4 t, 2 sp, 4 t, 1 sp, 3 long sp, 1 sp, 7 t, 4 sp, 4 t, 15 sp, 7 t, ch 1. *25th row*— Sl over 7 t, ch 3, 6 t, 12 sp, 4 t, 6 sp, 4 t, 3 long sp, 1 sp, 4 t, 6 sp, 1 t, ch 3. *26th row*—One t, 7 sp, 4 t, 1 sp, 1 long sp, 4 t, 2 sp, 4 t, 6 sp, 4 t, 12 sp, 7 t, ch 1. *27th row*—Sl over 7 t, ch 3, 6 t, 10 sp, 4 t, 6 sp, 4 t, 1 long sp, 7 t, 1 sp, 7 t, 7 sp, 1 t, ch 3. *28th row*—One t, 8 sp, 4 t, 2 long sp, 4 t, 3 sp, 4 t, 2 sp, 4 t, 11 sp, 7 t, ch 1. *29th row*—Sl over 7 t, ch 3, 6 t, 10 sp, 7 t, 5 sp, 4 t, 1 long sp, 1 sp, 4 t, 8 sp, 1 t, ch 3. *30th row*—One t, 9 sp, 4 t, 1 sp, 4 t, 18 sp, 7 t, ch 1.

31st row—Sl over 7 t, ch 3, 6 t, 16 sp, 7 t, 10 sp, 1 t, ch 3. *32d row*— One t, 11 sp, 4 t, 16 sp, 7 t, ch 1. At the heading of the 32d row is the right angle of the mitred corner (B in Fig. 6); the next two rows (33d and 34th) are finished at the inside with but one treble (see B in Fig. 7), the rows that finish the last half of corner are crocheted across these two meshes. *33d row*—Sl over 7 t, ch 3, 6 t, 14 sp,

4 t, 11 sp, ch 5. *34th row*—21 sp, 7 t, 3 sp, 7 t, ch 9. *35th row*—Like 3d row, omitting last 3 sp, turn with ch 5. *36th row*—Follow the design of 4th row. *37th row*—Like 5th row, omitting last 2 sp. Follow the design to and including 50th row; turn with ch 3 when a solid block is in the diagonal, turn with ch 5 when a sp is in the diagonal. In the 51st row omit 1 sp and 7 t; omit 2 sp thereafter. *61st row*— Sl over 7 t, ch 3, 6 t, ch 3. *62d row*—6 t, ch 1. *63d row*—Sl over 7 t.

SECOND HALF OF CORNER. — Chain 9. *1st row*—T in 5th st from hook, 5 t, 1 sp, t into t on first half of corner. *2d row*—Ch 2, t into middle of 5 ch, turn, 1 sp, 7 t, ch 9. *3d row*—T in 5th st, 5 t, 5 sp, 1 t into first half. *4th row*—Ch 2, t into middle of 5 ch, turn, 5 sp and block of 7, ch 9. *5th row*—Block of 7, spaces, join as in 3d row. *6th row*—Like 4th row with added sp. *7th and 8th rows*—Like 5th and 6th rows, with added sp. In *9th row* begin working groups of treble for "Butterfly" following illustration. *10th and 11th rows*—Follow design; at end of 11th row, turn work half way around and make 4 t over 4 t, ch 2, turn. *12th and 13th rows*—Follow design, at the end of 13th row make 3 t over the t that lies below, sl into point, sl across this t and next t to inside corner of point, sl across next sp and in next t, turn. *14th row*—7 t over sl sts, follow design. *15th row*—Follow design, and at the end, 2 sp, ch 2 for another sp, sl in corner of next point and across t and to 3d st on next point (as in 13th row), turn. *16th row*—40 t, spaces, and block at the edge as before. *17th row*—Follow design, 7 t over last 7 t, sl across end of point and to 3d t of next point as before, turn. *18th row*—6 t over 6 sl sts, 22 t, follow design to edge. *19th row*—After last 4 t, sl across end of point, across sp

FIG. 9. CORNER OF BUTTERFLY INSERTION. See Fig. 8

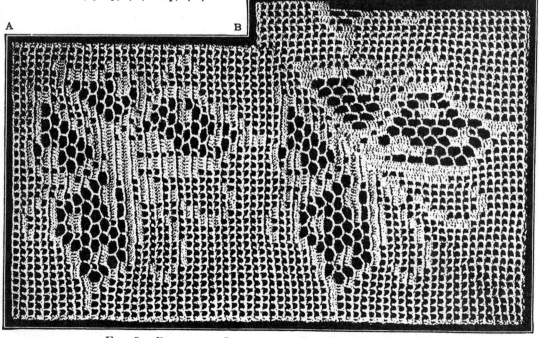

FIG. 8. BUTTERFLY INSERTION. See Fig. 9 and page 10

and in 1st t of next point, turn. *20th row*—Trebles over sl sts, over trebles and over next sp, follow design. *21st row*—After last 4 t of design, miss last 2 t of last row, ch 2, sl in next 3 sts only, which brings thread half way on side of point, ch 2, t on t between 2 sp of next point, ch 2, turn. *22d row*—4 t over sp, follow design and turn. *23d row*—After last 4 t, ch 2, sl in point and across sp, ch 2, t on t between 2 sp of next point, ch 2, turn. *24th row*—4 t over sp, finish as before, turn. *25th row*—At the end join and turn as in 23d row. *26th row*—Follow design, turn. *27th row*—At the end after 19 t, 1 sp, ch 2, sl across next sp, ch 2, t between sps of next point, ch 2, turn. *28th row*—Follow design, turn. *29th row*—At the end after the t over last t of 28th row, t on t between next 2 sp of next point, ch 2, t in 3d of 5-ch at point, ch 2, turn. *30th row*—Follow design to edge. This row finishes the corner, notice the block of 4 t that commences the wing of the next butterfly. *31st row*—Make the last 2 sp across the ends of 33d and 34th rows of first half of corner, and make 2 t at the heading just after the corner. The 30th row is the first of 32 rows required for the next butterfly and pointed scallop, and corresponds with the

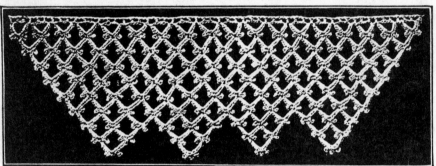

FIG. 10. EDGING. See page 10

33d row of directions for first butterfly; and the order of rows must be reversed from that to the second row.

For the last butterfly, commence with 2d row of directions and follow as for the first butterfly. The butterflies are turned toward the corners from the middle of each side; and if a longer border is made the number turned in each direction must be determined by the length of the border.

Figure 8. Butterfly Insertion.—The corner of Insertion is turned as in the edging, with a slight difference at the outer edge, which is shown at Fig. 9. This shows the outer point as it should be when ready for the second half of the corner. After it is worked as far as shown in the detail, ch 2, d in t between the 2 sp, ch 2, d at corner of 2d sp, ch 3, t at corner of same sp, * ch 2, t between next 2 sp; repeat from * twice more, t on t between next 2 sp, ch 2, t in next point, ch 2, turn. Work back to the edge with spaces, making 2 t at edge, ch 3, turn and work back and forth as in edging.

Figure 10. Edging.—No. 70 crochet cotton and No. 12 hook.

Chain 13, join with sl to form a ring. In this ring make 5 d, picot of 4 joined by d through 2 upper loops of last d, 1 d, ch 4 (not joining for p), 1 d, picot, 5 d. * Chain 13, sl through top loop of first st, 5 d, p,

1 d, leaving remainder of ring unfinished *. **Chain 9, take hook out of work, insert through ch between picots on preceding ring, catch 9th st and draw through, 5 d, p, 1 d, ch 4, 1 d, p, 5 d **, (ch 2, in unfinished ring make 1 d, p, 5 d). Repeat from * to *. *** Chain 9, take hook out of work and draw 9th ch st through 2-ch between picots in preceding ring, 5 d, p, 1 d ***. Repeat from ** to **, then repeat directions in parenthesis in each of the next unfinished rings. Repeat from * to *, then from *** to *** twice, from ** to **, then directions in parenthesis 3 times. Repeat the directions beginning with "from * to *" in the order in which they are given until there is a triangle of 9 rings. The 9th ring, which forms the point of the triangle, is finished with 3 picots. The only rings having 4-ch between picots are the outside rings.

The next row will have but 7 rings, the next 8, the next 9, and repeat to the required length; do not break thread, but work along the top for heading. There should be 5 ch sts showing at the top of each ring. HEADING.—Chain 5, t in first ch st, * ch 1, miss 1, t in next st, ch 1, t between rings *; repeat from * to * the whole length.

Figure 11. Edging.—No. 50 crochet cotton and No. 12 hook.

CENTRE MOTIF.—Make a chain of 8 sts, 1 dt in the first st made, * in the same st make (ch 3, 1 long t, over 3 times, ch 3, 1 long t, over 4 times, ch 5, 1 long t, over 4 times, ch 3, 1 long t, over 3 times, ch 3, 1 dt, ch 7, 1 d), * (ch 15, 1 d t in 8th st from hook; repeat from * to *) twice, ch 7, join with sl in first st of first leaf. *1st round*—In the first space of leaf make * (5 d, picot of 5 joined by d through two upper loops of last d, 3 d); in each of next two sp make (2 d, p, 2 d); in centre sp make (4 d, p, 4 d); in each of next two make (2 d, p, 2 d); in last sp make (3 d, p, 5 d); 6 d in sp at base of leaf *; repeat from * to * in each leaf, connecting with previous leaf after the 5th d in first sp of leaf as follows: Ch 1, take hook out of work, insert down through opposite p on preceding leaf, catch dropped st and draw through, ch 2, and finish p with 1 d through 2 upper loops of last d. The joining of the third leaf to the first leaf must be done in the same way at the last p on third leaf. After making the 6th d over last base line sl in first st of first leaf, break thread. *2d row*—Ch 7, take hook out of work, insert down through centre p of a leaf, draw st through, ch 6, sl in 1st st of 7 ch, * ch 1, working to the left make 1 sl in each of next 6 sts to p, taking 1 loop of st only, draw 6th st through p, sl in each of next 6 sts, sl through top st, ch 18, (do not twist ch), draw 18th st through next p to the left, ch 6, sl in 7th st from p *; repeat from * to * around at each p, except 1 p before and after the joined p; after working the last loop, ch 11, join with sl in centre of first loop. *3d row*—One d in each st around, using top loop only, making 2 sts in each corner st over the centre of the loops. There should be 44 or 45 sts on each side. *4th round*—Turn work wrong side up, 1 d in each st around (taking back loop), 2 d in each corner, join last st to first one with sl. *5th round*—Turn work right side up, make 3 d in each corner, 1 d in each st around, taking back loop only, join with sl. *6th round*—Sl to centre corner st, ch 7, d in same st, ch 4, miss 2 d, 1 d in next st (back loop only), ch 4, miss 3 d, * (t, ch 4, t) in next st, (this is a shell or sh), ch 4, miss 3, d in next, ch 4, miss 3 *, repeat from * to * around two sides of the triangle; after making the sh in the corner st, work the top row as follows: ch 4, miss 2, 1 d in next, ch 4, miss 3, 1 sh in next, (ch 2, miss 3, sh in next) 8 times, ch 4, miss 3, 1 d in next st, ch 4, sl in third st of 7 ch, break thread and fasten.

There should be about 48 sts from point to point in the last row of d on triangle; if there are more or less, arrange before reaching the corner so that there will be but 2 sts between the last d and the st at each corner where the sh is placed.

Make a row of these scallops or triangles as long as required, joining each one as it is made to the preceding one at the corner shell and the shell below the corner, in working the second side, as follows: After making the first t of the shell before the corner one, ch 2, take hook out of work, insert in corresponding sh at the left side of preceding scallop, draw st through, ch 3, and finish sh, ch 4, miss 3, d in next, ch 4, miss 2, t in next, ch 2, and join to corner sh opposite like the other, then finish top row of scallop.

HEADING. — Fasten thread with 1 d in first 4 ch beyond corner sh, ch 5, 1 long t (3 loops) in next 4 ch, * (ch 11, miss 1 sh, d in next) 4 times, ch 11, 1 long t in first 4 ch after sh, retaining last 2 loops on hook, thread over 3 times, insert hook in next 4 ch, working off all loops by twos, ch 5, 2 long t in next two 4 ch, like last 2 in first scallop; repeat from * to end of edge and break thread.

2d row—Beginning again at right end, make 1 t in top of 2 long t, * (ch 2, miss 2, 1 t in next st) 3 times, ch 2, t in next d *; repeat from * to * across top of scallop to long t, ch 2, 1 t in 3d st of 5 ch, ch 2, t in long t; repeat to end of edging.

EDGE.—Fasten thread on the last scallop in the second d below the corner, ch 7, 1 d in next sh, * (ch 4, shell in next d, ch 4, d in next sh) 8 times, ch 4, t in next d, working off 2 loops, retaining 2 on hook, thread over, insert in opposite d and work off all loops by twos (a cross treble), ch 4, 1 d in next sh *; repeat from * to *. *2d row*—Begin again at right-hand end with 1 d in first d in scallop after 7 ch beginning last row, ch 7, 1 d in next sh, * (ch 4, sh in next d, ch 4, d in next sh) 7 times, ch 4, cross treble, one-half in next d, the

other half in opposite d, ch 4, 1 d in next sh; repeat from * to end. *3d row*—One d in first d after 7 ch at beginning of last row, ch 3, ** 2 dt in next sh, * ch 5, put hook through 2 loops of last dt, draw a loop through to make a p, but do not finish it, keep the 2 loops on the hook, thread over twice and make a dt, working off 2 loops twice and the last 3 all together, make another dt like first one; repeat from * to * twice, then make one more dt like first one, (there should be 3 p and 9 dt), ch 4, d in next d, ch 4, **; repeat from ** to ** the whole length.

Figure 12. Acorn Edging. — No. 50 crochet cotton and No. 12 hook.

CUP. — Chain 20, turn. *1st row*—One d in 7th st from hook, (ch 4, miss 2, d in next st) 4 times, turn. *2d row*—Ch 5, d in first sp, (ch 4, d in next sp) 3 times, ch 2, t in last sp, turn. *3d row*—Ch 4, d in second sp, (ch 4, d in next sp) twice, ch 2, t in last sp, turn. *4th row*—Ch 4, d in second sp, (ch 4, d in next sp) twice. Break thread, leaving an end about an inch long. Make another cup, but do not break the thread at end of 4th row; ch 1,

FIG. 11. EDGING. See page 10

turn, 4 d in first sp. ACORN.—* Ch 9, turn. *1st row*—One d in second st from hook, 7 d in next 7 sts to cup, d in centre sp, turn. *2d row*—Miss 1 d, 7 d in 7 d (taking both loops), 2 d in end st, sl in next st, ch 1, turn. *3d row*—Miss sl, 9 d in 9 d, d in centre sp, ch 1, turn. *4th row*—9 d in 9 d, working over last row of sts by inserting hook in the same sts where they were placed, 2 d in end st, d in next st; without turning, work down side to cup with 7 d in 7 d, sl in each of next 2 d in next sp, turn. *5th row*—7 t in 7 d, 1 h t in next d, 3 d in next 3 d across top of acorn, 1 ht in next d, 7 t in 7 d to cup, 3 d in each of next 3 sps, 4 d in next, (working over the end of thread), 3 d in next, 1 d in centre sp, * ch 12 for stem, 1 d in second st from hook, 2 d in next 2 sts, ** ch 7, take first cup made and holding the lower side up, with the piece of thread left at beginning at the right, make 2 d in centre sp, 3 d in next, 4 d in next, 3 d in each of next 2 sps, 4 d in next, which is the first sp of top row of cup; repeat from * to *, d in each of 7 sts of stem to the junction of first stem, sl across into first stem, d in each st to cup, 2 d in centre sp, 3 d in next, 2 d in next, now join to second cup by taking hook out of work, insert in third st of second sp from centre sp, draw dropped st through, 2 d in same sp, 3 d in each of next 2 sp, sl in next d.

11

Break thread, leaving an end long enough to fasten off securely on the back of cup with a needle. Repeat directions from beginning for each two cups and acorns, with this exception,—Ch 23 for stem (instead of 12, which was for the first or end stem only), and make 1 d in second st from hook, d in each of next 13 sts, then repeat from ** to end, joining the end of the long stem to the centre of the cups of the preceding 2 acorns where they are joined together. It is easier to join them with a needle and thread at the back of the work than to try to join them in making. Make a row of acorns as long as required, and at the end make a short stem of 12 ch and join in the centre of cups.

FILLING. *1st row*—Begin at right hand, holding work right side up, the acorns pointing toward the left, ch 25, picot of 4 (joined with d), ch 3, d in 15th st from p, make a picot loop (p 1) as follows,— (ch 2, picot, ch 4, picot, ch 3), d in 9th st from last d, a half p loop as follows,—* (ch 2, p, ch 3), then pick up the work and make 1 d in the end st of short stem, half p loop, d in 5th d from stem on cup, turn, half p loop, d in centre of next p loop, 1 p loop, d in third st beyond p in end loop, turn; ch 10, p, ch 3, d in centre of first loop, half p loop, d in last d in third sp from centre, turn; p loop, d in third st beyond p in end loop, turn, ch 10, p, ch 3, d between 6th and 7th t from bottom of acorn, turn; 1 p loop, d in third st beyond p in end loop, turn; ch 10, p, ch 3, d in centre of next loop, 1 p loop, d between 6th and 7th t from bottom of acorn on opposite side *; repeat from * to *, placing the first half p loop in repeating, in the third st of long stem below the junction. At end of row, place the half p loop in the last d on short stem.

HEADING.—Fasten thread in

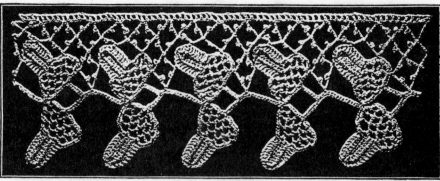

FIG. 12. ACORN EDGING. See page 11

centre st of first loop at the right, ch 4, miss 1, t in next st, * ch 1, miss 1, t in next st; repeat to end.

Figure 13. Acorn Insertion. — No. 50 crochet cotton and No. 12 hook. Repeat entire directions for Acorn Edging, Figure 12, making a double row of acorns the length required. Repeat directions for "Filling" on both sides of insertion, working first a side having the acorns pointing to the left. On the second side, turn the work wrong side up when working the "Filling," then turn work right side up and work the "Heading" on both edges.

Figure 14. Edging. — No. 150 crochet cotton and No. 14 hook. *1st row*—Chain 9, join in a ring with sl, ch 3, 2 t in ring, ch 5 for picot, insert hook down through top of last t, bringing it out at the side under 2 loops of the t and make a sl, (3 t, picot made in the same manner) twice, 3 t, * ch 21, join with sl in 9th st from hook, ch 3, drop st, take it up through 3d st of ch from joining, t in ring, (the chains and t correspond with the first 3 t), picot, (3 t, picot) twice, 3 t *; repeat from * to * for required length. At the end of the edging, fill out last ring with,— picot, (3 t, picot) 3 times, 3 t, making 7 picots altogether in the ring, join the last t to third st of ch with sl; ** sl in each st of ch to next ring, sl in top of the last t made in ring, (3 t, picot) 3 times, 3 t, sl in third st of ch **; repeat from ** to ** to the end and make a picot in last t, joining with sl to first 3-ch made.

LOWER EDGE. — Fasten thread with 1 d in picot at right-hand end, ch 5, d in next p, ch 5, dt in next p, ch 7, dt in same p, ch 5, d in next p, ch 5, d in middle st of bar between rings, * ch 5, d in first picot on next ring, ch 5, dt in centre p, ch 7, dt in same p, ch 5, d in next p, ch 5, d in middle st of bar; repeat from * to * throughout. *2d row*—Begin again at the same end, make 3 d over first 5-ch, picot of 4 joined with d, 3 d, (3 d, p, 3 d) over next ch, (3 d, p, 3 d, p, 3 d, p, 3 d) over centre ch, (3 d, p, 3 d) over next sp, (3 d, p, 3 d) over next ch; repeat from beginning of row to the end.

HEADING. *1st row*—Holding work right side towards you, fasten thread with 1 d in first free picot at right, ch 5, d in next picot, * ch 4, 1 ht in next p, ch 4, long t (over 4 times) in middle st on bar, crochet off by twos, ch 4, 1 ht in next p, ch 4, d in next p *; repeat from * to * throughout, turn. *2d row*—Ch 3, t in each st, turn. *3d row*—Ch 4, thread over twice, miss 2 t, insert hook in next t and make a dt, ch 6, thread over twice, insert hook under the 2 top loops of the dt, draw a loop through, (thread over and draw through 2 loops)

FIG. 13. ACORN INSERTION. See page 12

3 times, * ch 2, thread over 4 times, miss 2 t, insert hook in next t, draw a loop through, (thread over and draw through 2 loops) twice, thread over twice, miss 2 t, insert hook in next t, draw a loop through, (thread over, draw through 2 loops) 6 times, ch 2, thread over twice, insert hook under 2 centre loops, (thread over, draw through 2 loops) 3 times *; repeat from * to * throughout, turn. *4th row*—Ch 3, t in each st. *5th row*—Ch 5, miss 2 t, t in next t, (ch 2, miss 2, t in next t) to the end.

Figure 15. Edging. — No. 100 crochet cotton and No. 14 hook.

SPRAY.— Chain 7, miss first st, sl in each of next 6 sts. FIRST LEAF.— Chain 6, miss first st, sl in each of next 5 sts, bring thread underneath to opposite side, * insert hook in the first of 6-ch last made, and draw a loop through work and st on hook, ch 3, t in each of the next 4 sts (taking outer loop of the sts only), 5 t in the st at top of leaf, 4 t in next 4 sts, ch 3, sl in st where first 3-ch began *. SECOND LEAF.— Chain 12, miss first st, sl in each of next 5 sts, bring thread underneath and repeat from * to * of first leaf. THIRD LEAF.— Repeat directions for second leaf, then sl down next 6 sts on stem, to next leaf. FOURTH LEAF.—Chain 6, miss first st, sl in next 5 sts, bring thread underneath to upper side and repeat from * to *, ** sl down 6 sts on stem to next leaf. FIFTH LEAF.— Repeat directions for fourth leaf to **, break thread and fasten off. Make another spray to the third t in top of fifth leaf, then join to preceding spray at third t in top of second leaf, by taking hook out of work, inserting it in the third t in top of second leaf, draw dropped st through, then make 2 more t in top st of fifth leaf, and finish remainder of leaf and break thread. Make as many sprays as required for length, joining them together as in preceding sprays.

HEADING.— Holding stems upwards, insert hook in third t in top of first leaf at right hand, ch 11, d in end of stem, ch 8, t in third t at end of next leaf, * ch 8, d in next stem, ch 8, t in third t at end of next leaf; repeat from * throughout, turn. *2d row*—Ch 3, t in each st to end of row, turn. *3d row*—Ch 5, miss 2, t in next, (ch 2, miss 2, t in next) repeat throughout.

LOWER EDGE.— Fasten thread in third t at top of

FIG. 14. EDGING. See page 12

Figure 16. Wide Edging. — No. 50 crochet cotton and No. 10 hook.

The medallions are made separately, and the second is joined to the first with sl when the 8th and the 11th picots are made. *1st round*—(includes the four rings and connecting ch), ch 15, join with sl, 24 d in ring, * ch 33, sl into 15th st from hook, bring the working thread down under and back of the ch between rings, 8 d in ring, join to first ring (in 8th st from top), by dropping st from hook, insert hook in 8th st, catch dropped st and draw through, 16 more d in ring; repeat from * twice more, joining 16th st of fourth ring to side of first ring. After fourth ring is finished, ch 18, sl in top of first ring. Care must be taken that the ch between rings do not become twisted. *2d round*—* 9 d in next 9 ch, ch 3, 9 d in next 9 d; repeat from * 3 times more, join. *3d round*—Ch 4, miss 1 t, t in next st, (ch 1, miss 1, t in next st) twice more, ch 1, t under 3-ch at corner, ch 3, t in same place, * ch 1, miss 1, t in next; repeat from * across one side. (In order to have 12 t on each side, t into first st after 3-ch and do not miss 1 in the middle of the side, but make 2 t with 3-ch between, over 3 ch at corner.) After last 1-ch, sl in third st of 4-ch at beginning of row. *4th round*—Make 1 d in each st (taking up the back thread), join, and sl to next corner of figure. *5th round*—D in each st of one side of figure (taking up back loop of st), * ch 12, join (with sl) one-third of the way back on side just worked; repeat from * twice more, the last time joining at the corner, (17 d over 12-ch, d in st between loops) twice, 8 d over next 12-ch, (ch 12, join back at middle st of 17 d) twice, 17 d over last ch, d between loops, 8 d over next ch, ch 12, join back in middle st of 17 d, 17 d over ch, (9 d over next ch) twice, d in st at end of ch, ch 5; repeat from beginning of round on the three remaining sides of figure.

After fourth scallop is finished, turn, sl back over 9 d to next loop, ch 5, turn, * long t (over 3 times) under 5-ch at corner, (ch 5, long t in same place) 3 times, ch 5, sl in lower st of second loop at side of next scallop, sl across next 8 sts to top of loop, ch 5, turn, long t (over 3 times) in last 5-ch of last row, (ch 5, long t in next 5-ch) 4 times, ch 5, sl at end of top of next scallop, sl in next 3 sts, ch 3, turn, over each 5-ch make (1 dt, picot, 2 dt, p, 2 dt, p, 1 dt), after last dt ch 3, sl in 4th st of top loop of next scallop, sl across loop and across next loop, ch 5 and repeat from * twice more, making scallops around three corners of central square; after last

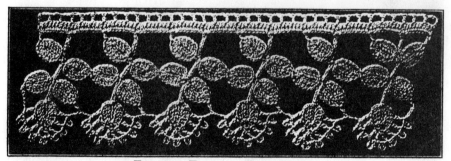

FIG. 15. EDGING. See page 13

second leaf on spray at the right, ch 6, * t in third t on third leaf (counting 3 ch as 1 t), ch 5, d in first st for picot, miss 1 t on leaf, t in next t, picot, miss 1 t, t in next t, picot, t in next t, t in same t, picot, t in next t, picot, miss 1 t on leaf, t in next t, picot, miss 1 t, t in next t, (take one loop of sts only in this row), ch 3, t in third t in end of next leaf, ch 3; repeat from *.

dt ch 3, sl in 4th st of top loop, cut and fasten thread.

HEADING.—When the required number of medallions are joined, instead of breaking thread, sl across next 8 sts, ch 8, t in 4th d on next loop, ch 6, t in 4th d of next loop, ch 5, t in 5-ch at corners, ch 5, t in 5th st of next loop, ch 6, t in 5th st of next loop, ch 6, t in 1st p, ch 9, miss 1 p, long t (over 4 times) in next p, miss 1 p, long t (over 5 times) in next p, miss 1 p, long t (over 7 times) in next p, long t (over 7 times) in 7th p down side of next medallion, long t (over 5 times) in 5th p, long t (over 4 times) in 3d p, ch 9, t in first p, ch 6; repeat across each medallion. *2d row*—(Begin each row at the right), 1 t over each st of 1st row, with 6 d t over 6 long t between medallions. *3d row*—Dt over every 3d t of last row, with 2-ch between dt. *4th row*—T in each st of 3d row.

Figure 17. Ivy Leaf Edging.—No. 20 crochet cotton and No. 9 hook.

FOR A LEAF CLUSTER.—Chain 12, turn and make 11 sl in 11 sts of ch (under one thread), ch 14, turn, 13 sl in 13 sts, ch 12, turn, 11 sl in 11 sts. This triple stem is the foundation for the three sections of leaf.

FIG. 16. WIDE EDGING. See page 13

1st row—Work up one side of first stem with 5 d over 5 sts, 3 d over next st, 5 d over next 5 sts, 3 d at end, work down next side with 5 d, 3 d opposite 3 d on first side, 4 d in next 4, draw loop through next st, leaving it on the hook, miss next st, draw loop through 1st st on next stem, thread over and through 3 loops on hook. By missing a st and working two off together, this narrows 2 sts. Each narrowing is made in the same way. Work down middle stem with 5 d over 5 sts, 3 d over next st, d in each st to end of stem, 3 d in end, work up next side in the same way, narrow as before between stems, work third stem like first to within 1 st of the end, turn. *2d row*—Sl in 1st st, work entirely around with d, taking up back loop only of st, make 3 d in middle st of each 3 d at sides, and 5 d at end of each section; narrow between sections as before, work to within 1 st of the end, turn. *3d row*—Sl in next st, and work like 2d row. *4th row*—Like 2d row. Join first and third sections with a sl and ch 13 for stem, turn, 6 d over 6 sts, 6 sl over 6 sts, fasten and cut thread. These leaves should be made very close and solid; join tips of leaves at each side with sl while working the last row. When leaves are joined make the Outer Edge in two rows of work. *1st row*—Before joining thread to leaves, ch 8, sl in 5th from hook for picot, ch 3,

drop st, insert hook in 5th st from the tip of leaf at left, catch dropped st and draw through, sl back over the 3-ch, picot of 5, sl in next 3 sts of 1st ch, ch 8, dt in point at side of same section, dt in next point, ch 17, * sl back into 5th for picot, ch 3, drop st and pick it up through a st half way down side of next section, sl in 3 ch sts, picot of 5, sl in next 3 ch sts, ch 17 and repeat from *, catching the ch at places shown. After fifth pair of picots around the lower point, ch 8, make 2 dt in points, ch 17, pair of picots near end of last section; repeat from beginning of row, ch 8, etc. *2d row*—Over first 8-ch make (1 d, ch 2, 9 t, ch 2, 1 d); over each of next 6-ch loops make (1 d, ch 2, 4 t, cluster of 3 picots, 4 t, ch 2, 1 d), over last 8-ch make (1 d, ch 2, 9 t, ch 2, 1 d); repeat from beginning of row and join first cluster of picots (with sl) to last cluster on preceding leaf.

HEADING. *1st row*—Ch 6, sl in 5th for picot, ch 2, drop st and draw it through a st at right hand, opposite the last pair of picots made, 2 sl on 2 ch, picot, sl in 1st of 5 ch st, sl in ch st above 1st p, ch 11, * t in point at side of leaf, ch 6, d in 4th d on leaf stem, ch 6, d in next point of leaf, ch 16, sl back in 5th for p, ch 2, drop st, pick it up through 5th st back from outer point of leaf, sl in last 2 ch, picot, sl in ch st above 1st p, ch 1, p, ch 2, drop st and pick it up through 5th st on next section, 2 sl on 2 ch, picot, sl in ch st above first picot, ch 11 and repeat from *. *2d row*—T in 1st st, (ch 2, miss 2, t in next); repeat.

Figure 18. Narrow Edgings.—No. 70 crochet cotton and No. 12 hook.

A. — Chain 5, t in 1st st of ch, * ch 5, t in last space; repeat from * for length required. *1st and 2d rows*—Ch 7, turn, sl in the first loop of 5-ch, * ch 5, sl in next loop; repeat from * across. *3d row*—Ch 6, turn, 1 d in first loop, * ch 4, 1 d in next loop; repeat from * across. *4th row*—Ch 1, (2 d, ch 4, 2 d) in first loop, * (2 d, ch 4, 2 d) in next loop; repeat from * across and fasten off.

B. — Chain 7, join, ch 6, t in ring, (ch 3, t in ring) 4 times; ch 1, turn, * (1 d, ch 1, 3 t, ch 1, 1 d) in first space, ch 1; repeat from * 4 times.

SECOND FLOWER.—Chain 1, picot of 4 joined by d, ch 2, picot, ch 12, turn, t in 8th st from hook, ch 6, turn, t in ring, (ch 3, t in ring) 3 times, ch 3, d in 2d st from p, ch 1, turn, 1 d, ch 1, 2 t on 3-ch, turn, 1 d in the centre of the first petal on preceding flower, turn, (1 t, ch 1, 1 d) in same 3-ch sp, (ch 1, 1 d, ch 1, 3 t, ch 1, 1 d in next sp) 4 times; repeat "second flower" for length required.

HEADING. — T in end sp of flower, ch 7, * 3 t (leaving last loop of each on hook and working all off together) in the centre of flower, ch 7, 1 d on loop between p, ch 7; repeat from * across, join the last sp of last flower with 1 t, turn, 1 d on each st of last row.

C. — Chain 5, 1 loose ch, ch 12, sl in the loose ch, ch 1, 5 d, ch 6, 13 d, ch 6, 5 d in ring, sl on 5-ch close to ring, * ch 11, 1 loose st, ch 12, sl in loose st, ch 1, 5 d, ch 3, sl st off hook, insert hook in 6-ch p on last ring and draw loop through, ch 3, 13 d, ch 6, 5 d, all in ring, sl on 11-ch close to ring; repeat from * for length required, ch 10, turn, miss 5 sts of ch, 1 t in next st,

14

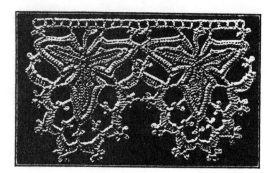

FIG. 17. IVY LEAF EDGING. See page 14

(ch 1, miss 1, 1 t in next st) repeat to end and fasten off.

Join thread to p on side of ring, ch 4, miss 2 d, 1 d in next st, ** (ch 3, miss 1, 1 d in next st) 4 times, ch 4, 1 d on p between rings, ch 4, miss 2 d on next ring, 1 d in next st; repeat from ** across and fasten off. Three d on first 4 ch at end, *** 1 d in 3-ch loop, (ch 5, p, ch 1, 1 d in next 3-ch loop) 3 times, 3 d on 4-ch, 3 d on next 4-ch; repeat from *** across and fasten off.

D. — Chain 10, sl into first st, * ch 1, 1 d in ring, (ch 4, 2 d in ring) 3 times; ch 5, 1 loose ch, ch 9, sl into the loose st; repeat from * for length required. An even number of flowers is to be made.

Row Back. — (Ch 4, 2 d in ring) 4 times, * ch 2, 1 d on connecting ch, ch 2, 2 d into next flower, instead of completing, ch 5, 1 loose ch, ch 9, sl into loose st, ch 1, 1 d in ring, ch 2, 1 d to join into 1st p of completed flower, ch 2, 2 d back into point flower, (ch 4, 2 d) 6 times into same, ch 2, 1 d into connecting ch, ch 2, 2 d into next flower, (ch 4, 2 d into same) twice only, ch 2, sl into connecting ch, ch 2, 2 d into next flower, (ch 4, 2 d into same) 3 times, repeat from *. HEADING. — One t in 1st p on side of r, * ch 7, miss 1 p, t in next p on same r, t in 1st p on next r; repeat from *. *2d row* — One t in 1st st, (ch 1, miss 1, t in next st) repeat.

Figure 19. Wide Edging. — No. 50 crochet cotton and No. 12 hook.

SQUARE. — Chain 50, turn. *1st row* — One dt in 5th st from hook, one dt in each st to end of ch, there should be 47 dt, counting the first 4-ch as 1 dt, turn. *2d row* — One tight sl in first dt, ch 4, 3 dt on next 3 dt, ch 3, miss 3, dt on next dt; repeat until there are 10 spaces, 3 dt on last dt, turn. Repeat the 2d row 9 times, turn. *12th row* — One tight sl in first dt, ch 4, 3 dt on 3 dt, (3 dt over first sp, dt on next dt) 10 times, 3 dt on last 3 dt. This completes the square. *1st round* — Without turning ch 9, miss 2 rows on side, d in st at bottom of 2d row, (ch 9, d at end of next 2d row) repeat to corner, then continue around making 6 loops of 9-ch across 1st row, 6 loops across third side of square, and 6 loops across 12th row, joining as evenly as possible, join at first corner with sl. *2d round* — 13 d in each 9-ch loop around, join with sl, break thread or sl over 6 sts. *3d round* — D in 7th st of first 13 d, * ch 9, d in 7th st of next loop to corner, across corner ch 11, d in 7th st of next loop; repeat from * around, join with sl. *4th round* — Over each 9-ch loop make (4 d, picot of 3 joined with d, 3 d, p, 3 d, p, 4 d); over each 11-ch loop make (5 d, p, 3 d, p, 3 d, p, 5 d); repeat around and join with

sl, break thread. Make as many squares as are necessary for length, joining each one as it is made to preceding square at corresponding picots directly above the corner.

FLOWER. — Chain 8, join with sl to form a ring. *1st round* — Ch 1, 18 d in ring, join with sl. *2d round* — Ch 4, 3 dt in next st, ch 4, sl in same st, (ch 1, miss 1 d in ring, sl in next d, ch 4, 3 dt in same st, ch 4, sl in same st) repeat until there are 8 petals, ch 1, miss 1 d, d in next st, ch 25 for stem and leaf, * d in 3d st of ch (taking but one loop), 1 ht, 2 t, 6 dt, 2 t, 1 ht, d in next 13 sts of ch, sl across the end of leaf into next ch st, ch 1, d in each of next 4 sts (taking but one loop), picot of 3, 4 d in next 4 sts, p, 4 d, p, 3 d in next 3 sts, d under 2-ch at top, picot, 4 d in next 4 sts, p, 4 d, p; 4 d, p, 3 d, d across end of leaf into the ch on next side, * ch 17 for stem, turn, d in 3d st of ch, d in each st to leaf; ch 18 for 2d leaf; repeat from * to * for 2d leaf, d into st made across 1st leaf, d into each st of ch to flower, d on last d in ring. Break thread, leaving an end long enough to sew flower on square as indicated in cut.

LEAVES BETWEEN SCALLOPS. — Chain 18, repeat directions for leaf as far as 2d picot, then ch 2, dt in middle p of 2d loop from corner loop on the 2d square at the right, ch 2, d in last d on leaf to finish p, 4 d in next 4 d, p, 3 d in next 3 d, d under 2-ch at top of leaf, ch 1, ** take hook out of work, insert it down through the middle picot of next lower loop, draw dropped st through, ch 2, and finish picot, ** (from ** to ** will be called "joining" hereafter), 4 d in next 4 d, p, 4 d, ch 2, dt in middle p on next loop, ch 2, finish picot, 4 d, p, 3 d to end of leaf, 1 d across leaf into ch st opposite, ch 25, repeat directions for leaf to 1st picot, ch 2, dt in same p with last dt, ch 2, finish p, 4 d, p, 4 d, ch 2, join as from ** to **, 3 d in next 3 d, 1 d under 2 ch at top of leaf, ch 2, make a cross dt into picots before and after joining of squares, ch 2, finish p, 4 d in 4 d, ch 2, join in middle picot of next loop. Finish leaf joining as before, ch 25 for 3d leaf and make leaf and join in the places corresponding with the 1st leaf, break thread and fasten. Repeat the three leaves between scallops to end, then

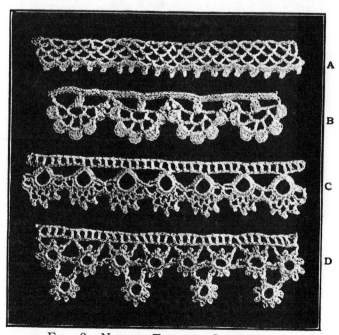

FIG. 18. NARROW EDGINGS. See page 14

make 2 leaves at beginning and end of edging.

HEADING. — Chain 8 for the half scallop at the right-hand end of lace, d in 1st d of end leaf, * ch 13, d in 2d p of leaf, ch 15, d in middle p of next loop, ch 9, d in middle p of top loop, ch 9, d in middle p of next loop, ch 15, d in same p with dt, ch 13, d in end st of next leaf, ch 13, d in end st of next leaf; repeat from * to end of edging. *2d row*—Begin again at right hand, fasten thread with sl in 1st st of 8 ch, 9 d over ch, * 21 d over 1st loop, 23 d over next, 12 d over each of next 2 loops, 23 d over next, 21 d over next, 19 d over next; repeat from * to end. *3d row*—D in 1st d of half loop at right hand, * (ch

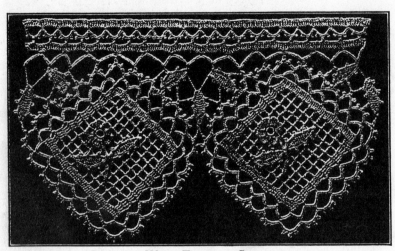

FIG. 19. WIDE EDGING. See page 15

12, d in 13th d of next loop) twice, ch 14, d in d over p, ch 14, d in 9th d of next loop, ch 12, d in middle st of next loop; repeat from * to end. *4th row*—Make dt in each st across row. Now make a ch as long as the last row, turn, dt in 5th st of ch, dt in each st to end, ch 4, d in first st at beginning to bring thread in position at lower edge of dt sts, (ch 9, d between 7th and 8th dt) repeat to end, break thread and begin again at right hand. Fasten thread with d at first of row, * 4 d, p of 3, 3 d, ch 2, take hook out of work, pick up the edge and holding the left end of it towards you, insert hook in top of 4th dt, catch dropped st and draw through, ch 2, finish p, 3 d, p, 4 d over same loop *; repeat in each loop from * to * the whole length, connecting each loop at middle p, between the 7th and 8th dt on edge, the p of 1st loop being joined at the 4th dt because it is at the end.

Figure 20. Edging. — No. 70 crochet cotton and No. 13 hook.

TOP MOTIF. — Chain 17, join with sl, cover loop with 29 d, sl across the end into 1st d, * ch 17, join as at first, 29 d in loop, sl across the end; repeat from * twice more, break thread and fasten.

LOWER MOTIF. — Chain 17, turn. *1st row*—T in 8th st from hook, * ch 2, miss 2, t in next; repeat from * to end, turn. *2d row*—Ch 5, t on next t, * ch 2, t on next t; repeat from * to end of row. *3d and 4th rows*—Like 2d row. Without turning ch 1 and work along the next side of square, making 3 d in each sp to corner; * ch 14, join in 1st st by a sl through under outside loop of st, 23 d in loop; sl across end into first d in loop, then insert hook down through

top of 3d d in last sp and out at side of st, and make a tight double (all picots are fastened in this way except in the triple p, the 3d p is fastened in the same way but finished with a sl), * ch 14 and make another loop like the last, 3 d in each sp to next corner, make but one loop on this corner, repeating directions from * to *, 3 d in each sp to next corner and make two loops, 3 d in each sp to last corner and make but one loop, join with sl, break thread and fasten.

CENTRE MOTIF. — Chain 20, join with sl, ch 9, sl in same st where ch was joined, putting hook right down through the st, sl in each of the next 5 sts, * ch 9, sl in centre of last st, sl in each of next 5 sts; repeat from * until the 1st 9-ch is reached, sl up 2 sts of the 9-ch, ch 5, miss 2 sts of 9-ch, in the next make (t, ch 5, t), ch 2, miss 2, t in next st, ch 5, ** t in second st of next 9-ch, ch 2, miss 2, (t, ch 5, t) in next st, ch 2, miss 2, t in next st, ch 5 **; repeat from ** to ** around, joining last 5-ch to the 3d st of 1st 5-ch. *1st round*—Ch 1, d in same st with joining, d in each st around, taking back loop only, and making 3 d in each corner, join with sl. *2d round*—Turn, like 1st round. *3d round*—Turn, ch 1, d in same st with joining, ch 5, dt in the corner st, picot of 5 (joined under 2 threads in top of dt with d), ch 2, pick up Top Motif, * take hook out of work, insert hook down through the 15th st of left-hand loop, draw dropped st through *, (from * to * will be called "joining" hereafter), ch 3, finish p, a third picot fastened in the same place with sl, (ch 4, dt in same st with last dt, 3 p in top of dt) twice, ch 5, d in each of the 7 d in middle of side of square, ch 5, dt in corner st, 3 p in top of dt, (ch 4, dt in same st, 3 p in top of dt) twice, ch 5, 7 d in 7 middle sts of square, ch 5, (dt in corner st, 3 p on dt, ch 4) twice, dt in same corner st, p, ch 2, take up the Lower Motif, joining as before in the 12th st of one of the single loops at the side, ch 3, finish p, make a 3d p and fasten in the same place with sl, ch 5, 7 d in middle 7 sts of square, ch 5, dt in corner st, p, ch 2, join in middle d of next loop on lower motif, ch 3, finish p, make one more p in same st, ch 4, dt in same corner st, 3 p on dt, ch 4, dt in same st, p, ch 2, join in second loop of top motif, ch 3, finish p, one more p in same st, ch 5, 6 d in 6 d in middle of side of square, sl in next d, break thread and fasten.

Make another top and lower motif, then the centre square; after completing the 2d round of doubles, ch 1 and turn, *** ch 5, dt in corner st, p, ch 2, pick up the top motif and join to the middle st of loop at the left as before, finish p, make one more p in same st. Work on the 3d round as before, 3 triple p at each corner, joining in the following places,—3d triple p to right loop of 1st top motif, —at next corner of the 1st triple p to free loop of top motif,—next triple p to corresponding p of 1st square,—3d triple p to next free loop of lower motif—1st triple p of next corner to single loop of lower motif,—3d triple p to single loop of second lower motif—at last corner, 1st triple p to one of two loops on second lower motif; 3d triple p to second loop of upper motif; repeat from *** to *** to join all motifs.

HEADING. — Make 1 d in top p at right hand, * ch 9, t in 4th d from p on next loop, ch 12, cross dt in end sts of the 2 top loops of upper motifs, ch 12, t in 4th d from p on next loop, ch 9, d in centre p; repeat from *. *2d row*—Begin again at the right, make 1 dt in 1st st, * ch 1, miss 1, dt in next; repeat from *.

LOWER EDGE. — *1st row*—One d in middle p at point of square at right, * ch 7, 3 dt in 7th d on side of loop, (making a Cluny group), ch 9, d in middle d of next loop, ch 8, make a Cluny group of 3 in 6th st from the last d, a Cluny group on next loop, ch 8, d in middle st of same loop, ch 9, Cluny group in 7th d in side of next loop, ch 7, d in centre p; repeat from * and break thread. *2d row*—Begin again at the right, d in 1st d, * over ch make (d, 3 t, 3 p in top of last t, fastening 2 p with d, the 3d p with sl, 3 t, d), sl in centre of group; over next ch make (1 d, 3 t, 3 p, 3 t, d, 3 t, 3 p); over next ch make (3 t, 1 d, 3 t, 3 p, 3 t, d), sl in centre of group; over next ch (d, 3 t, 3 p, 3 t, d, 3 t, 3 p); over next ch (3 t, d, 3 t, 3 p, 3 t, d), sl in centre of group; over next ch make (d, 3 t, 3 p, 3 t, d); repeat from * to end.

Figure 21. Edging. — No. 70 crochet cotton and No. 12 hook.

LEAVES. — * Chain 13, sl in 5th st from hook, sl in each of next 4 sts, sl across to opposite side of ch, ch 2, t in sl taken across, t in each of next 5 sts, 5 t in little ring at top, 5 t down next side, ch 2, sl in next st, sl in each of next 4 sts *. This completes one of the larger leaves; without breaking thread repeat from * to *, which makes the lower leaf; ** again without breaking thread, ch 10, sl in 5th st from hook, sl in each of 3 sts, sl to opposite side of ch, ch 2, t in sl taken across, t in each of next 3 sts, 5 t in ring, t in each of next 4 sts, ch 2, sl in same st with last t, sl in each of next 2 sts, ** sl across stem to opposite side; repeat from ** to **, fasten with sl in centre of stems and break thread. *1st round*—Make a cross dt between the small side leaf at the right side and the larger top leaf as follows, — Having a loop on the hook, put thread over twice, insert hook in 3d t from bottom of side leaf (counting last 2 ch as 1 t), thread over and draw loop through, (thread over and draw through 2 loops) twice, retaining 2 loops on hook, thread over twice, insert hook in 3d t from bottom of top leaf, thread over and draw a loop through, thread over and draw through all loops by twos, * (ch 3, miss 1 t, dt in next) twice, ch 3, 2 dt in centre st at top of leaf with 5 ch between, (ch 3, miss 1 t, dt in next) twice, ch 3, miss 1 t, 1 cross dt between leaves, ch 3, miss 1 t, dt in next, ch 3, 2 dt with 5 ch between in centre st at top of leaf, ch 3, miss 1 t, dt in next, ch 3, * miss 1 t, cross dt between leaves; repeat from * to * around and join to top st of 1st cross dt with sl. *2d round*—4 d over each sp to corner, 7 d over each corner sp. *3d round*—D

in each d all around (taking back loop of st), join to 1st d with sl. *4th round*—Ch 9, d in 5th st from hook for picot, ch 1, miss 3 d, dt in next d, (ch 5, d in 5th st from hook, ch 1, miss 3 d, dt in next d) twice, * ch 5, d in 5th st, ch 1, dt in 4th d, (ch 4, d in 2 upper loops of last dt, dt in same st) 4 times, (ch 5, d in 5th st, ch 1, miss 3 d, dt in next d) 6 times *; repeat from * to * around, joining to 4th st of next sp with sl, break thread and fasten. Make as many diamonds as required for length, joining each one as it is made, to preceding one at the second and third picots of the cluster at side.

HEADING. — Having a loop on the hook, put thread over 12 times, insert in the 4th p of cluster at right side, thread over and draw loop through, (thread over and through 2 loops) 6 times, leaving 7 loops on hook, * thread over 6 times, miss 1 p, insert in next p, draw loop through, (thread over and through 2 loops) 6 times, * miss 1 p and repeat from * to * once, thread over and through 3 loops, (thread over and through 2 loops) 7 times, ch 2, thread over 5 times, insert in the loop over the top of the three loops (formed by the thread drawn through the 1st 2 loops of top bar), draw loop through, (thread over and through 2 loops) 6 times, ch 2, thread over 6 times, and make last bar in same loop, (drawing thread through 2 loops) 7 times, ** ch 5, miss 2 picots, t in next p, ch 5, miss 1 p, d in next, ch 3, d in next, ch 5, miss 1 p, t in next, ch 5, miss 2 p, thread over 12 times, insert in next p, draw loop through, (thread over and through 2 loops) 6 times, leaving 7 loops on hook, * thread over 6 times, miss 1 p, insert in next p, draw loop through, (thread over and through 2 loops) 6 times *; repeat from * to * 4 times, making the 4th bar in the 1st p on next diamond, thread over and draw a loop

FIG. 20. EDGING. See page 16

through 6 loops, (thread over and draw through 2 loops) 7 times, ch 2, thread over 5 times, insert in loop over the 6 lower bars and draw through 2 loops 6 times; make 4 more bars in same loop, with 2 ch between bars, for the 4th bar putting thread over 6 times and drawing through 2 loops 7 times **; repeat from ** to ** to end of diamonds, making but 3 bars above and below at end of last diamond; break thread and begin again at the right hand. *2d row*—T in 1st st, * ch 1, miss 1 st, t in next; repeat from * to end.

Figure 22. Torchon Edging. — No. 70 crochet cotton and No. 13 hook. Chain 48, turn. *1st row*—Sl in 8th st of ch, (ch 5, sl in 5th st) 3 times, ch 5, miss 4, 4 t in next 4 sts, ch 5, miss 4, 4 t in next 4 sts, ch 5, miss 4, t in next st, ch 1, miss 1, t in next, ch 1, miss 1, t in next, ch 5, turn. *2d row*—(1 t, ch 1, 1 t) over 1-ch, ch 1, 1 t over next ch, ch 1, (1 t, ch 1, 1 t) over next ch, ch 5, * 2 t over 3d and 4th t, 2 t over ch, ch 5; repeat from *, sl over middle of 5-ch, * ch 5, sl on ch *, (from * to * will be called a mesh), make 2 more meshes, ch 5, turn. *3d row*—Sl on 1st mesh, make 2 more meshes, * ch 5, 2 t over last sts of ch, 2 t over 2 t; repeat from *, ch 5, (1 t, ch 1, 1 t) over last of 5-ch, (ch 1, 1 t) over each of next 3 chs, ch 1, (1 t, ch 1, 1 t) over next ch, ch 5, turn. *4th row*—Like 2d row except there will be 9 t in lower section of design and but 3 meshes in upper design. *5th row*—Like 3d except 3 meshes in upper design and 11 t in lower. *6th row*—Like 4th row except 13 t below and 2 meshes above. *7th row*—Like 5th except 2 meshes above and 15 t below. *8th row*—Like 6th except 17 t below and 1 mesh above. It is helpful to notice that the 8th row is the centre of the scallop and is worked from below to the top. *9th row*—Sl on 1st mesh, ch 5, * 2 t over 3d and 4th t, 2 t over ch, * ch 5, make from * to * again, ch 5, t between 2d and 3d t, * ch 1, t over next ch *; repeat from * to * until there are 15 t altogether, ch 5, turn. *10th row*—T over 1st ch, * ch 1, t over next ch *; repeat until there are 13 t, (ch 5, 2 t over ch, 2 t over

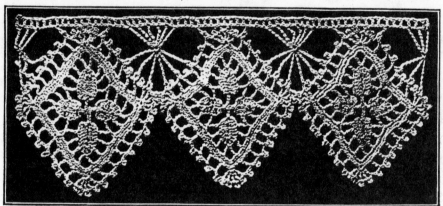

FIG. 21. EDGING. See page 17

2 t) repeat, 2 meshes, ch 5, turn. *11th row*—Like 9th except 11 t below and 3 meshes above. *12th, 13th and 14th rows*—Continue in the same way, increasing the meshes above and decreasing the t below. *15th row*—Like 1st, except ch 5, sl on 1st mesh. *16th row*—Like 2d row. *17th row*—Like 3d row. *18th row*—Commencing corner, same as 4th, omitting last mesh, turn. *19th row*—Sl to 3d st of ch, ch 5, 2 t over ch, 2 t over 2 t, continue as in 5th row. *20th row*—Like 6th row to, and including upper block. *21st row*—Sl down block and 5 sts of ch, ch 2 for 1 t, 1 t over ch, 2 t over 2 t, continue as in 7th row. *22d row*—Like 8th row to, and including 2 t over ch, ch 3, turn. *23d row*—T between 2d and 3d t, continue as in 9th row. *24th row*—Like 10th row, to within 2 t of top of lower design, ch 3, turn. *25th row*—T between 2d and 3d t, continue as in 11th row. *26th row*—Like 12th row to within 2 t of top, ch 3, turn. *27th row*—T between 2d and 3d t, continue as in 13th row. *28th row*—Like 14th row to within 2 t of top, ch 3, turn. *29th row*—T between 2d and 3d t, continue as in 15th row. *30th row*—Like 2d row up to 2 t over ch (inclusive), ch 4, sl in upper mesh opposite, ch 3, turn. *31st row*—2 t over ch, continue as in 3d row. *32d row*—Like 4th row up to 2 t over ch, ch 4, sl in upper mesh opposite, ch 3, turn. *33d row*—2 t over ch, continue as in 5th row. *34th row*

—Like 6th row to 2 t over ch, ch 4, sl in upper mesh opposite, ch 3, turn. *35th row*—2 t over ch, continue as in 7th row. *36th row*—Like 8th row to 2 t over ch, ch 7, sl in last t of block, ch 7, catch in last t of next block, turn. *37th row*—Sl down 5 sts of 7-ch (last 2 sts equal to 1 t), 3 t over ch, ch 5, t between 2d and 3d t, continue as in 9th row. *38th row*—Like 10th row until there are 13 t, ch 5, 2 t over ch, 2 t over 2 t, ch 5, 4 t over ch, ch 5, sl in 2d mesh, ch 5, sl in last mesh, ch 5, turn. *39th row*—Like 11th row. *40th row*—Like 12th row. *41st row*—Like 13th row. *42d row*—Like 14th row. *43d row*—Like 15th row.

Figure 22½. Torchon Insertion.—Materials as in Figure 22. Chain 87, turn. *1st row*—Sl in 8th st, (ch 5, miss 4, sl in next st) 3 times, * ch 5, miss 4, 4 t (block) in next 4 sts, repeat once from *, ch 5, miss 4, 1 t in next st, ch 1, miss 1, 1 t in next st, ch 1, miss 1, 1 t in next st, ch 5, block, ch 5, block, (ch 5, miss 4, sl in next st) 5 times, ch 7, turn. *2d row* — Sl in 1st mesh, and continue as in 1st row, except decrease one 5-ch mesh on each side, by working the blocks 2 t over ch, 2 t over 2 t, and increase the number of t (with 1-ch between) by making 2 additional t (with 1 ch between) over ch both preceding and following the t of previous row. Continue until 8 rows are worked; after which, increase the number of 5-ch meshes by working the blocks 2 t over 2 t, 2 t over ch, and decrease the number of trebles (with 1-ch between) by beginning between 2d and 3d trebles and omitting 2 t below after the last t made. This design would be beautiful in carpet warp, or any of the heavier threads, for Counterpane stripe, and make the corresponding edge for a border.

Narrow Lace (not illustrated). — No. 70 crochet cotton and No. 13 hook.

Chain 23. *1st row*—Sl in the 5th ch st from hook, ch 5, sl in 6th ch st, (ch 3, sl in 3d ch st) 4 times. *2d row*—Turn, ch 5, sl under first 3-ch, (ch 3, sl under next 3-ch) 3 times, ch 3, 6 d under 5-ch. *3d row*—Turn, picot of 5 joined by sl, ch 5, miss 6 d, sl in next 3-ch, (ch 3, sl in next 3-ch) 3 times, ch 3, sl under 5-ch at the end. Repeat 2d and 3d rows for required length.

Picot Lace (not illustrated). No. 50 crochet cotton and No. 12 hook.

Chain 4, (picot of 5 joined by d) 3 times, ch 3, 3 picots, ch 3, 7 picots, turn to make the 7 picots form a ring, 3 d over 3-ch, (3 picots, 3 d over 3-ch) twice. This completes a round, that is a row back and forth across the lace. *2d round*—Ch 4, picot, ch 7, (3 picots, joining the second one in middle picot of first ring in 1st round, ch 3) twice; to join the picots, take the hook out of st after making 3 ch, insert hook in opposite picot and draw the st through, ch 2 to finish picot and join with d, 7 picots, joining the 2d p to corresponding picot of 1st round, (3 d over 3-ch, 3 picots) twice, 3 d over 3-ch; repeat from first of 2d round.

Figure 23. Double Fan Lace. — No. 70 crochet cotton and No. 13 hook. Make a chain the required length.

1st row—One t in the 7th st of ch, * ch 3, 4 t under t, miss 3 st, 1 t in the 4th st; repeat from * the length of chain. *2d row* — Seven ch, * 1 d on top of 3-ch, ch 3; repeat from * across, ch 3, 1 t under 7-ch at end. *3d row*—Ch 4, 1 t on 1 d, then 1 t, ch 1, in every 2d st. Break off thread and begin at the other end. *4th row*—Ch 4, 1 t on 1 t, * ch 3, 4 t under 1 t, miss 1 t, 1 t on next t; repeat from * across. *5th row* — Ch 7, 1 d on 3-ch, ch 3; repeat across. *6th row*—Ch 4, 1 t on 1 d, then ch 1, 1 t in every 2d st. Break off thread and work next row on other edge of beading. *7th row*—Ch 1, 1 t in every 2d st of foundation chain. *8th row*—Two d under each of 6 spaces of 1-ch, * ch 4, miss 1 sp, 2 d under each of next 12 sp; repeat from *. *9th row*—One d in each of first 10 d, * miss 2, ch 3, 3 t under 4-ch of last row, ch 3, miss 2, 1 d in each of next 20 d; repeat from *. *10th row*—One d in each of first 9 d, * miss 1, ch 3, 5 t in top of 3 t, ch 3, miss 1, 1 d in each of next 18 d; repeat. *11th row*—One d in each of first 8 d, * miss 1, ch 4, 6 t in top of 5 t, ch 4, miss 1, 1 d in each of next 16 d; repeat. *12th row*—One d in each of first 7 d, * miss 1, ch 5, 6 t in top of 6 t, ch 5, miss 1, 1 d in each of next 14 d; repeat. *13th row*—One d in each of first 6

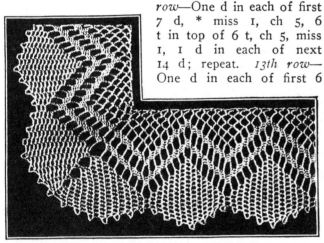

FIG. 22. TORCHON EDGING. See page 17

d, * miss 1, ch 6, 1 t in each of 6 t (with ch 1 between), ch 6, miss 1, 1 d in each of next 12 d; repeat. *14th row*—One d in each of first 5 d, * miss 1, ch 7, 1 t in each of 6 t (with ch 2 between), ch 7, miss 1, 1 d in each of next 9 d; repeat. *15th row*—One d in each of first 4 d, * miss 1, ch 7, 3 t under each 2-ch, ch 7, miss 1, 1 d in each of next 7 d; repeat. *16th row*—One d in each of first 3 d, miss 1, ch 10, make a Cluny group on each group of 3 t, as follows: Thread over twice, insert hook in top of 1st t, take up thread and draw through, take up thread and draw through 2 sts, * thread over, insert hook in next t, take up thread and draw through, thread over, draw through 3 sts; repeat from * once, thread over, and draw through 2 sts, over, draw through 2 sts, ch 4, 1 Cluny group on next 3 t, ch 4; repeat until there are 5 groups separated by 4 ch, ch 10, miss 1, 1 d in each of next 6 d; repeat. *17th row*—One ch, 1 t in 2d st of 10-ch, ch 2, (1 t, ch 2, 1 t) in 4th st, ch 2, 1 t in 6th st, ch 2, (1 t, ch 2, 1 t) in 8th st, * ch 2, 1 t in Cluny st, ch 2, (1 t, ch 2, 1 t) in 4-ch; repeat from * 3 times, ch 2, 1 t in Cluny st, ch 2, (1 t, ch 2, 1 t) in 2d of 10-ch, ch 2, t in

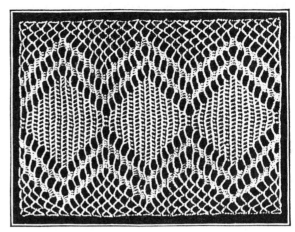

FIG. 22½. TORCHON INSERTION. See page 18

5th st of 10-ch, ch 2, (1 t, ch 2, 1 t) in 7th st of 10-ch, ch 2, t in 9th st of 10-ch, ch 2, 1 t in centre of 6 d; repeat from first of row. *18th row*—One d under second 2-ch, * 2 d under each of next 2-ch, (1 d, ch 3, 1 d, ch 3, 1 d, ch 3, 1 d) under next 2-ch; repeat from * around scallop, making six groups of picots, 2 d under next two 2-ch, 1 d under next 2-ch, 1 d in second 2-ch of next scallop; repeat from *. *19th row*—Ch 7, 1 d in centre of 1st group of picots, ch 10, * 1 t in 2d group, ch 5, 1 d in 3d group, ch 5, 1 d in 4th group, ch 5, 1 t in 5th group, ch 5, 1 dt in 6th group, 1 dt in centre of 1st group of picots on next scallop, ch 5; repeat from *. *20th row*—Ch 1, 1 t in every 2d st of ch. Repeat from the 8th to the 18th rows, inclusive, except that the solid portion, of doubles, is made a little longer, to make the second row of fans come exactly beneath the first row.

If a narrower lace is preferred, the work may end with the 18th row. This pattern would be very handsome crocheted in No. 5 crochet cotton or carpet warp with hook No. 7 or No. 8. For different purposes and where actual measure is not to be considered, the worker may experiment at will.

FIG. 23. DOUBLE FAN LACE. See page 19

Figure 24. Church Lace. — No. 60 crochet cotton and No. 11 hook.

Chain 102, turn. *1st row*—T in 9th st from hook, 3 t in next 3 sts, ch 6, miss 6, 5 sl in next 5 sts, ch 6, miss 6, 4 t (block) in next 4 sts, ch 6, miss 6, 5 sl in 5 sts, ch 6, miss 6, block (blk), (ch 2, miss 2, t in next) twice, (this is called 2 spaces or 2 sp), 16 t, including the t that finishes sp, 1 sp, 16 t, 2 sp, blk, ch 10, turn. *2d row*—T in 8th st from hook, 3 more t (the last one over last t in 1st row), sp, blk, 2 sp, blk, 3 sp, blk, 3 sp, blk, 2 sp, blk, sp, blk, ch 5, miss 1 sl, 3 sl over next 3, ch 5, blk, (this blk is 3 t over ch, 1 t over 1st t of blk below), sp, blk, ch 5, miss 1 sl, 3 sl, ch 5, blk, 2 sp, ch 5, turn. *3d row*—3 sp, blk (1 t over last t below and 3 t over ch), ch 4, dt in middle of 3 sl, ch 4, blk, ch 4, dt over 2-ch, ch 4, blk, ch 4, dt in middle

FIG. 24. CHURCH LACE. See page 20

of 3 sl, ch 4, blk, 4 ch, dt over 2-ch, ch 4, blk, 5 sp, blk, 5 sp, blk, ch 4, dt over 2-ch, ch 4, blk, ch 10, turn. *4th row*—Blk, (this blk is t in 8th st from hook, 2 t in next 2 sts, 1 t over last t of last row), ch 5, 3 sl over dt, ch 5, blk, 4 sp, blk, 4 sp, blk, ch 5, 3 sl over dt, ch 5, blk, sp, blk, ch 5, 3 sl over dt, ch 5, blk, sp, blk, 4 sp, ch 5, turn. *5th row*—5 sp, blk, ch 6, 5 sl, ch 6, blk, ch 6, 5 sl, ch 6, blk, 2 sp, 3 blk, 2 sp, blk, ch 6, 5 sl, ch 6, blk, ch 10. *6th row*—Blk, sp, blk, ch 5, 3 sl, ch 5, blk, sp, blk, 2 sp, blk, 2 sp, blk, sp, blk, ch 5, 3 sl, ch 5, blk, sp, blk, ch 5, 3 sl, ch 5, blk, sp, blk, 4 sp, ch 5. *7th row*—3 sp, blk, ch 4, dt over 2-ch, ch 4, blk, ch 4, dt in middle of 3 sl, ch 4, blk, ch 4, dt over 2-ch, ch 4, blk, ch 4, dt over middle of 3 sl, ch 4, blk, ch 4, dt over 2-ch, ch 4, blk, 3 sp, blk, ch 4, dt over 2-ch, ch 4, blk, ch 4, dt over middle of 3 sl, ch 4, blk, ch 4, dt over 2-ch, ch 4, blk, ch 10. *8th row*—Blk, ch 5, 3 sl over dt, ch 5, blk, sp over dt, blk, ch 5, 3 sl over dt, ch 5, blk, sp, blk, ch 5, 3 sl over dt, ch 5, blk, sp, blk, ch 5, 3 sl over dt, ch 5, blk, 2 sp, ch 5. *9th row*—Sp, blk, (ch 6, 5 sl, ch 6) blk over sp, (ch 6, 5 sl, ch 6), blk, (ch 6, 5 sl, ch 6), blk, (ch 6, 5 sl, ch 6), blk, (ch 6, 5 sl, ch 6), blk in loop, ch 5. *10th row*—Miss 1 blk, blk over ch, ch 5, 3 sl, ch 5, blk, sp, blk, ch 5, 3 sl, ch 5, blk, sp, blk, ch 5, 3 sl, ch 5, blk, sp, blk, ch 5, 3 sl, ch 5, blk, 2 sp, ch 5. *11th row*—3 sp, blk, ch 4, dt in middle sl, ch 4, blk, ch 4, dt over 2-ch, ch 4, blk, ch 4, dt in middle sl, ch 4, blk, ch 4, dt over 2-ch, ch 4, blk, ch 4, dt in middle sl, ch 4, blk, 3 sp, blk, ch 4, dt in middle sl, ch 4, blk, ch 4, dt over 2-ch, ch 4, blk, ch 4, dt in middle sl, blk, ch 5. *12th row*—Blk over 4-ch, sp, blk, ch 5, 3 sl, ch 5, blk, sp, blk, 2 sp, blk, 2 sp, blk, sp, blk, ch 5, 3 sl, ch 5, blk, sp, blk, ch 5, 3 sl, ch 5, blk, sp, blk, 4 sp, ch 5. *13th row*—5 sp,

blk, ch 6, 5 sl, ch 6, blk, ch 6, 5 sl, ch 6, blk, 2 sp, 3 blk, 2 sp, blk, ch 6, 5 sl, ch 6, blk, ch 5. *14th row*—Blk, ch 5, 3 sl, ch 5, blk, 4 sp, blk, 4 sp, blk, ch 5, 3 sl, ch 5, blk, sp, blk, ch 5, 3 sl, ch 5, blk, sp, blk, 4 sp, ch 5. *15th row*—3 sp, blk, ch 4, dt, ch 4, blk, ch 4, dt in middle sl, ch 4, blk, ch 4, dt, ch 4, blk, ch 4, dt in middle sl, ch 4, blk, 5 sp, blk, 5 sp, blk, ch 4, dt in middle sl, ch 4, blk, ch 5. *16th row*—Blk, sp, blk, 2 sp, blk, 3 sp, blk, 3 sp, blk, 2 sp, blk, sp, blk, ch 5, 3 sl, ch 5, blk, sp, blk, ch 5, 3 sl, ch 5, blk, 2 sp, ch 5. *17th row*—Sp, blk, ch 6, 5 sl, ch 6, blk, ch 6, 5 sl, ch 6, blk, 2 sp, 5 blk, sp, 5 blk, 2 sp, blk, ch 10. *18th row*—Blk over 10 ch, sp, blk, 2 sp, blk, 3 sp, blk, 3 sp, blk, 2 sp, blk, sp, blk, ch 5, 3 sl, ch 5, blk, sp, blk, ch 5, 3 sl, ch 5, blk, 2 sp, ch 5. *19th row*—3 sp, blk, ch 4, dt in middle sl, ch 4, blk, ch 4, dt, ch 4, blk, ch 4, dt in middle sl, ch 4, blk, 3 sp, blk, 5 sp, blk, 5 sp, blk, ch 4, dt, ch 4, blk, ch 10. *20th row*—Blk on 10-ch, ch 5, 3 sl, ch 5, blk, 4 sp, blk, 4 sp, blk, 5 sp, blk, sp, blk, ch 5, 3 sl, ch 5, blk, sp, blk, 4 sp, ch 5. *21st row*—5 sp, blk, ch 6, 5 sl, ch 6, blk, 7 sp, blk, 2 sp, 3 blk, 2 sp, blk, ch 6, 5 sl, ch 6, blk, ch 10. *22d row*— Blk, sp, blk, ch 5, 3 sl, ch 5, blk, sp, blk, 2 sp, blk, 2 sp, blk, 9 sp, blk, ch 5, 3 sl, ch 5, blk, sp, blk, 4 sp, ch 5. *23d row*—3 sp, blk, ch 4, dt, ch 4, blk, ch 4, dt in middle sl, ch 4, blk, 2 sp, blk, 3 sp, 3 blk, 2 sp, blk, 3 sp, blk, ch 4, dt, ch 4, blk, ch 4, dt in middle sl, ch 4, blk, ch 4, dt, ch 4, blk, ch 10. *24th row*—Blk, ch 5, 3 sl, ch 5, blk, sp, blk, ch 5, 3 sl, ch 5, blk, sp, blk, 3 sp, blk, 3 sp, blk, 2 sp, blk, sp, blk, ch 5, 3 sl, ch 5, blk, 2 sp, ch 5. *25th row*—Sp, blk, ch 6, 5 sl, ch 6, blk, 3 sp, blk, 3 sp, blk, 3 sp, blk, ch 6, 5 sl, ch 6, blk, ch 6, 5 sl, ch 6, blk, ch 5. *26th row*—Miss 1 blk, blk over ch, ch 5, 3 sl, ch 5, blk, sp, blk, ch 5, 3 sl, ch 5, blk, 4 sp, blk, 3 sp, blk, 3 sp, blk, ch 5, 3 sl, ch 5, blk, 2 sp, ch 5. *27th row*—3 sp, blk, ch 4, dt in middle · sl, ch 4, blk, 6 sp, 3 blk, 3 sp, blk, 6 sp, blk, ch 4, dt in middle sl, ch 4, blk, ch 4, dt, ch 4, blk, ch 4, dt in middle sl, ch 4, blk, ch 5. *28th row*—Miss 1 blk, blk, sp, blk, ch 5, 3 sl, ch 5, blk, sp, blk, 21 sp, blk, sp, blk, 4 sp, ch 5. *29th row*—5 sp, blk, 7 sp, blk, 7 sp, blk, 7 sp, blk, ch 6, 5 sl, ch 6, blk, ch 5. *30th row*—Blk, ch 5, 3 sl, ch 5, blk, 4 sp, blk, 4 sp, 7 blk, 3 sp, blk, 5 sp, blk, 4 sp, ch 5. *31st row*—3 sp, blk, 5 sp, 3 blk, sp, blk, 3 sp, blk, 3 sp, blk, 3 sp, 2 blk, 4 sp, blk, ch 4, dt in middle sl, ch 4, blk, ch 5. *32d row*—Blk, sp, blk, 4 sp, blk, sp, blk, 7 sp, blk, 6 sp, blk, 3 sp, blk, 3 sp, blk, 2 sp, ch 5. *33d row*—Sp, blk, 3 sp, 13 blk, 7 sp, blk, 2 sp, blk, 4 sp, blk, ch 10. *34th row*—Blk, sp, blk, 4 sp, blk, sp, blk, 7 sp, blk, 6 sp, blk, 3 sp, blk, 3 sp, blk, 2 sp, ch 5. *35th row*—3 sp, blk, 5 sp, 3 blk, sp, blk, 3 sp, blk, 3 sp, blk, 3 sp, 2 blk, 4 sp, blk, ch 4, dt, ch 4, blk, ch 10. *36th row*—Blk, ch 5, 3 sl, ch 5, blk, 4 sp, blk, 4 sp, 7 blk, 3 sp, blk, 5 sp, blk, 4 sp, ch 5. *37th row*—5 sp, blk, 7 sp, blk, 7 sp, blk, 7 sp, blk, ch 6, 5 sl, ch 6, blk, ch 10. *38th row*—Blk, sp, blk, ch 5, 3 sl, ch 5, blk, sp, blk, 21 sp, blk,

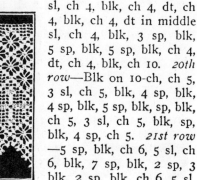

sp, blk, 4 sp, ch 5. *39th row*—3 sp. blk, ch 4, dt, ch 4, blk, 5 sp, blk, 7 sp, blk, 5 sp, blk, ch 4, dt, ch 4, blk, ch 4, dt in middle sl, ch 4, blk, ch 4, dt, ch 4, blk, ch 10. *40th row*—Blk, ch 5, 3 sl, ch 5, blk, sp, blk, ch 5, 3 sl, ch 5, blk, 5 sp, 7 blk, 5 sp, blk, ch 5, 3 sl, ch 5, blk, 2 sp, ch 5. *41st row*—Sp, blk, ch 6, 5 sl, ch 6, blk, 3 sp, blk, 7 sp, blk, 3 sp, blk, ch 6, 5 sl, ch 6, blk, ch 6, 5 sl, ch 6, blk, ch 5. *42d row* —Blk, ch 5, 3 sl, ch 5, blk, sp, blk, ch 5, 3 sl, ch 5, blk, sp, blk, 13 sp, blk, sp, blk, ch 5, 3 sl, ch 5, blk, 2 sp, ch 5. *43d row*—3 sp, blk, ch 4, dt in middle sl, ch 4, blk, ch 4, dt, ch 4, blk, 11 sp, blk, 3 sp, blk, ch 4, dt in middle sl, ch 4, blk, ch 4, dt, ch 4, blk, ch 4, dt in middle sl, ch 4, blk, ch 5. *44th row*—Blk, sp, blk, ch 5, 3 sl, ch 5, blk, sp, blk, 2 sp, blk, 2 sp, blk, 9 sp, blk, ch 5, 3 sl, ch 5, blk, sp, blk, 4 sp, ch 5. *45th row*—5 sp, blk, ch 6, 5 sl, ch 6, blk, 7 sp, blk, 2 sp, 3 blk, 2 sp, blk, ch 6, 5 sl, ch 6, blk, ch 5. *46th row*—Blk, ch 5, 3 sl, ch 5, blk, 4 sp, blk, 4 sp, blk, 5 sp, blk, sp, blk, ch 5, 3 sl, ch 5, blk, sp, blk, 4 sp, ch 5. *47th row*—3 sp, blk, ch 4, dt, ch 4, blk, ch 4, dt in middle sl, ch 4, blk, ch 4, dt, ch 4, blk, 3 sp, blk, 5 sp, blk, 5 sp, blk, ch 4, dt in middle sl, ch 4, blk, ch 5. *48th row*—Blk, sp, blk, 2 sp, blk, 3 sp, blk, 3 sp, blk, 2 sp, blk, sp, blk, ch 5, 3 sl, ch 5, blk, sp, blk, ch 5, 3 sl, ch 5, blk, 2 sp, ch 5. *49th row*—Sp, blk, ch 6, 5 sl, ch 6, blk, ch 6, 5 sl, ch 6, blk, 2 sp, 5 blk, sp, 5 blk, 2 sp, blk, ch 10. The pattern is completed in 48 rows, and the 49th row corresponds with the 1st row, the 50th row with the 2d row, etc. When the lace is finished the required length, make the picot edge as follows: Sl in first 10-ch loop, ch 5, sl in same loop, ch 5, sl in same loop, * ch 5, sl in next loop, ch 5, sl in same, ch 5, sl in same; repeat from *.

Figure 25. Insertion. — No. 50 crochet cotton and No. 9 hook.

Chain 128, turn. *1st row*—T in 4th st from hook, t in each ch st across. *2d row*—Ch 3, 2 t in next 2 t, * ch 3, miss 2, d in 3d ch st, ch 3, t in 3d ch st (from * is one festoon), make 4 more festoons (fest), 13 t (including the last t of fest), 6 fest, 13 t, 5 fest, 3 t (including last t of fest). *3d row*—Ch 3, 2 t, * ch 5, t over t (from * is one bar), 4 more bars, 13 t, 6 bars, 13 t, 5 bars, 3 t. *4th row*—Like 2d row. *5th row*—Like 3d row. *6th row*—Ch 3, 2 t, 4 fest, 7 t, (ch 1, miss 1, t in next) 6 times, 6 t, 4 fest, 7 t, (ch 1, miss 1, t in next) 6 times, 6 t, 4 fest, 3 t. *7th row*—Ch 3, 2 t, 4 bars, 7 t, (ch 1, miss 1, 1 t) 6 times, 6 t, 4 bars, 7 t, (ch 1, miss 1, 1 t) 6 times, 6 t, 4 bars, 3 t. *8th row*—Ch 3, 2 t, 3 fest, 7 t, (ch 1, miss 1, 1 t) 12 times, 6 t, 2 fest, 7 t, (ch 1, miss 1, 1 t) 12 times, 6 t, 3 fest, 3 t. *9th row*—Ch 3, 2 t, 3 bars, 7 t, (ch 1, miss 1, 1 t) 12 times, 6 t, 2 bars, 7 t, (ch 1, miss 1, 1 t) 12 times, 6 t, 3 bars, 3 t. *10th row*—Ch 3, 2 t, fest, 15 t, (ch 1, miss 1, 1 t) 7 times, ch 3, miss 1 t, t in next t, ch 3, (1 t, 1 ch) 7 times, 15 t, (ch 1, miss 1, 1 t) 7 times, ch 3, miss 1 t, t in next, ch 3, (1 t, ch 1) 7 times, 15 t, 1 fest, 3 t. *11th row*—Ch 3, 2 t, 1 bar, 15 t, (ch 1, miss 1, 1 t) 7 times, ch 3, d in t, ch 2, d in same t, ch 3, (1 t, ch 1) 7 times, 15 t, (ch 1, miss 1, 1 t) 7 times, ch 3, d in t, ch 2, d in same t, ch 3, (1 t, ch 1) 7 times, 15 t, 1 bar, 3 t. *12th row* — Ch 3, 2 t, 1 fest, 15 t, (ch 1, miss 1, 1 t) 7 times, ch 3, d in d, 5 t over 2-ch, d in d, ch 3, (1 t, ch 1) 7 times,

15 t, (ch 1, miss 1, 1 t) 7 times, ch 3, d in d, 5 t over 2-ch, d in d, ch 3, (1 t, ch 1) 7 times, 15 t, 1 fest, 3 t. *13th row*—Ch 3, 2 t, 1 bar, 15 t, (ch 1, miss 1, 1 t) 7 times, ch 3, d in centre of 5 t, ch 3, (1 t, ch 1) 7 times, 15 t, (ch 1, miss 1, 1 t) 7 times, ch 3, d in centre of 5 t, ch 3, (1 t, ch 1) 7 times, 15 t, 1 bar, 3 t. *14th row*—Ch 3, 2 t. 3 fest, 7 t, (ch 1, miss 1, 1 t) 12 times, 6 t, 2 fest, 7 t, (ch 1, miss 1, 1 t) 12 times, 7 t, 3 fest, 3 t. *15th row*—Ch 3, 2 t, 3 bars, 7 t, (ch 1, miss 1, 1 t) 12 times, 6 t, 2 bars, 7 t, (ch 1, miss 1, 1 t) 12 times, 6 t, 3 bars, 3 t. *16th row*—Ch 3, 2 t, 4 fest, 7 t, (ch 1, miss 1, 1 t) 6 times, 6 t, 4 fest, 7 t, (ch 1, miss 1, 1 t) 6 times, 6 t, 4 fest, 3 t. *17th row*—Ch 3, 2 t, 4 bars, 7 t, (ch 1, miss 1, 1 t) 6 times, 6 t, 4 bars, 7 t, (ch 1, miss 1, 1 t) 6 times, 6 t, 4 bars, 3 t. Repeat from 2d row.

Figure 26. Leaf and Shell Lace. — No. 150 crochet cotton and No. 14 hook.

Chain 42 sts, turn. *1st row*—One sl in the 10th st from hook, ch 3, miss 2, 1 t in next st (ch 3, miss 2, 1 sl in next st, ch 3, miss 2, 1 t in next st, — a festoon) 4 times, 1 t in next st, ch 2, miss 2, 1 t in next st, turn. *2d row*—Ch 5, 1 t in each of 2 t, (ch 5, 1 t in next t, — a space) 4 times, ch 5, 1 t in the 3d of 10-ch loop, ch 6, 1 t in 8th st of same loop, turn. *3d row*—* A shell, which is always made thus: Twelve d on 6-ch, turn, 12 d on 12 d, turn, (1 d in each of 3 sts, ch 4, 1 d in same st with last d) 3 times, 1 d in each of 3 remaining sts of shell *, 5 festoons (fest), 1 t on next t, ch 2, t in 3d of 5-ch, turn. *4th row*—Ch 5, 1 t in each of 2 t, 6 spaces (sp), putting last t between first 2 p on shell, ch 6, t between next 2 p on shell, turn. *5th row*—A shell like 3d row from * to *, 2 fest, 1 t in each of next 6 sts, 3 fest, t on t, ch 2, t in 3d of 5-ch, turn. *6th*

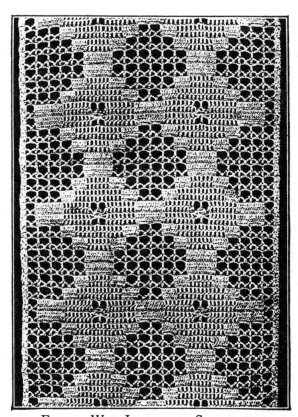

FIG. 25. WIDE INSERTION. See page 21

21

row—Ch 5, 2 t on 2 t, 3 sp, 1 t in each of 6 t, ch 5, t on t, * ch 5, 1 t in first d of shell, ch 5, t between first 2 p on shell, ch 6, t between next 2 p, turn. *7th row*—Shell, * 2 fest, 1 t in each of 6 sts, (ch 1, miss 1, t in next st) 3 times, 1 t in each of next 6 sts, 2 fest, t in t, ch 2, t in 3d of 5-ch, turn. *8th row*—Ch 5, 1 t in each of 2 t, 2 sp, 1 t in each of 6 t, (ch 1, miss 1, t on t) 3 times, 1 t in each of 6 t, * 3 sp, putting last t between p on shell, ch 6, 1 t between next 2 p on shell, turn. *9th row*—Shell,

FIG. 26. LEAF AND SHELL LACE. See page 21

2 fest, 1 t in each of next 6 sts, (ch 1, miss 1, t in next st) 9 times, 1 t in each of the next 6 sts, 1 fest, t in t, ch 2, t in 3d of 5-ch, turn. *10th row*—Ch 5, 1 t in each of 2 t, ch 5, 1 t in each of 7 t, (ch 1, miss 1, t in next st) 9 times, 1 t in each of 6 sts, 2 sp, ch 6, t between first 2 p of shell, turn. *11th row*—Shell, t on t, like 7th row from *. *12th row*—Like 8th row to *, then 1 sp, ch 5, 1 t between first 2 p on shell, ch 6, 1 t between next 2 p on shell, turn. *13th row* — Like 5th row, missing first 5-ch after shell. *14th row*—Like 6th row to *, 2 sp, ch 6, 1 t between next 2 p on shell. *15th row*—Like 3d row, missing first 5-ch after shell. *16th row*—Ch 5, 1 t in each of 2 t, 5 sp, ch 3, 1 d between first 2 p on shell, turn. *17th row*—Ch 3, 1 t in first t, 5 fest, t on t, ch 2, t in 3d of 5-ch, turn. *18th row*—Ch 5, 1 t in each of 2 t, 5 sp, ch 6, 1 t between first 2 p on shell, turn. Repeat from 3d row for length required.

When the lace is completed, leaves are worked over the centre blocks as follows: Fasten thread in centre, ch 11, catch in corner of block, * turn and work 1 d, 1 ht, 7 t, 1 ht, 1 d on 11-ch, ch 11, miss one block, fasten in corner of next one; repeat from * until there are 4 leaves, join first to last with a sl. If preferred the leaves may be worked and sewn to the squares with needle and thread, or they may be omitted altogether.

Figure 27. Diamond Lace. — No. 100 crochet cotton and No. 14 hook.

DIAMONDS. — Chain 10, join to form a ring, ch 4, 5 dt in ring, ch 3, 6 dt in ring, * ch 8 tight and 1 loose ch, ch 9 tight, 1 d in the loose st (this forms the centre for the second diamond), 1 sl in each of 4 sts of ch, 5 dt in ring, ch 3, 6 dt in ring; repeat from * for length required. Then turn, ch 3, ** 6 dt, 3 ch, 6 dt in ring, ch 1, 2 d on ch between diamonds (dia), ch 1; repeat from ** to end of row, ch 3, catch in first t on first row ***, 1 d in each of 6 dt, 6 d on 3-ch, 1 d on each of 6 dt, 3 d on

1-ch, 3 d on 1-ch of next dia; repeat from *** along both sides of dia.

UPPER PART OF LACE. — After finishing last dia, ch 7, 1 t above the 5th d t of first cluster, ch 7, 1 d between the 3d and 4th, d in point of dia, * ch 7, 1 t over the 2d dt of next cluster, then 1 cross dt made as follows: Thread twice around the hook, insert hook over the 5th dt of dia, work off 2 loops, thread around hook, insert hook over the 2d dt of first cluster on next dia, work off all the loops on hook by twos, ch 7, complete dt by working a t in the centre of dt where the 2 t meet, 1 t in the 5th d t of dia, ch 7, 1 d between 3d and 4th d at point of dia; repeat from * across, ch 9, turn. *2d row*—* One t in the 4th st of 7-ch loop, ch 5, 1 d in the first st of 5-ch, 1 t in same st with last t, ch 7; repeat from * across, ch 11, turn. *3d row*—* In the 4th st of 7-ch work 3 dt, as one Cluny group, ch 7; repeat from * to end, ch 9, turn. *4th row* — Like 2d row.

HEADING. *1st row*—T in 4th st of 7-ch, * ch 5, t in 4th st of next 7-ch; repeat from *, turn. *2d row*—Ch 5, miss 2, t in next st, * ch 2, miss 2, t in next st; repeat from *.

LOWER EDGE OF LACE. *1st row*—One t over the 2d dt of cluster, * ch 5, 1 t over the 5th dt of cluster, ch 5, 1 dt between the 3d and 4th d on point, ch 5, 1 dt in the same st with last dt, ch 5, 1 t over the 2d dt of next cluster, ch 5, 1 t over the 5th dt of cluster, 1 t over the 2d dt of next dia; repeat from * across. *2d row*—* Six d in first loop, 7 t, 1 d in next loop, 1 d, 7 t, 1 d in next loop, 1 d, 7 t in next loop, 6 d in last loop on dia; repeat from * across and fasten off. A handsome insertion may be made by omitting the scallops and working both edges alike.

Figure 28. Snowflake Lace. — No. 150 crochet cotton and No. 14 hook.

Make a chain the required length, turn. *1st row*—Seven t in the 4th st from hook, * ch 3, miss 3, 1 d in the next st, ch 3, miss 3, 7 t in the next st; repeat from * across, ending with cluster of 7 t, turn. *2d row*—Ch 3, 1 d in the 3d, 4th, and 5th t of cluster, * ch 11, 1 d in the 3d, 4th, and 5th t of next cluster; repeat from * across, turn. *3d row*—Ch 3, * 7 t in the 6th st of 11-ch, ch 3, 1 d in the second of 3 d on cluster, ch 3; repeat from * across, turn. *4th row*—Ch 14, 1 d in the 3d, 4th, and 5th t of cluster, ch 11; repeat from * across, then after working 3 d on last cluster, ch 6, 1 long t in the shell at end in the 1st row, this is done to keep edge straight, turn. *5th row*—Ch 3, 7 t in the first of 6-ch, * ch 3, 1 d

FIG. 27. DIAMOND LACE. See page 22

in the 2d d on cluster, ch 3, 7 t in the 6th of 11-ch; repeat from * across. Repeat from 2d row until as wide as desired. Then work the edge as follows: One d in the 2d t of cluster, * (ch 5, miss 1, 1 d in next t of cluster) twice, ch 5, (2 t, ch 3, 2 t) in the 4th t of next cluster, ch 5, 1 d in the 2d t on next cluster; repeat from * across, ending row with 2d d on shell, turn. *2d row*—Ch 5, 1 d in 5-ch loop, * ch 5, 9 dt with 1 ch between each in the 3-ch loop, ch 5, 1 d in 5-ch loop, ch 5, 1 d in next 5-ch loop; repeat from * across, turn. *3d row*—Sl to centre of 5-ch

FIG. 28. SNOWFLAKE LACE. See page 22

loop, * ch 2, 1 t on 5-ch, (ch 1, 1 t on next 1-ch between dt) 8 times, ch 1, 1 t on 5-ch, ch 2, 1 d in 5-ch loop; repeat from * across, turn. *4th row*—Ch 3, 1 t on 2-ch, * (ch 5, 1 d in first of 5-ch to form a p, 2 t in next space), 9 times, p of 5 ch, 1 t on 2-ch, 1 t on next 2-ch; repeat from * across, and fasten off. HEADING. — One t in first st, (ch 1, miss 1, 1 t in next st); repeat across.

Figure 29. Rose Medallion Lace. — No. 70 crochet cotton and No. 12 hook.

ROSE. — Wind the working thread 20 times around the top of the crochet-hook, slip off and work 16 d in the ring, sl in 1st d to join. Chain 8, miss 1, 1 t in next st, (ch 5, miss 1, 1 t in next st) 6 times, ch 5, sl in the 3d of first 8-ch, * 7 d on 5-ch, ch 6, 1 d in top of last d; repeat from * around, making 8 loops in all, sl to the fourth of 7 d, ** 11 t in the 6-ch loop, sl in the 4th of next 7 d; repeat from ** around. Sl to the 6th of 11 t, ch 14, 1 t in centre of next petal, ch 9, 1 dt in centre of next petal, ch 9, 1 dt in same place with last dt, ch 9, 1 t in centre of next petal, ch 9, 1 d in the centre of next petal, ch 9, 1 dt in same place with last dt, ch 9, 1 d in next petal, ch 9, 1 dt in next petal, ch 9, 1 dt in same place with last dt, ch 9, 1 t in next petal, ch 9, 1 dt in centre of next petal, ch 9, sl in 5th of first 14 ch, fasten off. In working the second and following flowers they must be joined to the 5th of the 9 ch between the dt of the preceding one with a sl, after working 4 of the 9 ch between 2 dt.

Make as many roses as required for length; join the thread to the first ch st after the 2 dt at end of strip, ch 3, miss 1, 1 t in the next st, (ch 1, miss 1, 1 t in the next st) 23 times, * 1 t in the first ch after the dt on next rose, (ch 1, miss 1, 1 t in next st) 24 times; repeat from * across, to pass end, ch 9, 1 d in the 5th of 9 ch on rose, ch 9, 1 t in the first ch

after dt; repeat from * along other side of lace.

HEADING.—Chain 8, 1 t in 3d space, ch 2, miss 2 sp, 1 dt in next sp, ch 13, * miss 3 sp, 2 d in each of next 6 sp, ch 13, 1 dt in 3d sp, ch 2, miss 2 sp, 1 t in next sp, 1 dt between patterns, ** 1 t in 4th sp, ch 2, 1 dt in 3d sp, ch 3, 1 sl in the 4th st of 13 ch, ch 10; repeat from * across, ending at **, turn, ch 6, 1 sl in the 4th st of 13 ch, now work 1 d in each st across top of lace, fasten off.

LOWER EDGE.—Chain 1, 1 long t (over 3 times) in top of 1st t, * miss 3 sp, 1 dt in next sp, miss 2 sp, 1 long t in next sp, ch 5, 1 long t in same sp, ch 7, 1 long t in same sp, ch 5, 1 long t in same sp, miss 4 sp, 1 long t in next sp, ch 5, 1 long t in same sp, ch 7, 1 long t in next sp, ch 5, 1 long t in same sp, miss 4 sp, 1 long t in next sp, ch 5, 1 long t in same sp, ch 7, 1 long t in same sp, ch 5, 1 long t in same sp, miss 2 sp, 1 dt in next sp, 1 long t between patterns; repeat from * and fasten off. *2d row*—9 d on each 5-ch and 11 d on each 7-ch on edge of lace.

Figure 30. Edging. — No. 100 crochet cotton and No. 14 hook.

Chain 52. *1st round*—Do not join the ch with a sl; instead, make 3 d in 1st st, working over end of thread and taking up 2 threads of st, (12 d in next 12 sts, 3 d in next st) 3 times, 12 d in next 12 sts, join to 1st d with sl. *2d round*—Sl in each of next 2 d, ch 3 for t, 4 more t in same st where 3 ch began, (14 t in next 14 d, 5 t in next st) 3 times, 14 t in next 14 d, join with sl in top st of the 3-ch. *3d round*—Ch 2 for 1st d, d in each of next 2 t, (picot of 6 joined with d) twice, * ch 13, put hook down through 2d st from last picot and make a sl across to bring thread on the right side of ring, make 1 d, 1 ht, 19 t, 1 ht, 1 d in ring, ch 1, (picot of 6, joined by d) twice, * d in same st with last d on corner of square, 5 d in next 5 sts; repeat from * to * twice more on the side, missing 1 t between the p bars, and making 6 t in next 6 t. At the corners repeat from * to *, making 1 d in same st with last d; on the sides miss 1 t between each pair of picot bars, and 6 d in next 6 t; repeat on each side, making 3 d after last picot bar on last side, joining to 2d ch st with sl, and

FIG. 29. ROSE MEDALLION LACE. See page 23

break thread. *4th round*—Having a st on the hook, put thread over and make * 1 t in 7th st of first circle at corner, (ch 1, picot of 6 joined by d, ch 1, miss 1 t, t in next) 5 times, ch 1 *; repeat from * to * in each circle around the square, join to 1st t with sl, and break thread.

Fill in the centre of squares with double net stitches. Make as many squares as required for length, joining each square to preceding one in the 4th round as follows: After the 1st sp on the circle at third corner, ch 4, take hook out of work and insert in second picot of corresponding circle of preceding square, catch dropped st, and draw through picot, ch 3, 1 d in 2d st, ch 1, miss 1 t, t in next t; repeat in next picot; this leaves 2 free picots above the joining and this side must be placed towards the top of the lace.

HEADING. *1st row* — Begin at right hand of top edge, having a st on hook, * thread over twice, insert hook in last picot on corner circle and draw a loop through, thread over and through 2 loops, insert hook in first picot on next circle, draw loop through, (thread over and through 2 loops) 3 times, * (ch 9, miss 1 p, 3 t in next, ch 9, repeat from * to *) 5 times, ** ch 3; repeat from * to * in the two opposite picots, ch 5, take hook out of work, insert in 5th st of 9 ch, ch 4, miss 1 p, 3 t in next, ch 9;

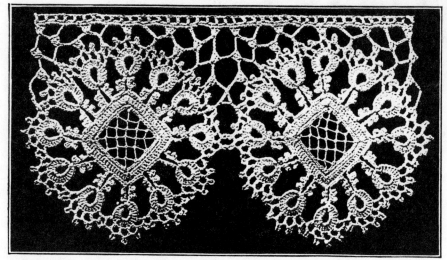

FIG. 30. EDGING. See page 23

repeat from * to *, then repeat directions in last parenthesis 4 times **, then repeat from ** to ** to end and break thread. *2d row* — Begin again at right corner, 3 t in 5th st of second 9-ch, * (ch 9, 3 t in 5th st of next 9-ch) twice, ch 5, sl in 5th st of next 9-ch, pull out loop and slip ball through to fasten and carry thread loosely along top to the 5th st of next 9-ch, sl in that st, ch 5, 3 t in 5th st of next 9-ch, (ch 9, 3 t in 5th st of next 9-ch) twice, ch 3, 3 t in 5th st of opposite 9-ch *; repeat from * to * to the end. *3d row* — 3 t in 5th st of first 9-ch, ch 5, sl in 5th st of next 9-ch, slip ball through loop and carry the thread along to 5th st of first 9-ch beyond 3 t at centre, and sl in that st, letting the thread lie quite loosely along the top edge, ch 5, 3 t in 5th st of last 9-ch on first scallop, ch 3; repeat from beginning of row to end and break thread. *4th row* — One d in each of 3 t, 6 d in next sp, 6 d in next sp, making first one in same st with sl, 3 d in next 3 t, 6 d in next sp, 1 d in sl, 5 d in sp, 3 d in 3 t, 5 d in sp, 1 d in sl, 6 d in sp, 3 d in 3 t, 5 d in sp, 1 d in sl, 6 d in sp, 3 d in 3 t, 3 d in 3-ch sp; repeat from beginning of row. *5th row* — One t in 1st d, * ch 2, miss 2, t in next; repeat from * to end.

Figure 31. Rose and Leaf Edge. — No. 70 crochet cotton and No. 14 hook.

LEAF. — Chain 12, turn, miss 1 st, 11 d in 11 sts, ch 2, d in same st with last d, 9 d in 9 sts down the other side, * ch 1, turn, 10 d in 10 d (into back loop only), d under 2-ch, ch 2, d in same place, 9 d in next 9 d on the other side *; repeat from * to * 4 times, ch 1, turn, 10 d in 10 d, d under 2-ch, ch 4, miss 1 st of 4-ch, 3 d in next 3 sts, d under 2-ch, 1 sl through last st, break thread and fasten securely at the back. Make another leaf but omit the stem; at the end after making "10 d in 10 d, d under 2-ch," make 1 sl in the 2d ch and fasten off. Make a third leaf like first one, but make only 3 ch st at the end instead of 4, pick up the leaf with no stem, holding it right side up, take hook out of work and insert it down through the top of last d (made under the 2-ch), and out at the side, catch the 3d st that was dropped and draw it through the d, ch 1 to fasten, then pick up leaf with stem, take hook out of work and insert in end of stem, pull st through, 1 d in each of next 2 sts (of stem), 1 d under 2 ch, 1 sl in next d and fasten off at back.

Beginning at the top of last leaf made and joined to the others, join thread in the outer st of last rib, * (ch 1, picot of 5 joined with d, ch 2, d in end of next rib) twice, make another picot loop the same way, placing the d after it in the end of the centre of leaf, ch 5, 1 d in same place, make 3 more p loops on the same leaf, * ch 1, picot, ch 1, d in end of first rib on next leaf **; repeat from first * to ** once, then from * to * and break thread.

ROSE. — Chain 7, t in 1st st of ch, (ch 4, t in same st) 3 times, (in making the last t, catch the loose end of thread and work it in with the t, then cut off remainder of it), ch 4, 1 sl in 2d st of ch. *2d round* — (D, 5 t, d) over each sp around, take hook out of work, insert through t at end of petal and draw last st through to the back. *3d round* — * Ch 5, insert hook between the doubles at end of petal, at the back, and make 1 d under the ch over which the last row was worked; repeat around. *4th round* — (D, 6 t, d) over each 5 ch around, draw last st through to the back. *5th round* — Ch 7, and fasten between doubles as in 3d round; repeat around. *6th round* — (D, 10 t, d) over each of 3 sp, in the 4th sp after making the 5th t, take hook out of work, insert between 5th and 6th d (counting from stem) on last made leaf, draw st through, then finish petal the same as the others. In the next petal after making the 5th t take hook out and draw st through between the 5th and 6th d on next leaf (without stem) then finish petal, 1 sl in 1st d, fasten off.

Make three more leaves and join. In working the row of p loops around leaves, join to the rose as follows: After making 3 p loops on the leaf at the top, ch 2, take hook out, and draw through second free petal between 4th and 5th t, counting from the

24

bottom upwards, ch 2, d in top section of leaf in the same st with last d, the next picot loop will be free (not joined to the rose), but with 1 d in end of next rib, ch 4, take hook out, draw st through between 4th and 5th t on next petal (counting downwards), ch 2, 1 d in 2d st of ch, ch 2, 1 d in end of next rib, make one more p loop on same leaf, and one between leaves, then join next 3 p loops on second leaf the same as the last loop on rose was joined, finish the same as on first three leaves.

Repeat leaves and roses to the length required, joining as indicated in directions.

HEADING. *1st row*—Join thread between 4th and 5th t on second petal from joining at right hand, ch 10, d between 4th and 5th t on next petal, * ch 10, d in 1st p on leaf, (ch 4, d in next p) twice, ch 7, t in next petal between 3d and 4th t from joining of p, ch 8, d on next petal between 4th and 5th t; repeat from * to end of row. *2d row*— Begin again at right hand, join thread in 2d st of 10 ch, ch 2, 1 ht in next st, 1 ht in each st to end of row, taking 1 loop of st only, break thread. *3d row*—Fasten thread in 2d ch st at right, ch 3, miss 1, t in next, * ch 1, miss 1, t in next; repeat from * to end.

Figure 32. Edging. — No. 70 crochet cotton and No. 12 hook.

Chain 17, turn. *1st row*—T in 8th st from hook, ch 3, t in same st, ch 2, miss 1, in next 6 sts of ch make 1 d, 1 ht, 1 t, 1 dt, 2 long t (3 loops), turn. *2d row*—Ch 8, (1 t, ch 3, 1 t) over 3 ch between 2 t at end of pyramid, ch 6, d over loop at end of 1st row, turn. *3d row*—Ch 1, 2 d over 6 ch, ch 4, make a picot by inserting hook down through top and out at the side of last d, and make 1 d, 2 d, p, 2 d, p, 2 d over same ch-loop, ch 2, (1 t, ch 3, 1 t) over 3 ch between next 2 t, ch 2, miss 1 st on 8-ch, in next 6 sts of ch make 1 d, 1 ht, 1 t, 1 dt, 2 long t (3 loops), turn. *4th row*—Ch 8, (1 t, ch 3, 1 t) over 3 ch, ch 6, 1 d over 2-ch, 1 sl in 1st d over 6-ch, turn; repeat from 3d row.

HEADING. *1st row*—After making last pyramid of row, ch 8, t between next 2 pyramids, (ch 5, t between next two) repeat to end and break thread. *2d row*—Fasten thread in 3d st of 8 ch, 5 d over ch, 1 d over t, (5 d over next 5-ch, 1 d over t) repeat to the end.

Figure 33. Curtain Trimming. — Cable or Brussels net, or scrim and No. 50 crochet cotton and No. 10 hook. No. 30 or No. 20 cotton may be used if preferred.

BACK EDGE OF CURTAIN. — * Six d into material, picot of 4, 6 d, p; repeat along outer edge of curtain.

For Insertion and Edging, see Fig. 1, Frontispiece, and directions for Fig. 1 (page 25).

Figure 1. Scarf. (See Frontispiece.) — No. 50 crochet cotton and No. 10 hook and linen, 19 x 30 inches.

The Insertion and Edging used in this Scarf are like the Curtain Trimming of Fig. 33.

MEDALLION.—Chain 8, join with sl. *1st round*—Ch 5, (t into ring, ch 2) 7 times, join with sl in 3d of 5-ch, making 8 spaces. *2d round*—Ch 7, (t into t of 1st row, ch 4) 7 times, sl in 3d of 7-ch. *3d round*—Ch 12, dt into each t of previous round, 8 ch between, sl in 4th st of 12-ch. *4th round*—Ch 1, cover each 8-ch with 11 d, join with sl in 1st ch;

FIG. 31. ROSE AND LEAF EDGE. See page 24

cut and fasten thread. Repeat medallion and when, in the last round, all but the last 2 loops are covered with d, make 5 d, sl onto middle of scallop of first medallion, 5 d over same loop, 5 d over next loop, sl into middle of next scallop of 1st medallion, 5 d over same loop, join with sl, cut and fasten thread. In joining be careful to keep right side of work up. At the corner join to make a right angle instead of straight line.

1st row of outer edge—Ch 4, t into middle of 1st scallop of medallion, ch 4, t down between scallops, ch 4, t into middle of next scallop, ch 4, * thread over 4 times, making 5 loops on hook, insert hook between next scallops, thread over and draw through, thread over and draw through 2 loops twice, (now there are 4 loops left on hook), thread over twice (making 6 loops), insert hook between next scallops of next medallion, thread over and draw through, (over and through 2 loops) 6 times, ch 4, t in middle of cross treble just made, ch 4, t into middle of next scallop, ch 4, t between scallops, ch 4, t in middle of next scallop, ch 4; repeat from *. In turning outer

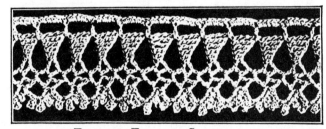

FIG. 32. EDGING. See page 25

corner after making t in middle of last scallop, ch 6, thread over 4 times, insert hook between scallops, thread over and draw through, (over and draw through 2) 5 times, ch 6, t into middle of next scallop, ch 4, and repeat as before. In turning inside corner, after making t in middle of last scallop, ch 4, thread over 4 times, insert hook between scallops, thread over and through, (over and through 2) twice, (this leaves 4 loops on hook), thread over twice, with 6 loops on hook, insert hook between scallops in the corner medallion, thread over and through, (over and through

2) twice, leaving 5 loops on hook, thread over twice, insert hook between scallops on next medallion, thread over and through, (over and through 2) twice, over and through 3, (over and through 2) 3 times, ch 4, t into middle of next scallop, continue as before. *2d row of outer edge*—* Ch 2, t into t of 1st row, ch 2, t down between t; repeat from *. *3d row*—T into

through middle of completed scallop, cover this 7-ch with 11 d, make 5 d over unfinished scallop, sl at base of scallop, (ch 2, miss 2, t in next) 4 times; repeat from * to end of ch.

Figure 34. Edge and Insertion. — No. 100 crochet cotton and No. 13 hook.

EDGING. — Ch 6, t in 1st st of ch, (ch 6, t in last space) twice, ch 9, turn. *2d row*—One d in 1st loop, (ch 6, d in next loop) twice, ch 9, turn. *3d row*—One d in first loop, 5 t in loop of row directly beneath next d, d in next loop, ch 6, d in next loop, ch 9, turn. *4th row*—D in 1st loop, ch 6, d in centre of shell, ch 6, d in next loop, ch 9, turn. *5th, 6th, 7th and 8th rows*—D in 1st loop, (ch 6, d in next loop) twice, ch 9, turn. Repeat from 3d row for length required. On narrow side of net work (ch 5, 1 d in next loop); repeat across: this brings the shell in the centre of the net. On the other side of net work the edge as follows: One d in 1st loop, * ch 10, d in next loop, ch 3, d in next loop; repeat from *. *2d row*—* (2 d, ch 4) 5 times, 2 d, all over 10-ch; 4 d over 3-ch; repeat from *.

The Insertion is worked like the Edging, omitting the lower edge.

Figure 35. Block Insertion. — Crochet cotton No. 30 and No. 9 hook.

Chain 55, turn. *1st row*—T in 9th st from hook, 7 t over 7 ch sts, ch 6, miss 4 ch, 8 t (block) over next 8 ch, ch 6, miss 4, 8 t over next 8 ch, ch 6, miss 4, 8 t over next 8 ch, ch 2, t over last ch, ch 5, turn. *2d row*—(* 3 t over 1st 3 t, ch 2, miss 2, 3 t over next 3 t, * ch 5) 3 times; repeat from * to *, ch 2, t in 3d of 5-ch, ch 5, turn. *3d row*—(* 2 t over 1st 2 t, ch 2, 2 t over ch, ch 2, 2 t over last 2 t in block, * ch 5) 3 times; repeat from * to *, ch 2, t in 3d ch, ch 5, turn. *4th row*—(* 3 t over 2 t and 1st ch, ch 2, 3 t over ch and last 2 t, * ch 3, catch together the three bars made in previous rows with a d and draw up tight, ch 3) 3 times; repeat from * to *, ch 2, t in 3d ch, ch 5, turn. *5th row*—(* 8 t over last block made, * ch 6) 3 times; repeat from * to *, ch 2, t over 3d ch, ch 5, turn. *6th row*—One t over 1st t, (ch 6, 1 t over last t of block, 6 t over ch, 1 t over 1st t of next block, making a block of 8) 3 times, ch 6, t over last t of block, ch 2, t over 3d ch, ch 5, turn. *7th row*—T over t, (ch 5, 3 t over 3 t, ch 2, 3 t over 3 t) 3 times, ch 5, t over t, ch 2, t over 3d ch, ch 5, turn. *8th row*—T over t, (ch 5, 2 t over 2 t, ch 2, 2 t over ch, ch 2, 2 t over last 2 t in block) 3 times, ch 5, t over t, ch 2, t over 3d ch, ch 5, turn. *9th row*—T over t, (* ch 3, catch 3 bars with d, ch 3 *, 3 t, ch 2, 3 t) 3 times; repeat from * to *, t over t, ch 2, t over 3d ch, ch 5, turn. *10th row*—T over t, (ch 6, 8 t) 3 times, ch 6, t over t, ch 2, t over 3d ch, ch 5, turn. *11th row*—(Block of 8 t over 1st t and ch and 1st t of block below, ch 6) 3 times, block of 8 t, ch 2, t over 3d ch, ch 5, turn. *12th row*—Like 2d row. *13th row*—Like 3d row, etc. The Insertion is three and one-half inches wide.

Figure 36. Edging. — No. 70 crochet cotton and No. 12 hook.

Make a ch of 35 sts, turn. *1st row*—Miss 1,

FIG. 33. CURTAINS OF NET WITH CROCHETED EDGING AND INSERTION. See Fig. 1 and page 25

each t of 2d row, with 2-ch between. In 2d and 3d rows ch 5 in turning corner.

EDGING. — Make ch required length, turn, t into 9th st from hook, (ch 2, miss 2, t into next) 3 times, having 4 open meshes, * (ch 7, drop st and pick it up through top of 2d t back) twice, cover 7-ch with 11 d, over next ch make 5 d, ch 7, drop st and pick it up

FIG. 34. EDGING AND INSERTION. See page 26

1 d in each of 34 sts, turn. *2d row*—Ch 5, miss 1, 1 dt in next st, (ch 1, miss 1, dt in next st) 16 times, turn. *3d row*—Ch 1, d in each dt and each ch st of last row, turn. *4th row*—Ch 5, starting in the 3d d work 1 t in each of 3 sts, (ch 3, miss 3, 3 t over next 3 sts) 5 times, turn. *5th row*—Ch 9, 3 t in the 1st 3-ch space of last row, (ch 3, 3 t in next 3-ch space) 5 times, turn. *6th row*—Ch 5, 3 t in 1st space, (ch 3, 3 t in next space) 5 times, (ch 2, 1 dt) 8 times in the 9-ch loop where last 3 t are worked, ch 2, 1 d in the end of 2d row of d, turn. *7th row*—(3 d over 2-ch, picot of 5 joined with d) 8 times, 3 d over each space and 1 d over each t of last row. This 7th row corresponds with the 1st row; repeat from 2d row for required length.

HEADING. *1st row*—4 d over each t along the top of lace. *2d row*—One dt in the 1st st, (ch 1, miss 1, 1 dt in the next st) repeat throughout.

Figure 37. Border for Tea Cloth.— Crochet cotton No. 150, and No. 14 hook. Work trebles into back loop, only, of trebles of preceding row; this gives the work a ribbed appearance.

The rows forming one complete pattern of the design are numbered from 1 to 50. But if the worker wishes to begin at the middle of one side of a square (at point marked A in Fig. 38), four rows,—A, B, C, and D, must be made before beginning row No. 1. Worked in this way the joining of first and last rows of work will be in the middle of a side of a finished square.

Chain 118, plus 3 as 1 t, turn. *Row A* (worked toward inner edge)—Beginning in the 4th st from hook, make 6 t in next 6 ch, 35 sp, 7 t, ch 3. This 3 ch when beginning another row is always counted as 1 t, and hereafter, when a given number of trebles is indicated at beginning of a row, it is understood that a ch of 3 is included as 1 t; thus, —7 t, when beginning a row means, ch 3, 6 more t. Turn at the end of every row.

Row B—7 t, 35 sp, 7 t. *Row C*—7 t, 21 sp, 4 t, 4 sp, 4 t, 8 sp, 7 t. *Row D*—7 t, 8 sp, 4 t, 2 sp, 4 t, 1 sp, 7 t, 6 sp, 4 t, 13 sp, 7 t. Begin with row No. 1 and continue working the pattern as shown at Fig. 37. When fin-

ishing the first of the two leaves at middle of next side after corner, work the last 4 rows of the leaf from design shown at Fig. 38, then a row of spaces, and begin again at Row A.

1st row—7 t, 9 sp, 4 t, 4 sp, 13 t, 3 sp, 10 t, 1 sp, 4 t, 9 sp, 7 t. *2d row*—7 t, 9 sp, 4 t, 1 sp, 10 t, 1 sp, 28 t, 11 sp, 7 t. *3d row*—Sl over 7 t, ch 3, 6 t (7 t in all), 10 sp, 40 t, 10 sp, 7 t. *4th row*— 7 t, 10 sp, 4 t, 1 sp, 28 t, 12 sp, 7 t. *5th row*—Sl over 7 t as in 3d row, 7 t, 9 sp, 34 t, 2 sp, 7 t, 7 sp, 7 t. *6th row*—7 t, 6 sp, 19 t, 1 sp, 25 t, 10 sp, 7 t. *7th row*—Sl over 7 t, 7 t, 12 sp, 10 t, 1 sp, 4 t, 1 sp, 19 t, 5 sp, 7 t. *8th row*—7 t, 7 sp, 13 t, 1 sp, 4 t, 4 sp, 4 t, 11 sp, 7 t. *9th row*—Sl over 7 t, 7 t, 6 sp, 10 t, 4 sp, 4 t, 1 sp, 13 t, 2 sp, 4 t, 5 sp, 7 t. *10th row*—7 t, 4 sp, 4 t, 1 sp, 19 t, 2 sp, 4 t, 1 sp, 19 t, 5 sp, 7 t. *11th row*—Ch 8, t in 4th st from hook, 4 t in next 4 ch, 1 t in last t of preceding row (block of 7 t), 4 sp, 31 t, 2 sp, 22 t, 1 sp, 4 t, 4 sp, 7 t. *12th row*—7 t, 3 sp, 4 t, 1 sp, 25 t, 1 sp, 31 t, 5 sp, 7 t. *13th row*— Ch 8, 6 t as at beginning of 11th row, 9 sp, 25 t, 1 sp, 16 t, 4 sp, 4 t, 3 sp, 7 t. *14th row*—7 t, 3 sp, 4 t, 4 sp, 16 t, 1 sp, 31 t, 7 sp, 7 t. *15th row*—Ch 8, 6 t as in 11th row, 8 sp, 34 t, 1 sp, 4 t, 1 sp, 13 t, 3 sp, 7 t, 2 sp, 7 t. *16th row*—7 t, 2 sp, 7 t, 3 sp, 13 t, 3 sp, 28 t, 10 sp, 7 t. *17th row*—Ch 8, 6 t as before, 11 sp, 31 t, 4 sp, 10 t, 3 sp, 7 t, 2 sp, 7 t. *18th row* —7 t, 1 sp, 4 t, 1 sp, 4 t, 4 sp, 7 t, 5 sp, 31 t, 10 sp, 7 t. *19th row*—7 t, 9 sp, 22 t, 1 sp, 10 t, 5 sp, 4 t, 5 sp, 4 t, 1 sp, 4 t, 1 sp, 7 t. *20th row*—7 t, 1 sp, 4 t, 2 sp, 4 t, 11 sp, 4 t, 2 sp, 7 t, 1 sp, 16 t, 8 sp, 7 t. *21st row*—7 t, 8 sp, 10 t, 3 sp, 4 t, 15 sp, 4 t, 2 sp, 4 t, 1 sp, 7 t. *22d row*—7 t, 1 sp, 4 t, 2 sp, 4 t, 9 sp, 4 t, 12 sp, 4 t, 7 sp, 7 t. *23d row*—7 t, 21 sp, 10 t, 6 sp, 4 t,

FIG. 35. BLOCK INSERTION. See page 26

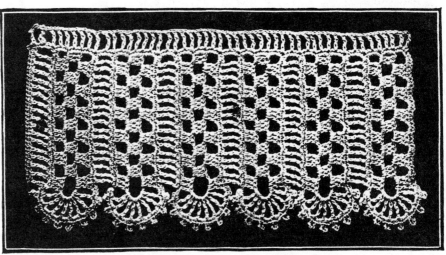

FIG. 36. EDGING. See page 26

2 sp, 4 t, 1 sp, 7 t. *24th row*—7 t, 1 sp, 4 t, 2 sp, 7 t, 4 sp, 19 t, 19 sp, 7 t. *25th row*—7 t, 17 sp, 28 t, 2 sp, 4 t, 1 sp, 4 t, 2 sp, 4 t, 1 sp, 7 t. *26th row*—7 t, 1 sp, 4 t, 3 sp, 4 t, 1 sp, 4 t, 2 sp, 19 t, 1 sp, 4 t, 3 sp, 4 t, 13 sp, 7 t. *27th row*—7 t, 14 sp, 10 t, 1 sp, 4 t, 2 sp, 10 t, 1 sp, 7 t, 2 sp, 4 t, 2 sp, 4 t, 2 sp, 7 t. *28th row*—7 t, 2 sp, 4 t, 2 sp, 4 t, 4 sp, 19 t, 1 sp, 4 t, 3 sp, 4 t, 11 sp, 7 t. *29th row*—7 t, 15 sp, 28 t, 3 sp, 4 t, 2 sp, 4 t, 2 sp, 7 t. *30th row*—7 t, 2 sp, 4 t, 3 sp, 4 t, 3 sp, 19 t, 15 sp, 7 t. *31st row*—7 t, 17 sp, 10 t, 4 sp, 4 t, 3 sp, 4 t, 2 sp, 7 t. *32d row*—7 t, 3 sp, 4 t, 3 sp, 4 t, 6 sp, 4 t, 14 sp, 7 t. *33d row*—7 t, 21 sp, 4 t, 3 sp, 4 t, 3 sp, 7 t. *34th row*—7 t, 3 sp, 4 t, 4 sp, 4 t, 10 sp, 4 t, 7 sp, 7 t. *35th row*—Ch 15, sl in 3d st from work, making a double ch for foundation of 7 t of next row, count the last 3 sts of the 15 ch as a t, miss last t of preceding row, 6 t over next 6 t, 8 sp, 13 t, 6 sp, 4 t, 4 sp, 4 t, 3 sp, 7 t. *36th row*—7 t, 3 sp, 4 t, 5 sp, 7 t, 3 sp, 22 t, 8 sp, 7 t worked over the upper ch and into sts of lower ch. *37th row*—Ch 15, begin row like 35th row, after 6 t,—4 sp, 4 t, 3 sp, 4 t, 1 sp, 16 t, 2 sp, 4 t, 1 sp, 4 t, 5 sp, 4 t, 3 sp, 7 t. *38th row*—7 t, 4 sp, 4 t, 5 sp, 4 t, 1 sp, 7 t, 1 sp, 7 t, 2 sp, 4 t, 1 sp, 10 t, 7 sp, 7 t. *39th row*—Begin as 35th row, after 6 t,—6 sp, 4 t, 3 sp, 4 t, 1 sp, 16 t, 3 sp, 4 t, 5 sp, 4 t, 4 sp, 7 t. *40th row*—7 t, 4 sp, 4 t, 6 sp, 4 t, 2 sp, 22 t, 12 sp, 7 t. *41st row*—Begin as 35th, after 6 t,—14 sp, 13 t, 3 sp, 4 t, 6 sp, 4 t, 4 sp, 7 t. *42d row*—7 t, 5 sp, 4 t, 6 sp, 4 t, 6 sp, 4 t, 15 sp, 7 t. *43d row*—7 t, 21 sp, 4 t, 7 sp, 4 t, 5 sp, 7 t. *44th row*—7 t, 5 sp, 4 t, 8 sp, 4 t, 20 sp, 7 t. *45th row*—7 t, 9 sp, 4 t, 9 sp, 4 t, 8 sp, 4 t, 6 sp, 7 t. *46th row*—7 t, 6 sp, 4 t, 9 sp, 4 t, 6 sp, 7 t, 10 sp, 7 t. *47th row*—7 t, 8 sp, 13 t, 4 sp, 7 t, 9 sp, 4 t, 7 sp, 7 t. *48th row*—7 t, 7 sp, 4 t, 11 sp, 13 t, 1 sp, 7 t, 1 sp, 4 t, 7 sp, 7 t. *49th row*—7 t, 8 sp, 13 t, 9 sp, 4 t, 4 sp, 4 t, 8 sp, 7 t. *50th row*—7 t, 8 sp, 4 t, 2 sp, 4 t, 1 sp, 7 t, 6 sp, 4 t, 1 sp, 7 t, 10 sp, 7 t.

This completes the pattern; to repeat, begin again at 1st row. Work 42 rows, then begin corner in next row. *43d row*—(of 2d pattern), 7 t, 21 sp, 4 t, 7 sp, 4 t, 2 sp, miss 3 sp, and 7 t of last row, to begin mitred corner (see detail of corner, Fig. 39). *44th row*—Ch 5 for a sp, t in next t, 1 more sp, 4 t, 8 sp, 4 t, 20 sp, 7 t. *45th row*—7 t, 9 sp, 4 t, 9 sp, 4 t, 8 sp, 4 t, 3 sp. *46th row*—3 sp (5 ch for 1st sp), 4 t, 9 sp, 4 t, 6 sp, 7 t, 10 sp, 7 t. *47th row*—7 t, 8 sp,

13 t, 4 sp, 7 t, 11 sp, 4 t, 2 sp. *48th row*—2 sp, 4 t, 13 sp, 13 t, 1 sp, 4 t, 2 sp, 4 t, 7 sp, 7 t. *49th row*—7 t, 8 sp, 13 t, 9 sp, 4 t, 8 sp, 4 t. *50th row*—Sl over 4 t, 6 sp (5 ch for 1st sp), 4 t, 1 sp, 7 t, 6 sp, 4 t, 1 sp, 7 t, 10 sp, 7 t. *51st row*—7 t, 9 sp, 4 t, 4 sp, 13 t, 3 sp, 10 t, 3 sp, 7 t. *52d row*—Sl over 4 t, 7 t, 2 sp, 10 t, 1 sp, 28 t, 11 sp, 7 t. *53d row*—Sl over 7 t, 7 t, 10 sp, 43 t. *54th row*—Sl over 4 t, 4 t, 1 sp, 28 t, 12 sp, 7 t. *55th row*—Sl over 7 t, 7 t, 9 sp, 34 t. *56th row*—4 t, 1 sp, 25 t, 10 sp, 7 t. *57th row*—Sl over 7 t, 7 t, 12 sp, 10 t, 1 sp, 4 t. *58th row*—4 t, 4 sp, 4 t, 11 sp, 7 t. *59th row*—Sl over 7 t, 7 t, 6 sp, 10 t, 4 sp, 4 t. *60th row*—Sl over 4 t, 4 t, 1 sp, 19 t, 5 sp, 7 t. *61st row*—Ch 8, 6 t (as at 1st of 11th row), 4 sp, 31 t. *62d row*—Sl over 4 t, 25 t, 5 sp, 7 t. *63d row*—Ch 8, 6 t as in 61st row, 9 sp, 16 t. *64th row*—Sl over 4 t, 19 t, 7 sp, 7 t. *65th row*—Ch 8, 6 t as before, 8 sp, 19 t. *66th row*—Sl over 4 t, 10 t, 10 sp, 7 t. *67th row*—Ch 8, 6 t, 11 sp, 10 t. *68th row*—Sl over 4 t, 10 t, 10 sp, 7 t. *69th row*—7 t, 9 sp, 7 t. *70th row*—Sl over 4 t, 7 t, 8 sp, 7 t. *71st row*—7 t, 8 sp, 4 t. *72d row*—Sl over 4 t, 4 t, 7 sp, 7 t. *73d row*—7 t, 6 sp. *74th row*—6 sp, 7 t. *75th row*—7 t, 2 sp. *76th row*—7 t. *77th row*—7 t. This completes first half of corner.

SECOND HALF OF CORNER. *1st row*—Ch 8, 6 t on ch as before, 2 sp on end of next block of t, miss 1 sp of the 4 sp of upright row, t in next t, making another sp. *2d row*—Ch 2, t in t after next sp of upright row, turn, 2 sp, 7 t. *3d row*—Ch 8, 6 t, 4 sp, t in t after next sp of upright row. *4th row*—Ch

NOTE.—Fig. 37 is a good example of Filet Crochet; directions are given in detail, but it would not be difficult to copy from the illustration by the use of a reading glass, after the work is commenced.

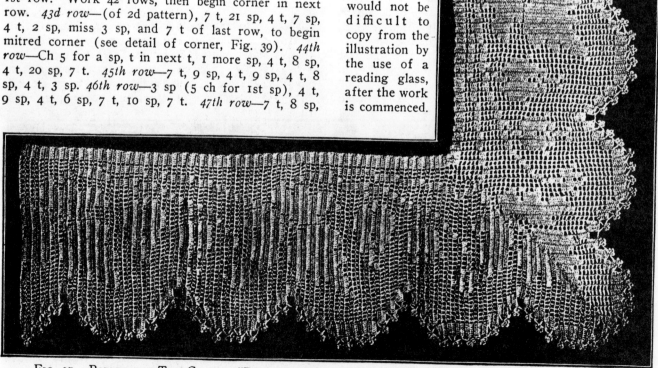

FIG. 37. BORDER FOR TEA CLOTH. "BLEEDING HEART" DESIGN. See Figs. 38 and 39, and page 27

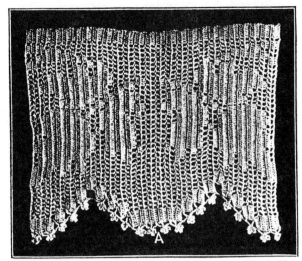

FIG. 38. MIDDLE OF ONE SIDE OF EDGING. See Fig. 37

2, t in middle of 5 ch at corner of upright row, turn, 4 sp, 7 t. *5th row*—7 t, 6 sp, t after sp of upright row. *6th row*—Ch 2, t in corner of upright row, 6 sp, 7 t. *7th row*—7 t, 7 sp, ch 2, join to corner with sl st. *8th row*—Sl across side of t to inside corner of point, ch 2, join to corner of next point on edge with sl st, turn, 3 t over side of t, 8 sp, 7 t. *9th row*—7 t, 8 sp, 7 t, join to corner with sl st. *10th row*—Sl to inside corner of point, ch 2, join to 4th t of upright row with a sl st, 7 t, 9 sp, 7 t. *11th row*—7 t, 9 sp, 7 t, sl st to corner. *12th row*—Sl to inside corner, ch 2, join to upper corner with sl st, 7 t, 8 sp, 7 t. *13th row*—7 t, 6 sp, 16 t, sl st at corner. *14th row*—Sl to inside corner, ch 2, sl st at point, 16 t, 5 sp, 7 t. *15th row*—7 t, 7 sp, 13 t, sl st at point. *16th row*—Sl to inside corner, ch 2, sl st at point, 19 t, 4 sp, 7 t. *17th row*—7 t, 3 sp, 25 t, sl st at point. *18th row*—Sl to inside corner, ch 2, sl st at point, 25 t, 2 sp, 7 t. *19th row*—Ch 15, begin row like 41st, 6 t, 4 sp, 19 t, ch 2, sl st at point. *20th row*—Ch 2, t in next point, 13 sp, 7 t. *21st row*—Begin row as 19th, 6 t, 8 sp, 16 t, 1 sp, ch 2, sl st at point. *22d row*—Sl over 4 t, ch 2, sl st at point, 1 sp, 19 t, 11 sp, 7 t. *23d row*—Begin as 19th, 6 t, 9 sp, 34 t, ch 2, sl st at point. *24th row*—Ch 2, t in point, 1 sp, 43 t, 8 sp, 7 t. *25th row*—Begin as 19th, 6 t, 9 sp, 43 t, 1 sp, t in 4th t on upright row. *26th row*—Ch 2, t in point, 1 sp, 13 t, 1 sp, 10 t, 2 sp, 10 t, 12 sp, 7 t. *27th row*—7 t, 9 sp, 4 t, 7 sp, 10 t, 2 sp, 7 t, 3 sp, ch 2, sl st at point. *28th row*—Ch 2, t in point, 5 sp, 4 t, 1 sp, 4 t, 2 sp, 4 t, 5 sp, 7 t, 10 sp, 7 t. *29th row*—7 t, 8 sp, 13 t, 17 sp, ch 2, sl st at point. *30th row*—Ch 2, t in next point (middle of 5 ch), 3 t, 13 sp, 13 t, 1 sp, 4 t, 2 sp, 4 t, 7 sp, 7 t. *31st row*—7 t, 8 sp, 13 t, 4 sp, 7 t, 11 sp, 4 t, 6 sp, t in t after 1st sp of upright row (42d row of 1st half of corner). *32d row*—Ch 2, t in t after next sp of upright row, 7 sp, 4 t, 9 sp, 4 t, 6 sp, 7 t, 10 sp, 7 t. *33d row*—7 t, 9 sp, 4 t, 9 sp, 4 t, 8 sp, 4 t, 7 sp, ch 2, sl st to corner of 7 t of upright row. *34th row*—Ch 2, sl st in 4th of 7 t, turn, 6 t, 5 sp, 4 t, 8 sp, 4 t, 20 sp, 7 t. *35th row*—7 t, 21 sp, 4 t, 7 sp, 4 t, 5 sp, 7 t, sl st in next corner of 7 t. The next row corresponds with the 42d row of pattern at the beginning of the corner. The pattern is now reversed by working this 42d row, then the 41st, the 40th and so on until the pattern is complete.

The same design for Insertion (Fig. 41½) is worked same as in edging, being carried out for 1 sp beyond design and finished with a block of 7 t on outer edge. The corner of design is mitred in same way, but to avoid confusing the worker, directions are given for a few rows at point of corner.

Work from directions for corner of edging (finishing outer edge as shown in Fig. 41½), to 71st row. *71st row*—7 t, 2 sp, 4 t. *72d row*—Sl over 4 t, 4 t, 1 sp, 7 t. *73d row*—7 t, turn and sl across the 7 t. This completes half of corner; for second half,— *1st row*—8 ch, 6 t in 6 sts of 8 ch, join with sl st to 4th of 7 t of upright row. *2d row*—Ch 2, sl st in top corner of 7 t, turn and counting the 2 ch as 1 t, make 6 more t. *3d row*—7 t, ch 2, join with sl st to lower corner of next 4 t. *4th row*—Sl across the 4 t to next corner, ch 2, turn, 7 t. *5th row*—7 t, 1 sp, ch 2, sl st in lower corner of next 4 t. *6th row*—Sl across side of t to inside corner, ch 2, turn, 3 t, 2 sp, 7 t. This row corresponds with the 8th row after corner of edging. Continue from 9th row.

PICOT EDGE.—Beginning at lower edge at left hand of Fig. 37, fasten thread, ch 3, 1 t between 2 blocks of 7 t, make 3 picots of 5 ch each, join all three with sl at top of t, ch 3, sl in outer corner of next block, * (ch 3, dt at intersection of blocks, 3 picots joined with sl at top of dt, ch 3, sl in outer corner of next block) 3 times, ch 6, sl in corner of first block on next scallop, (ch 3, dt at intersection of blocks, 3 picots joined with sl at top of dt, ch 3, sl in outer corner of next block) 3 times; over the ends of 11 rows of blocks make (ch 3, t, 3 picots, ch 3, sl) 4 times, spacing the trebles and sl as evenly as possible; repeat from * around the border.

Figure 41. Insertion. — Chain 99 (for 33 meshes) plus 3 (as 1 t), turn. *1st row*—7 t, 3 sp, 4 t, 4 sp, 13 t, 3 sp, 10 t, 1 sp, 4 t, 9 sp, 7 t, turn with 3 ch. *2d row* — 7 t, 9 sp, 4 t, 1 sp, 10 t, 1 sp, 28 t, 5 sp, (with the 5 sp the Insertion differs from the Border) 7 t. *3d row*—7 t, 6 sp, etc., following the pattern of Border, but keeping the outer edge of insertion straight and in line with these first three rows. The Corner of Insertion can be made from Corner of the Border; the outer block of the leaf in the corner is within one space (below and at one side) of the solid edge of Insertion. See Fig. 41½.

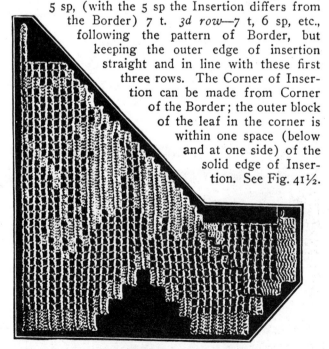

FIG. 39. TO MITRE THE CORNER OF FIGURE 37
This detail of corner shows the first half and ten rows of the second half

Figure 40. Reticella Crochet.—No. 70 crochet cotton and No. 13 hook. *Foundation row*—Chain 6, 1 d in the first st of ch, * turn, ch 6, 1 t in the last 6-ch space; repeat from * for length required. *1st row*—Ch 10, sl in the 9th st from hook, ch 1, 2 d, p, 6 d, p, 6 d, p, 2 d, all in ring, join first and last d; 3 d in each of next 3 spaces of foundation row, ch 7, 1 t between picots on side

FIG. 40. EDGING IN RETICELLA CROCHET. See page 30

of ring, ch 7, 1 dt in next p, turn; 9 d on each 7-ch, * 3 d in each of 6 spaces of foundation row, ch 10, sl in the 9th st from hook, ch 1, 2 d, p, 6 d, p, 6 d, p, 2 d, all in ring, join first and last d, 3 d in each of next 3 spaces of foundation row, ch 7, 1 t between picots on side of ring, ch 15, 1 t be-

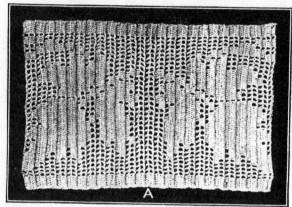

FIG. 41. MIDDLE OF ONE SIDE OF INSERTION.
See Fig. 41½

tween next 2 picots, ch 7, fasten over the 3d t from ring, turn, and make 9 d on 7-ch, 19 d on 15-ch, 9 d on 7 ch; repeat from * to end. *2d row*—Beginning on the end of half point, ch 4, t at 1st of ch, (ch 1, t in same place) twice, ch 1, t in next st, ch 1, miss 1, (t in next st, ch 1, miss 1) 8 times, 3 sl over 3 d on 1st row; around the whole scallop, * (ch 1, miss 1, t in next st) 9 times, ch 1, t in next, (ch 1, t in same place) twice, ch 1, t in next, ch 1, miss 1, (t in next, ch 1, miss 1) 8 times, 3 sl over 3 d; repeat from *. *3d row*—Three d in each of 2 spaces on end of point, * 2 d in each space down side, 1 d on foundation row, 2 d in each of 5 spaces on next point, 1 d in next space, ch 7, fasten into the corresponding d on first point, turn and work 6 d on ch, ch 18, turn, miss 1, 1 d in each of 13 sts of ch, miss 2, sl in next st, turn,

ch 1, 1 d in each d of last row, ch 8, sl in first st of ch to form a ring, ch 1, 12 d in ring, join, ch 1, 1 d in each d on ch, 3 sl sts on ch, finish filling 7-ch with 6 d, 1 d in same space with last d on point, 2 d in each 3 spaces, 1 d in next space, ch 9, fasten with sl to side of bar, ch 3, pass back of bar and fasten again, ch 9, fasten opposite 10th space on point (counting from base), turn, and make 7 d, p, 6 d on 9-ch, catch in side of bar, ch 3 to pass bar, 7 d, p, 6 d on next 9-ch, 1 d in same space with next d on point, 3 d in each of 2 spaces at tip of point; repeat from * for length required, working a half point at end to correspond with first one. *4th row*—Three d in each space across top of lace.

Narrow Ring Lace. (Not illustrated.) — No. 30 crochet cotton and No. 10 hook. Lay the hook on a lead pencil and wind the thread 10 times over it, slip off with the hook and fasten with a sl, fill the ring half full of d (perhaps 12 d), wind a ring again as close as possible to last d, * fill ring one-third full of d, ch 5 for scallop and fasten back over a third of the first ring, turn and fill the ch with (2 d, picot of 3-ch, d, p, d, p, d, p, 2 d), finish filling half the ring with d, wind another ring and repeat from * to the required. length. Fill around the last end with d and fill the upper half of rings with d. HEADING—*Two d in upper half of 1st ring with 2-ch between d, ch 5; repeat from *. *2d row*—One d in each st of row whether ch or d.

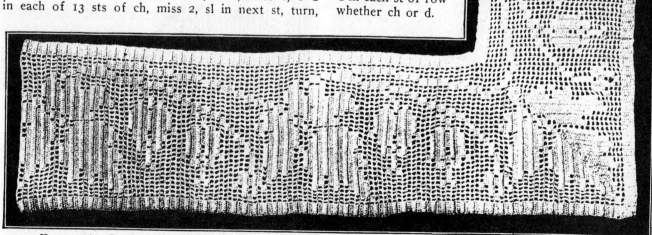

FIG. 41½. INSERTION FOR TEA CLOTH. "BLEEDING HEART" DESIGN. See Fig. 41 and page 29

Figure 42. Narrow Insertion. — Material for the following seven narrow Edges and Insertions.—No. 150 crochet cotton and No. 14 hook.

Chain 8, turn, miss 1 st, 2 d in next 2 sts, picot of 5 joined with sl in last d made, 2 d in next 2 ch, ch 9, d in 1st ch st made, turn, 9 d over 9-ch, picot, 3 d over 9-ch, ch 9, d in 1st d made, turn, * 9 d over 9 ch, picot, 3 d over 9-ch, ch 9, d in 4th d beyond picot, turn; repeat from *.

FIG. 42. INSERTION. See page 31

Figure 43. Narrow Edge. — Chain 10, d in 1st ch st made, making a ring, ch 7, d under 10-ch, turn, ch 7, d under 1st 7-ch, ch 8, d under 10-ch, turn, * 3 d over 8-ch, picot of 5 joined with sl in last d, 6 d over 8-ch, picot, 3 d over 8-ch, ch 7, d under last 7-ch, turn, ch 7, d under last 7-ch, ch 8, d in last scallop midway between picots, turn and repeat from *.

FIG. 43. EDGING. See page 31

Figure 44. Insertion. — Chain 23, turn, t in 4th st from hook, ch 3, d in 3d ch from last t, ch 3, t in 3d ch from last d, ch 5, t in 5th ch from t, ch 3, d in 3d ch from last t, ch 3, t in 3d ch from d, ch 1, t in end of 1st ch made, ch 4, turn, * t in next t, ch 5, t over next t, ch 3, d under 5-ch, ch 3, t over next t, ch 5, t over next t, ch 1, t under 4-ch, ch 4, turn, t over next t, ch 3, d under 5-ch, ch 3, t over next t, ch 5, t over next t, ch 3, d under 5-ch, ch 3, t over next t, ch 1, t under 4-ch, turn and repeat from *.

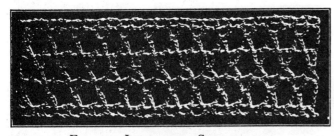

FIG. 44. INSERTION. See page 31

Figure 45. Edging. — The heading in this pattern is worked last. Chain 10, join with d in 1st ch, ch 7, d under 10 ch, ch 7, turn, d under loop of 7-ch, ch 4, d under loop of 10-ch, ch 1, turn, * 3 d under 4 ch (working over both chains that lie together), ch 5 for picot, 4 d over both chains, ch 7, d under last loop of 7-ch, ch 7, turn, d under last loop of 7-ch, ch 4, sl in last d of last scallop, ch 1, turn and repeat from * for required length. For the heading make 1 d over end loop of 7-ch, ch 4, t over d be-

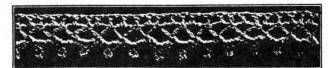

FIG. 45. EDGING. See page 31

tween loops, * ch 1, t under next loop, ch 1, t over d; repeat from * to the end.

Figure 46. Edging. — Chain 6, join in 1st ch with d, ch 4, * t in loop, ch 2; repeat from * until there are 4 t in loop, turn, ** ch 3, t over 2d 2-ch, ch 2, repeat until there are 4 t in the same loop, making a 2d shell, ch 1, dt (thread over twice) under 4-ch of 1st shell, turn, ch 3, t over 2d 2-ch in the last shell, repeat until there are 4 t over the same ch, ch 7, d under 3-ch of previous shell, turn, 10 d over 7-ch; repeat from **.

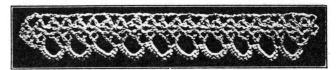

FIG. 46. EDGING. See page 31

Figure 47. Edging. — Make the heading first as follows: With double thread make a chain the required length, then drop one thread and make the remainder with one thread only, ch 5, t in 2d of double ch, ch 2, t in 2d ch from t, continue the whole length of the double ch, turn, make 2 d under the 1st 2 ch, 1 d over t, ch 8, dt (thread over twice) in 7th st from hook, ch 8, sl across ch next to heading, 10 d over 1st 8-ch, 10 d over 2d 8-ch, forming a ring with a bar across it, ** 2 d over 1-ch next to heading, * 2 d over next 2-ch of heading, 1 d over t; repeat from * twice more. Make another ring as follows: Chain 8, 1 dt in 7th st from hook, ch 8, sl across ch next to heading, 5 d over 8-ch, turn and make 1 t in the centre of nearest side of previous ring, turn back and make 4 d over 8-ch, turn, ch 7, make 1 d in top of previous ring, turn, 5 d over 7-ch, 5 ch for picot, 5 d over 7-ch, 1 d in 1st half of 2d ring, 10 d over next 8-ch, completing the 2d ring; repeat from **.

FIG. 47. EDGING. See page 31

Figure 48. Armenian Edge for Handkerchiefs. — Chain 4, * turn, miss 1 st, d in next, t in next, dt in next (taking up two threads each time), ch 3;

FIG. 48. ARMENIAN EDGE FOR HANDKERCHIEFS.

31

repeat from * taking the dt in the corner of last point.

This edge is pretty in a delicate shade of pink, blue, or lavender.

Figure 49. Reticella Insertion. — No. 70 crochet cotton and No. 12 hook.

The squares forming this insertion are made

around square, with 3 d in the st at each corner.

SQUARE WITH PYRAMIDS. — First 4 rounds are made like 1st 4 rounds of Square with Diamond Centre. *5th row*—Ch 14, 1 dt above t of 3d round (ch 10, 1 dt above next t); repeat around, join last 10-ch to the 4th of 14-ch. *6th row*—* Work a pyramid in afghan-stitch on the 10-ch, pick up a loop through each st of 10-ch, which will make 11 sts on the hook,

FIG. 49. RETICELLA INSERTION. See page 32

separately, and overcast together with a needle and thread.

SQUARE WITH DIAMOND CENTRE. — Chain 4, join to form a ring, 8 d in ring, join 1st and last d. *2d row*—Ch 1, 2 d in each of 8 d, join. *3d row*—Ch 8, miss 1, 1 t in next st, (ch 5, miss 1, 1 t in next st) 6 times, ch 5, sl in 3d of 8-ch. *4th row*—4 d, picot, 3 d in each space of last round. *5th row*— Ch 15, 1 t over next t, (ch 10, a long t (over 3 times) above next t, ch 10, a t over next t) repeat around, join last 10-ch to 5th st of 15-ch. *6th row* —Ch 2, miss 1, 1 ht in next st; repeat around. *7th row*—Ch 2, 1 ht in next st; repeat around, widening at the corners by working 2 ht with 2-ch between in each space above the long trebles. *8th row* —Two d in each space, making 2 picots on each side of square at equal distance from the corners. *9th row*—* Ch 30, turn, and work a long t in the 11th st from hook, ch 4, a sl in the 6th st from long t, turn and work 3 d, p, 3 d on 4-ch, a dt in side of square opposite treble, 1 d in long t of corner, 3 d, p, 3 d in next space, ch 13, a d in corner of diamond; repeat from * around. *10th row*—One d in each st

thread over, and work off all by twos, miss 1 st in each row until you have narrowed to 1 st. In order to make the pyramid a good shape the sts must be missed at the beginning and end of rows alternately. Make a picot of 4-ch at the beginning of the 6th row; when the pyramid is complete, sl down the side and make a picot to correspond with the one already made, d in top of dt; repeat from * around. *7th row*—Ch 17, 1 d in point of pyramid, holding wrong side of work next you, * ch 23, a long t in the 11th st from hook, ch 4, a sl in the 6th st from long t, turn and work 3 d, p, 3 d in 1st sp, a long t between pyramids, a d in long t of corner, 3 d, p, 3 d in next sp, ch 5, d in next pyramid, ch 8, a long t (over 4 times) between next 2 pyramids, ch 8, d in point of next pyramid; repeat from * around. *8th row*—One d in each st around square, with 3 d at the corner.

The two squares are joined alternately for length required; then a row of ch 1, miss 1, 1 t in next st, is worked along both sides of insertion.

Figure 50. Reticella Insertion. — No. 70 crochet cotton and No. 12 hook.

A   B

FIG. 50. RETICELLA INSERTION. See page 32

SQUARE A. — Chain 2, 8 d in the 1st st of ch, join 1st and last d. *2d row* — Ch 1, 2 d in each d of last round, join. *3d row* — Ch 7, miss 1 d, 1 t in next st, (ch 4, miss 1, 1 t in next st) 6 times, ch 4, 1 sl in the 7-ch loop; 8 spaces altogether. *4th row* — Seven d in each space of last round, join. *5th row* — Ch 6, 1 t in the 4th of 7 d, * ch 3, 1 t in the st above next t, ch 3, 1 t in the 4th of 7 d; repeat from * around, joining last 3-ch to the 3d of 1st 6-ch; 16 spaces altogether. *6th row* — Four d in each 3-ch space of last row, join. *7th row* — Ch 13, 1 sl in the st above next t, * ch 7, a long t (over 4 times) in the st above next t, ch 7, 1 sl in the st above next t; repeat from * around, ending with ch 7, 1 sl in the 13-ch loop. *8th row* — Five d, p of 4-ch, 6 d on 7-ch, * 6 d, p, 5 d on next 7-ch, 5 d, p, 6 d on next 7-ch; repeat from * around. *9th row* — Ch 33, * a dt in the 11th st from hook, ch 4, a sl in the 6th st from dt, turn and work 3 d, p, 3 d on 4-ch, dt in next joint of star, a d in the top of dt of corner, 3 d, p, 3 d in next sp, ch 13, 1 dt in next point of star, ch 30, and repeat from * around. *10th row* — One d in each st around square, with 3 d in each corner st. Commencing at one corner of square, work 1 t in the corner st, (ch 1, miss 1, 1 t in next d) repeat to next corner and fasten off, leaving a length of thread to be used in joining the squares.

SQUARE B. — Chain 4, join to form a ring, 8 d in ring, join. *2d row* — Two d in each of 8 d, join. *3d row* — Ch 10, miss 1, 1 t in next st, (ch 5, miss 1, 1 dt in next st, ch 5, miss 1, 1 t in next st) repeat around, joining last 5-ch to the 5th of 10-ch; 8 spaces altogether. *4th row* — * Work a pyramid in afghan-stitch (same as in Fig. 49 without picots) on 2 spaces and t, starting with 12 sts on the hook and decreasing 2 sts in each row until but one is left, sl down side of pyramid and work a d on dt, ch 10, a t in the 6th st from hook, ch 5, sl in the same st with t, ch 1, 8 d in each 5-ch sp, join 1st and last d, 3 sl over ch, d in top of dt; repeat from * around. *5th row* — Sl to point of pyramid, (ch 13, d in next ring, ch 13, d in next pyramid) repeat around. *6th row* — 8 d, p, 8 d on each 13-ch of last round. *7th row* — * Ch 30, a long t in the 11th st from hook, ch 4, a sl st in the 6th st from long t, ch 1, 3 d, p, 3 d on 4-ch, a long t in the side of square above pyramid, a d in the long t of corner, 3 d, p, 3 d in next space, ch 13, d in corner of square above ring; repeat from * around. Finish like the 1st square, commencing at the 10th row. Overcast the squares together as shown by the illustration, and work a row of ch 1, miss 1, 1 t in next st along both sides of insertion.

Figure 51. Edging. — No. 100 crochet cotton and No. 14 hook.

Chain 50, turn. *1st row* — T in 4th st from hook, (ch 5, miss 4, t in next) twice, 6 t in next 6 sts, (ch 5, miss 4, t in next) 6 times, turn. *2d row* — * Ch 8, t in 4th st from hook, 4 t in next 4 sts, t on t *, make a festoon as follows: ch 3, 1 d in 3d st of 5-ch, ch 3, t on next t, (5 t in next 5 sts, t on t) 4 times (or 25 t), festoon in next sp, 6 t in next 6 t

(taking up back loop), festoon in each of next 2 sp, t on last t, turn. *3d row* — Ch 3 for 1st t, t on next t, ch 5, t on next t (space) twice, 6 t on next 6 t, ch 5, 25 t on 25 t, ch 5, 7 t on 7 t. *4th row* — Repeat from * to * of 2d row, 2 festoons, block of 7 t (this includes the t of the festoon), 2 festoons, block of 7 t, 1 festoon, block of 7 t, 2 festoons, t on last t. *5th row* — Ch 3, t on t, 2 sp, block of 7 t, 1 sp, block of 7 t, 2 sp, block of 7 t, 2 sp, block of 7 t. *6th row* — Repeat from * to * of 2d row, festoon, block of 7, festoon, block of 7, festoon, 13 t in next 13 sts, festoon, block of 7, 2 festoons, t on last t. *7th row* — Ch 3, t on t, 2 sp, block of 7, 1 sp, 13 t, 1 sp, 7 t, sp, 7 t, sp, 7 t. *8th row* — Repeat from * to * of 2d row, festoon, 7 t, 2 festoons, 7 t, festoon, 7 t, 2 festoons, 7 t, 2 festoons, t on t. *9th row* — Ch 3, t on t, 2 sp, 7 t, 2 sp, 7 t, sp, 7 t, 2 sp, 7 t, sp, 7 t. *10th row* — Miss 1st t, sl in each of next 6 t, ch 3 for t, 6 t, * festoon, 7 t, festoon, 7 t, festoon, 25 t, 2 festoon, t on last t. *11th row* — Ch 3, t on t, 2 sp, 25 t, sp, 7 t, sp, 7 t, sp, 7 t. *12th row* — Like 10th row to *, 2 festoons, 7 t, 7 festoons, t on t. *13th row* — Ch 3, t on t, 7 sp, 7 t, 2 sp, 7 t. *14th row* — Like 10th row to *, festoon, 37 t, 2 festoons, t on t. *15th*

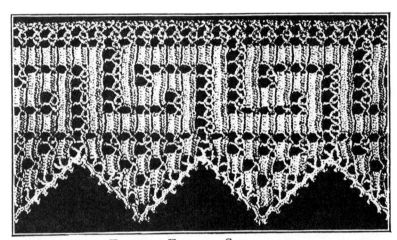

FIG. 51. EDGING. See page 33

row — Ch 3, t on t, 2 sp, 37 t, sp, 7 t. *16th row* — Miss 1st t, sl in each of next 6 t, ch 4, 1 d in 3d st of 5-ch, ch 3, t on t, 5 festoons, 7 t, 2 festoons, t on t. *17th row* — Like 1st row, placing the last t in 1st of 4-ch below. *18th row* — Like 2d row. Repeat for the required length.

OUTER EDGE. *1st row* — One d in last t of outer edge, * ch 4, dt at end of block, between 2 rows, crochet off twice, dt into middle of next block of t, crochet off twice, thread through remaining 3 loops at once, ch 4, 1 d in end st of next row of t *; repeat from * to * twice more, ch 6, 1 d in end of 1st st of next row; repeat from * to * 3 times on 2d side of scallop, placing 1st dt between 4th and 5th t, and the 2d dt in centre of next 2 rows, ch 4, 2 dt between scallops, ch 4, 1 d in end of row on next scallop; repeat from 1st *. *2d row* — Begin again at right hand, over each 4-ch loop make (2 d, picot of 3 joined by d, 2 d); over 6-ch at point make (3 d, p, 1 d, p, 1 d, p, 3 d); in the 2 loops between scallops make 2 d in 1st loop, picot of 3, 2 d in next loop.

Figure 52. Edging. — Material for this and following four Figures. — No. 70 crochet cotton and

33

FIG. 52. EDGING. See page 33

No. 14 hook; or carpet warp and No. 5 or 7 hook. Chain any length required, turn, 8 d in 8 ch sts, * 21 ch, turn hook back and fasten with sl and 1 ch in third ch st from foundation. This leaves 18 ch in loop, on right-hand side of loop make 8 d, 10 ch, fasten back with sl in 3d ch (of 21 ch), 4 d over 10 ch, ch 2, sl in 3d d in foundation, 2 d over 2-ch, 4 d over 10-ch, ch 3 and sl in side of last d for picot, 4 d in rest of 10-ch, 1 d over 18-ch, picot, 5 d, p, 5 d, p, 9 d, sl in same 3d ch st (of 21-ch), 10 ch, sl in 8th d back from hook, 4 d over 10-ch, p, 8 d, sl in same 3d ch st, 2 d over 3-ch, 5 d on foundation, 2 ch, sl in 4th d on last loop, 2 d over 2-ch, 5 d on foundation, ch 6, turn back and sl in same st the ch starts from, 8 d over 6-ch, fasten with sl, 9 d in foundation and repeat from *. After each sl make 1 ch st before making a d.

FIG. 53. EDGING. See page 34

Figure 53. Edging. — Chain any required length, turn, 8 d in 8 ch sts, ch 10, sl in 1st d, ch 1, 10 d over 10-ch, sl in 3d st of 10-ch, ch 9, sl in 3d d (from 1st), 13 d over 9-ch, sl in 3d st of 10-ch, ch 9, sl in 6th d of 13 d, 13 d over 9-ch, sl in 3d st of 10-ch, ch 9, sl in 7th d of 13 d, 12 d over 9-ch, sl in 3d st of 10-ch, 2 d over 10-ch loop, 16 d into 16 ch sts, * ch 10, sl in 9th d from 1st figure, 10 d over 10-ch, sl in 3d st of 10-ch, ch 9, sl in 3d d of 1st loop, 3 d over 9 ch, ch 2, sl in 6th d on last loop of 1st figure, 3 d over 2-ch, 10 d over 9-ch, sl in 3d st of 10-ch, ch 9, sl in 3d d from ch which joins the 1st figure, 13 d over 9-ch, sl in 3d st of 10-ch, ch 9, sl in 7th d of 13 d, 12 d over 9-ch, sl in 3d st of 10-ch, 2 d over 2-ch, 16 d in 16 ch sts; repeat from *. After each sl make 1 ch before making a d.

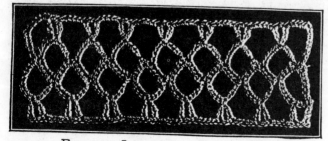

FIG. 54. INSERTION. See page 34

Figure 54. Insertion. — Chain 6, turn, miss 1 ch st, 5 d in 5 ch sts, ch 10, fasten in 1st d with sl and ch 1, 14 d over 10-ch, fasten with sl, ch 1, turn, sl over 5 d, (using 1 thread of st only), * ch 10, sl in 1st sl, ch 1, turn, 14 d over 10-ch, fasten

with sl, ch 1, turn, sl over 5 d; repeat from * the required length. HEADING. *1st row*—Fasten thread at beginning of work, ch 7, sl in top of loop along the edge, ch 1, turn, 3 d over ch, * ch 7, sl in top of next loop, ch 1, turn, 3 d over ch, ch 3, sl in same st, ch 1, turn, 3 d over 3-ch; repeat from *. *2d row* —Cover chains with d, 2 d between bars and 6 d over 7-ch.

FIG. 55. INSERTION. See page 34

Figure 55. Insertion. — * Ch 21, fasten back with sl in 14th st from hook, ch 1, 20 d over 14 ch; repeat from * for required length. This makes a line of oval loops connected by 7 ch sts. When covering the last loop with d, make but 10 d, turn and with the work wrong side up ch 7, 1 d in top of previous loop, * ch 7, 1 d in top of next loop; repeat from * the whole length, turn, * 1 d in top of loop, 11 d over ch 7; repeat the whole length, finish the last loop by making 10 d over last half. Work on around covering the 7-ch spaces with 11 d and making 1 d at end of each oval loop, turn, ch 6, 3 sl in middle 3 sts of 11 d, * ch 5, 3 sl in middle of next 11 d; repeat from * the whole length, turn (with 1-ch) and cover with d, * 5 d over 5 ch, 3 d over 3

FIG. 56. EDGING. See page 34

sl; repeat from *. Make the last 2 rows on the other edge of Insertion.

Figure 56. Edging. — Chain 7, turn, miss 1 ch, 6 d in 6 ch sts, turn, * ch 10, fasten with sl in 1st d, ch 1, turn, 14 d over 10-ch, fasten, turn, 7 sl in 7 d (using half of st only), turn; repeat from * for the required length.

HEADING. *1st row*—Fasten thread at middle of scallop, * ch 7, sl in middle of next scallop; repeat from * throughout, turn. *2d row*—* 5 d over 7-ch, ch 6, fasten with sl where ch starts (to form a ring),

FIG. 57. APPLIQUÉ OR INSERTION. See page 35

make 11 d over ring, fasten where ch starts, 4 d over the remainder of 7 ch; repeat from * throughout, turn. *3d row*—Sl in top of ring, * ch 7, sl in top of next ring; repeat from * throughout, turn. *4th row*—One d in each ch st.

Figure 57. Appliqué or Insertion. — No. 40 crochet cotton and No. 10 hook.

Chain 14, miss 1 ch, 13 d in 13 ch, turn, ch 10, sl in centre of 13 d, ch 10, sl in 1st d, (always make a sl st and ch 1 before filling in with d), 14 d over 10-

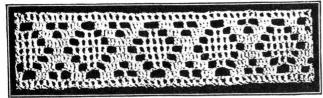

FIG. 58. INSERTION. See page 35

ch, sl in centre, 14 d over next 10-ch, fasten, turn, sl over 7 d (using half of st only), ch 6, fasten to 7th st of next loop, ch 10, fasten to 1st d of 1st loop, turn, 14 d over 10 ch, fasten, ch 10, fasten to 7th d of loop below, 14 d over 10-ch, fasten, ch 9, fasten to 7th d below, 13 d over 9-ch, fasten (in making each fastening be careful not to shorten the 6-ch connecting loops), 6 d over 6 ch, ch 10, fasten back to base, 14 d over 10-ch, ch 10, sl in 7th d of loop below, 14 d over 10-ch, ch 9, sl in 7th d of loop below, 13 d over 9-ch, fasten. This completes 2 figures. Sl over 7 d up the side of last 13 d, * ch 5, fasten to 7th d of opposite loop, turn, 6 d over 5-ch, ch 15, sl in 1st d on 6-ch, 6 d over 15-ch with 7th st sl in ch, ch 10, sl in 1st of 7 d just made, 14 d over 10-ch, ch 10, sl in 7th st below, 14 d over 10-ch, ch 9, sl in 7th d below, 13 d over 9-ch, 6 d over 15-ch, fasten with 7th st in ch, ch 2 for corner, 6 d under last of 15-ch, fasten, turn, sl over 7 d, ch 10, sl in 1st d, 14 d over 10-ch, ch 10, sl in 7th d below, 14 d over 10-ch, ch 9, sl in 7th d below, 13 d over 9-ch *; repeat from * to * as long as required.

Figure 58. Insertion. — No. 50 crochet cotton and No. 12 hook.

This insertion is worked lengthwise, each row beginning at the right and the thread fastened after each row. Where a number of ch is given, as ch 3, miss the same number of sts, whether ch or t.

Make chain the required length, let it be a multiple of 20 and 1 additional st, turn. (After the last repeat at the last end of rows, make the lace correspond with the 1st end in order to have a straight line at the beginning and the ending.) *1st row*—Ch 4, t in 7th st of ch, * ch 1, miss 1, t in next st; repeat from *. *2d row*—T over 1st t, * ch 3, 4 t, ch 5, 4 t, ch 3, 1 t; repeat from *. *3d row*—T over 1st t, ch 1, * 4 t, ch 3, 1 t, ch 1, 1 t, ch 3, 4 t, ch 3; repeat from *. *4th row*—4 t over 1st 4 sts, * ch 3, 1 t, ch 1, 1 t, ch 1, 1 t, ch 1, 1 t, ch 3, 7 t; repeat from *. *5th row*—2 t over 1st 2 sts, * ch 3, (1 t, ch 1) 5 times, 1 t, ch 3, 3 t; repeat from *. *6th row*—Like 4th row. *7th*

row—Like 3d row. *8th row*—Like 2d row. *9th row*—One t, * ch 1, 1 t; repeat from * throughout.

Figure 59. Insertion. — No. 70 crochet cotton and No. 13 hook.

This lace is worked lengthwise from right to left, the thread being broken at the end of each row, beginning again at the right-hand end. Stitches are taken into (not over) chain-stitches, and under 2 loops in top of trebles.

Make a chain the length required. *1st row*—One d in the 3d st from hook, 1 d in each st to end. *2d row*—One t in 1st d, * ch 1, miss 1, t in next st; repeat from *. *3d row*—Ch 5, miss 2, * 3 t in next 3 sts, ch 4, miss 4, 4 t in next 4 sts, ch 4, miss 4, 3 t in next 3 sts, ch 8, miss 8, 2 t in next 2 sts, ch 8, miss 8, 3 t in next 3 sts, ch 4, miss 4, 4 t in next 4 sts, ch 4, miss 4, 3 t in next 3 sts, ch 10, miss 10, t in next st, ch 10, miss 10; repeat from *.

It will be seen that where a number of ch is mentioned, the same number of sts (in the previous row) is missed. Each row contains the same number of sts, so from this point on, only the number of ch and t will be given.

4th row—Fasten thread in 3d st of 1st 5-ch of previous row, ch 7, miss 4, * 3 t, ch 3, 2 t, ch 3, 3 t, ch 9, 4 t, ch 9, 3 t, ch 3, 2 t, ch 3, 3 t, ch 11, 3 t, ch 11; repeat from *. *5th row*—Ch 11 (the 1st 3 sts as 1 t), miss 8, * 2 t, ch 4, 2 t, ch 10, 8 t, ch 10, 2 t, ch 4, 2 t, ch 7, 3 t, ch 3, 5 t, ch 3, 3 t, ch 7; repeat from *. *6th row*—Fasten thread in 3d st of previous row, ch 13, miss 10, * 1 t, ch 2, 1 t, ch 6, 3 t, ch 4, 6 t, ch 4, 3 t, ch 6, 1 t, ch 2, 1 t, ch 8, 5 t, ch 3, 3 t, ch 3, 5 t, ch 7; repeat from *. *7th row*—Ch 7, miss 4, 3 t, ch 4, * 2 t, ch 7, 6 t, ch 2, 4 t, ch 2, 6 t, ch 7, 2 t, ch 4, 3 t, ch 3, 17 t, ch 3, 3 t, ch 4; repeat from *. *8th row*—Ch 7, miss 4, 4 t, ch 7, * 3 t, ch 3, 18 t, ch 3, 3 t, ch 7, 4 t, ch 4, 6 t, ch 3, 6 t, ch 4, 4 t, ch 7; repeat from *. *9th row*—Ch 6, miss 3, 4 t, ch 8, * 6 t, ch 3, 12 t, ch 3, 6 t, ch 8, 9 t, ch 5, 1 t,

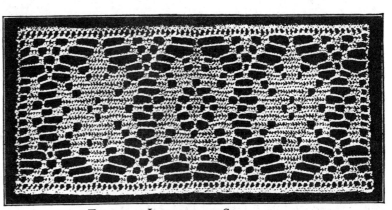

FIG. 59. INSERTION. See page 35

ch 5, 9 t, ch 8; repeat from *. *10th row*—Ch 6, miss 3, 2 t, ch 4, 1 t, ch 7, * 12 t, ch 2, 12 t, ch 7, 1 t, ch 4, 5 t, (ch 5, 5 t) twice, ch 4, 1 t, ch 7; repeat from *. *11th row*—Ch 6, miss 3, 6 t, ch 4, * 4 t, ch 3, 6 t, ch 2, 4 t, ch 2, 6 t, ch 3, 4 t, ch 4, 8 t, ch 3, 2 t, ch 2, 3 t, ch 2, 2 t, ch 3, 8 t, ch 4; repeat from *. *12th row*—Like 10th row. The 11th row is the middle; from this reverse the order of rows until the 21st row is like the first row. Figs. 58 to 62 (inclusive) are foreign models of very old laces.

Figure 60. Insertion. — No. 70 crochet cotton and No. 13 hook.

In working this lace the thread is broken at the end of each row, beginning again at the right-hand end. The stitches are taken into ch sts and under 2 loops in top of trebles.

Make a chain the required length. *1st row*—Make 1 t in 8th st from hook, 1 t in next st, * ch 2, miss 2, 2 t in next 2; repeat from * to end of ch. *2d row*—12 t in 1st 12 sts, ch 15, miss 15 sts, 2 t in next 2 sts, * ch

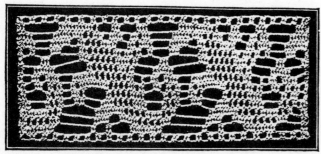

FIG. 60. INSERTION. See page 36

4, miss 4, 2 t in next 2, ch 7, miss 7, 11 t in next 11, ch 15, miss 15, 2 t in next 2 sts; repeat from *. (Hereafter the number of ch will be given, and the same number of sts are to be missed; and any given number of t will cover the same number of stitches.) *3d row* —3 t, (ch 1, 1 t) 3 times, * ch 1, 4 t, ch 13, 6 t, ch 4, 7 t, (ch 1, 1 t) 3 times; repeat from *. *4th row* — 10 t, * ch 1, 1 t, ch 1, 2 t, ch 13, 11 t, (ch 1, 1 t) 3 times, ch 1, 6 t; repeat from *. *5th row*—4 t, * ch 5, 2 t, ch 1, 1 t, ch 1, 2 t, ch 4, 4 t, ch 6, 5 t, (ch 1, 1 t) 3 times, ch 1, 5 t; repeat from *. *6th row*—3 t, * ch 7, 2 t, ch 1, 3 t, ch 3, 3 t, ch 1, 1 t, ch 8, 2 t, (ch 1, 1 t) 3 times, ch 1, 5 t; repeat from *. *7th row*—3 t, * ch 3, 3 t, ch 2, 2 t, ch 1, 2 t, ch 3, 2 t, ch 1, 11 t, (ch 1, 1 t) 3 times, ch 1, 3 t, ch 1, 2 t; repeat from *. *8th row*—2 t, * ch 3, 3 t, ch 2, 5 t, ch 5, 8 t, (ch 1, 1 t) 5 times, ch 1, 3 t, ch 3, 1 t; repeat from *. *9th row* — 2 t, ch 4, * 7 t, ch 12, 2 t, (ch 1, 1 t) 4 times, ch 1, 3 t, ch 1, 2 t, ch 7; repeat from *. *10th row*—2 t, ch 7, 3 t, * ch 11, 4 t, (ch 1, 1 t) 4 times, ch 1, 5 t, ch 1, 2 t, ch 8, 3 t; repeat from *. *11th row*—2 t, * ch 2, 2 t, ch 5, 4 t, ch 7, 3 t, (ch 1, 1 t) 4 times, (ch 1, 3 t) twice, ch 1, 2 t; repeat from *. *12th row*—6 t, ch 5, * 7 t, ch 3, 3 t, (ch 1, 1 t) twice, ch 1, 6 t, ch 4, 3 t, ch 1, 5 t, ch 6; repeat from *. *13th row*—5 t, ch 7, * 6 t, without making any ch st, miss 1 st, 4 t, ch 1, 1 t, ch 1, 4 t, ch 2, 5 t, ch 3, 3 t, ch 1, 3 t, ch 8; repeat from *. *14th row*—3 t, * ch 11, 11 t, ch 1, 1 t, ch 5, 3 t, ch 6, 4 t; repeat from *. *15th row*—Like 1st row.

Figure 61. Insertion. — No. 50 crochet cotton and No. 12 hook.

In working this lace, the thread is to be broken at the end of each row and all rows are worked in the same direction. The stitch is taken into the ch and

into the back loop of trebles, giving a pretty effect.

Make a chain the required length. *1st row*—One t in 6th st from hook, * ch 1, miss 1, t in next; repeat from * to end of ch. *2d row*—3 t in 1st 3 sts, * ch 5, miss 5, t in next st; repeat from *. (Since the number of sts missed and the number of ch are the same, the directions will give only the number of ch and number of t. There are the same number of sts in each row and each t covers 1 st.) *3d row*—3 t, ch 2, 1 t, (ch 5, 1 t) 5 times, * ch 6, 5 t, ch 6, 1 t, (ch 5, 1 t) 6 times; repeat from *. *4th row*—3 t, (ch 5, 1 t) 4 times, * ch 6, 5 t, ch 2, 9 t, ch 2, 5 t, ch 6, 1 t, (ch 5, 1 t) 3 times; repeat from *. *5th row*—3 t, ch 3, 5 t, ch 6, 1 t, * ch 6, 5 t, ch 2, 9 t, ch 2, 5 t, ch 2, 9 t, ch 2, 5 t, ch 6, 1 t; repeat from *. *6th row*—13 t, * ch 4, 1 t, ch 4, 9 t, ch 2, 5 t, (ch 1, 1 t) 6 times, ch 1, 5 t, ch 2, 9 t; repeat from *. *7th row*—4 t, ch 2, 5 t, * ch 2, 9 t, ch 2, 5 t, (ch 1, 1 t) 6 times, ch 7, 1 t, (ch 1, 1 t) 5 times, ch 1, 5 t; repeat from *. *8th row*—4 t, (ch 1, 1 t) 3 times, * ch 1, 13 t, (ch 1, 1 t) 6 times, ch 7, 3 t, ch 7, 1 t, (ch 1, 1 t) 5 times; repeat from *. *9th row*—3 t, (ch 1, 1 t) 3 times, * ch 1, 6 t, ch 3, 6 t, (ch 1, 1 t) 4 times, ch 7, 3 t, ch 3, 3 t, ch 7, 1 t, (ch 1, 1 t) 3 times; repeat from *. *10th row*—Like 8th row. *11th row*—Like 7th row. *12th row*—Like 6th row. *13th row*—Like 5th row. *14th row*—Like 4th row. *15th row*—Like 3d row. *16th row*—Like 2d row. *17th row*—Like 1st row.

Figure 62. Insertion. — No. 50 crochet cotton and No. 12 hook.

This insertion is made lengthwise; at the end of each row the thread is broken off and the next row is worked in the same direction as the first row. In this work the hook is put through chain sts, not

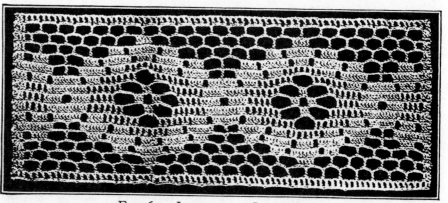

FIG. 61. INSERTION. See page 36

over, and under two loops in top of trebles.

Make a chain a little longer than the length required, and after the first row is finished, decide upon the exact length, having 2 t at the last end. Repeat the pattern according to the directions, and in the last repeat of each row, work to the last 2 t, and finish with 2 t in each row; this will insure a straight line at the last end, as the directions insure a straight line at the first. A indicates the beginning of directions.

1st row—2 t in 1st 2 ch, * ch 2, miss 2, 2 t in next 2 sts; repeat from *. *2d row*—2 t in first 2 t, * ch 12, 2 t in 2 ch between 4th and 5th groups of t, ** ch 10, 2 t in 2 ch after 3d group of t; repeat from

** 3 times more, ch 12, miss 12, 8 t in next 8 sts, ch 2, miss 2, 18 t in next 18 sts, ch 6, miss 6, 18 t, ch 2, 8 t; repeat from *. (It will be noted that where a number of ch is mentioned, the same number of sts in the previous row is missed. Each row contains the same number of stitches, so from this point on only the number of ch and t will be given.)

3d row—2 t, ch 2, 2 t, * ch 6, 2 t, ch 2, 2 t; repeat from * 4 times more, ch 6, 2 t, ch 2, 14 t, ch 10, 6 t, ch 2, 6 t, ch 10, 14 t, ch 2, 2 t; repeat from first *. *4th row*—8 t, ch 6, 2 t, * ch 10, 2 t; repeat from * 3 times more, ch 6, 16 t, ch 4, 10 t, ch 2, 4 t, ch 2, 4 t, ch 2, 10 t, ch 4, 16 t, ch 6, 2 t; repeat from first *. *5th row*—8 t, ch 12, 2 t, * ch 10, 2 t; repeat from * twice more, ch 12, 12 t, ch 4, 4 t, ch 4, 12 t, ch 2, 12 t, ch 4, 4 t, ch 4, 12 t, ch 12, 2 t; repeat from first *. *6th row*—8 t, ch 4, 6 t, * ch 4, 2 t, ** ch 6, 2 t, ch 2, 2 t; repeat once from **, ch 6, 2 t, ch 4, 6 t, ch 4, 6 t, ch 2, 2 t, ch 2, 4 t, ch 10, 6 t, ch 2, 2 t, ch 2, 2 t, ch 2, 6 t, ch 10, 4 t, ch 2, 2 t, ch 2, 6 t, ch 4, 6 t; repeat from *. *7th row*—8 t, ch 2, 10 t, * ch 12, 2 t, ch 10, 2 t, ch 12, 10 t, ch 2, 6 t, ch 4, 4 t, ch 6, 4 t, ch 4, 2 t, ch 4, 2 t, ch 2, 2 t, ch 4, 2 t, ch 4, 4 t, ch 6, 4 t, ch 4, 6 t, ch 2, 10 t; repeat from *. *8th row*—6 t, ch 4, 12 t, * ch 4, 2 t, ch 10, 2 t, ch 10, 2 t, ch 4, 12 t, ch 4, 4 t, ch 2, 16 t, ch 8, 2 t, ch 6, 2 t, ch 8, 16 t, ch 2, 4 t, ch 4, 12 t; repeat from *. *9th row*—6 t, ch 2, 14 t, * ch 2, 2 t, ch 2, 2 t, ch 6, 2 t, ch 2, 2

t, ch 4, 4 t, ch 4, 6 t, * ch 8, 2 t, ch 8, 6 t, ch 4, 4 t, ch 4, 4 t, ch 4, 4 t, ch 4, 4 t, ** ch 6, 2 t, ch 2, 2 t; repeat from ** twice more, ch 6, 4 t, ch 4, 4 t, ch 4, 4 t, ch 4, 4 t, ch 4, 6 t; repeat from *. *17th row*—8 t, ch 2, 4 t, ch 4, 4 t, ch 2, 6 t, * ch 18, 6 t, ch 2, 4 t, ch 4, 4 t, ch 2, 8 t, ch 6, 2 t, ch 8, 2 t, ch 10, 2 t, ch 10, 2 t, ch 8, 2 t, ch 6, 8 t, ch 2, 4 t, ch 4, 4 t, ch 2, 6 t; repeat from *. *18th row*—14 t, ch 2, 14 t, * ch 4, 2 t, ch 6, 2 t, ch 4, 14 t, ch 2, 14 t, ** ch 10, 2 t; repeat from ** 3 times more, ch 10, 14 t, ch 2, 14 t; repeat from *. *19th row*—4 t, ch 8, 4 t, ch 2, 14 t, * ch 14, 14 t, ch 2, 4 t, ch 8, 8 t, ch 4, 2 t, ch 2, 2 t, ** ch 6, 2 t, ch 2, 2 t; repeat from ** twice more, ch 4, 8 t, ch 8, 4 t, ch 2, 14 t; repeat from *. *20th row*—14 t, ch 8, 14 t, * ch 6, 14 t, ch 8, 20 t, ch 4, 2 t, ** ch 10, 2 t; repeat from ** twice more, ch 4, 20 t, ch 8, 14 t; repeat from *. *21st row*—20 t, ch 6, * 26 t, ch 6, 26 t, ** ch 10, 2 t; repeat from ** twice more, ch 10, 26 t, ch 6; repeat from *. *22d row*—4 t, ch 2, 20 t, ch 10, * 6 t, ch 10, 20 t, ch 2, 6 t, ch 6, 2 t, ch 4, 2 t, ch 2, 2 t, ch 6, 2 t, ch 2, 2 t, ch 6, 2 t, ch 2, 2 t, ch 4, 2 t, ch 6, 6 t, ch 2, 20 t, ch 10; repeat from *. *23d row*—2 t, ch 4, 10 t, ch 10, 10 t, * ch 6, 10 t, ch 10, 10 t, ch 12, 2 t, ch 8, 2 t, ch 10, 2 t, ch 10, 2 t, ch 8, 2 t, ch 12, 10 t, ch 10, 10 t; repeat from *. *24th row*—4 t, * ch 2, 2 t; repeat from *.

Figure 63. Insertion. — Crochet cotton No. 50,

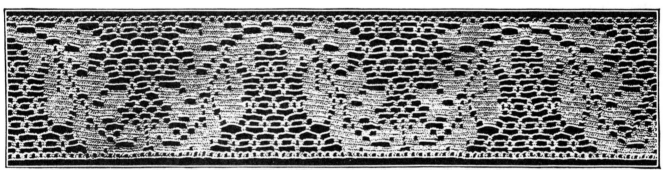

FIG. 62. INSERTION. See page 36   A

t, ch 6, 2 t, ch 2, 2 t, ch 2, 14 t, ch 2, 4 t, ch 2, 14 t, ch 6, 2 t, ch 6, 2 t, ch 6, 2 t, ch 6, 14 t, ch 2, 4 t, ch 2, 14 t; repeat from *. *10th row*—2 t, ch 2, 2 t, ch 2, 12 t, * ch 6, 2 t, ch 10, 2 t, ch 10, 2 t, ch 6, 12 t, ch 2, 2 t, ch 2, 4 t, ch 6, 10 t, ch 6, 2 t, ch 6, 2 t, ch 6, 10 t, ch 6, 4 t, ch 2, 2 t, ch 2, 12 t; repeat from *. *11th row* — 2 t, ch 4, 2 t, ch 2, 12 t, * ch 10, 2 t, ch 10, 2 t, ch 10, 12 t, ch 2, 2 t, ch 6, 20 t, ch 8, 2 t, ch 8, 20 t, ch 6, 2 t, ch 2, 12 t; repeat from *. *12th row*—4 t, ch 2, 8 t, ch 2, 6 t, * ch 8, 2 t, ch 2, 2 t, ch 6, 2 t, ch 2, 2 t, ch 8, 6 t, ch 2, 8 t, ch 2, 10 t, ch 4, 10 t, ch 2, 2 t, ch 10, 2 t, ch 2, 10 t, ch 4, 10 t, ch 2, 8 t, ch 2, 6 t; repeat from *. *13th row*—6 t, ch 2, 6 t, ch 2, 6 t, * ch 10, 2 t, ch 10, 2 t, ch 10, 6 t, ch 2, 6 t, ch 2, 14 t, ch 12, 2 t, ch 2, 2 t, ch 6, 2 t, ch 2, 2 t, ch 12, 14 t, ch 2, 6 t, ch 2, 6 t; repeat from *. *14th row*—8 t, ch 2, 4 t, ch 2, 6 t, ch 6, 2 t, * ch 8, 2 t, ch 8, 2 t, ch 6, 6 t, ch 2, 4 t, ch 2, 18 t, ch 12, 2 t, ch 10, 2 t, ch 12, 18 t, ch 2, 4 t, ch 2, 6 t, ch 6, 2 t; repeat from *. *15th row*—2 t, ch 4, 4 t, ch 2, 2 t, ch 2, 4 t, ch 6, 6 t, * ch 4, 2 t, ch 2, 2 t, ch 4, 6 t, ch 6, 4 t, ch 2, 2 t, ch 2, 4 t, ch 6, 10 t, ch 6, 2 t, ch 10, 2 t, ch 10, 2 t, ch 6, 10 t, ch 6, 4 t, ch 2, 2 t, ch 2, 4 t, ch 6, 6 t; repeat from *. *16th row*—4 t, ch 4, 4

No. 12 hook, novelty braid No. 4; actual size of braid at Figure 64.

Fasten thread in end of braid, ch 7, * 3 t in 3d and 4th picots (used as one p), ch 7, 3 t over bar of braid, ch 7, * repeat to end of length required. *2d row*—* Ch 6, 2 t over 7-ch, 3 t over 3 t of previous row, 2 t over 7-ch, ch 6, t over 2d t over bar *, repeat. *3d row*—* Ch 5, 2 t over 6-ch, 7 t over 7 t of previous row, 2 t over 6-ch *, repeat. *4th row* — 2 t over 5-ch, * 11 t over 11 t, 4 t over 5-ch *, repeat. *5th row*—T in every other st, with 2 ch between.

CORNER OF INSERTION. *1st row* — Same as insertion to 3 t in top of braid, where turn is to be made, ch 6, (3 t, ch 2, 3 t) over bar, 6 ch, 3 t in top of braid and proceed. (In making turn, if braid is given a half twist, it will lie more evenly.) *2d row*—7 t in top of braid, ch 7, t over 2d t, ch 6, t over 5th t, ch 7, and proceed with 7 t. *3d row*—11 t, ch 4, 1 dt (thread over twice, working off 2 sts each time) over t, ch 5, dt in middle of 6-ch, ch 5, dt over t, ch 4 and proceed with 11 t. *4th row*—After 11 t, 5 t over ch, t over dt, 5 t over ch, 3 dt over dt, 5 t over ch, t over dt, 5 t. 11 t, etc. *5th row*—

Same as for straight edge, making 2 t, with 3 ch between, in corner st.

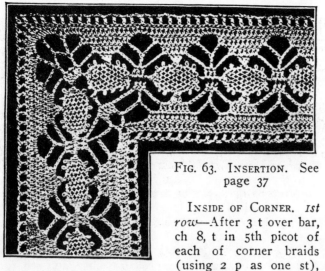

FIG. 63. INSERTION. See page 37

INSIDE OF CORNER. *1st row*—After 3 t over bar, ch 8, t in 5th picot of each of corner braids (using 2 p as one st), ch 8, 3 t over bar, etc. *2d row*—After 7 t, ch 6, t over 2d t, ch 6, 2 t over 8-ch, t over t, 2 t over next 8-ch, ch 6, t over 2d of 3 t, etc. *3d row*—After 11 t, ch 5, t over 6-ch, t over next 6-ch, ch 5, 11 t, etc. *4th row*—After 11 t over 11 t, 4 t over ch, 4 t over ch on other side, 11 t over 11 t, etc. *5th row*—T in every other st, ch 2 between, miss last 2 sts on each side at corner.

Figure 65. Edging. — The heading or upper part of this Edging is made like Insertion, Figure 63.

LOWER PART OF EDGING. *1st row*—Like 1st row of Insertion. *2d row* — Like Insertion until corner is reached, 7 t in top of braid, ch 5, 2 t over 6-ch, 3 t over 3 t, 2 t over 2-ch, 3 t over 3 t, 2 t over 6-ch, ch 5, etc. *3d row*—Like Insertion as far as corner, after 11 t, ch 2, 16 t, ch 2, 11 t, etc. *4th row*—Like Insertion, making 4 t over 2-ch at corner, 16 t over 16 t, 4 t over 2-ch, 11 t, etc. *5th row*—From beginning of row, ch 4 between groups of 11 t; after 11 t at corner, ch 3, t over 2d of 4 t, ch 3, 16 t across corner, ch 3, t, ch 3, 11 t, etc. *6th row* — 7 t in top of diamond, ch 4, turn, make 3 t drawn together as one st at top, ch 4, catch in 1st st of 7 t in previous row, ch 6, turn, t in point of diamond, ch 6, catch in other end of 7 t, ch 4, 1 d over 4-ch, ch 4, 7 t, repeat. At corner, after 7 t, ch 5, d over t, ch 5, 12 t, ch 4, turn, 8 t, ch 4, turn, 3 t drawn together in point, ch 4, catch in end of 8 t, and cut thread. Join thread at beginning of 12 t, ch 4, catch at corner of row above, ch 6, t in point, ch 6, catch at corner below, ch 5, d over t, ch 5, 7 t, etc. *7th row*—7 t over 6-ch, 3 dt in t at top, 7 t over 6-ch, 4 t over 4-ch, 4 t over next 4-ch, 7 t over 6-ch, etc. *8th row*—Ch 4, d in every other st, at top ch 4, t in point, ch 4, etc.

Figure 66. Reticella Insertion. — No. 50 crochet cotton and No. 12 hook.

FIGURE A, with small block in centre. Chain 4, turn, miss 1 st, 3 d in next 3 sts, ch 1, turn. *2d row* —3 d in 3 d of last row (under two threads of the st). *3d row*—Like 2d row. Chain 9, t in next corner, (ch 6, t in next corner) twice, ch 6, sl in 3d st of 9-ch, * 5 d under next loop, picot, 3 d, ch 13,

drop st, insert hook through 4th d back of p, catch dropped st and draw through, over 13-ch make 2 sl in 2 ch, ch 4, (3 sl in 3 ch, ch 4) 3 times, 2 sl in last 2 ch, 2 d over ch below, 1 d over next t; repeat from * 3 times more, join row and fasten.

FIGURE B.—Chain 10, dt in 1st st, (ch 6, dt in same st) twice, ch 6, sl in 4th of 10-ch, 9 d under next loop, * ch 7, drop st and pick it up through 4th d back, ch 7, drop st and pick it up through 4th st back from last loop, sl in each of the last 7 ch sts and in 4 sts in next loop, ch 7, drop st and pick it up through middle of the 7 sl sts on last loop, 7 sl in 7 sts of last ch, sl in st from which this ch started and in next 3 sts of first 7-ch, 1 d in top of next dt, 9 d under next ch; repeat from * 3 times more. When making the outer loop on last scallop after first 4 sl in this loop, ch 3, drop st and pick it up through the middle of a point on Figure A, sl back over the 3 ch sts and finish scallop as before. This joins the two figures, fasten thread. Alternate the two figures, (joining by 3-ch with 3 sl sts in ch), until the strip is as long as required.

FOR OUTER ROWS. — Join thread to middle of the upper point of figure at left end of strip, * ch 24, turn, drop st and pick it up through a d between this point and next one on figure, 12 sl sts on 12 sts of ch (under one thread only), ch 12, drop st, pick it up through middle of the 3 sl sts joining figures, sl back across 12 ch, ch 12, drop st, pick up through a d between next 2 points of next figure, sl back across 12 ch, sl at end of first 12 sl sts, ch 6, drop st and pick it up through 3d st down from top of last 12 sl sts, ch 3, drop and pick up through 3d st down on second 12 sl sts, ch 3, and pick up on 1st row of 12 sl sts, ch 3, pick up through 3d st back on the 12 ch above. These chs are foundation for the 4 little scallops. Under each 3-ch make (1 d, 3 t, 1 d), and after working 2d scallop, fasten it with a sl

FIG. 64. ACTUAL SIZE OF BRAID USED IN FIGS. 63 AND 65

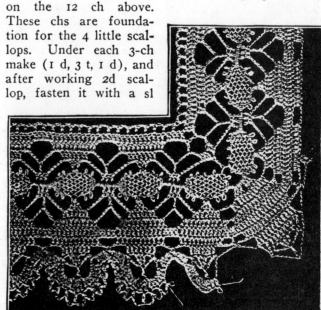

FIG. 65. EDGING. See page 38

to a st in the stem just back of it; this keeps the little figure in place. The 4th scallop is made under half of the 6-ch, leaving the remainder of ch to form part of the edge.

After 4th scallop, ch 12, drop st and pick up through middle of top point of next figure, sl back on 2 of the ch sts; repeat from *, ch 24, etc.

HEADING. — T in first st of ch, * ch 1, miss 1, t in next st; repeat from * the whole length and along the opposite side.

Figure 67. Insertion.—No. 50 crochet cotton and No. 9 hook.

Chain 67, turn, miss 1. *1st row* —D in every st across row. *2d row*—Ch 4, miss 1 d, t in next, (ch 1, miss 1, t in next), repeat until there are 9 t (including 4-ch at beginning) with 1 ch between t, ch 7, miss 3 d, sl in 4th d, ch 4, miss 3 d, 5 dt in next 5 d, ch 4, miss 3 d, sl in next, ch 4, miss 3 d, 5 dt, ch 4, miss 3 d, sl in next, ch 7, miss 3, 9 t with 1 ch between, 1 t in last st. *3d row*—Ch 4, t after 2d t, ch 1, t in next sp, until there are 8 t (always including 4-ch), ch 7, sl in centre of loop, (ch 5, sl in 1st d t, ch 5, sl after 5th dt) twice, ch 5, 10 t with 1 ch between (the first 2 t in loop), 1 t in last st. *4th row*—Ch 4, 12 t with 1 ch between, 7 ch, (sl in loop, ch 4, 5 dt in loop, ch 4) twice, sl in loop, ch 7, 6 t with 1 ch between, 1 t in last st. *5th row*—Ch 4, 5 t with 1 ch between, ch 7, sl in loop, (ch 5, sl in 1st dt, ch 5, sl after 5th d) twice, ch 7, 13 t with 1 ch between, 1 t in last st. *6th row*—Ch 4, 15 t with 1 ch between, ch 7, (sl in loop, ch 4, 5 dt, ch 4) twice, sl in loop, ch 7, 3 t with 1 ch between, 1 t in last st. *7th row* — Ch 4, 5 t with 1 ch between, ch 7, (sl in 1st dt, ch 5, sl after 5th dt, ch 5) twice, sl in loop, ch 7, 13 t with 1 ch between, 1 t in last st. *8th row*—Ch 4, 12 t with 1 ch between, ch 7, (sl in loop, ch 4, 5 dt, ch 4) twice, sl in loop, ch 7, 6 t with 1 ch between, 1 t in last st. *9th row*—Ch 4, 8 t with 1 ch between, ch 7, (sl in 1st dt, ch 5, sl after 5th dt, ch 5) twice, sl in loop, ch 7, 10 t with 1 ch between, 1 t in last st. *10th row*—Ch 4, 9 t with 1 ch between, ch 7, (sl in loop, ch 4, 5 dt, ch 4) twice, sl in loop, ch 7, 9 t with 1 ch between, 1 t in last st. *11th row*—Ch 4, 11 t with 1 ch between, ch 7, (sl in 1st dt, ch 5, sl after 5th dt, ch 5) twice, sl in loop, ch 7, 7 t with 1 ch between, 1 t in last st. *12th row* — Ch 4, 6 t with 1 ch between, ch 7, (sl in loop, ch 4, 5 dt, ch 4) twice, sl in loop, ch 7, 12 t with 1 ch between, 1 t in last st. *13th row*—Ch 4, 14 t with 1 ch between, ch 7, (sl in 1st dt, ch 5, sl after 5th dt, ch 5) twice, sl in loop, ch 7, 4 t with 1 ch between, 1 t in last st. *14th row*—Ch 4, 3 t with 1 ch between, ch 7, ·(sl in loop, ch 4, 5 dt, ch 4) twice, sl in loop, ch 7, 15 t with 1 ch between, 1 t in last st. *15th row*—Ch 4, 14 t with 1 ch between, ch 7, sl in loop, (ch 5, sl in 1st dt, ch 5, sl after 5th dt) twice, ch 7, 4 t with 1 ch between, 1 t in last st. *16th row* — Ch 4, 6 t with 1 ch between, ch 7, (sl in loop, ch 4, 5 dt, ch 4) twice, sl in loop,

FIG. 66. RETICELLA INSERTION. See page 38.

ch 7, 12 t with 1 ch between, 1 t in last st. *17th row* —Ch 4, 11 t with 1 ch between, ch 7, sl in loop, (ch 5, sl in 1st dt, ch 5, sl after 5th dt) twice, ch 7, 7 t with 1 ch between, 1 t in last st. Repeat from 2d row.

Figure 68. Edging for Handkerchief. — No. 150 crochet cotton and No. 14 hook.

Prepare the edge of a square of handkerchief linen by drawing three threads, ¼ of an inch from the edge; roll the hem tightly up to the drawn threads and * double crochet 3 sts over the hem, ch 6 for a picot, and join at base of ch; repeat from * around the handkerchief. *2d row*—Ch 12 very tightly, sl in 4th ch st from work but do not finish the sl, keep 2 sts on the hook, draw a loop under the ch, (thread over hook, loop under the ch) 4 times, then draw a loop through the 11 sts on the hook, ch 2 tightly, dt between the picots of 1st row, * ch 9, sl in top of dt, keeping both sts on the hook, loop under dt, (thread over hook, loop under dt) 4 times, loop through 11 sts on hook, ch 2, dt between next 2 picots; repeat from * around. Crowd the work at the corners so that it will round nicely. Crochet the chs very tightly and when it is completed, round out the picots with the crochet-hook or stiletto.

Turn the work face down on a bath-towel, cover with a damp cloth and press, remove the cloth and finish pressing but do not iron the edge with the last pressing.

Figure 69. Edging for Handkerchief. — No. 50 crochet cotton and No. 13 hook.

Double crochet over a very narrow flat or rolled hem. If the hem is turned to the right side and two or three threads drawn as for hemstitching, the crocheting will be very easy. After the row of doubles,

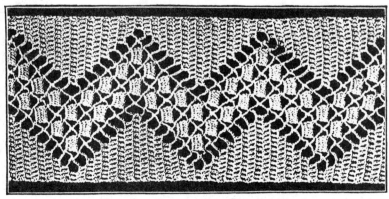

FIG. 67. INSERTION. See page 39

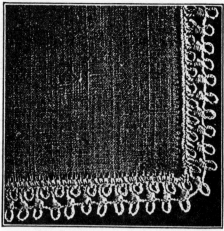

FIG. 68. EDGING FOR HANDKERCHIEF.
See page 39

the work is in two rows, both worked in the same direction, both beginning at the right and without turning the work. When a corner is to be turned put 3 d in the same place at the corner.

1st row—2 sl in first 2 d, ch 2, picot of 5 joined by d, (all the picots are of 5 ch, joined by d unless otherwise noted), ch 2, miss 3 d on hem, 2 sl in next 2 d, * ch 4, picot, ch 6, picot, ch 1, t in 4th ch st from last sl, ch 3, miss 4 d on hem, 2 sl in next 2 d, ch 2, picot, ch 2, miss 3 d on hem, 2 sl in next 2 d; repeat from *. At the corner, finish one of the larger figures with 1 sl in the st next to the corner, omit the smaller figure or loop, commence again at * and make the larger figure, finish with 1 sl in the corner st without missing any d, commence again at *. *2d row*—Fasten thread at the 1st st of 6-ch loop, * 5 d over 6-ch, ch 4 for picot, without joining, make 5 more d over same 6-ch, ch 1, picot, ch 1; repeat from *.

If the row of doubles is not crowded too closely, the picot loop of 2d row (between scallops) may be made "ch 2, p, ch 2" instead of "ch 1, p, ch 1." And upon the spacing of doubles will depend the number to be missed between pairs of sl sts.

Figure 70. Edging with Coronation Braid. — No. 50 crochet cotton and No. 10 hook, and braid of the size shown in the illustration.

1st row — Work 3 d over cord between first two

FIG. 69. EDGING FOR HANDKERCHIEF.
See page 39

sections of braid, * give a downward twist with the next two sections, bringing the cord after second section up underneath, d over the crossed cords, 2 d over single cord beyond crossing, twist another loop like first one, d over the crossed cords, 3 d over cord beyond crossing, ch 3, t in next section close to the first end, ch 1, picot of 5 joined with a d, ch 1, t close to first t in same section, (ch 1, picot, ch 1, dt close to last t) twice, ch 1, picot, ch 1, t close to last dt, ch 1, picot, ch 1, t close to last t, ch 3, 3 d over single cord at end of section; repeat from * the length required.

HEADING. *1st row*—3 d over cord at top of first loop, 3 d over next loop, ch 13, d in middle of section at the side of second loop, ch 5, t in middle of next section at the bottom, ch 5, d in middle of section at the side of next loop, ch 5, take hook out of st, insert in 5th st of 13 ch (counting up from the bottom), catch the st and draw through, ch 9; repeat from beginning of row. *2d row*—Beginning again at right-hand end, work * 6 d in 6 d, 3 d over 13-ch, ch 8, 3 d over next ch loop; repeat from *. *3d row*—T in 1st d at right, * ch 2, miss 2, t in next st; repeat from *.

Figure 71. Insertion. — No. 100 crochet cotton and No. 14 hook.

Chain 14, join in a ring with sl. *1st round*—24 d in ring, join last d to the first one with sl. *2d round*

FIG. 70. EDGING WITH CORONATION BRAID. See page 40

—Ch 5, thread over hook 3 times, insert in same st where 5-ch began, draw a loop through, (thread over and draw through 2 loops) 4 times, ch 5, d in next d, * 1 d in next d, ch 5, thread over 3 times, insert hook in next d, draw a loop through, (thread over and draw through 2 loops) 3 times, retaining 2 loops on hook, thread over 3 times, insert hook in same d with last st, draw a loop through, (thread over and draw through 2 loops) 3 times, thread over and draw through remaining 3 loops on hook, ch 5, d in next d *; repeat from * to * until there are 8 clusters; after the end of the 8th cluster, make 1 d in next d, ch 5, sl in top of first cluster to finish it. Break thread and fasten securely. Make as many stars as are necessary for the length, joining each as it is made to preceding star at the centre point.

HEADING. *1st row*—Having a loop on the hook, insert hook in top of first cluster at the right and make sl to fasten thread, * (ch 7, d in 5th st from needle to form picot, ch 3, d in centre of next cluster) twice, ch 2, picot of 5, ch 3, d in first cluster on next star; repeat from * to end and break thread. *2d row*—Begin again at right hand, fasten thread before the picot in first loop with sl, ch 3, t in same place, * ch 5, 2 t before picot in next loop, ch 4, thread over twice, insert hook before picot in loop between stars and work off loops by twos, leaving 2 loops on hook, thread over twice, insert hook in same loop after the picot and work off loops by twos, working the last 3 loops off at once, ch 5, 2 t before picot in first loop on next star; repeat from * to end and break thread. *3d row*—Sl in first loop at right, ch 3, thread over twice, insert hook under same loop, work off loops by twos, leaving 2 on hook, thread over twice, make another st in same place, working off by twos and the last 3 loops together, * ch 3, thread over twice, make another Cluny st in same loop, retaining 2 loops on hook, thread over twice, insert hook in next loop, work off two loops twice, then the last 3 together, ch 3, thread over twice, make a cluster of 3 sts in same loop; repeat from * to end. Repeat the 3 rows of heading for second side of Insertion.

Figure 72. Edging. — No. 100 crochet cotton and No. 14 hook.

Make a row of stars the required length, repeating the 3 rows of Heading at the top.

LOWER EDGE. *1st row*—Like first row of Heading for Insertion, Figure 71. *2d row*—One d before picot in first loop at right hand, * ch 9, thread over twice,

FIG. 71. INSERTION. See page 40

insert hook after picot in same loop, work off by twos, retaining 2 on hook, thread over twice, insert hook before picot in next loop and finish st, working last 3 loops off together, ch 9, 1 d after p in same loop, ch 3, make 2 cross t in loop between stars, placing one st before and one st after the picot, ch 3, 1 d in first loop on next star before the picot; repeat from * to end. *3d row*—In first loop make * 4 d, picot of 4 joined with d, 1 d, picot, 6 d; in next loop make 5 d, ch 9, take hook out and insert in 2d st from picot in preceding loop, catch st and draw through; in this loop make 5 d, p, 1 d, p, 5 d; in unfinished loop make 1 d, p, 1 d, p, 4 d; in loop between stars make 3 d, 1 d in cross t, p in last d, 3 d; repeat from * to end.

Figure 73. Edging for Handkerchief. — No. 150 crochet cotton and No. 14 hook.

Over a very narrow hem, with 3 threads drawn as for hemstitching, * make 3 d, picot of 5 joined by a d made through the top of last d and under the hem, 7 d, picot of 5 joined as before, 3 d, ch 9, turn point of hook back over the thread and sl in 4th st from last picot, cover ch with (2 d, picot of 5 without joining, 4 d, picot, 4 d, picot, 2 d); repeat from *. Crowd the stitches at the corners closely to make the work lie flat.

Figure 74. Edging. — No. 70 crochet cotton and No. 13 hook.

FIG. 72. EDGING. See page 41

This edge is worked lengthwise and the thread is broken at the end of each row, beginning again at the same end.

Make a chain the required length. *1st row*—One d in each of first 6 sts, * ch 2, miss 2 sts on foundation ch, t in next st, (ch 2, t in next st) 3 times, ch 2, miss 2, d in each of next 12 sts; repeat from * to end of ch, ending with 6 d. *2d row*—5 d over first 5 d, * (ch 3, t over next t) 4 times, ch 3, miss 1st d, 10 d over 10 d; repeat from *. *3d row*—4 d over first 4 d, * (ch 4, t over next t) 4 times, ch 4, miss 1 d, 8 d over 8 d; repeat from *. *4th row*—3 d over first 3 d, * (ch 5, t over next t) 4 times, ch 5, miss 1 d, 6 d over 6 d; repeat from *. *5th row*—2 d over first 2 d, * (ch 6, t over next t) 4 times, ch 6, miss 1 d, 4 d over 4 d; repeat from *. *6th row*—One d over 1st d, * (ch 7, t over t) 4 times, ch 7, miss 1 d, 2 d over 2 d; repeat from *. *7th row*—* One d over 1st ch loop, (ch 3, d over same loop) 3 times over first space; over each of second, third, and fourth spaces make 1 d, (ch 3, 1 d) 4 times; over fifth space make 1 d, (ch 3, 1 d) 3 times; repeat from *.

Figure 75. Edging. — No. 30 crochet cotton and No. 9 hook.

Make a foundation chain the length required, turn, t in 7th st from hook, * miss 3, t in next st, ch 3, t in same st; repeat these shells from * the whole length, break thread and fasten between first 2 shells. Or the foundation ch and shells may be turned, without breaking thread, and sl back over first shell, * ch 25, turn, sl into 10th st from hook and sl into the following 3 sts, ch 4, miss 4 ch st, dt into next ch st, ch 2, miss 2, long t (3 loops) into next ch st, ch 2, miss 2, long t (4 loops) into

FIG. 73. EDGING FOR HANDKERCHIEF. See page 41

FIG. 74. EDGING. See page 41

next ch st, ch 1, miss 2 shells, sl between 2d and 3d shell, ch 1, turn, 2 d over first ch (3 d over next ch) twice, 5 d over next ch, 4 sl over next 4 sts, (5 ch, d in ring) 4 times, 5 ch, 4 sl over next 4 sts, 5 d over ch, (3 d over next ch) twice, 2 d over next ch, sl over 2 sts of shell, turn, miss 2 sl, 5 d over first 5 d, picot of 5 joined with sl. (3 d over next ch, picot) twice, 2 d over same ch, 4 sl over 4 sl, over each 5-ch make (1 d, 3 t, picot, 3 t, 1 d), 4 sl over 4 sl, 2 d over ch, picot, 3 d over same ch, picot, 3 d over next ch, picot, 3 d over next ch, 2 d over next ch, join with sl in middle of shell, sl to point between shells and repeat from *.

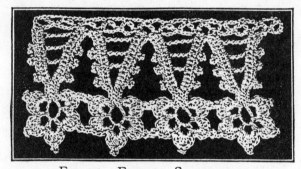

FIG. 75. EDGING. See page 41

When making the first and second picots of the second rosette, join each one to the corresponding picot on the first rosette; this may be done in the following manner: After making 5-ch for picot drop the stitch from the hook and draw it up through the picot of first rosette, finish the picot as before and complete the petal.

Figure 76 A. Cluny Insertion. — No. 70 crochet cotton and No. 12 hook.

The row of medallions through the centre is made first and three rows of work crocheted along each side.

Chain 12, turn, miss 1 st, 6 d in next 6 sts, turn, (ch 5, 1 d in 1st st) 6 times, 1 d in the end of work, 6 d on opposite side of ch, turn, (ch 5, 1 d in 1st st) 6 times, 1 d in the end of work. This completes the centre or heart of the medallion. Make as many medallions as required for the length.

1st row—Join the thread at the first loop or picot at the right, ch 4, make 2 Cluny sts (of dt, crocheting two off twice) and with the 3 sts on hook crochet off two and two,

ch 5, miss 1 picot, in the next picot make a group of 3 Cluny sts (3 dt, crochet off each by twos, twice, leaving 4 sts on the hook), crochet off 2, crochet off 3 together, ch 5, Cluny group of 3 dt in next picot, ch 5, miss 1 picot, Cluny group of 3 dt in last picot, without ch, * make Cluny group of 3 dt in first picot of next medallion, ch 5, group in 3d picot, ch 5, group in 4th picot, ch 5, group in 6th picot; repeat from * to the end, turn, ch 3. *2d row*—D in first 5-ch, * ch 5, d in next 5-ch; repeat from * to the end, turn, ch 4. *3d row*—Ch 4, t in first loop, * ch 4, t in next loop; repeat from *. Make these three rows on the opposite side of medallions.

Figure 76 B. Cluny Edging. — No. 70 crochet cotton and No. 12 hook.

Make a chain the required length. *1st row*—T in the 9th st from hook, * ch 2, miss 2, t in next st; repeat from *, turn. *2d row*—Ch 4, * miss 1 space, Cluny group of 3 dt in next space, ch 5, Cluny group in same space; repeat from * and break thread. *3d row*—Begin at the first end of last row, * 4 ht over 5-ch, picot of 5 without joining, 4 ht over same 5-ch, 1 d in top of Cluny group; repeat from * to the end.

Figure 77. Insertion of Cluny Crochet. — No. 70 crochet cotton and No. 12 hook.

This lace can be rapidly made in carpet warp or heavier crochet cotton for curtains or towels.

Chain 12, sl in 1st st to form a ring, cover half the ring with 4 d, picot of 4 joined with sl, 4 d, p, 4 d, make a Cluny group (gr) as follows: * Chain 6, thread over twice, join in first of 6-ch, crochet off two, and two, thread over twice, join in same st, (crochet off two) 4 times; repeat from * 3 times more; repeat from the beginning for the required length. This alternates a ring and 4 Cluny gr of three, and should end with a ring.

To make the other side, work on around the end and fill the last half of last ring with 4 d, p, 4 d, p, 4 d, * make 2 Cluny gr, 1 d between 2d and 3d groups, 2 Cluny gr, fill half of next ring; repeat from * the whole length. Without breaking thread, after last ring is finished, * ch 9, d between 2 p of ring, ch 9, d between 1st and 2d Cluny gr, ch 9, d between 3d and 4th Cluny gr; repeat from *.

Make this first row on both edges. *2d row*—Ch 5,

FIG. 76. CLUNY INSERTION AND EDGING. See page 42

FIG. 77. INSERTION OF CLUNY CROCHET. See page 42

miss 2, t in next st, * ch 2, miss 2, t in next st; repeat from * the whole length on both edges.

Figure 78. Edging of Cluny Crochet. — Follow directions for Insertion, Figure 77, until the last ring is completely filled. Make 1 Cluny gr, ch 12, sl back into the ring (between 2 p), cover the ch with 4 d, p, 4 d, p, 4 d, p, 4 d, * 1 Cluny gr, d between 2d and 3d gr of first half, Cluny gr, ch 12, sl between 1st and 2d gr, cover 12 ch as before, Cluny gr, fill one-fourth of the ring with (4 d, p, 2 d), ch 12, sl between last 2 gr, cover 12 ch as before, complete the ring with 2 d, p, 4 d, Cluny gr, 12 ch, sl in ring (between p), partly cover 12-ch with (4 d, p, 2 d), ch 12, sl back in last loop between 2d and 3d p, cover 12 ch as before, finish covering loop with 2 d, p, 4 d, p, 4 d; repeat from *.

HEADING.—Fasten thread between p of ring and follow directions for Heading of Insertion, Figure 77.

In making this lace with heavier thread it is well to make the 12-ch ring rather loose, or to make 16 close tight ch; in coarser cotton the 12-d fill the half ring too tightly unless this point is noted.

Figure 79. Edging. — No. 30 crochet cotton and No. 10 hook.

Chain 24, turn. *1st row* — T in 5th st from hook, t in next st, (ch 5, miss 3 sts on foundation ch, d in next st) 3 times, ch 10, d in last st of ch, ch 1, turn. *2d row*—5 d over 10 ch, ch 5, t over same ch, ch 1, t over same ch, (ch 5, d over next 5-ch) 3 times, ch 3, 3 t on 3 t, (the 3-ch at the end of row represent 1 t). *3d row*—Ch 3, 2 t over 2 t, (ch 5, d over 5-ch) twice, ch 5, t over next 5-ch, ch 1, t over same ch, ch 1, t over 1-ch between 2 t, ch 1, t over next ch-loop, ch 1, t over same loop, ch 10, d between first 2 d, ch 1, turn. *4th row*—8 d over 10 ch, ch 5, t over same ch-loop, ch 1, t over same loop, (ch 1, t over 1-ch between next 2 t) 4 times, ch 1, t over next loop, ch 1, t over same loop, (ch 5, d over next loop) twice, ch 3, 3 t over 3 t, turn. *5th row*—Ch 3, 2 t over 2 t, ch 5, d over next 5-ch loop, ch 5, 2 t over next loop with 1-ch between t, (ch 1, miss 1 t, t over next 1-ch) 7 times, ch 1, 2 t over next loop with 1-ch between, ch 10, d between first 2 d, ch 1, turn. *6th row*—8 d over 10 ch, ch 5, 2 t over same loop with 1-ch between, (ch 1, t over 1-ch) 10 times, ch 1, 2 t over next loop with 1-ch between t, ch 5, d over next loop, ch 3, 3 t over 3 t, turn. *7th row*—Ch 3, 2 t over 2 t, ch 5, 2 t over next loop with 1-ch between, (ch 1, t over 1-ch) 13 times, ch 1, 2 t over next loop with 1 ch between, ch 10, d between first 2 d, ch 1, turn. *8th row*—12 d over 10-ch, ch 4, miss 2 t, t over next 1-ch, (ch 1, t over next 1-ch) 13 times, ch 5, d over 5-ch, ch 3, 3 t over 3 t, turn. *9th row*—Ch 3, 2 t over 2 t, ch 5, d over 5-ch, ch 5, miss 2 t, t over 1-ch, (ch 1, t over next 1-ch) 10 times, ch 10, d between first 2 d, ch 1, turn.

10th row—8 d over 10-ch, ch 5, miss 2 t, t over next 1-ch, (ch 1, t over next 1-ch) 7 times, (ch 5, d over next 5-ch) twice, ch 3, 3 t over 3 t, turn. *11th row*—Ch 3, 2 t over 2 t, (ch 5, d over next 5-ch) twice, ch 5, miss 2 t, t over 1-ch, (ch 1, t over next 1-ch) 4 times, ch 10, d between first 2 d, ch 1, turn. *12th row*—8 d over 10-ch, ch 5, miss 2 t, t over 1-ch, ch 1, t over next 1-ch, (ch 5, d over next 5-ch) 3 times, ch 3, 3 t over 3 t, turn. *13th row*—Ch 3, 2 t over 2 t, (ch 5, d over next 5-ch) 3 times, ch 10, d between first 2 d, ch 1, turn. Repeat from 2d row for length required.

Figure 80. Insertion and Edging. — No. 50 crochet cotton and No. 10 hook.

INSERTION. — Chain 17, turn, * 1 d in 3d st from hook, 1 t in next st, 3 dt in next 3 sts, t in next, d in next, * ch 9, turn, work from * to * for a second petal, ** ch 17, turn, make from * to * for a petal, ch 9, turn, make from * to * for a second petal **: repeat from ** to ** for the required length. At the end make three more petals (on 9-ch each), these will be the one at the end and two on the other side. Over the chain between petals make one petal as before of (1 d, 1 t, 3 dt, 1 t, 1 d), (ch 9, turn, work from * to *) twice, make from * to * over chain between petals. Complete the second side and make the heading on each side as follows.

HEADING.—Fasten thread at tip of first petal, * ch 7, sl in tip of next petal, ch 1, sl in tip of next petal; repeat from *. *2d row*—T in 1st st of ch, * ch 2, miss 2, t in next st; repeat from * the whole length.

EDGING.—Chain 23, * turn, 1 d in 3d st from hook, t in next st, 3 dt in next 3 sts, t in next st, d in next st, * (ch 9, repeat the work from * to *) 3 times, 3 d in 3 sts of ch above flower, ch 13, turn,

FIG. 78. EDGING OF CLUNY CROCHET. See page 43

sl in point of 1st petal, (ch 7, sl in point of next petal) 3 times, ch 4, sl in 2d ch st from beginning, (in succeeding scallops, sl in 2d st from last scallop), sl in next st, turn, 6 d over 4-ch (in succeeding scallops make 3 d, join to previous scallop, 3 d over same ch), over each 7-ch make (1 d, 1 t, 1 dt, ch 2, 2 d, 1 t, 1 dt, ch 2, 1 d), over 13-ch make 6 d. Begin next scallop with ch 23, and repeat

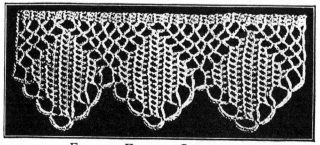

FIG. 79. EDGING. See page 43

FIG. 80. INSERTION AND EDGING. See page 43

to the required length; keep the petals even in size.

HEADING. — Over the chain along the top make 1 t, * ch 2, miss 2, t in next st; repeat from * the whole length.

Figure 81. Edging. — No. 50 crochet cotton and No. 10 hook.

Chain 10, turn. *1st row*—Miss 1 ch, d in each of 9 ch, turn. *2d row*—Ch 1, d in each d, taking up back loop of st to make a ridge. Repeat 2d row until there are 6 ridges (or 12 rows), always making 1 ch at the turn and being careful not to lose any sts. Turn, ch 9, sl between 3d and 4th ridges on the side, ch 9, sl at end of 1st row. Turn, 12 d over 9-ch, 6 d over next 9-ch, turn, ch 9, sl in 7th from hook to form a loop, ch 4, dt in loop, * ch 3, dt in loop; repeat

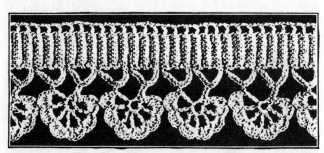

FIG. 81. EDGING. See page 44

from * 4 times more, sl to middle of 12 d, turn, (1 d, 3 t, 1 d) over each 3-ch, 2 d over 2 ch of loop, 6 d over last half of 9-ch loop. Repeat from beginning, joining centre of first petal of flower to centre of last petal on flower just made.

HEADING. — One t and 2 ch in every other row (or in every ridge) along length of edging.

Figure 82. Edging. — No. 30 crochet cotton and No. 9 hook.

Make a chain the required length. *1st row*—One dt in 12th st from hook, (ch 3, miss 3, dt in next st) repeat to end of ch, turn. *2d row*—Ch 7, dt in 2d dt, (ch 3, dt in next dt) repeat to end of row, turn. *3d row*—Ch 4, 5 dt over 3-ch, * ch 1, miss 1 sp, 6 dt over next 3 ch; repeat from * to end of row, turn. *4th row*—Ch 10, sl in ch st between dt; repeat from beginning of row to end of edging, turn. *5th row*—* Make 18 d over 1st 10-ch, 18 d over 2d 10-ch, 9 d over 3d 10-ch (half across), ch 10, sl back

in middle of 2d 18 d, ch 10, sl back in middle of 1st 18 d, make 18 d over 10 ch, 9 d over next 10-ch (half across), ch 12, sl back in middle of 18 d, 22 d over 12 ch, 9 d over next ch, 9 d over next ch; repeat from * to end of row.

Figure 83. Narrow Edging. — No. 70 crochet cotton and No. 13 hook.

Chain 5 and join in a ring. *1st row*—Ch 5, in ring make (1 t, ch 1, 1 t, ch 3, 1 t, ch 1, 1 t), ch 5, turn. *2d row*—Over 3-ch of 1st row make (1 t, ch 1, 1 t, ch 3, 1 t, ch 1, 1 t), turn, ch 5. Repeat 2d row for length required.

HEADING. — Fasten thread in first point, * ch 5, fasten with sl in next point; repeat from * the whole length.

OUTER EDGE. — Fasten thread in 1st 5 ch, * ch 6, d in next point; repeat from * to end and turn. *2d row*—Over 1st loop of 6-ch make (3 d, picot of 4, 4 d, p, 3 d), over 2d 6-ch make (3 d, p, 2 d), ch 6,

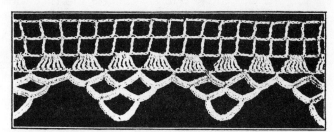

FIG. 82. EDGING. See page 44

turn, d between 2 p of 1st loop, turn, over loop make (3 d, p, 2 d, p, 2 d, p, 3 d), over remainder of 2d loop make (2 d, p, 3 d); repeat from beginning of row.

Figure 84. Insertion. — No. 50 crochet cotton and No. 10 hook.

Chain 19, turn. *1st row*—One t in 8th st of ch. (ch 3, 1 t in same st) 3 times, (forming shell of 3 meshes), ch 3, 1 t in 4th st, ch 2, 1 t in 3d st, ch 2, shell in 4th st, ch 5, turn. *2d row*—Shell in shell, ch 3, 1 dt in t of previous row, 2 dt over ch, 1 dt in next t (making a block of 4 dt), ch 3, shell in shell, ch 5, turn. *3d row*—Shell in shell, ch 3, 1 t in 1st dt, ch 2, 1 t in last dt, ch 3, shell in shell, ch 5, turn. Repeat the 2d and 3d rows for the required length, and finish each side with ch of 7 st, and d (or sl) in middle of 5-ch made in the turn of each row.

Figure 85. Edging. — No. 50 crochet cotton and No. 10 hook.

Chain 16, turn. *1st row*—One t in 6th st, (ch 3, t in same st) twice (making 3 meshes), ch 3, 1 t in 3d st, ch 2, 1 t in 3d st, ch 2, 1 t in 3d st, ch 6, turn. *2d row*—1 dt over 1st t, 2 dt over ch, 1 dt over next t (making block of 4 dt), ch 3, shell

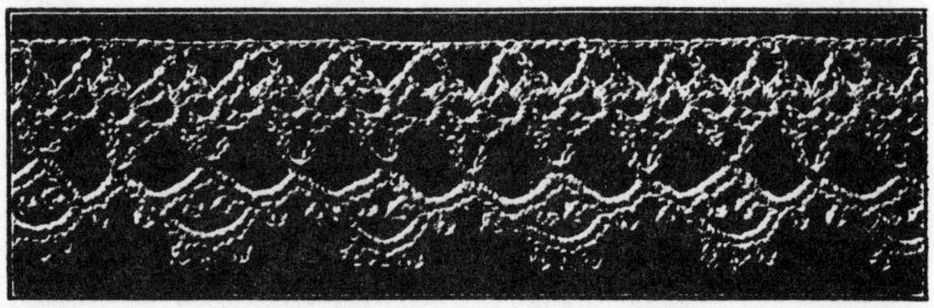

FIG. 83. EDGING. See page 44

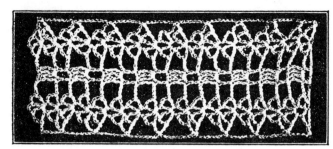

FIG. 84. INSERTION. See page 44

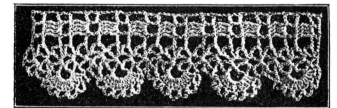

FIG. 85. EDGING. See page 44

in shell, ch 5, turn. *3d row*—Shell in shell, ch 3, t in 1st dt, ch 2, t in last dt, ch 2, t in 3d of 6-ch, ch 5, turn. *4th row*—Same as 2d row until shell is finished, then ch 2, 12 t in 5-ch of last row, d into first mesh of 1st row, ch 4, turn, miss 1 st, d in next, (ch 4, miss 1, d in next) 5 times. *5th row*—Ch 3, shell in shell, ch 3, t in 1st dt, ch 2, t in last dt, ch 2, t in 3d st, ch 6, turn. Repeat from 2d row to 5th row inclusive for the required length.

Figure 86. Narrow Edging. — No. 150 crochet cotton and No. 14 hook. Chain 6, turn, make a t in 4th st from hook.

* Chain 9, turn, make a t in the 4th st from hook *; repeat from * to * until it is a little longer than the required length, ending with ch 3, turn. *2d row* —* 9 t over one-half of the ring made by ch and t, sl in middle st of ch between rings; repeat from *, working on around the first end and opposite side of ch. *3d row*—When the second end is reached, without breaking thread work around the end, * ch 5, d in 5th of 9 t, 3 picots of 5-ch in same st, ch 5, d between rings; repeat from * along one side.

HEADING.—Chain 8, d in 5th of 9 t, ch 4, dt between rings, * ch 4, d in 5th of 9 t, ch 4, dt between rings; repeat from *.

Figure 87. Filet Insertion. — No. 70 crochet cotton and No. 13 hook.

Chain 82, turn. *1st row*—T in 8th st from hook, (this makes the first space), 5 more sp, 10 t, ch 5, miss 2, d in next, ch 5, miss 2, 10 t, ch 5, miss 2, d in next st, ch 5, miss 2, 10 t, 6 sp, turn always with ch 5. *2d row*—7 sp, 10 t (the last 3 t on 3 ch sts), ch 2, 16 t (3 on ch, 10 on 10 t, 3 on ch), ch 2, 10 t

FIG. 86. EDGING. See page 45

(3 on ch, 7 on 7 t), 7 sp. *3d row*—8 sp, 16 t, ch 5, miss 2 t, 16 t, 8 sp. *4th row*—9 sp, 10 t, ch 5, d in middle of 5-ch, ch 5, miss 3 t, 10 t, 9 sp. *5th row*—8 sp, 16 t, ch 2, 16 t, 8 sp. *6th row*—7 sp, 10 t, ch 5, miss 2 t, 16 t, ch 5, miss 2 t, 10 t, 7 sp. *7th row*—6 sp, 10 t, * ch 5, d under 5-ch, ch 4, d in same place * (this will be known as "from * to *"), ch 5, miss 3 t, 10 t, ch 5, d under 5-ch, ch 4, d in same place, ch 5, miss 3 t, 10 t, 6 sp. *8th row*—5 sp, 10 t, make from * to * twice, ch 5, miss 3 t, 4 t, make from * to * twice, ch 5, miss 3 t, 10 t, 5 sp. *9th row*—4 sp, 10 t, make from * to * 6 times, ch 5, miss 3 t, 10 t, 4 sp. *10th row*—3 sp, 10 t, make from * to * 7 times, ch 5, miss 3 t, 10 t, 3 sp. *11th row*—2 sp, 10 t, make from * to * 8 times, ch 5, miss 3 t, 10 t, 2 sp. *12th row*—One sp, 10 t, make from * to * 9 times, ch 5, miss 3 t, 10 t, 1 sp. *13th row*—2 sp, 10 t (7 t on 7 t, 3 t on 3 ch st), make from * to * 8 times, ch 5, 10 t (3 on last 3 ch, 7 on 7 t), 2 sp. *14th row*—3 sp, 10 t, make from * to * 7 times, ch 5, 10 t, 3 sp. *15th row*—4 sp, 10 t, make from * to * 6 times, ch 5, 10 t, 4 sp. *16th row*—5 sp, 10 t, make from * to * twice, ch 5, 4 t under next 5 ch, make from * to * twice, ch 5, 10 t, 5 sp. *17th row*—6 sp, 10 t, from * to * once, ch 5, 10 t (3 t on last 3 ch, 4 t on 4 t, 3 on next 3 ch), from * to * once, ch 5, 10 t, 6 sp. *18th row*—7 sp, 10 t, ch 2, 16 t (3 on last 3 ch, 10 t on 10 t,

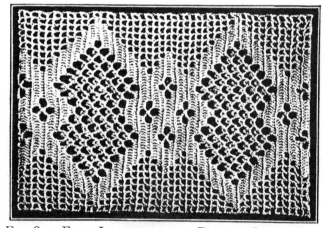

FIG. 87. FILET INSERTION WITH PICOTS. See page 45

3 on next 3 ch), ch 2, 10 t, 7 sp. *19th row*—Like 3d row. *20th row*—Like 4th row. *21st row*—Like 5th row. *22d row*—Like 6th row. *23d row*—Like 1st row. Repeat from 2d row for length.

Figure 88. Ring Edging. — No. 30 crochet cotton and No. 9 hook.

Chain 30, join in ring. *1st round* — Ch 3, t in st of joining, 10 t in 10 sts, * 2 t in 1 st, t in 1 st, 2 t in 1 st, t in 1 st, * 2 t in 1 st, 10 t in 10 sts; repeat from * to *, join with sl. *2d round*—Ch 3, 2 t in 1, 10 t in 10 t, (working throughout under two loops in top of t), * 2 t in 1, 1 t in 1, 2 t in 1, 2 t in 2 t, 2 t in 1, * 1 t in 1, 2 t in 1, 10 t in 10 t; repeat from * to *, join with sl, break thread and fasten. Make a second ring like the first, when joining the ch of ring interlace it in the first completed ring. Do not connect them in any other way except interlacing the chain. Make as many rings as necessary for the required length. When finishing

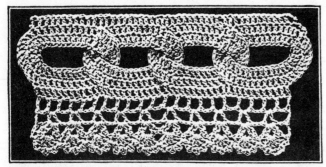

FIG. 88. RING EDGING. See page 45

the last one do not cut the thread but sl over 2 t.

HEADING.—Chain 3, * 10 t in 10 t, 1 t joined in 2d t of 2d round of previous ring and through 11th t of last ring, 10 t on previous ring; repeat from * the whole length, without breaking thread, ch 3, sl around the end of the last ring and make the same heading for 1st row of the outer edge, turn. 2d row—Ch 5, miss 1 t, t in next t, * ch 2, miss 1, t in next; repeat from * throughout, turn. 3d row—Ch 5, miss 1 mesh, t in next mesh, ch 2, t in same mesh, * ch 2, miss 1 mesh, t in next mesh, ch 2, t in same mesh; repeat from * the whole length, turn. 4th row—Ch 5, (2 t, ch 1, 2 t) over 2-ch between t that are joined in the same mesh, * miss 1 mesh, (2 t, ch 1, 2 t) over next mesh; repeat from * to end, turn. 5th row—Ch 1, * 5 t over 1-ch, d between shell; repeat from * to the end, turn. 6th row—* Ch 2, d in 2d t, ch 2, d in next t, ch 2, d in next t, d in d between scallops; repeat from *.

Figure 89. Edging for Handkerchief. — No. 150 crochet cotton and No. 14 hook.

This Edging may be made directly into the hemstitched hem of handkerchief, or it may be crocheted over a rolled hem in this way. Draw 3 threads ¼ of an inch from the edge of linen, roll hem or turn up to the right side and work over the hem. * One d, 1 ht, 1 t, 1 dt, 1 tt (triple t, thread over 3 times), picot of 4 joined with sl in top of last tt, 1 tt, 1 dt, 1 t, 1 ht; repeat from *. Around the corner make 2 d, p, 2 d.

Figure 90. Insertion and Edging. — No. 50 crochet cotton and No. 10 hook.

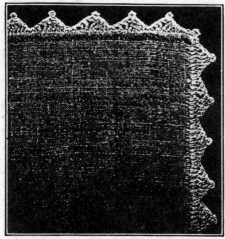

FIG. 89. EDGING FOR HANDKERCHIEF.
See page 46

INSERTION. — Chain 17, turn. 1st row — T in 5th st from hook, ch 4, 3 dt across the t, miss 3 ch, t in next st, ch 4, 3 dt across the t, miss 3 ch, t in next st, ch 4, 3 dt across the t, miss 3 ch, 1 dt in last st of foundation ch, ch 5, turn. 2d row—One t in point of last group made, ch 4, 3 dt across t, (t in point of next group, 3 dt across t) twice, 1 dt into the end of last 5-ch, ch 5, turn. 3d row—Like 2d row. Repeat the 2d row to the required length.

EDGING.—Make the Edging like the Insertion to the end of the 2d row, where the last dt is omitted, ch 5, turn. The dt is necessary to form the line for the heading, but is omitted at the lower edge. Make 4 rows and after the last block of the 4th row make 8 dt over the 5-ch, with 1 ch between dt, join with d at corner of first block on lower edge, turn, (ch 3, 3 d over 1-ch) 7 times, ch 3, sl across block, ch 7, dt in 5th st from hook, 2 dt over next 2 sts, t in point of next group, ch 4, 3 dt across t. This row corresponds with the 1st row. The 4 rows are to be repeated for the edging.

Figure 91, A and B. Rickrack Edgings. — No. 50 crochet cotton, No. 10 hook, and rickrack braid of the size shown in the illustration.

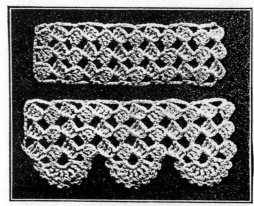

FIG. 90. INSERTION AND EDGING. See page 46

A.—Two t in point of braid, picot of 5 ch joined with d, 2 t in same place, ch 1, (2 t, p, 2 t) in next point.

HEADING.—Sl in point of braid, * ch 6, sl in next point; repeat from *.

B. 1st row—One t in point of braid, ch 3, 1 t in same place, ch 3, 1 t in side of braid, 1 t in opposite side, ch 3, * 1 t in next point, ch 3, 1 t in same place, ch 3, 1 t in side of braid, 1 t in opposite side, ch 3; repeat from *. 2d row—Shell of (2 t, ch 2, 2 t) in single shell of 1st row, ch 1, shell in next single shell; repeat from 1st. 3d row — T in 1st st, * ch 1, miss 1, t in next st; repeat from *.

Figure 92. Edging. — Coronation cord of the size shown in cut, No. 70 crochet cotton and No. 12 hook.

The rows of work are all commenced at the same end.

HEADING. 1st row — On a second section of the braid, make 1 t ⅛ inch from the first end, make another t ⅛ inch from the 1st st in the same section; * ch 7, d in cord at end; make a loop of 2 sections of braid, twisting them downward to the right, bringing the cord up under the cord at end

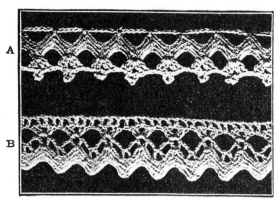

FIG. 91. RICKRACK AND CROCHET EDGINGS. See page 46

of second section, d over the crossed cords, d over the cord beyond the loop; make another loop of the next two sections like the first one, d over crossed cords, d over cord beyond; ch 7, 2 t in next section like those made at first; repeat from * the required length. *2d row*—D between 2 t at right-hand end, 2 d under ch, * ch 5, thread over hook twice, insert hook in same loop, draw a loop through, (thread over hook and through 2 loops) twice, thread over twice, insert hook in next loop, draw a loop through, (thread over and through 2 loops) 4 times, ch 5, 2 d under loop, d between 2 t, 2 d under next loop; repeat from * to end of row. *3d row*—T in 1st d at right, * ch 2, miss 2, t in next st; repeat from *.

LOWER EDGE. *1st row* — Holding the work right side toward you, with heading below, pick up braid at end and bring a section down by the side of the first loop and make 2 d over the cord at the end of it and into the loop, * ch 9, twist the second section (from hook) into a ring, twisting it over to the right, bringing the cord underneath, make 1 d over the crossed cords from the back, ch 9, 2 d in each of the next 2 loops and over the cord at the end of the next section; repeat from *. *2d row* —One t under 9-ch at right, * ch 5, d over cord in ring close to section, ch 11, d over cord on the other side of ring, ch 5, a cross-treble as in 2d row of heading; repeat from *. *3d row*—Fasten thread with sl in 1st t at right, (2 d, 3 ht, 2 d) over 5-ch, sl in d at side of ring, ch 1 (very tight), (2 d, 3 ht, 2 d) over 11-ch, d into middle of ring section, ch 5, d in the d just made to form a p, (2 d, 3 ht, 2 d) over remainder of 11-ch, sl in d in side of ring, ch 1, (2 d, 3 ht, 2 d) over next 5-ch, sl in top of cross t, ch 1; repeat from beginning of row.

Figure 93. Insertion.—

No. 50 crochet cotton and No. 12 hook. This is a very old pattern and has been used as an allover design for a bedspread.

Chain 96, turn, t in 9th st from hook (first open

mesh), 22 more open meshes or sp, 7 t, 1 sp (ch 2, miss 2), 4 t, 3 sp, ch 5, turn. *2d row*—Follow pattern down, etc.

With the 54th row the repetition of the word "Love" begins, and is to be repeated as many times as necessary for the required length; 2 rows between letters, and 2 rows between words, as well as 2 rows between the trefoil along each edge.

Figure 94. Edge for Round Lunch Cloth. — No. 20 crochet cotton and No. 8 hook, and Battenberg braid (½ inch wide), sufficient to go around the table top.

Chain 12, join to form a ring. *1st round*—Ch 4 (for 1st dt), fill ring with 32 dt; join. *2d round*— Ch 12, * miss 1st st of ch, d in next st, ht in next st, 2 t in next 2 sts, 2 dt in next 2 sts, 2 long t (3 loops) in next 2 sts, 1 t in 4th st in ring, ch 9 *; repeat from * to * until there are 8 spokes, sl in 3d st of first 12-ch to join. *3d round*—Ch 14, d in top of first spoke, * ch 7, make a long t (4 loops) between spokes, ch 7, d in top of spoke *; repeat from * to * and join to 7th st of 1st ch. *4th round*—8 d

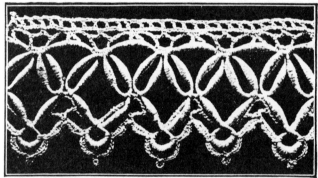

FIG. 92. EDGING OF CROCHET AND CORONATION BRAID
See page 46

over each 7-ch all around, join. *5th round*—* Ch 9, dt over spoke of 3d row, ch 9, d over long t; repeat from * and join. *6th round*—8 d over 9-ch, picot of 5 joined with sl, 5 d over same 9-ch, 5 d over next

FIG. 93. INSERTION. See page 47

9-ch, ch 9, take out hook and insert back in d next to picot, pick up st and sl st to form loop, cover loop with (4 d, p, 4 d, p, 4 d), finish lower loop with p and 8 d. (Notice that the first outer scallop hangs at the lowest tip of lace and is different from the other seven scallops). * Over next 9-ch make (8 d, p, 5 d), over next 9-ch make (5 d, p, 8 d); repeat from * around and fasten off.

SECOND MEDALLION. — Repeat directions for first medallion until six outer scallops are finished. *7th scallop.*—(This is joined to 1st medallion), 8 d over 9-ch, ch 2, d in 2d picot of 3d scallop of first medallion, ch 2, finish picot with sl, 5 d over same 9-ch, 5 d over next 9-ch, ch 2, t in next p of 1st medallion, ch 2, finish picot with sl, 8 d to finish scallop, complete 8th (last) scallop and fasten.

Overcast the lace braid around the circular piece of linen. To join edging to braid, — D in braid, * ch 4, d in 1st picot of top scallop, ch 4, d in space after 6th small mesh of braid (each joining to braid is in space after 6th mesh), ch 4, d in next

FIG. 94. EDGING FOR ROUND LUNCH CLOTH. See Fig. 95 and page 47

picot, ch 4, d in braid, ch 4, long t (3 loops) between scallops, ch 4, d in braid, ch 4, dt in next p, ch 4, d in braid, ch 18, sl in 7th st to form a ring, 6 d in ring, ch 2, d in nearest p of medallion, ch 2, finish p with sl, 6 d on ring, ch 2, long t (3 loops) in place where p of scallops were joined, ch 2, finish picot with sl, 6 d over ring, ch 2, d in 1st p next to joining of next medallion, ch 2, finish picot with sl, 6 d over ring, insert hook in top of 1st d of ring, draw through loop, ch 6, d in braid, ch 4, dt in next p, ch 4, d in braid, ch 4, long t (3 loops) between scallops, ch 4, d in braid; repeat from * around.

Care should be taken to thoroughly shrink the linen before cutting the circular piece; and the braid needs shrinking before applying to the linen. In crocheting of this character (with much open work) it is not necessary to shrink the crocheting, but good judgment should be used in attaching the crochet to the braid. The spacing of doubles in the braid may need to be changed from that of the directions.

FIG. 95. ROUND LUNCH CLOTH TRIMMED WITH FIG. 94